Structural Equation Modeling with AMOS

Basic Concepts, Applications, and Programming

SECOND EDITION

Multivariate Applications Series

Sponsored by the Society of Multivariate Experimental Psychology, the goal of this series is to apply complex statistical methods to significant social or behavioral issues, in such a way so as to be accessible to a nontechnical-oriented readership (e.g., nonmethodological researchers, teachers, students, government personnel, practitioners, and other professionals). Applications from a variety of disciplines such as psychology, public health, sociology, education, and business are welcome. Books can be single- or multiple-authored or edited volumes that (a) demonstrate the application of a variety of multivariate methods to a single, major area of research; (b) describe a multivariate procedure or framework that could be applied to a number of research areas; or (c) present a variety of perspectives on a controversial subject of interest to applied multivariate researchers.

There are currently 15 books in the series:

- *What if There Were No Significance Tests?* coedited by Lisa L. Harlow, Stanley A. Mulaik, and James H. Steiger (1997)
- *Structural Equation Modeling With LISREL, PRELIS, and SIMPLIS: Basic Concepts, Applications, and Programming*, written by Barbara M. Byrne (1998)
- *Multivariate Applications in Substance Use Research: New Methods for New Questions*, coedited by Jennifer S. Rose, Laurie Chassin, Clark C. Presson, and Steven J. Sherman (2000)
- *Item Response Theory for Psychologists*, coauthored by Susan E. Embretson and Steven P. Reise (2000)
- *Structural Equation Modeling With AMOS: Basic Concepts, Applications, and Programming*, written by Barbara M. Byrne (2001)
- *Conducting Meta-Analysis Using SAS*, written by Winfred Arthur, Jr., Winston Bennett, Jr., and Allen I. Huffcutt (2001)
- *Modeling Intraindividual Variability With Repeated Measures Data: Methods and Applications*, coedited by D. S. Moskowitz and Scott L. Hershberger (2002)
- *Multilevel Modeling: Methodological Advances, Issues, and Applications*, coedited by Steven P. Reise and Naihua Duan (2003)
- *The Essence of Multivariate Thinking: Basic Themes and Methods*, written by Lisa Harlow (2005)
- *Contemporary Psychometrics: A Festschrift for Roderick P. McDonald*, coedited by Albert Maydeu-Olivares and John J. McArdle (2005)

- *Structural Equation Modeling With EQS: Basic Concepts, Applications, and Programming, 2nd edition,* written by Barbara M. Byrne (2006)
- *Introduction to Statistical Mediation Analysis,* written by David P. MacKinnon (2008)
- *Applied Data Analytic Techniques for Turning Points Research,* edited by Patricia Cohen (2008)
- *Cognitive Assessment: An Introduction to the Rule Space Method,* written by Kikumi K. Tatsuoka (2009)
- *Structural Equation Modeling With AMOS: Basic Concepts, Applications, and Programming, 2nd edition,* written by Barbara M. Byrne (2010)

Anyone wishing to submit a book proposal should send the following: (a) the author and title; (b) a timeline, including completion date; (c) a brief overview of the book's focus, including table of contents and, ideally, a sample chapter (or chapters); (d) a brief description of competing publications; and (e) targeted audiences.

For more information, please contact the series editor, Lisa Harlow, at Department of Psychology, University of Rhode Island, 10 Chafee Road, Suite 8, Kingston, RI 02881-0808; phone (401) 874-4242; fax (401) 874-5562; or e-mail LHarlow@uri.edu. Information may also be obtained from members of the advisory board: Leona Aiken (Arizona State University), Gwyneth Boodoo (Educational Testing Services), Barbara M. Byrne (University of Ottawa), Patrick Curran (University of North Carolina), Scott E. Maxwell (University of Notre Dame), David Rindskopf (City University of New York), Liora Schmelkin (Hofstra University), and Stephen West (Arizona State University).

Structural Equation Modeling with AMOS

Basic Concepts, Applications, and Programming

SECOND EDITION

Barbara M. Byrne

University of Ottawa
Ottawa, Ontario, Canada

Routledge
Taylor & Francis Group
New York   London

Routledge
Taylor & Francis Group
711 Third Avenue, 8th Floor,
New York, NY 10017

Routledge
Taylor & Francis Group
27 Church Road
Hove, East Sussex BN3 2FA

International Standard Book Number: 978-0-8058-6372-7 (Hardback) 978-0-8058-6373-4 (Paperback)

Library of Congress Cataloging-in-Publication Data

Byrne, Barbara M.
  Structural equation modeling with AMOS: basic concepts, applications, and programming / Barbara M. Byrne. -- 2nd ed.
      p. cm. -- (Multivariate applications series)
   Includes bibliographical references and index.
   ISBN 978-0-8058-6372-7 (hardcover : alk. paper) -- ISBN 978-0-8058-6373-4 (pbk. : alk. paper)
   1. Structural equation modeling. 2. AMOS. I. Title.

QA278.B96 2009
519.5'35--dc22   2009025275

Visit the Taylor & Francis Web site at
http://www.taylorandfrancis.com

and the Psychology Press Web site at
http://www.psypress.com

Printed and bound in the United States of America by Edwards Brothers Malloy, Inc.

Contents

Section II: Applications in single-group analyses

**Chapter 3   Testing for the factorial validity of a
theoretical construct (First-order CFA model)** **53**

**Chapter 4   Testing for the factorial validity of scores
from a measuring instrument
(First-order CFA model)** **97**

Section III: Applications in multiple-group analyses

**Chapter 7   Testing for the factorial equivalence of
                    scores from a measuring instrument
                    (First-order CFA model)**

Preface

As with the first edition of this book, my overall goal is to provide readers with a nonmathematical introduction to basic concepts associated with structural equation modeling (SEM), and to illustrate basic applications of SEM using the AMOS program. All applications in this volume are based on AMOS 17, the most up-to-date version of the program at the time this book went to press. During the production process, however, I was advised by J. Arbuckle (personal communication, May 2, 2009) that although a testing of Beta Version 18 had been initiated, the only changes to the program involved (a) the appearance of path diagrams, which are now in color by default, and (b) the rearrangement of a few dialog boxes. The text and statistical operations remain unchanged. Although it is inevitable that newer versions of the program will emerge at some later date, the basic principles covered in this second edition of the book remain fully intact.

This book is specifically designed and written for readers who may have little to no knowledge of either SEM or the AMOS program. It is intended *neither* as a text on the topic of SEM, *nor* as a comprehensive review of the many statistical and graphical functions available in the AMOS program. Rather, my primary aim is to provide a practical guide to SEM using the AMOS Graphical approach. As such, readers are "walked through" a diversity of SEM applications that include confirmatory factor analytic and full latent variable models tested on a wide variety of data (single/multi-group; normal/non-normal; complete/incomplete; continuous/categorical), and based on either the analysis of covariance structures, or on the analysis of mean and covariance structures. Throughout the book, each application is accompanied by numerous illustrative "how to" examples related to particular procedural aspects of the program. In summary, each application is accompanied by the following:

- statement of the hypothesis to be tested
- schematic representation of the model under study

- full explanation bearing on related AMOS Graphics input path diagrams
- full explanation and interpretation of related AMOS text output files
- published reference from which the application is drawn
- illustrated use and function associated with a wide variety of icons and pull-down menus used in building, testing, and evaluating models, as well as for other important data management tasks
- data file upon which the application is based

This second edition of the book differs in several important ways from the initial version. *First*, the number of applications has been expanded to include the testing of: a multitrait-multimethod model, a latent growth curve model, and a second-order model based on categorical data using a Bayesian statistical approach. *Second*, where the AMOS program has implemented an updated, albeit alternative approach to model analyses, I have illustrated both procedures. A case in point is the automated multi-group approach to tests for equivalence, which was incorporated into the program after the first edition of this book was published (see Chapter 7). *Third*, given ongoing discussion in the literature concerning the analysis of continuous versus categorical data derived from the use of Likert scaled measures, I illustrate analysis of data from the same instrument based on both approaches to the analysis (see Chapter 5). *Fourth*, the AMOS text output files are now imbedded within cell format; as a result, the location of some material (as presented in this second edition) may differ from that of former versions of the program. *Fifth*, given that most users of the AMOS program wish to work within a graphical mode, all applications are based on this interface. Thus, in contrast to the first edition of this book, I do not include example input files for AMOS based on a program-ming approach (formerly called AMOS Basic). *Finally*, all data files used for the applications in this book can be downloaded from http://www.psypress.com/sem-with-amos.

The book is divided into five major sections; Section I comprises two introductory chapters. In Chapter 1, I introduce you to the fundamental concepts underlying SEM methodology. I also present you with a general overview of model specification within the graphical interface of AMOS and, in the process, introduce you to basic AMOS graphical notation. Chapter 2 focuses solely on the AMOS program. Here, I detail the key ele-ments associated with building and executing model files.

Section II is devoted to applications involving single-group analyses; these include two first-order confirmatory factor analytic (CFA) models, one second-order CFA model, and one full latent variable model. The first-order CFA applications demonstrate testing for the validity of the theoretical structure of a construct (Chapter 3) and the factorial structure of a measuring instrument (Chapter 4). The second-order CFA model bears on the factorial structure of a measuring instrument (Chapter 5). The final single-group application tests for the validity of an empirically-derived causal structure (Chapter 6).

In Section III, I present three applications related to multiple-group analyses with two rooted in the analysis of covariance structures, and one in the analysis of mean and covariance structures. Based on the analysis of *only* covariance structures, I show you how to test for measurement and structural equivalence across groups with respect to a measuring instrument (Chapter 7) and to a causal structure (Chapter 9). Working from a somewhat different perspective that encompasses the analysis of mean and covariance structures, I first outline the basic concepts associated with the analysis of latent mean structures and then continue on to illustrate the various stages involved in testing for latent mean differences across groups.

Section IV presents two models that are increasingly becoming of substantial interest to practitioners of SEM. In addressing the issue of construct validity, Chapter 10 illustrates the specification and testing of a multitrait-multimethod (MTMM) model. Chapter 11 focuses on longitudinal data and presents a latent growth curve (LGC) model that is tested with and without a predictor variable included.

Section V comprises the final two chapters of the book and addresses critically important issues associated with SEM methodology. Chapter 12 focuses on the issue of non-normal data and illustrates the use of bootstrapping as an aid to determining appropriate parameter estimated values. Chapter 13, on the other hand, addresses the issue of missing (or incomplete) data. Following a lengthy review of the literature on this topic as it relates to SEM, I walk you through an application based on the direct maximum likelihood (ML) approach, the method of choice in the AMOS program.

Although there are now several SEM texts available, the present book distinguishes itself from the rest in a number of ways. *First*, it is the only book to demonstrate, by application to actual data, a wide range of confirmatory factor analytic and full latent variable models drawn from published studies and accompanied by a detailed explanation of each model tested and the resulting output file. *Second* it is the only book to incorporate applications based solely on the AMOS program. *Third*, it is the only book to literally "walk" readers through: (a) model specification, estimation, evaluation, and post hoc modification decisions and processes associated with a variety of applications, (b) competing approaches to the analysis of multiple-group and categorical/continuous data based AMOS model files, and (c) the use of diverse icons and drop-down menus to initiate a variety of analytic, data management, editorial, and visual AMOS procedures. Overall, this volume serves well as a companion book to the AMOS user's guide (Arbuckle, 2007), as well as to any statistics textbook devoted to the topic of SEM.

In writing a book of this nature, it is essential that I have access to a number of different data sets capable of lending themselves to various applications. To facilitate this need, all examples presented throughout the book are drawn from my own research. Related journal references are cited for readers who may be interested in a more detailed discussion of theoretical frameworks, aspects of the methodology, and/or substantive issues and findings. It is important to emphasize that, although all applications are based on data that are of a social/psychological nature, they could just as easily have been based on data representative of the health sciences, leisure studies, marketing, or a multitude of other disciplines; my data, then, serve only as one example of each application. Indeed, I urge you to seek out and examine similar examples as they relate to other subject areas.

Although I have now written five of these introductory books on the application of SEM pertinent to particular programs (Byrne, 1989, 1994c, 1998, 2001, 2006), I must say that each provides its own unique learning experience. Without question, such a project demands seemingly endless time and is certainly not without its frustrations. However, thanks to the ongoing support of Jim Arbuckle, the program's author, such difficulties were always quickly resolved. In weaving together the textual, graphical, and statistical threads that form the fabric of this book, I hope that I have provided my readers with a comprehensive understanding of basic concepts and applications of SEM, as well as with an extensive working knowledge of the AMOS program. Achievement of this goal has necessarily meant the concomitant juggling of word processing, "grabber", and statistical programs in order to produce the end result. It has been an incredible editorial journey, but one that has left me feeling truly enriched for having had yet another wonderful learning experience. I can only hope that, as you wend your way through the chapters of this book, you will find the journey to be equally exciting and fulfilling.

Acknowledgments

As with the writing of each of my other books, there are many people to whom I owe a great deal of thanks. First and foremost, I wish to thank Jim Arbuckle, author of the AMOS program, for keeping me constantly updated following any revisions to the program and for his many responses to any queries that I had regarding its operation. Despite the fact that he was on the other side of the world for most of the time during the writing of this edition, he always managed to get back to me in quick order with the answers I was seeking.

As has been the case for my last three books, I have had the great fortune to have Debra Riegert as my editor. Once again, then, I wish to express my very special thanks to Debra, whom I consider to be the crème de la crème of editors and, in addition, a paragon of patience! Although this book has been in the works for two or three years now, Debra has never once applied pressure regarding its completion. Rather, she has always been encouraging, supportive, helpful, and overall, a wonderful friend. Thanks so much Debra for just letting me do my own thing.

I wish also to extend sincere gratitude to my multitude of loyal readers around the globe. Many of you have introduced yourselves to me at conferences, at one of my SEM workshops, or via email correspondence. I truly value these brief, yet incredibly warm exchanges and thank you so much for taking the time to share with me your many achievements and accomplishments following your walk through my selected SEM applications. Thank you all for your continued loyalty over the years—this latest edition of my AMOS book is dedicated to you!

Last, but certainly not least, I am grateful to my husband, Alex, for his continued patience, support and understanding of the incredible number of hours that my computer and I necessarily spend together on a project of this sort. I consider myself to be fortunate indeed!

section one

Introduction

chapter one

Structural equation models
The basics

Structural equation modeling (SEM) is a statistical methodology that takes a confirmatory (i.e., hypothesis-testing) approach to the analysis of a structural theory bearing on some phenomenon. Typically, this theory represents "causal" processes that generate observations on multiple variables (Bentler, 1988). The term *structural equation modeling* conveys two important aspects of the procedure: (a) that the causal processes under study are represented by a series of structural (i.e., regression) equations, and (b) that these structural relations can be modeled pictorially to enable a clearer conceptualization of the theory under study. The hypothesized model can then be tested statistically in a simultaneous analysis of the entire system of variables to determine the extent to which it is consistent with the data. If goodness-of-fit is adequate, the model argues for the plausibility of postulated relations among variables; if it is inadequate, the tenability of such relations is rejected.

Several aspects of SEM set it apart from the older generation of multivariate procedures. *First*, as noted above, it takes a confirmatory rather than an exploratory approach to the data analysis (although aspects of the latter can be addressed). Furthermore, by demanding that the pattern of intervariable relations be specified a priori, SEM lends itself well to the analysis of data for inferential purposes. By contrast, most other multivariate procedures are essentially descriptive by nature (e.g., exploratory factor analysis), so that hypothesis testing is difficult, if not impossible. *Second*, whereas traditional multivariate procedures are incapable of either assessing or correcting for measurement error, SEM provides explicit estimates of these error variance parameters. Indeed, alternative methods (e.g., those rooted in regression, or the general linear model) assume that error(s) in the explanatory (i.e., independent) variables vanish(es). Thus, applying those methods when there is error in the explanatory variables is tantamount to ignoring error, which may lead, ultimately, to serious inaccuracies—especially when the errors are sizeable. Such mistakes are avoided when corresponding SEM analyses (in general terms) are used. *Third*, although data analyses using the former methods are based on observed measurements only, those using SEM procedures can incorporate

3

both unobserved (i.e., latent) and observed variables. *Finally,* there are no widely and easily applied alternative methods for modeling multivariate relations, or for estimating point and/or interval indirect effects; these important features are available using SEM methodology.

Given these highly desirable characteristics, SEM has become a popular methodology for nonexperimental research, where methods for testing theories are not well developed and ethical considerations make experimental design unfeasible (Bentler, 1980). Structural equation modeling can be utilized very effectively to address numerous research problems involving nonexperimental research; in this book, I illustrate the most common applications (e.g., Chapters 3, 4, 6, 7, and 9), as well as some that are less frequently found in the substantive literatures (e.g., Chapters 5, 8, 10, 11, 12, and 13). Before showing you how to use the AMOS program (Arbuckle, 2007), however, it is essential that I first review key concepts associated with the methodology. We turn now to their brief explanation.

Basic concepts

Latent versus observed variables

In the behavioral sciences, researchers are often interested in studying theoretical constructs that cannot be observed directly. These abstract phenomena are termed *latent variables,* or *factors.* Examples of latent variables in psychology are self-concept and motivation; in sociology, powerlessness and anomie; in education, verbal ability and teacher expectancy; and in economics, capitalism and social class.

Because latent variables are not observed directly, it follows that they cannot be measured directly. Thus, the researcher must operationally define the latent variable of interest in terms of behavior believed to represent it. As such, the unobserved variable is linked to one that is observable, thereby making its measurement possible. Assessment of the behavior, then, constitutes the *direct* measurement of an observed variable, albeit the *indirect* measurement of an unobserved variable (i.e., the underlying construct). It is important to note that the term *behavior* is used here in the very broadest sense to include scores on a particular measuring instrument. Thus, observation may include, for example, self-report responses to an attitudinal scale, scores on an achievement test, in vivo observation scores representing some physical task or activity, coded responses to interview questions, and the like. These measured scores (i.e., measurements) are termed *observed* or *manifest* variables; within the context of SEM methodology, they serve as *indicators* of the underlying construct which they are presumed to represent. Given this necessary bridging process between observed variables and unobserved latent variables, it should now be clear why methodologists urge researchers to be circumspect in their selection of assessment measures. Although the choice of psycho-metrically sound instruments bears importantly on the credibility of all study findings, such selection becomes even more critical when the observed measure is presumed to represent an underlying construct.[1]

Exogenous versus endogenous latent variables

It is helpful in working with SEM models to distinguish between latent variables that are exogenous and those that are endogenous. *Exogenous* latent variables are synonymous with independent variables; they "cause" fluctuations in the values of other latent variables in the model. Changes in the values of exogenous variables are not explained by the model. Rather, they are considered to be influenced by other factors external to the model. Background variables such as gender, age, and socioeconomic status are examples of such external factors. *Endogenous* latent variables are synonymous with dependent variables and, as such, are influenced by the exogenous variables in the model, either directly or indirectly. Fluctuation in the values of endogenous variables is said to be explained by the model because all latent variables that influence them are included in the model specification.

The factor analytic model

The oldest and best-known statistical procedure for investigating relations between sets of observed and latent variables is that of *factor analysis*. In using this approach to data analyses, the researcher examines the covaria-tion among a set of observed variables in order to gather information on their underlying latent constructs (i.e., factors). There are two basic types of factor analyses: exploratory factor analysis (EFA) and confirmatory fac-tor analysis (CFA). We turn now to a brief description of each.

Exploratory factor analysis (EFA) is designed for the situation where links between the observed and latent variables are unknown or uncer-tain. The analysis thus proceeds in an exploratory mode to determine how, and to what extent, the observed variables are linked to their underlying factors. Typically, the researcher wishes to identify the minimal number of factors that underlie (or account for) covariation among the observed variables. For example, suppose a researcher develops a new instrument designed to measure five facets of physical self-concept (e.g., Health, Sport Competence, Physical Appearance, Coordination, and Body Strength). Following the formulation of questionnaire items designed to measure these five latent constructs, he or she would then conduct an EFA to deter-mine the extent to which the item measurements (the observed variables) were related to the five latent constructs. In factor analysis, these relations are represented by *factor loadings*. The researcher would hope that items designed to measure health, for example, exhibited high loadings on that factor, and low or negligible loadings on the other four factors. This factor analytic approach is considered to be exploratory in the sense that the researcher has no prior knowledge that the items do, indeed, measure the intended factors. (For texts dealing with EFA, see Comrey, 1992; Gorsuch, 1983; McDonald, 1985; Mulaik, 1972. For informative articles on EFA, see Byrne, 2005a; Fabrigar, Wegener, MacCallum, & Strahan, 1999; MacCallum, Widaman, Zhang, & Hong, 1999; Preacher & MacCallum, 2003; Wood, Tataryn, & Gorsuch, 1996.)

In contrast to EFA, confirmatory factor analysis (CFA) is appropriately used when the researcher has some knowledge of the underlying latent variable structure. Based on knowledge of the theory, empirical research, or both, he or she postulates relations between the observed measures and the underlying factors a priori and then tests this hypothesized structure statistically. For example, based on the example cited earlier, the researcher would argue for the loading of items designed to measure sport competence self-concept on that specific factor, and *not* on the health, physical appearance, coordination, or body strength self-concept dimensions. Accordingly, a priori specification of the CFA model would allow all sport competence self-concept items to be free to load on that factor, but restricted to have zero loadings on the remaining factors. The model would then be evaluated by statistical means to determine the adequacy of its goodness-of-fit to the sample data. (For more detailed discussions of CFA, see, e.g., Bollen, 1989a; Byrne, 2003, 2005b; Long, 1983a.)

In summary, then, the factor analytic model (EFA or CFA) focuses solely on how, and the extent to which, the observed variables are linked to their underlying latent factors. More specifically, it is concerned with the extent to which the observed variables are generated by the underlying latent constructs and thus strength of the regression paths from the factors to the observed variables (the factor loadings) are of primary interest. Although interfactor relations are also of interest, any regression structure among them is not considered in the factor analytic model. Because the CFA model focuses solely on the link between factors and their measured variables, within the framework of SEM, it represents what has been termed a *measurement model*.

The full latent variable model

In contrast to the factor analytic model, the full latent variable (LV) model allows for the specification of regression structure among the latent variables. That is to say, the researcher can hypothesize the impact of one latent construct on another in the modeling of causal direction. This model is termed *full* (or *complete*) because it comprises both a measurement model and a structural model: the measurement model depicting the links between the latent variables and their observed measures (i.e., the CFA model), and the structural model depicting the links among the latent variables themselves.

A full LV model that specifies direction of cause from one direction only is termed a *recursive model*; one that allows for reciprocal or feedback effects is termed a *nonrecursive model*. Only applications of recursive models are considered in the present book.

General purpose and process of statistical modeling

Statistical models provide an efficient and convenient way of describing the latent structure underlying a set of observed variables. Expressed either diagrammatically or mathematically via a set of equations, such models explain how the observed and latent variables are related to one another.

Typically, a researcher postulates a statistical model based on his or her knowledge of the related theory, on empirical research in the area of study, or on some combination of both. Once the model is specified, the researcher then tests its plausibility based on sample data that comprise all observed variables in the model. The primary task in this model-testing procedure is to determine the goodness-of-fit between the hypothesized model and the sample data. As such, the researcher imposes the structure of the hypothesized model on the sample data, and then tests how well the observed data fit this restricted structure. Because it is highly unlikely that a perfect fit will exist between the observed data and the hypothesized model, there will necessarily be a differential between the two; this differential is termed the *residual*. The model-fitting process can therefore be summarized as follows:

$$\text{Data} = \text{Model} + \text{Residual}$$

where

> *Data* represent score measurements related to the observed variables as derived from persons comprising the sample.
>
> *Model* represents the hypothesized structure linking the observed variables to the latent variables and, in some models, linking particular latent variables to one another.
>
> *Residual* represents the discrepancy between the hypothesized model and the observed data.

In summarizing the general strategic framework for testing structural equation models, Jöreskog (1993) distinguished among three scenarios which he termed *strictly confirmatory* (SC), *alternative models* (AM), and *model generating* (MG). In the strictly confirmatory scenario, the researcher postulates a single model based on theory, collects the appropriate data, and then tests the fit of the hypothesized model to the sample data. From the results of this test, the researcher either rejects or fails to reject the model; no further modifications to the model are made. In the alternative models case, the researcher proposes several alternative (i.e., competing) models, all of which are grounded in theory. Following analysis of a single set of empirical data, he or she selects one model as most appropriate in representing the sample data. Finally, the model-generating scenario represents the case where the researcher, having postulated and rejected a theoretically derived model on the basis of its poor fit to the sample data, proceeds in an exploratory (rather than confirmatory) fashion to modify and reestimate the model. The primary focus, in this instance, is to locate the source of misfit in the model and to determine a model that better describes the sample data. Jöreskog (1993) noted that, although respecification may be either theory or data driven, the ultimate objective is to find a model that is both substantively meaningful and statistically well fitting. He further posited that despite the fact that "a model is tested in each round, the whole approach is model generating, rather than model testing" (Jöreskog, 1993, p. 295).

Of course, even a cursory review of the empirical literature will clearly show the MG situation to be the most common of the three scenarios, and for good reason. Given the many costs associated with the collection of data, it would be a rare researcher indeed who could afford to terminate his or her research on the basis of a rejected hypothesized model! As a consequence, the SC case is not commonly found in practice. Although the AM approach to modeling has also been a relatively uncommon practice, at least two important papers on the topic (e.g., MacCallum, Roznowski, & Necowitz, 1992; MacCallum, Wegener, Uchino, & Fabrigar, 1993) have precipitated more activity with respect to this analytic strategy.

Statistical theory related to these model-fitting processes can be found (a) in texts devoted to the topic of SEM (e.g., Bollen, 1989a; Kline, 2005; Loehlin, 1992; Long, 1983b; Raykov & Marcoulides, 2000; Saris & Stronkhurst, 1984; Schumacker & Lomax, 2004), (b) in edited books devoted to the topic (e.g., Bollen & Long, 1993; Cudeck, du Toit, & Sörbom, 2001; Hoyle, 1995b; Marcoulides & Schumacker, 1996), and (c) in methodologically oriented journals such as *British Journal of Mathematical and Statistical Psychology, Journal of Educational and Behavioral Statistics, Multivariate Behavioral Research, Psychological Methods, Psychometrika, Sociological Methodology, Sociological Methods & Research,* and *Structural Equation Modeling.*

The general structural equation model

Symbol notation

Structural equation models are schematically portrayed using particular configurations of four geometric symbols—a circle (or ellipse), a square (or rectangle), a single-headed arrow, and a double-headed arrow. By convention, circles (or ellipses; $\bigcirc$) represent unobserved latent factors, squares (or rectangles; $\square$) represent observed variables, single-headed arrows ($\rightarrow$) represent the impact of one variable on another, and double-headed arrows ($\leftrightarrow$) represent covariances or correlations between pairs of variables. In building a model of a particular structure under study, researchers use these symbols within the framework of four basic configurations, each of which represents an important component in the analytic process. These configurations, each accompanied by a brief description, are as follows:

- $\bigcirc\!\!\rightarrow\!\!\square$ Path coefficient for regression of an observed variable onto an unobserved latent variable (or factor)
- $\bigcirc\!\!\rightarrow\!\!\bigcirc$ Path coefficient for regression of one factor onto another factor
- $\rightarrow\!\!\square$ Measurement error associated with an observed variable
- $\!\!\rightarrow\!\!\bigcirc$ Residual error in the prediction of an unobserved factor

The path diagram

Schematic representations of models are termed *path diagrams* because they provide a visual portrayal of relations which are assumed to hold among the variables under study. Essentially, as you will see later, a path diagram depicting a particular SEM model is actually the graphical equivalent of its mathematical representation whereby a set of equations relates dependent variables to their explanatory variables. As a means of illustrating how the above four symbol configurations may represent a particular causal process, let me now walk you through the simple model shown in Figure 1.1, which was formulated using AMOS Graphics (Arbuckle, 2007).

In reviewing the model shown in Figure 1.1, we see that there are two unobserved latent factors, math self-concept (MSC) and math achievement (MATH), and five observed variables—three are considered to measure MSC (SDQMSC; APIMSC; SPPCMSC), and two to measure MATH (MATHGR; MATHACH). These five observed variables function as indicators of their respective underlying latent factors.

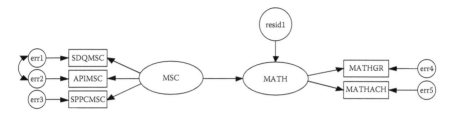

Figure 1.1 A general structural equation model.

Associated with each observed variable is an error term (err1–err5), and with the factor being predicted (MATH), a residual term (resid1);[2] there is an important distinction between the two. Error associated with observed variables represents *measurement error,* which reflects on their adequacy in measuring the related underlying factors (MSC; MATH). Measurement error derives from two sources: random measurement error (in the psychometric sense) and *error uniqueness,* a term used to describe error variance arising from some characteristic that is considered to be specific (or unique) to a particular indicator variable. Such error often represents *nonrandom* (or *systematic*) measurement error. *Residual* terms represent error in the prediction of endogenous factors from exogenous factors. For example, the residual term shown in Figure 1.1 represents error in the prediction of MATH (the endogenous factor) from MSC (the exogenous factor).

It is worth noting that both measurement and residual error terms, in essence, represent unobserved variables. Thus, it seems perfectly reasonable that, consistent with the representation of factors, they too should be enclosed in circles. For this reason, then, AMOS path diagrams, unlike those associated with most other SEM programs, model these error variables as circled enclosures by default.[3]

In addition to symbols that represent variables, certain others are used in path diagrams to denote hypothesized processes involving the entire system of variables. In particular, one-way arrows represent structural regression coefficients and thus indicate the impact of one variable on another. In Figure 1.1, for example, the unidirectional arrow pointing toward the endogenous factor, MATH, implies that the exogenous factor MSC (math self-concept) "causes" math achievement (MATH).[4] Likewise, the three unidirectional arrows leading from MSC to each of the three observed variables (SDQMSC, APIMSC, and SPPCMSC), and those leading from MATH to each of its indicators, MATHGR and MATHACH, suggest that these score values are each influenced by their respective underlying factors. As such, these path coefficients represent the magnitude of expected change in the observed variables for every change in the related latent variable (or factor). It is important to note that these observed variables typically represent subscale scores (see, e.g., Chapter 8), item scores (see, e.g., Chapter 4), item pairs (see, e.g., Chapter 3), and/or carefully formulated item parcels (see, e.g., Chapter 6).

The one-way arrows pointing from the enclosed error terms (err1–err5) indicate the impact of measurement error (random and unique) on the observed variables, and from the residual (resid1), the impact of error in the prediction of MATH. Finally, as noted earlier, curved two-way arrows represent covariances or correlations between pairs of variables. Thus, the bidirectional arrow linking err1 and err2, as shown in Figure 1.1, implies that measurement error associated with SDQMSC is correlated with that associated with APIMSC.

Structural equations

As noted in the initial paragraph of this chapter, in addition to lending themselves to pictorial description via a schematic presentation of the causal processes under study, structural equation models can also be represented by a series of regression (i.e., structural) equations. Because (a) regression equations represent the influence of one or more variables on another, and (b) this influence, conventionally in SEM, is symbolized by a single-headed arrow pointing from the variable of influence to the variable of interest, we can think of each equation as summarizing the impact of all relevant variables in the model (observed and unobserved) on one specific variable (observed or unobserved). Thus, one relatively simple approach to formulating these equations is to note each variable that has one or more arrows pointing toward it, and then record the summation of all such influences for each of these dependent variables.

To illustrate this translation of regression processes into structural equations, let's turn again to Figure 1.1. We can see that there are six variables with arrows pointing toward them; five represent observed variables (SDQMSC, APIMSC, SPPCMSC, MATHGR, and MATHACH), and one represents an unobserved variable (or factor; MATH). Thus, we know that the regression functions symbolized in the model shown in Figure 1.1 can be summarized in terms of six separate equation-like representations of linear dependencies as follows:

$$MATH = MSC + resid1$$

$$SDQMSC = MSC + err1$$

$$APIMSC = MSC + err2$$

$$SPPCMSC = MSC + err3$$

$$MATHGR = MATH + err4$$

$$MATHACH = MATH + err5$$

Nonvisible components of a model

Although, in principle, there is a one-to-one correspondence between the schematic presentation of a model and its translation into a set of structural equations, it is important to note that neither one of these model representations tells the whole story; some parameters critical to the estimation of the model are not explicitly shown and thus may not be obvious to the novice structural equation modeler. For example, in both the path diagram and the equations just shown, there is no indication that the variances of the exogenous variables are parameters in the model; indeed, such parameters are essential to all structural equation models. Although researchers must be mindful of this inadequacy of path diagrams in building model input files related to other SEM programs, AMOS facilitates the specification process by automatically incorporating the estimation of variances by default for all independent factors.

Likewise, it is equally important to draw your attention to the specified nonexistence of certain parameters in a model. For example, in Figure 1.1, we detect no curved arrow between err4 and err5, which suggests the lack of covariance between the error terms associated with the observed variables MATHGR and MATHACH. Similarly, there is no hypothesized covariance between MSC and resid1; absence of this path addresses the common, and most often necessary, assumption that the predictor (or exogenous) variable is in no way associated with any error arising from the prediction of the criterion (or endogenous) variable. In the case of both examples cited here, AMOS, once again, makes it easy for the novice structural equation modeler by automatically assuming these specifications to be nonexistent. (These important default assumptions will be addressed in chapter 2, where I review the specifications of AMOS models and input files in detail.)

Basic composition

The general SEM model can be decomposed into two submodels: a measurement model, and a structural model. The *measurement model* defines relations between the observed and unobserved variables. In other words, it provides the link between scores on a measuring instrument (i.e., the observed indicator variables) and the underlying constructs they are designed to measure (i.e., the unobserved latent variables). The measurement model, then, represents the CFA model described earlier in that it specifies the pattern by which each measure loads on a particular factor. In contrast, the *structural model* defines relations among the unobserved variables. Accordingly, it specifies the manner by which particular latent variables directly or indirectly influence (i.e., "cause") changes in the values of certain other latent variables in the model.

For didactic purposes in clarifying this important aspect of SEM composition, let's now examine Figure 1.2, in which the same model presented in Figure 1.1 has been demarcated into measurement and structural components.

Considered separately, the elements modeled within each rectangle in Figure 1.2 represent two CFA models. The enclosure of the two factors within the ellipse represents a full latent variable model and thus would not be of interest in CFA research. The CFA model to the left of the diagram represents a one-factor model (MSC) measured by three observed variables (SDQMSC, APIMSC, and SPPCMSC), whereas the CFA model on the right represents a one-factor model (MATH) measured by two observed variables (MATHGR-MATHACH). In both cases, the regression of the observed variables on each factor, and the variances of both the

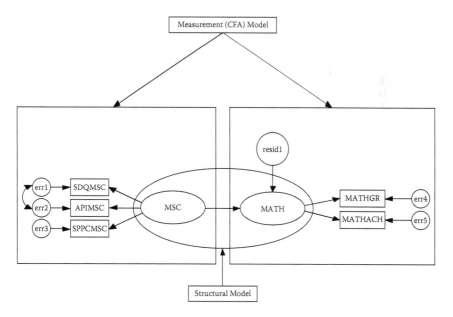

Figure 1.2 A general structural equation model demarcated into measurement and structural components.

factor and the errors of measurement are of primary interest; the error covariance would be of interest only in analyses related to the CFA model bearing on MSC.

It is perhaps important to note that, although both CFA models described in Figure 1.2 represent first-order factor models, second-order and higher order CFA models can also be analyzed using AMOS. Such hierarchical CFA models, however, are less commonly found in the literature (Kerlinger, 1984). Discussion and application of CFA models in the present book are limited to first- and second-order models only. (For a more comprehensive discussion and explanation of first- and second-order CFA models, see Bollen, 1989a; Kerlinger.)

The formulation of covariance and mean structures

The core parameters in structural equation models that focus on the analysis of covariance structures are the regression coefficients, and the variances and covariances of the independent variables; when the focus extends to the analysis of mean structures, the means and intercepts also become central parameters in the model. However, given that sample data comprise observed scores only, there needs to be some internal mechanism whereby the data are transposed into parameters of the model. This task is accomplished via a mathematical model representing the entire system of variables. Such representation systems can and do vary with each SEM computer program. Because adequate explanation of the way in which the AMOS representation system operates demands knowledge of the program's underlying statistical theory, the topic goes beyond the aims and intent of the present volume. Thus, readers interested in a comprehensive explanation of this aspect of the analysis of covariance structures are referred to the following texts (Bollen, 1989a; Saris & Stronkhorst, 1984) and monographs (Long, 1983b).

In this chapter, I have presented you with a few of the basic concepts associated with SEM. As with any form of communication, one must first understand the language before being able to understand the message conveyed, and so it is in comprehending the specification of SEM models. Now that you are familiar with the basic concepts underlying structural equation modeling, we can turn our attention to the specification and analysis of models within the framework of the AMOS program. In the next chapter, then, I provide you with details regarding the specification of models within the context of the graphical interface of the AMOS program. Along the way, I show you how to use the Toolbox feature in building models, review many of the drop-down menus, and detail specified and illustrated components of three basic SEM models. As you work your way through the applications included in this book, you will become increasingly more confident both in your understanding of SEM and in using the AMOS program. So, let's move on to Chapter 2 and a more comprehensive look at SEM modeling with AMOS.

Endnotes

1. Throughout the remainder of the book, the terms *latent, unobserved,* or *unmeasured* variable are used synonymously to represent a hypothetical construct or factor; the terms *observed, manifest,* and *measured* variable are also used interchangeably.
2. Residual terms are often referred to as *disturbance terms.*
3. Of course, this default can be overridden by selecting Visibility from the Object Properties dialog box (to be described in chapter 2).
4. In this book, a *cause* is a direct effect of a variable on another within the context of a complete model. Its magnitude and direction are given by the partial regression coefficient. If the complete model contains all relevant influences on a given dependent variable, its causal precursors are correctly specified. In practice, however, models may omit key predictors, and may be misspecified, so that it may be inadequate as a "causal model" in the philosophical sense.

chapter two

Using the AMOS program

The purpose of this chapter is to introduce you to the general format of the AMOS program and to its graphical approach to the analysis of confirmatory factor analytic and full structural equation models. The name, AMOS, is actually an acronym for *analysis of moment structures* or, in other words, the analysis of mean and covariance structures.

An interesting aspect of AMOS is that, although developed within the Microsoft Windows interface, the program allows you to choose from three different modes of model specification. Using the one approach, AMOS Graphics, you work directly from a path diagram; using the others, AMOS VB.NET and AMOS C#, you work directly from equation statements. The choice of which AMOS method to use is purely arbitrary and bears solely on how comfortable you feel in working within either a graphical interface or a more traditional programming interface. In the second edition of this book, I focus only on the graphical approach. For information related to the other two interfaces, readers are referred to the user's guide (Arbuckle, 2007).

Without a doubt, for those of you who enjoy working with draw programs, rest assured that you will love working with AMOS Graphics! All drawing tools have been carefully designed with SEM conventions in mind—and there is a wide array of them from which to choose. With the simple click of either the left or right mouse buttons, you will be amazed at how quickly you can formulate a publication-quality path diagram. On the other hand, for those of you who may feel more at home with specifying your model using an equation format, the AMOS VB.NET and/or C# options are very straightforward and easily applied.

Regardless of which mode of model input you choose, all options related to the analyses are available from drop-down menus, and all estimates derived from the analyses can be presented in text format. In addition, AMOS Graphics allows for the estimates to be displayed graphically in a path diagram. Thus, the choice between these two approaches to SEM really boils down to one's preferences regarding the specification of models. In this chapter, I introduce you to the various features of AMOS Graphics by illustrating the formulation of input specification related to three simple models. As with all subsequent chapters in the book, I walk you through the various stages of each featured application.

Let's turn our attention now to a review of the various components and characteristics of AMOS Graphics as they relate to the specification of three basic models—a first-order CFA model (Example 1), a second-order CFA model (Example 2), and a full SEM model (Example 3).

Working with AMOS Graphics: Example 1

Initiating AMOS Graphics

To initiate AMOS Graphics, you will need, first, to follow the usual Windows procedure as follows: Start → Programs → AMOS (Version) → AMOS Graphics. In the present case, all work is based on AMOS version 17.[1] Shown in Figure 2.1 is the complete AMOS selection screen with which you will be presented. As you can see, it is possible to get access to various aspects of previous work. Initially, however, you will want to click on AMOS Graphics. Alternatively, you can always place the AMOS Graphics icon on your desktop.

Once you are in AMOS Graphics, you will see the opening screen and toolbox shown in Figure 2.2. On the far right of this screen you will see a blank rectangle; this space provides for the drawing of your path diagram. The large highlighted icon at the top of the center section of the screen, when activated, presents you with a view of the input path diagram (i.e., the model specification). The companion icon to the right of the first one allows you to view the output path diagram, that is, the path diagram with the parameter estimates included. Of course, given that we have not yet conducted any analyses, this output icon is grayed out and not highlighted.

AMOS modeling tools

AMOS provides you with all the tools that you will ever need in creating and working with SEM path diagrams. Each tool is represented

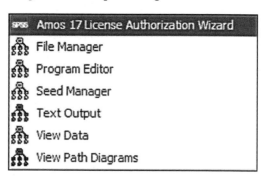

Figure 2.1 AMOS startup menu.

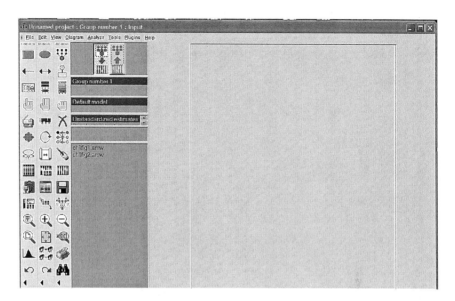

Figure 2.2 Opening AMOS Graphics screen showing palette of tool icons.

by an icon (or button) and performs one particular function; there are 42 icons from which to choose. Immediately upon opening the program, you see the toolbox containing each of these icons, with the blank workspace located to its right. A brief descriptor of each icon is presented in Table 2.1.

In reviewing Table 2.1, you will note that, although the majority of the icons are associated with individual components of the path diagram (e.g.,), or with the path diagram as a whole (e.g.,), others relate either to the data (e.g.,) or to the analyses (e.g.,). Don't worry about trying to remember this smorgasbord of tools as simply holding the mouse pointer stationary over an icon is enough to trigger the pop-up label that identifies its function. As you begin working with AMOS Graphics in drawing a model, you will find two tools in particular, the *Indicator Icon* and the *Error Icon* , to be worth their weight in gold! Both of these icons reduce, tremendously, the tedium of trying to align all multiple indicator variables together with their related error variables in an effort to produce an aesthetically pleasing diagram. As a consequence, it is now possible to structure a path diagram in just a matter of minutes.

Now that you have had a chance to peruse the working tools of AMOS Graphics, let's move on to their actual use in formulating a path diagram. For your first experience in using this graphical interface, we'll reconstruct the hypothesized CFA model shown in Figure 2.3.

Table 2.1 Selected Drawing Tools in AMOS Graphics

	Rectangle Icon: Draws observed (measured) variables
	Oval Icon: Draws unobserved (latent, unmeasured) variables
	Indicator Icon: Draws a latent variable or adds an indicator variable
	Path Icon: Draws a regression path
	Covariance Icon: Draws covariances
	Error Icon: Adds an error/uniqueness variable to an existing observed variable
	Title Icon: Adds figure caption to path diagram
	Variable List (I) Icon: Lists variables in the model
	Variable List (II) Icon: Lists variables in the data set
	Single Selection Icon: Selects one object at a time
	Multiple Selection Icon: Selects all objects
	Multiple Deselection Icon: Deselects all objects
	Duplicate Icon: Makes multiple copies of selected object(s)
	Move Icon: Moves selected object(s) to an alternate location
	Erase Icon: Deletes selected object(s)
	Shape Change Icon: Alters shape of selected object(s)
	Rotate Icon: Changes orientation of indicator variables
	Reflect Icon: Reverses direction of indicator variables
	Move Parameter Icon: Moves parameter values to alternate location
	Scroll Icon: Repositions path diagram to another part of the screen
	Touch-Up Icon: Enables rearrangement of arrows in path diagram

(continued)

Table 2.1 Selected Drawing Tools in AMOS Graphics (*Continued*)

Data File Icon: Selects and reads data file(s)

Analysis Properties Icon: Requests additional calculations

Calculate Estimates Icon: Calculates default and/or requested estimates

Clipboard Icon: Copies path diagram to Windows clipboard

Text Output Icon: View output in textual format

Save Diagram Icon: Saves the current path diagram

Object Properties Icon: Defines properties of variables

Drag Properties Icon: Transfers selected properties of an object to one or more target objects

Preserve Symmetry Icon: Maintains proper spacing among a selected group of objects

Zoom Select Icon: Magnifies selected portion of a path diagram

Zoom-In Icon: Views smaller area of path diagram

Zoom-Out Icon: Views larger area of path diagram

Zoom Page Icon: Shows entire page on the screen

Fit-to-Page Icon: Resizes path diagram to fit within page boundary

Loupe Icon: Examines path diagram with a loupe (magnifying glass)

Bayesian Icon: Enables analyses based on Bayesian statistics

Multiple Group Icon: Enables analyses of multiple groups

Print Icon: Prints selected path diagram

Undo (I) Icon: Undoes previous change

Undo (II) Icon: Undoes previous undo

Specification Search: Enables modeling based on a specification search

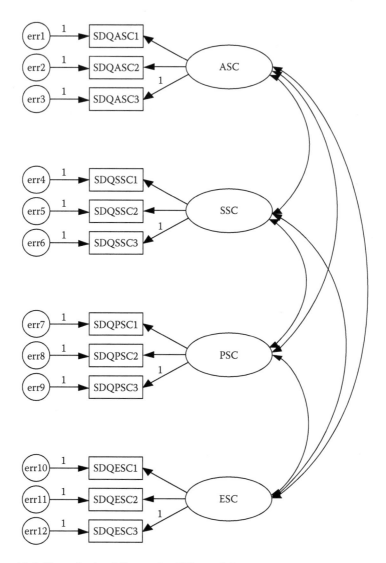

Figure 2.3 Hypothesized first-order CFA model.

The hypothesized model

The CFA structure in Figure 2.3 comprises four self-concept (SC) factors—academic SC (ASC), social SC (SSC), physical SC (PSC), and emotional SC (ESC). Each SC factor is measured by three observed variables, the reliability of which is influenced by random measurement error, as indicated by the associated error term. Each of these observed variables is regressed onto its respective factor. Finally, the four factors are shown to be intercorrelated.

Drawing the path diagram

To initiate the drawing of a new model, click on *File*, shown at the top of the opening AMOS screen, and then select *New* from the drop-down menu. Although the *File* drop-down menu is typical of most Windows programs, I include it here in Figure 2.4 in the interest of completeness.

Now, we're ready to draw our path diagram. The first tool which you will want to use is what I call the "million-dollar" (indicator) icon (see Table 2.1) because it performs several functions. Click on this icon to activate it and then, with the cursor in the blank drawing space provided, hold down the left mouse button and draw an ellipse by dragging it slightly to create an ellipse. If you prefer your factor model to show the factors as circles, rather than ellipses, just don't perform the dragging action. When working with the icons, you need to release the mouse button after you have finished working with a particular function. Figure 2.5 illustrates the completed ellipse shape with the *Indicator Icon* 🔲 still activated. Of course, you could also have activated the *Draw Unobserved Variables Icon* 🔲 and achieved the same result.[2]

Now that we have the ellipse representing the first latent factor, the next step is to add the indicator variables. To do so, we click on the *Indicator Icon*, after which the mouse pointer changes to resemble the *Indicator Icon*. Now, move the *Indicator Icon* image to the center of the ellipse, at which time its outer rim becomes highlighted in red. Next, click on the unobserved variable. In viewing Figure 2.6, you will see that this action produces a

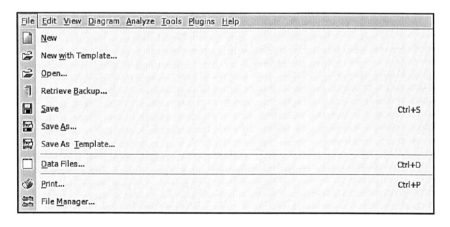

Figure 2.4 The AMOS Graphics file menu.

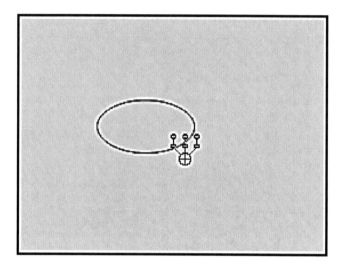

Figure 2.5 Drawing an ellipse to represent an unobserved latent variable (or factor).

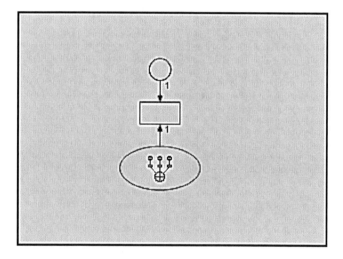

Figure 2.6 Adding the first error term to the latent factor.

rectangle (representing a single observed variable), an arrow pointing from the latent factor to the observed variable (representing a regression path), and a small circle with an arrow pointing toward the observed variable (representing a measurement error term).[3] Again, you will see that the *Indicator Icon*, when activated, appears in the center of the ellipse. This, of course, occurs because that's where the cursor is pointing.

Note, however, that the hypothesized model (see Figure 2.3) we are endeavoring to structure schematically shows each of its latent factors to have three, rather than only one, indicator variable. These additional indicators are easily added to the diagram by two simple clicks of the left mouse button while the *Indicator Icon* is activated. In other words, with this icon activated, each time that the left mouse button is clicked, AMOS Graphics will produce an additional indicator variable, each with its associated error term. Figures 2.7 and 2.8 show the results of having made one and two additional clicks, respectively, to the left mouse button.

In reviewing the hypothesized model again, we note that the three indicator variables for each latent factor are oriented to the left of the ellipse rather than to the top, as is currently the case in our diagram here. This task is easily accomplished by means of rotation. One very simple way of accomplishing this reorientation is to click the right mouse button while the *Indicator Icon* is activated. Figure 2.9 illustrates the outcome of this clicking action.

As you can see from the dialog box, there are a variety of options related to this path diagram from which you can choose. At this time, however, we are only interested in the *Rotate* option. Moving down the menu and clicking with the left mouse button on *Rotate* will activate the *Rotate* function and assign the related label to the cursor. When the cursor is moved to the center of the oval and the left mouse button clicked, the three indicator variables, in combination with their error terms and links

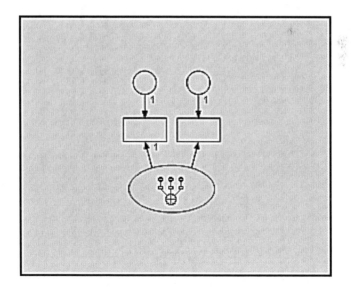

Figure 2.7 Adding the second error term to the latent factor.

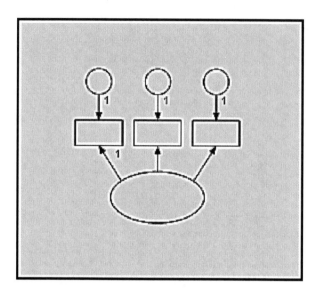

Figure 2.8 The latent factor with three indicator variables and their associated error terms.

to the underlying factor, will move 45 degrees clockwise, as illustrated in Figure 2.10; two additional clicks will produce the desired orientation shown in Figure 2.11. Alternatively, we could have activated the *Rotate Icon* 🔘 and then clicked on the ellipse to obtain the same effect.

Now that we have one factor structure completed, it becomes a simple task of duplicating this configuration in order to add three additional ones to the model. However, before we can duplicate, we must first group all components of this structure so that they operate as a single unit. This is easily accomplished by clicking on the *Multiple Selection Icon* 🖑, after which you will observe that the outline of all factor structure components is now highlighted in blue, thereby indicating that they now operate as a unit. As with other drawing tasks in AMOS, duplication of this structure can be accomplished either by clicking on the *Duplicate Icon* 🖨 or by right-clicking on the model and activating the menu, as shown in Figure 2.9. In both cases, you will see that with each click and drag of the left mouse button, the cursor takes on the form of a photocopier and generates one copy of the factor structure. This action is illustrated in Figure 2.12.

Once you have the number of copies that you need, it's just a matter of dragging each duplicated structure into position. Figure 2.13 illustrates the four factor structures lined up vertically to replicate the hypothesized

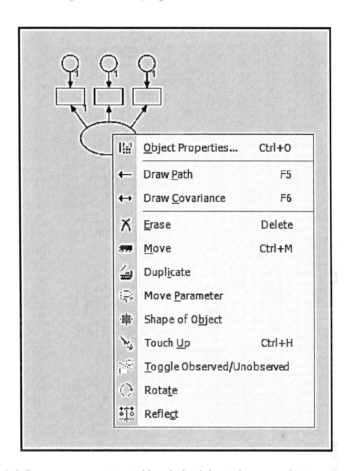

Figure 2.9 Pop-up menu activated by click of the right mouse button.

CFA model. Note the insert of the *Move Icon* in this figure; it is used to reposition objects from one location to another. In the present case, it was used to move the four duplicated factor structures such that they were aligned vertically. In composing your own SEM diagrams, you may wish to move an entire path diagram for better placement on a page. This realignment is made possible with the *Move Icon*, but don't forget to activate the *Multiple Selection Icon* illustrated earlier.[4]

Now we need to add the factor covariances to our path diagram. Illustrated in Figure 2.14 is the addition of a covariance between the first and fourth factors; these double-headed arrows are drawn by clicking on the *Covariance Icon* . Once this button has been activated, you then click on one object (in this case, the first latent factor), and drag the arrow to the second object of interest (in this case, the fourth latent factor). The

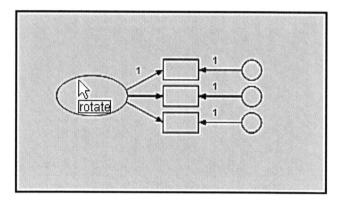

Figure 2.10 The latent factor with indicator variables and error terms rotated once.

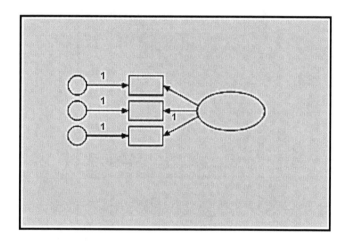

Figure 2.11 The reflected latent factor structure shown in Figure 2.10.

process is then repeated for each of the remaining specified covariances. Yes, gone are the days of spending endless hours trying to draw multiple arrows that look at least somewhat similar in their curvature! Thanks to AMOS Graphics, these double-headed arrows are drawn perfectly every single time.

At this point, our path diagram, structurally speaking, is complete; all that is left for us to do is to label each of the variables. If you look back at Figure 2.9, in which the mouse right-click menu is displayed, you will see a selection termed *Object Properties* at the top of the menu. This is the option you need in order to add text to a path diagram. To initiate this

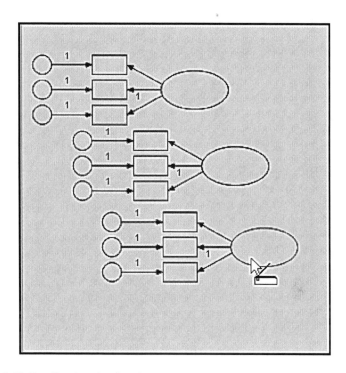

Figure 2.12 Duplicating the first factor structure.

process, point the cursor at the object in need of the added text, right-click to bring up the *View* menu, and, finally, left-click on *Object Properties*, which activates the dialog box shown in Figure 2.15. Of import here are the five different tabs at the top of the dialog box. We select the *Text* tab, which enables us to specify a font size and style specific to the variable name to be entered. For purposes of illustration, I have simply entered the label for the first latent variable (ASC) and selected a font size of 12 with regular font style. All remaining labeling was completed in the same manner. Alternatively, you can display the list of variables in the data and then drag each variable to its respective rectangle.

The path diagram related to the hypothesized CFA model is now complete. However, before leaving AMOS Graphics, I wish to show you the contents of four pull-down menus made available to you on your drawing screen. (For a review of possible menus, see Figure 2.2.) The first and third drop-down menus shown in Figure 2.16 relate in some way to path diagrams. In reviewing these *Edit* and *Diagram* menus, you will quickly see that they serve as alternatives to the use of drawing tools, some of which I have just demonstrated in the recon-struction of Figure 2.3. Thus, for those of you who may prefer to work

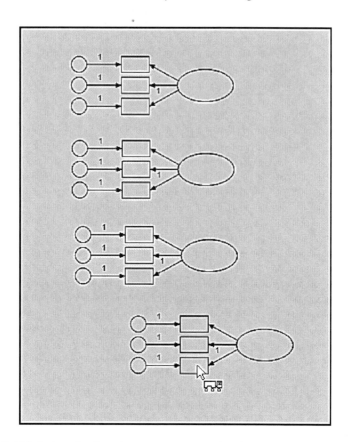

Figure 2.13 Moving the four factor structures to be aligned vertically.

with pull-down menus, rather than with drawing tool buttons, AMOS Graphics provides you with this option. As its name implies, the *View* menu allows you to peruse various features associated with the variables and/or parameters in the path diagram. Finally, from the *Analyze* menu, you can calculate estimates (i.e., execute a job), manage groups and/or models, and conduct a multiple group analysis and varied other types of analyses.

By now, you should have a fairly good understanding of how AMOS Graphics works. Of course, because learning comes from doing, you will most assuredly want to practice on your own some of the techniques illustrated here. For those of you who are still uncomfortable working with draw programs, take solace in the fact that I too harbored such fears until I worked with AMOS. Rest assured that once you have decided to take the plunge into the world of draw programs, you will be amazed at how simple the techniques are, and this is especially true of AMOS Graphics!

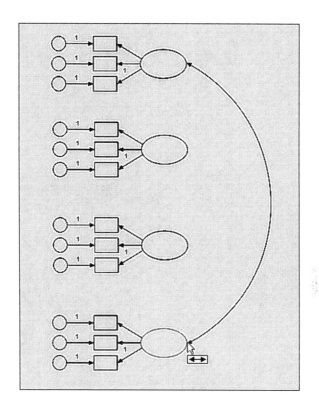

Figure 2.14 Drawing the first factor covariance double-headed arrow.

Understanding the basic components of model 1

Recall from Chapter 1 that the key parameters to be estimated in a CFA model are the regression coefficients (i.e., factor loadings), the factor and error variances, and, in some models (as is the case with Figure 2.3), the factor covariances. Given that the latent and observed variables are specified in the model in AMOS Graphics, the program automatically estimates the factor and error variances. In other words, variances associated with these specified variables are freely estimated by default. However, defaults related to parameter covariances are governed by the WYSIWYG rule—what you see is what you get. That is, if a covariance path is not included in the path diagram, then this parameter will not be estimated (by default); if it is included, then its value will be estimated.

One extremely important caveat in working with structural equation models is to always tally the number of parameters in the model to be estimated prior to running the analyses. This information is critical to your

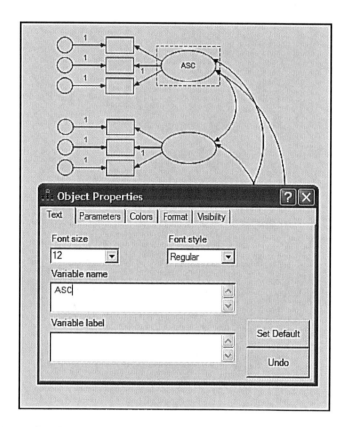

Figure 2.15 The object properties dialog box: text tab open.

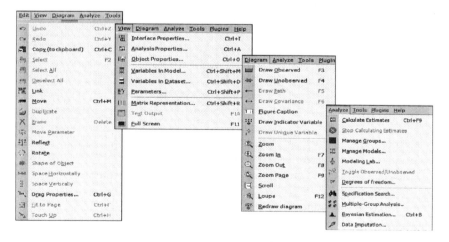

Figure 2.16 Four selected AMOS Graphics pull-down menus.

knowledge of whether or not the model that you are testing is statistically identified. Thus, as a prerequisite to the discussion of identification, let's count the number of parameters to be estimated for the model portrayed in Figure 2.3. From a review of the figure, we can ascertain that there are 12 regression coefficients (factor loadings), 16 variances (12 error variances and 4 factor variances), and 6 factor covariances. The 1's assigned to one of each set of regression path parameters represent a fixed value of 1.00; as such, these parameters are not estimated. In total, then, there are 30 parameters to be estimated for the CFA model depicted in Figure 2.3. Let's now turn to a brief discussion of the important concept of model (or statistical) identification.

The concept of model identification

Model identification is a complex topic that is difficult to explain in non-technical terms. Although a thorough explanation of the identification principle exceeds the scope of the present book, it is not critical to the reader's understanding and use of the book. Nonetheless, because some insight into the general concept of the identification issue will undoubtedly help you to better understand why, for example, particular parameters are specified as having fixed values, I attempt now to give you a brief, nonmathematical explanation of the basic idea underlying this concept. Essentially, I address only the so-called t-rule, one of several tests associated with identification. I encourage you to consult the following texts for a more comprehensive treatment of the topic: Bollen (1989a), Kline (2005), Long (1983a, 1983b), and Saris and Stronkhorst (1984). I also recommend a very clear and readable description of the identification issue in a book chapter by MacCallum (1995), and of its underlying assumptions in Hayashi and Marcoulides (2006).

In broad terms, the issue of identification focuses on whether or not there is a unique set of parameters consistent with the data. This question bears directly on the transposition of the variance–covariance matrix of observed variables (the data) into the structural parameters of the model under study. If a unique solution for the values of the structural parameters can be found, the model is considered to be identified. As a consequence, the parameters are considered to be estimable and the model therefore testable. If, on the other hand, a model cannot be identified, it indicates that the parameters are subject to arbitrariness, thereby implying that different parameter values define the same model; such being the case, attainment of consistent estimates for all parameters is not possible, and, thus, the model cannot be evaluated empirically. By way of a simple example, the process would be conceptually akin to trying to determine unique values for X and Y, when the only information you have is that X + Y = 15. Generalizing this example to covariance structure analysis, then, the model identification issue focuses on the extent to which a unique set of values can be inferred for the unknown parameters from a given covariance matrix of analyzed variables that is reproduced by the model.

Structural models may be *just-identified, overidentified,* or *underidentified.* A just-identified model is one in which there is a one-to-one correspondence between the data and the structural parameters. That is to say, the number of data variances and covariances equals the number of parameters to be estimated. However, despite the capability of the model to yield a unique solution for all parameters, the just-identified model is not scientifically interesting because it has no degrees of freedom and therefore can never be rejected. An overidentified model is one in which the number of estimable parameters is less than the number of data points (i.e., variances and covariances of the observed variables). This situation results in positive degrees of freedom that allow for rejection of the model, thereby rendering it of scientific use. The aim in SEM, then, is to specify a model and such that it meets the criterion of overidentification. Finally, an underidentified model is one in which the number of parameters to be estimated exceeds the number of variances and covariances (i.e., data points). As such, the model contains insufficient information (from the input data) for the purpose of attaining a determinate solution of parameter estimation; that is, an infinite number of solutions are possible for an underidentified model.

Reviewing the CFA model in Figure 2.3, let's now determine how many data points we have to work with (i.e., how much information do we have with respect to our data?). As noted above, these constitute the variances and covariances of the observed variables; with p variables, there are $p(p + 1) / 2$ such elements. Given that there are 12 observed variables, this means that we have $12(12 + 1) / 2 = 78$ data points. Prior to this discussion of identification, we determined a total of 30 unknown parameters. Thus, with 78 data points and 30 parameters to be estimated, we have an overidentified model with 48 degrees of freedom.

However, it is important to note that the specification of an overidentified model is a necessary, but not sufficient, condition to resolve the identification problem. Indeed, the imposition of constraints on particular parameters can sometimes be beneficial in helping the researcher to attain an overidentified model. An example of such a constraint is illustrated in Chapter 5 with the application of a second-order CFA model.

Linked to the issue of identification is the requirement that every latent variable have its scale determined. This constraint arises because these variables are unobserved and therefore have no definite metric scale; it can be accomplished in one of two ways. The first approach is tied to specification of the measurement model whereby the unmeasured latent variable is mapped onto its related observed indicator variable. This scaling requisite is satisfied by constraining to some nonzero value (typically, 1.0) one factor-loading parameter in each congeneric[5] set of loadings. This constraint holds for both independent and dependent latent variables. In reviewing Figure 2.3, then, this means that for one of the three regression paths leading from each SC factor to a set of observed indicators, some fixed value should be specified; this fixed parameter is termed a *reference* variable.[6] With respect to the model in Figure 2.3, for example, the scale has been established by constraining to a value of 1.0 the third parameter in each set of observed variables. Recall that AMOS Graphics automatically assigned this value when the *Indicator Icon* was activated and used to add the first indicator variable and its error term to the model. It is important to note, however, that although AMOS Graphics assigned the value of "1" to the lower regression path of each set, this assignment can be changed simply by clicking on the right mouse button and selecting *Object Properties* from the pop-up menu. (This modification will be illustrated with the next example.)

With a better idea of important aspects of the specification of a CFA model in general, specification using AMOS Graphics in particular, and basic notions associated with model identification, we continue on our walk through two remaining models reviewed in this chapter.

Working with AMOS Graphics: Example 2

In this second example of model specification, we examine the second-order model displayed in Figure 2.17.

The hypothesized model

In our previous factor analytic model, we had four factors (ASC, SSC, PSC, and ESC) which operated as independent variables; each could be considered to be one level, or one unidirectional arrow, away from the observed variables. Such factors are termed *first-order factors*. However, it may be the case that the theory argues for some higher level factor that is considered accountable for the lower order factors. Basically, the number of levels or unidirectional arrows that the higher order factor is removed from the observed variables determines whether a factor model is considered to be second order, third order, or some higher order; only a second-order model will be examined here.

Although the model schematically portrayed in Figure 2.17 has essentially the same first-order factor structure as the one shown in Figure 2.3, it differs in that a higher order general self-concept (GSC) factor is hypothesized as accounting for, or explaining, all variance and covariance related to the first-order factors. As such, GSC is termed the

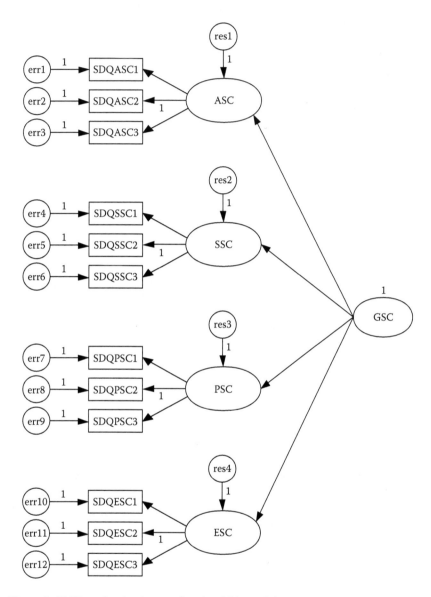

Figure 2.17 Hypothesized second-order CFA model.

second-order factor. It is important to take particular note of the fact that GSC does not have its own set of measured indicators; rather, it is linked indirectly to those measuring the lower order factors. Let's now take a closer look at the parameters to be estimated for this second-order model.

I wish to draw your attention to several aspects of the second-order model shown in Figure 2.17. First, note the presence of single-headed arrows leading from the second-order factor (GSC) to each of the first-order factors (ASC to ESC). These regression paths represent second-order factor loadings, and all are freely estimated. Recall, however, that for reasons linked to the model identification issue, a constraint must be placed either on one of the regression paths or on the variance of an independent factor, as these parameters cannot be estimated simultaneously. Because the impact of GSC on each of the lower order SC factors is of primary interest in second-order CFA models, the variance of the higher order factor is typically constrained to equal 1.0, thereby leaving the second-order factor loadings to be freely estimated.

A second aspect of this second-order model, perhaps requiring amplification, is the initial appearance that the first-order factors operate as both independent and dependent variables. This situation, however, is not so, as variables can serve as either independent or dependent variables in a model, but not as both.[7] Because the first-order factors function as dependent variables, it follows that their variances and covariances are no longer estimable parameters in the model; such variation is presumed to be accounted for by the higher order factor. In comparing Figures 2.3 and 2.17, then, you will note that there are no longer double-headed curved arrows linking the first-order SC factors, thereby indicating that neither the factor covariances nor variances are to be estimated.

Finally, the prediction of each of the first-order factors from the second-order factor is presumed not to be without error. Thus, a residual error term is associated with each of the lower level factors.

As a first step in determining whether this second-order model is identified, we now sum the number of parameters to be estimated; we have 8 first-order regression coefficients, 4 second-order regression coefficients, 12 measurement error variances, and 4 residual error terms, making a total of 28. Given that there are 78 pieces of information in the sample variance–covariance matrix, we conclude that this model is identified with 50 degrees of freedom.

Before leaving this identification issue, however, a word of caution is in order. With complex models in which there may be more than one level of latent variable structures, it is wise to visually check each level separately for evidence that identification has been attained. For example, although we know from our initial CFA model that the first-order level is identified, it is quite possible that the second-order level may indeed be underidentified. Because the first-order factors function as indicators of (i.e., the input data for) the second-order factor, identification is easy to assess. In the present model, we have four factors, thereby giving us

10 (4 × 5 / 2) pieces of information from which to formulate the parameters of the higher order structure. According to the model depicted in Figure 2.17, we wish to estimate 8 parameters (4 regression paths; 4 residual error variances), thus leaving us with 2 degrees of freedom, and an overidentified model. However, suppose that we only had three first-order factors. We would then be left with a just-identified model at the upper level as a consequence of trying to estimate 6 parameters from 6 (3[3 + 1] / 2) pieces of information. In order for such a model to be tested, additional constraints would need to be imposed (see, e.g., Chapter 5). Finally, let's suppose that there were only two first-order factors; we would then have an underidentified model since there would be only three pieces of information, albeit four parameters to be estimated. Although it might still be possible to test such a model, given further restrictions on the model, the researcher would be better advised to reformulate his or her model in light of this problem (see Rindskopf & Rose, 1988).

Drawing the path diagram

Now that we have dispensed with the necessary "heavy stuff," let's move on to creating the second-order model shown in Figure 2.17 which will serve as the specification input for AMOS Graphics. We can make life easy for ourselves here simply by pulling up our first-order model (see Figure 2.3). Because the first-order level of our new model will remain the same as that shown in Figure 2.3, the only thing that needs to be done by way of modification is to remove all the factor covariance arrows. This task, of course, can be accomplished in AMOS in one of two ways: either by activating the *Erase Icon* X and clicking on each double-headed arrow, or by placing the cursor on each double-headed arrow individually and then right-clicking on the mouse, which produces the menu shown earlier. Once you select the *Erase* option on the menu, the *Erase Icon* will automatically activate and the cursor converts to a claw-like X symbol. Simply place the X over the component that you wish to delete and left-click; the targeted component disappears. As illustrated in Figure 2.18, the covariance between ASC and SSC has already been deleted, with the covariance between ASC and PSC being the next one to be deleted. For both methods of erasure, AMOS automatically highlights the selected parameter in red.

Having removed all the double-headed arrows representing the factor covariances from the model, our next task is to draw the ellipse representing the higher order factor of GSC. We do this by activating the *Oval Icon* , which, for me, resulted in an ellipse with solid red fill. However, for publication purposes, you will likely want the ellipse to be clear. To accomplish this, place the cursor over the upper ellipse and right-click on

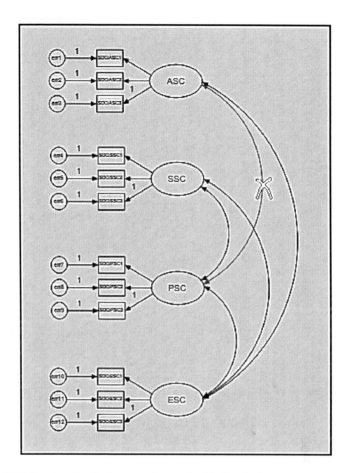

Figure 2.18 Erasing the factor covariance double-headed arrows.

the mouse, which again will produce a menu from which you select *Object Properties*. At this point, your model should resemble the one shown in Figure 2.19. Once in this dialog box, click on the *Color* tab, scroll down to *Fill* style, and then choose *Transparent*, as illustrated in Figure 2.20. Note that you can elect to set this color option as default by clicking on the *Set Default* tab to the right.

Continuing with our path diagram, we now need to add the second-order factor regression paths. We accomplish this task by first activating the *Path Icon* ← and then, with the cursor clicked on the central underside of the GSC ellipse, dragging the cursor up to where it touches the central right side of the ASC ellipse. Figure 2.21 illustrates this drawing process with respect to the first path; the process is repeated for each of the other three paths.

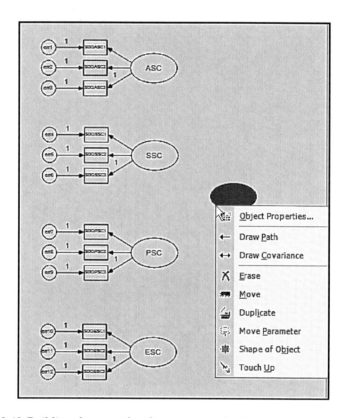

Figure 2.19 Building the second-order structure: the higher order latent factor.

Because each of the first-order factors is now a dependent variable in the model, we need to add the residual error term associated with the prediction of each by the higher order factor of GSC. To do so, we activate the *Error Icon* [icon] and then click with the left mouse button on each of the ellipses representing the first-order factors. Figure 2.22 illustrates implementation of the residual error term for ASC. In this instance, only one click was completed, thereby leaving the residual error term in its current position (note the solid fill as I had not yet set the default for transparent fill). However, if we clicked again with the left mouse button, the error term would move 45 degrees clockwise, as shown in Figure 2.23; with each subsequent click, the error term would continue to be moved clockwise in a similar manner.

The last task in completing our model is to label the higher order factor, as well as each of the residual error terms. Recall that this process is accomplished by first placing the cursor on the object of interest (in this case, the first residual error term) and then clicking with the right mouse

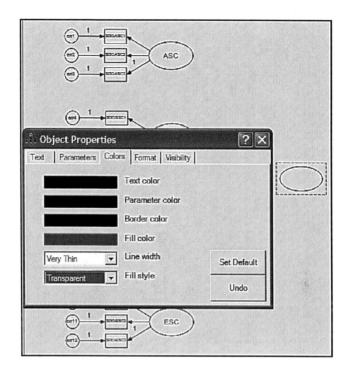

Figure 2.20 Removing colored fill from the higher order latent factor.

button. This action releases the pop-up menu shown in Figure 2.19, from which we select *Object Properties*, which, in turn, yields the dialog box displayed in Figure 2.24. To label the first error term, we again select the *Text* tab and then add the text "res1"; this process is then repeated for each of the remaining residual error terms.

Working with AMOS Graphics: Example 3

For our last example, we'll examine a full SEM model. Recall from Chapter 1 that, in contrast to a first-order CFA model which comprises only a measurement component, and a second-order CFA model for which the higher order level is represented by a reduced form of a structural model, the full structural equation model encompasses *both* a measurement and a structural model. Accordingly, the full model embodies a system of variables whereby latent factors are regressed on other factors as dictated by theory, as well as on the appropriate observed measures. In other words, in the full SEM model, certain latent variables are connected by one-way arrows, the directionality of which reflects hypotheses bearing on the causal structure of variables in the model. We turn now to the hypothesized model.

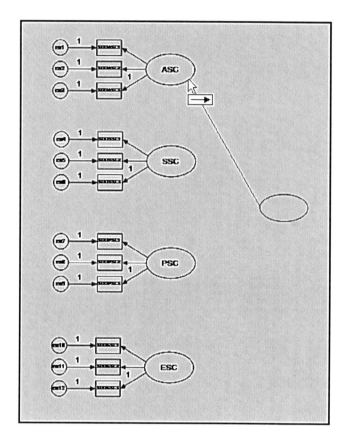

Figure 2.21 Building the second-order structure: the regression paths.

The hypothesized model

For a clearer conceptualization of full SEM models, let's examine the relatively simple structure presented in Figure 2.25. The structural component of this model represents the hypothesis that a child's self-confidence (SCONF) derives from his or her self-perception of overall social competence (social SC, or SSC), which, in turn, is influenced by the child's perception of how well he or she gets along with family members (SSCF), as well as with his or her peers at school (SSCS). The measurement component of the model shows each of the SC factors to have three indicator measures, and the self-confidence factor to have two.

Turning first to the structural part of the model, we can see that there are four factors; the two independent factors (SSCF; SSCS) are postulated as being correlated with each other, as indicated by the curved two-way arrow joining them, but they are linked to the other two factors by a series

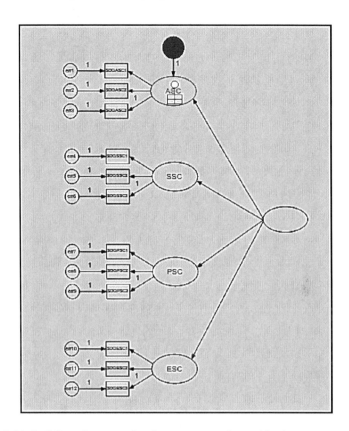

Figure 2.22 Building the second-order structure: the residual errors.

of regression paths, as indicated by the unidirectional arrows. Because the factors SSC and SCONF have one-way arrows pointing at them, they are easily identified as dependent variables in the model. Residual errors associated with the regression of SSC on both SSCF and SSCS, and the regression of SCONF on SSC, are captured by the disturbance terms res1 and res2, respectively. Finally, because one path from each of the two independent factors (SSCF; SSCS) to their respective indicator variables is fixed to 1.0, their variances can be freely estimated; variances of the dependent variables (SSC; SCONF), however, are not parameters in the model.

By now, you likely feel fairly comfortable in interpreting the measurement portion of the model, and so substantial elaboration is not necessary here. As usual, associated with each observed measure is an error term, the variance of which is of interest. (Because the observed measures technically operate as dependent variables in the model, as indicated by the arrows pointing toward them, their variances are not estimated.) Finally,

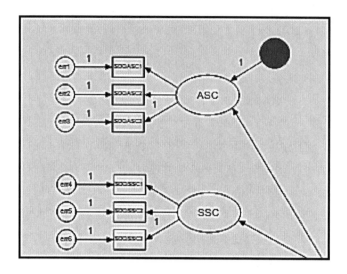

Figure 2.23 Changing the orientation of the residual error term.

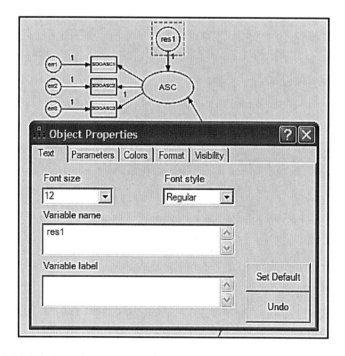

Figure 2.24 Labeling the second-order factor and residual errors: object properties dialog box's text tab open.

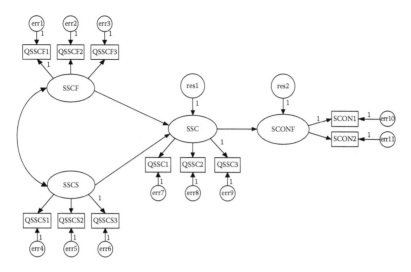

Figure 2.25 Hypothesized full structural equation model.

to establish the scale for each unmeasured factor in the model (and for purposes of statistical identification), one parameter in each set of regression paths is fixed to 1.0; recall, however, that path selection for the imposition of this constraint was purely arbitrary.

For this, our last example, let's again determine if we have an identified model. Given that we have 11 observed measures, we know that we have 66 (11[11 + 1] / 2) pieces of information from which to derive the parameters of the model. Counting up the unknown parameters in the model, we see that we have 26 parameters to be estimated: 7 measurement regression paths, 3 structural regression paths, 2 factor variances, 11 error variances, 2 residual error variances, and 1 covariance. We therefore have 40 (66 – 26) degrees of freedom and, thus, an overidentified model.

Drawing the path diagram

Given what you now already know about drawing path diagrams within the framework of AMOS Graphics, you likely would encounter no difficulty in reproducing the hypothesized model shown in Figure 2.25. Therefore, rather than walk you through the entire drawing process related to this model, I'll take the opportunity here to demonstrate two additional features of the drawing tools that have either not yet been illustrated or been illustrated only briefly. The first of these makes use of the *Object Properties Icon* in reorienting the assignment of fixed "1" values that the program automatically assigns to the factor-loading regression paths. Turning to Figure 2.25, focus on the SSCS factor in the lower left corner of the diagram. Note that the fixed path for this factor has been assigned to the one associated with the prediction of QSSCS3. For purposes of illustration, let's reassign the fixed value of "1" to the first regression path (QSSCS1). To carry out this reorientation process, we can either right-click on the mouse, or click on the *Object Properties Icon,* which in either case activates the related dialog box; we focus here on the latter. In using this approach, we click first on the icon and then on the parameter of interest (QSSCS3, in this instance), which then results in the parameter value becoming enclosed in a broken line box (see Figure 2.26). Once in the dialog box, we click on the *Parameter* tab at the top, which then generates the dialog box shown in Figure 2.26. Note that the regression weight is listed as "1." To remove this weight, we simply delete the value. To reassign this weight, we subsequently click on the first regression path (QSSCS1) and then on the *Object Properties Icon.* This time, of course, the *Object Properties* dialog box indicates no regression weight (see Figure 2.27) and all we need to do is to add a value of "1," as shown in Figure 2.26 for indicator variable QSSCS3. Implementation of these last two actions yields a modified version of the originally hypothesized model (Figure 2.25), which is schematically portrayed in Figure 2.28.

The second feature that I wish to demonstrate involves the reorientation of error terms, usually for purposes of improving the appearance

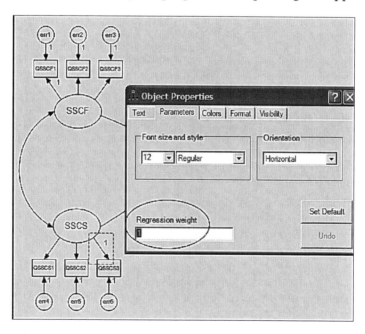

Figure 2.26 Reassigning a fixed regression weight: the existing parameter.

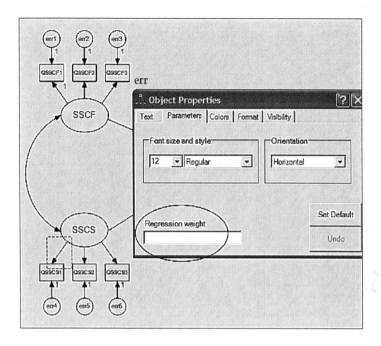

Figure 2.27 Reassigning a fixed regression weight: the target parameter.

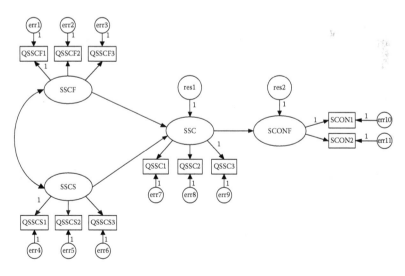

Figure 2.28 Reproduced model with rotated residual error terms and reassigned fixed "1" regression weight.

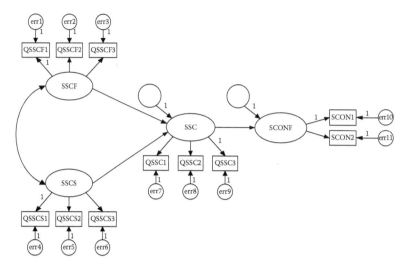

Figure 2.29 Rotating the residual error terms.

of the path diagram. Although I briefly mentioned this procedure and showed the resulting reorientation with respect to Example 2, I consider it important to expand on my earlier illustration as it is a technique that comes in handy when you are working with path diagrams that may have many variables in the model. With the residual error terms in the 12 o'clock position, as in Figure 2.25, we'll continue to click with the left mouse button until they reach the 10 o'clock position shown in Figure 2.29. Each click of the mouse results in a 45-degree clockwise move of the residual error term, with eight clicks thus returning us to the 12 o'clock position; the position indicated in Figure 2.29 resulted from seven clicks of the mouse.

In Chapter 1, I introduced you to the basic concepts underlying SEM, and in the present chapter, I extended this information to include the issue of model identification. In this chapter, specifically, I have endeavored to show you the AMOS Graphics approach in specifying particular models under study. I hope that I have succeeded in giving you a fairly good idea of the ease by which AMOS makes this process possible. Nonetheless, it is important for me to emphasize that, although I have introduced you to a wide variety of the program's many features, I certainly have not exhausted the total range of possibilities, as to do so would far exceed the intended scope of the present book. Now that you are fairly well equipped with knowledge of the conceptual underpinning of SEM and the basic functioning of the AMOS program, let's move on to the remaining chapters, where we explore the analytic processes involved in SEM using

AMOS Graphics. We turn now to Chapter 3, which features an application bearing on a CFA model.

Endnotes

1. It is important to note that a Beta Version 18 was developed after I had completed the writing of this second edition. However, I have been advised by J. Arbuckle, developer of the AMOS program, that the only changes made to Version 18 are: (a) the appearance of path diagrams, which are now in color by default, and (b) the rearrangement of a few dialog boxes. The text and statistical operations remain unchanged (J. Arbuckle, personal communication, May 2, 2009).
2. Throughout the book, the terms *click* and *drag* are used within the usual Windows framework. As such, *click* means to press and release the mouse button in a single, fairly rapid motion. In contrast, *drag* means to press the mouse button and hold it down while simultaneously moving the mouse.
3. The 1's that are automatically assigned to selected single arrows by the program relate to the issue of model identification, a topic which is addressed later in the chapter.
4. Whenever you see that various components in the path diagram are colored blue, this indicates that they are currently selected as a group of objects. As such, they will be treated as one object should you wish to reorient them in any way. In contrast, single parameters, when selected by a point-and-click action, become highlighted in red.
5. A set of measures is said to be "congeneric" if each measure in the set purports to assess the same construct, except for errors of measurement (Jöreskog, 1971a). For example, as indicated in Figure 2.1, SDQASC1, SDQASC2, and SDQASC3 all serve as measures of academic SC; they therefore represent a congeneric set of indicator variables.
6. Although the decision as to which parameter to constrain is purely an arbitrary one, the measure having the highest reliability is recommended, if this information is known; the value to which the parameter is constrained is also arbitrary.
7. In SEM, once a variable has an arrow pointing at it, thereby targeting it as a dependent variable, it maintains this status throughout the analyses.

section two

Applications in single-group analyses

chapter three

Testing for the factorial validity of a theoretical construct
(First-order CFA model)

Our first application examines a first-order CFA model designed to test the multidimensionality of a theoretical construct. Specifically, this application tests the hypothesis that self-concept (SC), for early adolescents (grade 7), is a multidimensional construct composed of four factors—general SC (GSC), academic SC (ASC), English SC (ESC), and mathematics SC (MSC). The theoretical underpinning of this hypothesis derives from the hierarchical model of SC proposed by Shavelson, Hubner, and Stanton (1976). The example is taken from a study by Byrne and Worth Gavin (1996) in which four hypotheses related to the Shavelson et al. (1976) model were tested for three groups of children—preadolescents (grade 3), early adolescents (grade 7), and late adolescents (grade 11). Only tests bearing on the multidimensional structure of SC, as they relate to grade 7 children, are relevant to the present chapter. This study followed from earlier work in which the same four-factor structure of SC was tested for adolescents (see Byrne & Shavelson, 1986), and was part of a larger study that focused on the structure of social SC (Byrne & Shavelson, 1996). For a more extensive discussion of the substantive issues and the related findings, readers should refer to the original Byrne and Worth Gavin article.

The hypothesized model

At issue in this first application is the plausibility of a multidimensional SC structure for early adolescents. Although numerous studies have supported the multidimensionality of the construct for grade 7 children, others have counterargued that SC is less differentiated for children in their pre- and early adolescent years (e.g., Harter, 1990). Thus, the argument could be made for a two-factor structure comprising only GSC and ASC. Still others postulate that SC is a unidimensional structure so that all facets of SC are embodied within a single SC construct (GSC). (For a review of the literature related to these issues, see Byrne, 1996.) The task presented to us here, then, is to test the original hypothesis that SC is a four-factor structure comprising a general component (GSC), an academic component (ASC), and two subject-specific components (ESC; MSC) against two alternative hypotheses: (a) that SC is a two-factor structure comprising GSC and ASC, and (b) that SC is a one-factor structure in which there is no distinction between general and academic SCs.

We turn now to an examination and testing of each of these hypotheses.

Hypothesis 1: Self-concept is a four-factor structure

The model to be tested in Hypothesis 1 postulates a priori that SC is a four-factor structure composed of general SC (GSC), academic SC (ASC), English SC (ESC), and math SC (MSC); it is presented schematically in Figure 3.1.

Before any discussion of how we might go about testing this model, let's take a few minutes first to dissect the model and list its component parts as follows:

1. There are four SC factors, as indicated by the four ellipses labeled GSC, ASC, ESC, and MSC.
2. The four factors are intercorrelated, as indicated by the two-headed arrows.
3. There are 16 observed variables, as indicated by the 16 rectangles (SDQ2N01–SDQ2N43); they represent item pairs from the General, Academic, Verbal, and Math SC subscales of the Self Description Questionnaire II (Marsh, 1992a).
4. The observed variables load on the factors in the following pattern: SDQ2N01–SDQ2N37 load on Factor 1, SDQ3N04–SDQ2N40 load on Factor 2, SDQ2N10–SDQ2N46 load on Factor 3, and SDQ2N07–SDQ2N43 load on Factor 4.
5. Each observed variable loads on one and only one factor.
6. Errors of measurement associated with each observed variable (err01–err43) are uncorrelated.

Summarizing these observations, we can now present a more formal description of our hypothesized model. As such, we state that the CFA model presented in Figure 3.1 hypothesizes a priori that

1. SC responses can be explained by four factors: GSC, ASC, ESC, and MSC.
2. Each item-pair measure has a nonzero loading on the SC factor that it was designed to measure (termed a *target loading*), and a zero loading on all other factors (termed *nontarget loadings*).

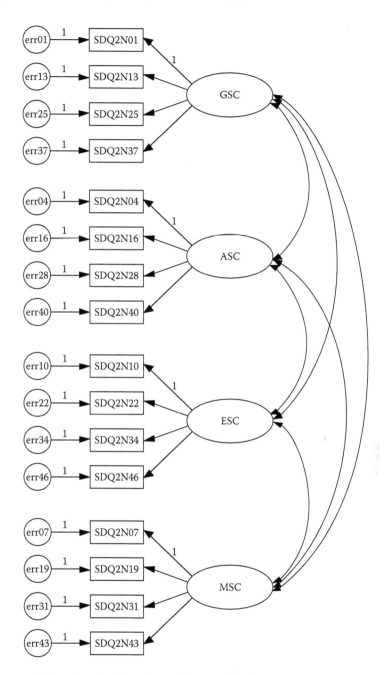

Figure 3.1 Hypothesized four-factor CFA model of self-concept.

3. The four SC factors, consistent with the theory, are correlated.
4. Error/uniquenesses[1] associated with each measure are uncorrelated.

Another way of conceptualizing the hypothesized model in Figure 3.1 is within a matrix framework as presented in Table 3.1. Thinking about the model components in this format can be very helpful because it is consistent with the manner by which the results from SEM analyses are commonly reported in program output files. Although AMOS, as well as other Windows-based programs, also provides users with a graphical output, the labeled information is typically limited to the estimated values and their standard errors. The tabular representation of our model in Table 3.1 shows the pattern of parameters to be estimated within the framework of three matrices: the factor-loading matrix, the factor variance–covariance matrix, and the error variance–covariance matrix. For purposes of model identification and latent variable scaling (see Chapter 2), you will note that the first of each congeneric[2] set of SC measures in the factor-loading matrix is set to 1.0; all other parameters are freely estimated (as represented by the dollar [$] sign). Likewise, as indicated in the variance–covariance matrix, all parameters are to be freely estimated. Finally, in the error–uniqueness matrix, only the error variances are estimated; all error covariances are presumed to be zero.

Modeling with AMOS Graphics

Provided with these two perspectives of the hypothesized model, let's now move on to the actual testing of the model. We'll begin by examining the route to model specification, data specification, and the calculation of parameter estimates within the framework of AMOS Graphics.

Model specification

The beauty of working with the AMOS Graphics interface is that all we need to do is to provide the program with a hypothesized model; in the present case, we use the one portrayed in Figure 3.1. Given that I demonstrated most of the commonly used drawing tools, and their application, in Chapter 2, there is no need for me to walk you through the construction of this model here. Likewise, construction of hypothesized models presented throughout the remainder of the book will not be detailed. Nonetheless, I take the opportunity, wherever possible, to illustrate a few of the other drawing tools or features of AMOS Graphics not specifically demonstrated earlier. Accordingly, in the first edition of this book, I noted two tools that, in combination, I had found to be invaluable in working on various parts of a model; these were the *Zoom-In* 🔍 and the *Scroll* 🔲

Table 3.1 Pattern of Estimated Parameters for Hypothesized Four-Factor CFA Model

Observed measure	GSC	ASC	ESC	MSC
	F_1	F_2	F_3	F_4
	Factor loading matrix			
SDQ2N01	1.0[a]	0.0	0.0	0.0
SDQ2N13	$[b]	0.0	0.0	0.0
SDQ2N25	$	0.0	0.0	0.0
SDQ2N37	$	0.0	0.0	0.0
SDQ2N04	0.0[c]	1.0	0.0	0.0
SDQ2N16	0.0	$	0.0	0.0
SDQ2N28	0.0	$	0.0	0.0
SDQ2N40	0.0	$	0.0	0.0
SDQ2N10	0.0	0.0	1.0	0.0
SDQ2N22	0.0	0.0	$	0.0
SDQ2N34	0.0	0.0	$	0.0
SDQ2N46	0.0	0.0	$	0.0
SDQ2N07	0.0	0.0	0.0	1.0
SDQ2N19	0.0	0.0	0.0	$
SDQ2N31	0.0	0.0	0.0	$
SDQ2N43	0.0	0.0	0.0	$
	Factor variance–covariance matrix			
GSC	$			
ASC	$	$		
ESC	$	$	$	
MSC	$	$	$	$

(continued)

Table 3.1 Pattern of Estimated Parameters for Hypothesized Four-Factor CFA Model (*Continued*)

Observed measure	GSC				ASC				ESC				MSC			
	Error variance–covariance matrix															
	01	13	25	37	04	16	28	40	10	22	34	46	07	19	31	43
SDQ2N01	$															
SDQ2N13	0.0	$														
SDQ2N25	0.0	0.0	$													
SDQ2N37	0.0	0.0	0.0	$												
SDQ2N04	0.0	0.0	0.0	0.0	$											
SDQ2N16	0.0	0.0	0.0	0.0	0.0	$										
SDQ2N28	0.0	0.0	0.0	0.0	0.0	0.0	$									
SDQ2N40	0.0	0.0	0.0	0.0	0.0	0.0	0.0	$								
SDQ2N10	0.0	0.0	0.0	0.0	0.0	0.0	0.0	0.0	$							
SDQ2N22	0.0	0.0	0.0	0.0	0.0	0.0	0.0	0.0	0.0	$						
SDQ2N34	0.0	0.0	0.0	0.0	0.0	0.0	0.0	0.0	0.0	0.0	$					
SDQ2N46	0.0	0.0	0.0	0.0	0.0	0.0	0.0	0.0	0.0	0.0	0.0	$				
SDQ2N07	0.0	0.0	0.0	0.0	0.0	0.0	0.0	0.0	0.0	0.0	0.0	0.0	$			
SDQ2N19	0.0	0.0	0.0	0.0	0.0	0.0	0.0	0.0	0.0	0.0	0.0	0.0	0.0	$		
SDQ2N31	0.0	0.0	0.0	0.0	0.0	0.0	0.0	0.0	0.0	0.0	0.0	0.0	0.0	0.0	$	
SDQ2N43	0.0	0.0	0.0	0.0	0.0	0.0	0.0	0.0	0.0	0.0	0.0	0.0	0.0	0.0	0.0	$

[a] Parameter fixed to 1.0.
[b] Parameter to be estimated.
[c] Parameter fixed to 0.0.

tools. To use this approach, you would click first on the *Zoom-In* icon, with each click enlarging the model a little more than the previous view. Once you had achieved sufficient magnification, you would then click on the *Scroll* icon to move around the entire diagram. Clicking on the *Zoom-Out* tool 🔍 would then return the diagram to the normal view. Although these drawing tools still operate in the more recent version of AMOS, their tasks are somewhat redefined. That is, you can now zoom in on specific objects of a diagram by simply using the mouse wheel. Furthermore, the mouse wheel can also be used to adjust the magnification of the *Loupe* tool 🔍. Although the *Scroll* tool still enables you to move the entire path diagram around, you can also use the scrollbars that appear when the diagram extends beyond the AMOS Graphics window. An example of magnification using the *Loupe* tool is presented in Figure 3.2. Finally, it is worth noting that when either the *Scroll* or *Zoom-In* tool is activated, a right-click of

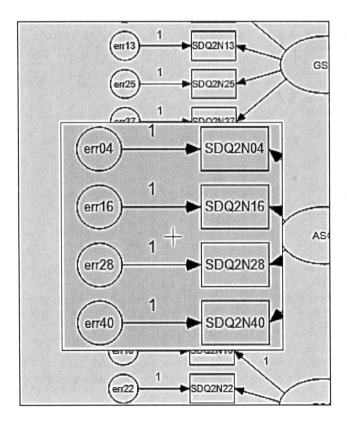

Figure 3.2 AMOS Graphics: Magnified portion of hypothesized model using the *Loupe* tool.

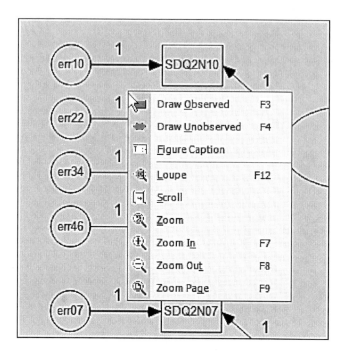

Figure 3.3 AMOS Graphics: Pop-up menu of drawing tools.

the mouse will provide a pop-up menu of different diagram features you
may wish to access (see Figure 3.3).

Data specification

Now that we have provided AMOS with the model to be analyzed, our
next job is to tell the program where to find the data. All data to be used
in applications throughout this book have been placed in an AMOS
folder called *Data Files*. To activate this folder, we can either click on the
Data File icon ▦, or pull down the *File* menu and select *Data Files*. Either
choice will trigger the *Data Files* dialog box displayed in Figure 3.4; it is
shown here as it pops up in the forefront of your workspace.

   In reviewing the upper section of this dialog box, you will see that the
program has identified the Group Name as *Group Number 1*; this labeling
is default in the analysis of single sample data. The data file to be used
for the current analysis is labeled *ASC7INDM.TXT,* and the sample size
is 265; the 265/265 indicates that 265, of a total sample size of 265, have
been selected for inclusion in the analysis. In the lower half of the dialog
box, you will note a *View Data* button that allows you to peruse the data

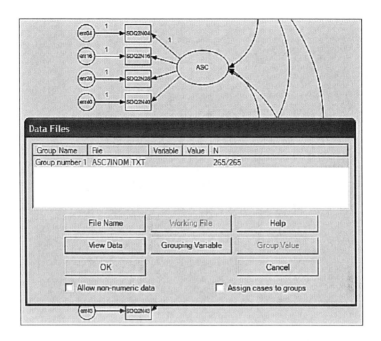

Figure 3.4 AMOS Graphics: *Data Files* dialog box.

in spreadsheet form should you wish to do so. Once you have selected the data file that will serve as the working file upon which your hypothesized model is based, you simply click the *OK* button.

In the example shown here, the selected data file was already visible in the *Data Files* dialog box. However, suppose that you wanted to select from a list of several available data sets. To do so, you would click on the File *Name* button in the *Data Files* dialog box (see Figure 3.4). This action would then trigger the *Open* dialog box shown in Figure 3.5. Here, you select a data file and then click on the *Open* button. Once you have opened a file, it becomes the working file and its filename will then appear in the *Data Files* dialog box, as illustrated in Figure 3.4.

It is important that I point out some of the requirements of the AMOS program in the use of external data sets. If your data files are in ASCII format (as all of mine were initially), you will need to restructure them before you are able to conduct any analyses using AMOS. Consistent with SPSS and many other Windows applications, the most recent version of AMOS requires that data be structured in the comma-delimited format. Although the semicolon (rather than the comma) delimiter is used in many European and Asian countries, this is not a problem as AMOS can detect which version of the program is running (e.g., the French version)

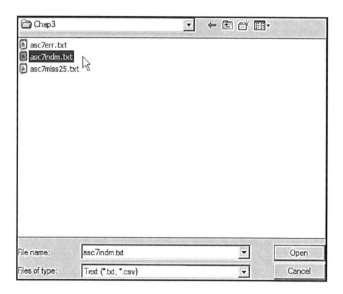

Figure 3.5 AMOS Graphics: *Open* (data) dialog box.

and then automatically define a compatible delimiter, which would be a semicolon in the case of the French version (J. L. Arbuckle, personal communication, February 22, 2008). Furthermore, all data must reside in an external file. For help in reformatting your data, the current AMOS online *Help* menu has a topic titled "Translating Your Old Text (ASCII) Data Files" that contains useful information related to the reformatting of ASCII files. The data used in this chapter are in the form of a text file. However, AMOS supports several common database formats, including SPSS *.sav files; I use different formats throughout this book.

Calculation of estimates

Now that we have specified both the model to be analyzed and the data file upon which the analyses are to be based, all that is left for us to do is to execute the job; we do so by clicking on the *Calculate Estimates* icon ▦. (Alternatively, we could select *Calculate Estimates* from the *Analyze* drop-down menu.) Once the analyses have been completed, AMOS Graphics allows you to review the results from two different perspectives—graphical and textual. In the graphical output, all estimates are presented in the path diagram. These results are obtained by clicking on the *View Output Path Diagram* icon ▦ found at the top of the middle section of the AMOS main screen. Results related to the testing of our hypothesized model are presented in Figure 3.6. To copy the graphical output to another file, such

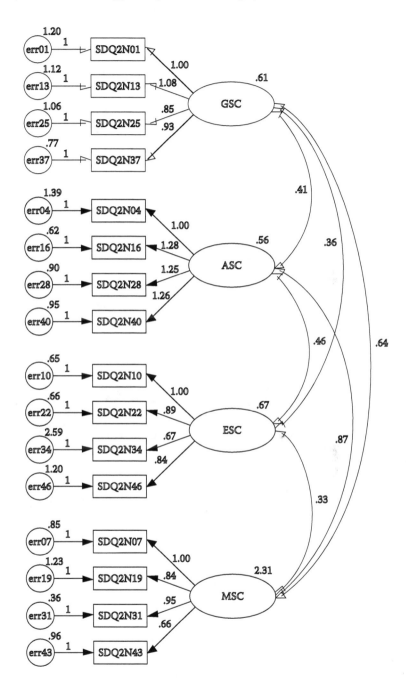

Figure 3.6 AMOS Graphics: Output path diagram for hypothesized model.

as a Word document, either click on the *Duplicate* icon 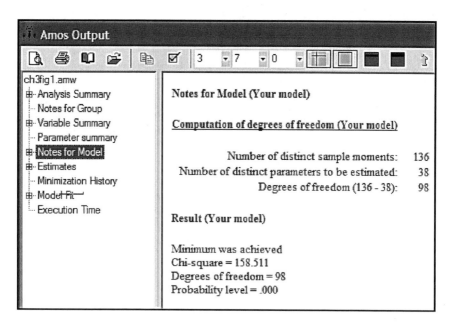, or pull down the *Edit* menu and select *Copy (to Clipboard)*. You can then paste the output into the document.

Likewise, you have two methods of viewing the textual output—either by clicking on the *Text Output* icon, or by selecting *Text Output* from the *View* drop-down menu. However, in either case, as soon as the analyses are completed, a red tab representing the AMOS output file will appear on the bottom status bar of your computer screen. Let's turn now to the output resulting from our test of the hypothesized model.

AMOS text output: Hypothesized four-factor model

Textual output pertinent to a particular model is presented very neatly in the form of summaries related to specific sections of the output file. This tree-like arrangement enables the user to select sections of the output that are of particular interest. Figure 3.7 presents a view of this tree-like formation of summaries, with summary information related to the hypothesized four-factor model open. To facilitate the presentation and discussion of results in this chapter, the material is divided into three primary sections: (a) "Model Summary," (b) "Model Variables and Parameters," and (c) "Model Evaluation."

Figure 3.7 AMOS Graphics: Tested model summary notes.

Model summary

This very important summary provides you with a quick overview of the model, including the information needed in determining its identification status. Here we see that there are 136 distinct sample moments, or, in other words, elements in the sample covariance matrix (i.e., number of pieces of information provided by the data), and 38 parameters to be estimated, thereby leaving 98 degrees of freedom based on an overidentified model, and a chi-square value of 158.511 with a probability level equal to .000.

Recall that the only data with which we have to work in SEM are the observed variables, which in the present case number 16. Based on the formula $p(p + 1) / 2$ (see Chapter 2), the sample covariance matrix for these data should yield 136 (16[17] / 2) sample moments, which, indeed, it does. A more specific breakdown of the estimated parameters is presented in the "Model Variables and Parameters" section discussed next. Likewise, an elaboration of the ML chi-square statistic, together with substantially more information related to model fit, is presented and discussed in the "Model Evaluation" section.

Model variables and parameters

The initial information provided in the AMOS text output file can be invaluable in helping you resolve any difficulties with the specification of a model. Listed first, and presented in Table 3.2, are all the *variables* in the model, accompanied by their categorization as either observed or unobserved, and as endogenous or exogenous. Consistent with the path diagram in Figure 3.1, all the observed variables (i.e., the input data) operate as dependent (i.e., endogenous) variables in the model; all factors and error terms are unobserved, and operate as independent (i.e., exogenous) variables in the model. This information is followed by a summary of the total number of variables in the model, as well as the number in each of the four categories.

The next section of the output file focuses on a summary of the *parameters* in the model and is presented in Table 3.3. Moving from left to right, we see that there are 32 *regression weights*, 20 of which are fixed and 12 of which are estimated; the 20 fixed regression weights include the first of each set of four factor loadings and the 16 error terms. There are 6 *covariances* and 20 *variances*, all of which are estimated. In total, there are 58 parameters, 38 of which are to be estimated. Provided with this summary, it is now easy for you to determine the appropriate number of degrees of freedom and, ultimately, whether or not the model is identified. Although, of course, this information is provided by the program as noted in Figure 3.7, it is always good (and fun?) to see if your calculations are consistent with those of the program.

Table 3.2 Selected AMOS Output for Hypothesized Four-Factor CFA Model: Summary of Model Variables

Your model contains the following variables

Observed, endogenous variables

SDQ2N37

SDQ2N25

SDQ2N13

SDQ2N01

SDQ2N40

SDQ2N28

SDQ2N16

SDQ2N04

SDQ2N46

SDQ2N34

SDQ2N22

SDQ2N10

SDQ2N43

SDQ2N31

SDQ2N19

SDQ2N07

Unobserved, exogenous variables

GSC	ASC	ESC	MSC
err37	err40	Err46	err43
err25	err28	Err34	err31
err13	err16	Err22	err19
err01	err04	Err10	err07

Variable counts

Number of variables in your model:	36
Number of observed variables:	16
Number of unobserved variables:	20
Number of exogenous variables	20
Number of endogenous variables:	16

Model evaluation

Of primary interest in structural equation modeling is the extent to which a hypothesized model "fits," or, in other words, adequately describes the sample data. Given findings of an inadequate goodness-of-fit, the next logical step is to detect the source of misfit in the model. Ideally, evaluation of model fit should derive from a variety of perspectives and be based

Table 3.3 Selected AMOS Output for Hypothesized Four-Factor
CFA Model: Summary of Model Parameters

		Parameter summary				
	Weights	Covariances	Variances	Means	Intercepts	Total
Fixed	20	0	0	0	0	20
Labeled	0	0	0	0	0	0
Unlabeled	12	6	20	0	0	38
Total	32	6	20	0	0	58

on several criteria that assess model fit from a diversity of perspectives. In particular, these evaluation criteria focus on the adequacy of (a) the parameter estimates, and (b) the model as a whole.

Parameter estimates

In reviewing the model parameter estimates, three criteria are of interest: (a) the feasibility of the parameter estimates, (b) the appropriateness of the standard errors, and (c) the statistical significance of the parameter estimates. We turn now to a brief explanation of each.

Feasibility of parameter estimates

The initial step in assessing the fit of individual parameters in a model is to determine the viability of their estimated values. In particular, parameter estimates should exhibit the correct sign and size, and be consistent with the underlying theory. Any estimates falling outside the admissible range signal a clear indication that either the model is wrong or the input matrix lacks sufficient information. Examples of parameters exhibiting unreasonable estimates are correlations > 1.00, negative variances, and covariance or correlation matrices that are not positive definite.

Appropriateness of standard errors

Standard errors reflect the precision with which a parameter has been estimated, with small values suggesting accurate estimation. Thus, another indicator of poor model fit is the presence of standard errors that are excessively large or small. For example, if a standard error approaches zero, the test statistic for its related parameter cannot be defined (Bentler, 2005). Likewise, standard errors that are extremely large indicate parameters that cannot be determined (Jöreskog & Sörbom, 1993).[3] Because standard errors are influenced by the units of measurement in observed and/or latent variables, as well as the magnitude of the parameter estimate itself, no definitive criteria of "small" and "large" have been established (see Jöreskog & Sörbom, 1989).

Statistical significance of parameter estimates

The test statistic here is the critical ratio (C.R.), which represents the parameter estimate divided by its standard error; as such, it operates as a z-statistic in testing that the estimate is statistically different from zero. Based on a probability level of .05, then, the test statistic needs to be > ±1.96 before the hypothesis (that the estimate equals 0.0) can be rejected. Nonsignificant parameters, with the exception of error variances, can be considered unimportant to the model; in the interest of scientific parsimony, albeit given an adequate sample size, they should be deleted from the model. On the other hand, it is important to note that nonsignificant parameters can be indicative of a sample size that is too small (K. G. Jöreskog, personal communication, January 1997).

Let's turn now to this section of the AMOS output file. After selecting *Estimates* from the list of output sections (see Figure 3.7), you will be presented with the information shown in Table 3.4. However, before examining the contents of this table, I wish to show you two examples of how you can obtain additional information related to these estimates. Illustrated in Figure 3.8 is the dialog box that appears after one click of the left mouse button and advises how you may obtain additional estimates. Clicking on the first option, *To Estimate Squared Multiple Correlations*, opens the *AMOS Reference Guide* dialog box shown in Figure 3.9. I show how to estimate these additional parameters, as well as other important information, later in this chapter as well as in other chapters that follow.

Let's move on now to the estimated values presented in Table 3.4. It is important to note that, for simplicity, all estimates related to this first hypothesized model are presented only in the unstandardized form; further options will be examined in subsequent applications.

As you can readily see, results are presented separately for the factor loadings (listed as regression weights), the covariances (in this case, for factors only), and the variances (for both factors and measurement errors). The parameter estimation information is very clearly and succinctly presented in the AMOS text output file. Listed to the right of each parameter is its estimated value (Column 1), standard error (Column 2), critical ratio (Column 3), and probability value (Column 4). An examination of this unstandardized solution reveals all estimates to be both reasonable and statistically significant; all standard errors appear also to be in good order.

Model as a whole

In the model summary presented in Figure 3.7, we observed that AMOS provided the overall chi-square (χ^2) value, together with its degrees of

Table 3.4 Selected AMOS Output for Hypothesized Four-Factor
CFA Model: Parameter Estimates

	Estimate	S.E.	C.R.	P
	Regression weights			
SDQ2N37<---GSC	.934	.131	7.117	***
SDQ2N25<---GSC	.851	.132	6.443	***
SDQ2N13<---GSC	1.083	.154	7.030	***
SDQ2N01<---GSC	1.000			
SDQ2N40<---ASC	1.259	.157	8.032	***
SDQ2N28<---ASC	1.247	.154	8.082	***
SDQ2N16<---ASC	1.279	.150	8.503	***
SDQ2N04<---ASC	1.000			
SDQ2N46<---ESC	.843	.117	7.212	***
SDQ2N34<---ESC	.670	.148	4.530	***
SDQ2N22<---ESC	.889	.103	8.642	***
SDQ2N10<---ESC	1.000			
SDQ2N43<---MSC	.655	.049	13.273	***
SDQ2N31<---MSC	.952	.049	19.479	***
SDQ2N19<---MSC	.841	.058	14.468	***
SDQ2N07<---MSC	1.000			
	Covariances			
ASC<-->ESC	.464	.078	5.909	***
GSC<-->ESC	.355	.072	4.938	***
ASC<-->MSC	.873	.134	6.507	***
GSC<-->MSC	.635	.118	5.377	***
GSC<-->ASC	.415	.079	5.282	***
ESC<-->MSC	.331	.100	3.303	***
	Variances			
GSC	.613	.138	4.456	***
ASC	.561	.126	4.444	***
ESC	.668	.116	5.738	***
MSC	2.307	.273	8.444	***
err37	.771	.088	8.804	***
err25	1.056	.107	9.878	***
err13	1.119	.124	9.002	***
err01	1.198	.126	9.519	***
err40	.952	.095	10.010	***

(continued)

Table 3.4 Selected AMOS Output for Hypothesized Four-Factor
CFA Model: Parameter Estimates (*Continued*)

	Estimate	S.E.	C.R.	P
Variances				
err28	.896	.090	9.940	***
err16	.616	.068	9.003	***
err04	1.394	.128	10.879	***
err46	1.201	.118	10.164	***
err34	2.590	.233	11.107	***
err22	.657	.075	8.718	***
err10	.653	.082	7.926	***
err43	.964	.092	10.454	***
err31	.365	.065	5.638	***
err19	1.228	.121	10.133	***
err07	.854	.100	8.535	***

*** probability <.000

freedom and probability value. However, this information is intended only as a quick overview of model fit. Indeed, the program, by default, provides many other fit statistics in its output file. Before turning to this section of the AMOS output, however, it is essential that I first review four important aspects of fitting hypothesized models; these are (a) the model-fitting process, (b) the issue of statistical significance, (c) the estimation process, and (d) the goodness-of-fit statistics.

The model-fitting process

In Chapter 1, I presented a general description of this process and noted that the primary task is to determine the goodness-of-fit between the hypothesized model and the sample data. In other words, the researcher specifies a model and then uses the sample data to test the model.

With a view to helping you to gain a better understanding of the goodness-of-fit statistics presented in the AMOS output file, let's take a few moments to recast this model-fitting process within a more formal-ized framework. As such, let S represent the sample covariance matrix (of observed variable scores), Σ (sigma) represent the population covariance matrix, and θ (theta) represent a vector that comprises the model param-eters. Thus, $\Sigma(\theta)$ represents the restricted covariance matrix implied by the model (i.e., the specified structure of the hypothesized model). In SEM, the null hypothesis (H_0) being tested is that the postulated model holds in the population [i.e., $\Sigma = \Sigma(\theta)$]. In contrast to traditional statisti-cal procedures, however, the researcher hopes *not* to reject H_0 (but see

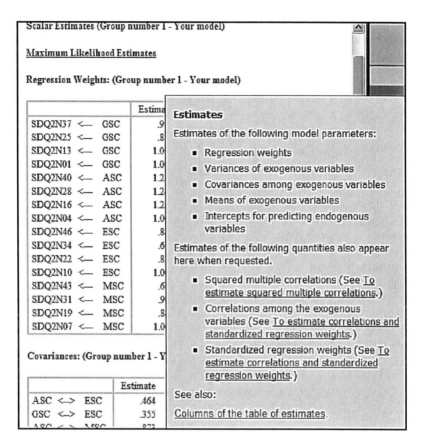

Figure 3.8 AMOS Graphics: Pop-up menu enabling provision of additional estimates.

MacCallum, Browne, & Sugarawa, 1996, for proposed changes to this hypothesis-testing strategy).

The issue of statistical significance

The rationale underlying the practice of statistical significance testing has generated a plethora of criticism over, at least, the past 4 decades. Indeed, Cohen (1994) has noted that, despite Rozeboom's (1960) admonition more than 33 years ago that "the statistical folkways of a more primitive past continue to dominate the local scene" (p. 417), this dubious practice still persists. (For an array of supportive as well as opposing views with respect to this article, see the *American Psychologist* [1995], *50*, 1098–1103.) In light of this historical bank of criticism, together with the current pressure by methodologists to cease this traditional ritual

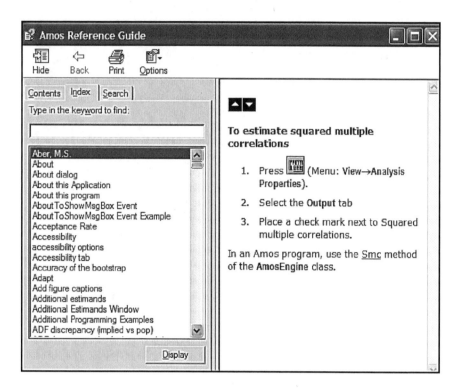

Figure 3.9 AMOS Graphics: Pop-up *AMOS Reference Guide* dialog box.

(see, e.g., Cohen, 1994; Kirk, 1996; Schmidt, 1996; Thompson, 1996), the Board of Scientific Affairs for the American Psychological Association appointed a task force to study the feasibility of phasing out the use of null hypothesis testing procedures, as described in course texts and reported in journal articles. Consequently, the end of statistical significance testing relative to traditional statistical methods may soon be a reality. (For a compendium of articles addressing this issue, see Harlow, Mulaik, & Steiger, 1997.)

Statistical significance testing with respect to the analysis of covariance structures, however, is somewhat different in that it is driven by degrees of freedom involving the number of elements in the sample covariance matrix and the number of parameters to be estimated. Nonetheless, it is interesting to note that many of the issues raised with respect to the traditional statistical methods (e.g., practical significance, the importance of confidence intervals, and the importance of replication) have long been addressed in SEM applications. Indeed, it was this very issue of practical "nonsignificance" in model testing that led Bentler and

Bonett (1980) to develop one of the first subjective indices of fit (the NFI); their work subsequently spawned the development of numerous additional practical indices of fit, many of which are included in the AMOS output. Likewise, the early work of Steiger (1990; Steiger & Lind, 1980) precipitated the call for use of confidence intervals in the reporting of SEM findings (see, e.g., MacCallum et al., 1996). Finally, the classic paper by Cliff (1983) denouncing the proliferation of post hoc model fitting, and criticizing the apparent lack of concern for the dangers of overfitting models to trivial effects arising from capitalization on chance factors, spirited the development of evaluation indices (Browne & Cudeck, 1989; Cudeck & Browne, 1983), as well as a general call for increased use of cross-validation procedures (see, e.g., MacCallum, Roznowski, Mar, & Reith, 1994; MacCallum, Roznowski, & Necowitz, 1992).

The estimation process

The primary focus of the estimation process in SEM is to yield parameter values such that the discrepancy (i.e., residual) between the sample covariance matrix S and the population covariance matrix implied by the model $[\Sigma(\theta)]$ is minimal. This objective is achieved by minimizing a discrepancy function, $F[S, \Sigma(\theta)]$, such that its minimal value (F_{min}) reflects the point in the estimation process where the discrepancy between S and $\Sigma(\theta)$ is least $[S - \Sigma(\theta) = minimum]$. Taken together, then, F_{min} serves as a measure of the extent to which S differs from $\Sigma(\theta)$.

Goodness-of-fit statistics

Let's now turn to the goodness-of-fit statistics which are presented in Table 3.5. For each set of fit statistics, you will note three rows. The first row, as indicated, focuses on the *hypothesized* model under test (i.e., your model); the second, on the *saturated* model; and the third, on the *independence* model. Explanation of the latter two models, I believe, is most easily understood within a comparative framework. As such, think of these three models as representing points on a continuum, with the *independence* model at one extreme, the *saturated* model at the other extreme, and the *hypothesized* model somewhere in between. The *independence* model is one of complete independence of all variables in the model (i.e., in which all correlations among variables are zero) and is the most restricted. In other words, it is a null model, with nothing going on here as each variable represents a factor. The *saturated* model, on the other hand, is one in which the number of estimated parameters equals the number of data points (i.e., variances and covariances of the observed variables, as in the case of the just-identified model), and is the least restricted.

Table 3.5 Selected AMOS Output for Hypothesized Four-Factor
CFA Model: Goodness-of-Fit Statistics

Model fit summary				

CMIN

Model	NPAR	CMIN	DF	P	CMIN/ DF
Your model	38	158.511	98	.000	1.617
Saturated model	136	.000	0		
Independence model	16	1696.728	120	.000	14.139

RMR, GFI

Model	RMR	GFI	AGFI	PGFI
Your model	.103	.933	.906	.672
Saturated model	.000	1.000		
Independence model	.628	.379	.296	.334

Baseline comparisons

Model	NFI Delta 1	RFI rho 1	IFI Delta 2	TLI rho 2	CFI
Your model	.907	.886	.962	.953	.962
Saturated model	1.000		1.000		1.000
Independence model	.000	.000	.000	.000	.000

Parsimony-adjusted measures

Model	PRATIO	PNFI	PCFI
Your model	.817	.740	.785
Saturated model	.000	.000	.000
Independence model	1.000	.000	.000

NCP

Model	NCP	LO 90	HI 90
Your model	60.511	29.983	98.953
Saturated model	.000	.000	.000
Independence model	1576.728	1447.292	1713.561

FMIN

Model	FMIN	F0	LO 90	HI 90
Your model	.600	.229	.114	.375
Saturated model	.000	.000	.000	.000
Independence model	6.427	5.972	5.482	6.491

(continued)

Table 3.5 Selected AMOS Output for Hypothesized Four-Factor
CFA Model: Goodness-of-Fit Statistics (*Continued*)

		RMSEA		
Model	RMSEA	LO 90	HI 90	PCLOSE
Your model	.048	.034	.062	.562
Independence model	.223	.214	.233	.000

		AIC		
Model	AIC	BCC	BIC	CAIC
Your model	234.511	239.742	370.541	408.541
Saturated model	272.000	290.721	758.843	894.843
Independence model	1728.728	1730.931	1786.004	1805.004

		ECVI		
Model	ECVI	LO 90	HI 90	MECVI
Your model	.888	.773	1.034	.908
Saturated model	1.030	1.030	1.030	1.101
Independence model	6.548	6.058	7.067	6.557

	HOELTER	HOELTER	
Model	HOELTER .05	HOELTER .01	
Your model	204	223	
Independence model	23	25	

For didactic as well as space reasons, all goodness-of-fit statistics are provided only for the initially hypothesized model in this first application; hereafter, only a selected group of fit statistics will be reported. We turn now to an examination of each cluster, as they relate to the *hypothesized* model only. (Formulae related to each fit statistic can be found in Arbuckle, 2007.)

Focusing on the first set of fit statistics, we see the labels NPAR (number of parameters), CMIN (minimum discrepancy), DF (degrees of freedom), P (probability value), and CMIN/DF. The value of 158.511, under CMIN, represents the discrepancy between the unrestricted sample covariance matrix S, and the restricted covariance matrix $\Sigma(\theta)$, and, in essence, represents the Likelihood Ratio Test statistic, most commonly expressed as a χ^2 statistic. It is important to note that, for the remainder of the book, I refer to CMIN as the χ^2. This statistic is equal to $(N–1)F_{min}$ (sample size minus 1, multiplied by the minimum fit function) and, in large samples, is distributed as a central χ^2 with degrees of freedom equal to $1/2(p)$ $(p + 1) - t$, where p is the number of observed variables, and t is the number of parameters to be estimated (Bollen, 1989a). In general, H_0: $\Sigma = \Sigma(\theta)$ is equivalent to the hypothesis that $\Sigma - \Sigma(\theta) = 0$; the χ^2 test, then, simultaneously tests the extent to which all residuals in $\Sigma - \Sigma(\theta)$ are zero (Bollen, 1989a). Framed a little differently, the null hypothesis (H_0) postulates that specification of the factor loadings, factor variances and covariances, and error variances for the model under study are valid; the χ^2 test simultaneously tests the extent to which this specification is true. The probability value associated with χ^2 represents the likelihood of obtaining a χ^2 value that exceeds the χ^2 value when H_0 is true. Thus, the higher the probability associated with χ^2, the closer the fit between the hypothesized model (under H_0) and the perfect fit (Bollen, 1989a).

The test of our H_0, that SC is a four-factor structure as depicted in Figure 3.1, yielded a χ^2 value of 158.511, with 98 degrees of freedom and a probability of less than .0001 (p < .0001), thereby suggesting that the fit of the data to the hypothesized model is not entirely adequate. Interpreted literally, this test statistic indicates that, given the present data, the hypothesis bearing on SC relations, as summarized in the model, represents an unlikely event (occurring less than one time in 1,000 under the null hypothesis) and should be rejected.

However, both the sensitivity of the Likelihood Ratio Test to sample size and its basis on the central χ^2 distribution, which assumes that the model fits perfectly in the population (i.e., that H_0 is correct), have led to problems of fit that are now widely known. Because the χ^2 statistic equals $(N-1)F_{min}$, this value tends to be substantial when the model does *not* hold and when sample size is large (Jöreskog & Sörbom, 1993). Yet, the analysis of covariance structures is grounded in large sample theory. As such, large samples are critical to the obtaining of precise parameter estimates, as well as to the tenability of asymptotic distributional approximations (MacCallum et al., 1996). Thus, findings of well-fitting hypothesized models, where the χ^2 value approximates the degrees of freedom, have proven to be unrealistic in most SEM empirical research. More common are findings of a large χ^2 relative to degrees of freedom, thereby indicating a need to modify the model in order to better fit the data (Jöreskog & Sörbom, 1993). Thus, results related to the test of our hypothesized model are not unexpected. Indeed, given this problematic aspect of the Likelihood Ratio Test, and the fact that postulated models (no matter how good) can only ever fit real-world data *approximately* and *never exactly*, MacCallum et al. (1996) recently proposed changes to the traditional hypothesis-testing approach in covariance structure modeling. (For an extended discussion of these changes, readers are referred to MacCallum et al., 1996.)

Researchers have addressed the χ^2 limitations by developing goodness-of-fit indices that take a more pragmatic approach to the evaluation process. Indeed, the past 3 decades have witnessed a plethora of newly developed fit indices, as well as unique approaches to the model-fitting process (for reviews, see, e.g., Gerbing & Anderson, 1993; Hu & Bentler, 1995; Marsh, Balla, & McDonald, 1988; Tanaka, 1993). One of the first fit statistics to address this problem was the χ^2/degrees of freedom ratio (Wheaton, Muthén, Alwin, & Summers, 1977), which appears as CMIN/DF, and is presented in the first cluster of statistics shown in Table 3.5.[4] For the most part, the remainder of the AMOS output file is devoted to these alternative indices of fit, and, where applicable, to their related confidence intervals. These criteria, commonly referred to as *subjective, practical,* or *ad hoc* indices of fit, are typically used as adjuncts to the χ^2 statistic.

Turning now to the next group of statistics, we see the labels *RMR, GFI, AGFI,* and *PGFI*. The root mean square residual (RMR) represents the average residual value derived from the fitting of the variance–covariance matrix for the hypothesized model $\Sigma(\theta)$ to the variance–covariance matrix of the sample data (S). However, because these residuals are relative to the sizes of the observed variances and covariances, they are difficult to interpret. Thus, they are best interpreted in the metric of the correlation matrix (Hu & Bentler, 1995; Jöreskog & Sörbom, 1989). The standardized RMR, then, represents the average value across all standardized residuals, and ranges from zero to 1.00; in a well-fitting model, this value will be small (say, .05 or less). The value of .103 shown in Table 3.5 represents the unstandardized residual value. Not shown on the output, however, is the standardized RMR value, which is .043 and represents the average discrepancy between the sample observed and hypothesized correlation matrices. It can be interpreted as meaning that the model explains the correlations to within an average error of .043 (see Hu & Bentler, 1995).

The Goodness-of-Fit Index (GFI) is a measure of the relative amount of variance and covariance in S that is jointly explained by Σ. The Adjusted Goodness-of-Fit Index (AGFI) differs from the GFI only in the fact that it adjusts for the number of degrees of freedom in the specified model. As such, it also addresses the issue of parsimony by incorporating a penalty for the inclusion of additional parameters. The GFI and AGFI can be classified as absolute indices of fit because they basically compare the hypothesized model with no model at all (see Hu & Bentler, 1995). Although both indices range from zero to 1.00, with values close to 1.00 being indicative of good fit, Jöreskog and Sörbom (1993) noted that, theoretically, it is possible for them to be negative; Fan, Thompson, and Wang (1999) further cautioned that GFI and AGFI values can be overly influenced by sample size. This, of course, should not occur as it would reflect the fact that the model fits worse than no model at all. Based on the GFI and AGFI values reported in Table 3.5 (.933 and .906, respectively), we can once again conclude that our hypothesized model fits the sample data fairly well.

The last index of fit in this group, the Parsimony Goodness-of-Fit Index (PGFI), was introduced by James, Mulaik, and Brett (1982) to address the issue of parsimony in SEM. As the first of a series of "parsimony-based indices of fit" (see Williams & Holahan, 1994), the PGFI takes into account the complexity (i.e., number of estimated parameters) of the hypothesized model in the assessment of overall model fit. As such, "two logically inter-dependent pieces of information," the goodness-of-fit of the model (as measured by the GFI) and the parsimony of the model, are represented by the single index PGFI, thereby providing a more realistic evaluation of the hypothesized model (Mulaik et al., 1989, p. 439). Typically, parsi-mony-based indices have lower values than the threshold level generally perceived as "acceptable" for other normed indices of fit. Mulaik et al. suggested that nonsignificant χ^2 statistics and goodness-of-fit indices in the .90s, accompanied by parsimonious-fit indices in the 50s, are not unex-pected. Thus, our finding of a PGFI value of .672 would seem to be consis-tent with our previous fit statistics.

We turn now to the next set of goodness-of-fit statistics (baseline com-parisons), which can be classified as incremental or comparative indices of fit (Hu & Bentler, 1995; Marsh et al., 1988). As with the GFI and AGFI, incremental indices of fit are based on a comparison of the hypothesized model against some standard. However, whereas this standard represents no model at all for the GFI and AGFI, it represents a baseline model (typi-cally, the independence or null model noted above for the incremental indices).[5] We now review these incremental indices.

For the better part of a decade, Bentler and Bonett's (1980) Normed Fit Index (NFI) has been the practical criterion of choice, as evidenced in large part by the current "classic" status of its original paper (see Bentler, 1992; Bentler & Bonett, 1987). However, addressing evidence that the NFI has shown a tendency to underestimate fit in small samples, Bentler (1990) revised the NFI to take sample size into account and proposed the Comparative Fit Index (CFI; see last column). Values for both the NFI and CFI range from zero to 1.00 and are derived from the comparison of a hypothesized model with the independence (or null) model, as described earlier. As such, each provides a measure of complete covariation in the data. Although a value > .90 was originally considered representative of a well-fitting model (see Bentler, 1992), a revised cutoff value close to .95 has recently been advised (Hu & Bentler, 1999). Both indices of fit are reported in the AMOS output; however, Bentler (1990) has suggested that, of the two, the CFI should be the index of choice. As shown in Table 3.5, the CFI (.962) indicated that the model fitted the data well in the sense that the hypothesized model adequately described the sample data. In somewhat less glowing terms, the NFI value suggested that model fit was only marginally adequate (.907).

The Relative Fit Index (RFI; Bollen, 1986) represents a derivative of the NFI; as with both the NFI and CFI, the RFI coefficient values range from zero to 1.00, with values close to .95 indicating superior fit (see Hu & Bentler, 1999). The Incremental Index of Fit (IFI) was developed by Bollen (1989b) to address the issues of parsimony and sample size which were known to be associated with the NFI. As such, its computation is basically the same as that of the NFI, with the exception that degrees of freedom are taken into account. Thus, it is not surprising that our finding of IFI of .962 is consistent with that of the CFI in reflecting a well-fitting model. Finally, the Tucker-Lewis Index (TLI; Tucker & Lewis, 1973), consistent with the other indices noted here, yields values ranging from zero to 1.00, with values close to .95 (for large samples) being indicative of good fit (see Hu & Bentler, 1999).

The next cluster of fit indices relates to the issue of model parsimony. The first fit index (PRATIO) relates to the initial parsimony ratio proposed by James et al. (1982). More appropriately, however, the index has subsequently been tied to other goodness-of-fit indices (see, e.g., the PGFI noted earlier). Here, it is computed relative to the NFI and CFI. In both cases, as was true for PGFI, the complexity of the model is taken into account in the assessment of model fit (see James et al.; Mulaik et al., 1989). Again, a PNFI of .740 and PCFI of .785 (see Table 3.5) fall in the range of expected values.[6]

The next set of fit statistics provides us with the noncentrality parameter (NCP) estimate. In our initial discussion of the χ^2 statistic, we focused on the extent to which the model was tenable and could not be rejected. Now, however, let's look a little more closely at what happens when the hypothesized model is incorrect [i.e., $\Sigma \neq \Sigma(\theta)$]. In this circumstance, the χ^2 statistic has a noncentral χ^2 distribution, with a noncentrality parameter, λ, that is a fixed parameter with associated degrees of freedom, and can be denoted as $\chi^2_{(df, \lambda)}$ (Bollen, 1989a; Hu & Bentler, 1995; Satorra & Saris, 1985). Essentially, it functions as a measure of the discrepancy between Σ and $\Sigma(\theta)$ and, thus, can be regarded as a "population badness-of-fit" (Steiger, 1990). As such, the greater the discrepancy between Σ and $\Sigma(\theta)$, the larger the λ value. (For a presentation of the various types of error associated with discrepancies among matrices, see Browne & Cudeck, 1993; Cudeck & Henly, 1991; MacCallum et al., 1994.) It is now easy to see that the central χ^2 statistic is a special case of the noncentral χ^2 distribution when $\lambda = 0.0$. (For an excellent discussion and graphic portrayal of differences between the central and noncentral χ^2 statistics, see MacCallum et al., 1996.) As a means to establishing the precision of the noncentrality parameter estimate, Steiger (1990) has suggested that it be framed within the bounds of confidence intervals. Turning to Table 3.5, we find that our hypothesized model yielded a noncentrality parameter of 60.511. This value represents the χ^2 value minus its degrees of freedom (158.511 – 98). The confidence interval indicates that we can be 90% confident that the population value of the noncentrality parameter (λ) lies between 29.983 and 98.953.

For those who may wish to use this information, values related to the minimum discrepancy function (FMIN) and the population discrepancy (FO) are presented next. The columns labeled "LO 90" and "HI 90" contain the lower and upper limits, respectively, of a 90% confidence interval around FO.

The next set of fit statistics focuses on the root mean square error of approximation (RMSEA). Although this index, and the conceptual framework within which it is embedded, was first proposed by Steiger and Lind in 1980, it has only recently been recognized as one of the most informative criteria in covariance structure modeling. The RMSEA takes into account the error of approximation in the population and asks the question "How well would the model, with unknown but optimally chosen parameter values, fit the population covariance matrix if it were available?" (Browne & Cudeck, 1993, pp. 137–138). This discrepancy, as measured by the RMSEA, is expressed per degree of freedom, thus making it sensitive to the number of estimated parameters in the model (i.e., the complexity of the model); values less than .05 indicate good fit, and values as high as .08 represent reasonable errors of approximation in the population (Browne & Cudeck, 1993). MacCallum et al. (1996) have recently elaborated on these cutpoints and noted that RMSEA values ranging from .08 to .10 indicate mediocre fit, and those greater than .10 indicate poor fit. Although Hu and Bentler (1999) have suggested a value of .06 to be indicative of good fit between the hypothesized model and the observed data, they cautioned that, when sample size is small, the RMSEA (and TLI) tend to overreject true population models (but see Fan et al., 1999, for comparisons with other indices of fit). Although these criteria are based solely on subjective judgement, and therefore cannot be regarded as infallible or correct, Browne and Cudeck (1993) and MacCallum et al. (1996) argued that they would appear to be more realistic than a requirement of exact fit, where RMSEA = 0.0. (For a generalization of the RMSEA to multiple independent samples, see Steiger, 1998.)

Overall, MacCallum and Austin (2000) have strongly recommended routine use of the RMSEA for at least three reasons: (a) It would appear to be adequately sensitive to model misspecification (Hu & Bentler, 1998), (b) commonly used interpretative guidelines would appear to yield appropriate conclusions regarding model quality (Hu & Bentler, 1998, 1999), and (c) it is possible to build confidence intervals around RMSEA values.

Addressing Steiger's (1990) call for the use of confidence intervals to assess the precision of RMSEA estimates, AMOS reports a 90% interval around the RMSEA value. In contrast to point estimates of model fit (which do not reflect the imprecision of the estimate), confidence intervals can yield this information, thereby providing the researcher with more assistance in the evaluation of model fit. Thus, MacCallum et al. (1996) strongly urged the use of confidence intervals in practice. Presented with a small RMSEA, albeit a wide confidence interval, a researcher would conclude that the estimated discrepancy value is quite imprecise, thereby negating any possibility to determine accurately the degree of fit in the population. In contrast, a very narrow confidence interval would argue for good precision of the RMSEA value in reflecting model fit in the population (MacCallum et al., 1996).

In addition to reporting a confidence interval around the RMSEA value, AMOS tests for the closeness of fit (PCLOSE). That is, it tests the hypothesis that the RMSEA is "good" in the population (specifically, that it is < .05). Jöreskog and Sörbom (1996a) have suggested that the p-value for this test should be > .50.

Turning to Table 3.5, we see that the RMSEA value for our hypothesized model is .048, with the 90% confidence interval ranging from .034 to .062 and the p-value for the test of closeness of fit equal to .562. Interpretation of the confidence interval indicates that we can be 90% confident that the true RMSEA value in the population will fall within the bounds of .034 and .062, which represents a good degree of precision. Given that (a) the RMSEA point estimate is < .05 (.048); (b) the upper bound of the 90% interval is .06, which is less than the value suggested by Browne and Cudeck (1993), albeit equal to the cutoff value proposed by Hu and Bentler (1999); and (c) the probability value associated with this test of close fit is > .50 (*p* = .562), we can conclude that the initially hypothesized model fits the data well.[7]

Before leaving this discussion of the RMSEA, it is important to note that confidence intervals can be influenced seriously by sample size, as well as model complexity (MacCallum et al., 1996). For example, if sample size is small and the number of estimated parameters is large, the confidence interval will be wide. Given a complex model (i.e., a large number of estimated parameters), a very large sample size would be required in order to obtain a reasonably narrow confidence interval. On the other hand, if the number of parameters is small, then the probability of obtaining a narrow confidence interval is high, even for samples of rather moderate size (MacCallum et al., 1996).

Let's turn, now, to the next cluster of statistics. The first of these is Akaike's (1987) Information Criterion (AIC), with Bozdogan's (1987) consistent version of the AIC (CAIC) shown at the end of the row. Both criteria address the issue of parsimony in the assessment of model fit; as such, statistical goodness-of-fit as well as the number of estimated parameters are taken into account. Bozdogan, however, noted that the AIC carried a penalty only as it related to degrees of freedom (thereby reflecting the number of estimated parameters in the model), and not to sample size. Presented with factor analytic findings that revealed the AIC to yield asymptotically inconsistent estimates, he proposed the CAIC, which takes sample size into account (Bandalos, 1993). The AIC and CAIC are used in the comparison of two or more models, with smaller values representing a better fit of the hypothesized model (Hu & Bentler, 1995). The AIC and CAIC indices also share the same conceptual framework; as such, they reflect the extent to which parameter estimates from the original sample will cross-validate in future samples (Bandalos, 1993). The Browne-Cudeck Criterion (BCC; Browne & Cudeck, 1989) and the Bayes Information Criterion (BIC; Raftery, 1993; Schwartz, 1978) operate in the same manner as the AIC and CAIC. The basic difference among these indices is that both the BCC and BIC impose greater penalties than either the AIC or CAIC for model complexity. Turning to the output once again, we see that in the case of all four of these fit indices, the fit statistics for the hypothesized model are substantially smaller than they are for either the independence or the saturated models.

The Expected Cross-Validation Index (ECVI) is central to the next cluster of fit statistics. The ECVI was proposed, initially, as a means of assessing, in a single sample, the likelihood that the model cross-validates across similar-sized samples from the same population (Browne & Cudeck, 1989). Specifically, it measures the discrepancy between the fitted covariance matrix in the analyzed sample, and the expected covariance matrix that would be obtained in another sample of equivalent size. Application of the ECVI assumes a comparison of models whereby an ECVI index is computed for each model, and then all ECVI values are placed in rank order; the model having the smallest ECVI value exhibits the greatest potential for replication. Because ECVI coefficients can take on any value, there is no determined appropriate range of values.

In assessing our hypothesized four-factor model, we compare its ECVI value of .888 with those of both the saturated model (ECVI = 1.030) and the independence model (ECVI = 6.548). Given the lower ECVI value for the hypothesized model, compared with both the independence and saturated models, we conclude that it represents the best fit to the data.

Beyond this comparison, Browne and Cudeck (1993) have shown that it is now possible to take the precision of the estimated ECVI value into account through the formulation of confidence intervals. Turning to Table 3.5 again, we see that this interval ranges from .773 to 1.034. Taken together, these results suggest that the hypothesized model is well fitting and represents a reasonable approximation to the population. The last fit statistic, the MECVI (modified ECVI), is actually identical to the BCC, except for a scale factor (Arbuckle, 2007).

The last goodness-of-fit statistic appearing on the AMOS output is Hoelter's (1983) Critical N (CN) (albeit labeled as Hoelter's .05 and .01 indices). This fit statistic differs substantially from those previously discussed in that it focuses directly on the adequacy of sample size, rather than on model fit. Development of Hoelter's index arose from an attempt to find a fit index that is independent of sample size. Specifically, its purpose is to estimate a sample size that would be sufficient to yield an adequate model fit for a χ^2 test (Hu & Bentler, 1995). Hoelter proposed that a value in excess of 200 is indicative of a model that adequately represents the sample data. As shown in Table 3.5, both the .05 and .01 CN values for our hypothesized SC model were > 200 (204 and 223, respectively). Interpretation of this finding, then, leads us to conclude that the size of our sample ($N = 265$) was satisfactory according to Hoelter's benchmark that the CN should exceed 200.

Having worked your way through this smorgasbord of goodness-of-fit measures, you are no doubt feeling totally overwhelmed and wondering what you do with all this information! Although you certainly don't need to report the entire set of fit indices, such an array can give you a good sense of how well your model fits the sample data. But, how does one choose which indices are appropriate in evaluating model fit? Unfortunately, this choice is not a simple one, largely because particular indices have been shown to operate somewhat differently given the sample size, estimation procedure, model complexity, and/or violation of the underlying assumptions of multivariate normality and variable independence. Thus, Hu and Bentler (1995) cautioned that, in choosing which goodness-of-fit indices to use in the assessment of model fit, careful consideration of these critical factors is essential. For further elaboration on the above goodness-of-fit statistics with respect to their formulae and functions, or the extent to which they are affected by sample size, estimation procedures, misspecification, and/or violations of assumptions, readers are referred to Arbuckle (2007); Bandalos (1993); Beauducel and Wittmann (2005); Bentler and Yuan (1999); Bollen (1989a); Boomsma and Hoogland (2001); Browne and Cudeck (1993); Curran, West, and Finch (1996); Davey, Savla, and Luo (2005); Fan and Sivo (2005); Fan et al. (1999); Finch, West, and MacKinnon (1997); Gerbing and Anderson (1993); Hu and Bentler (1995, 1998, 1999); Hu, Bentler, and Kano (1992); Jöreskog and Sörbom (1993); La Du and Tanaka (1989); Lei and Lomax (2005); Marsh et al. (1988); Mulaik et al. (1989); Raykov and Widaman (1995); Stoel, Garre, Dolan, and van den Wittenboer (2006); Sugawara and MacCallum (1993); Tomarken and Waller (2005); Weng and Cheng (1997); West, Finch, and Curran (1995); Wheaton (1987); and Williams and Holahan (1994). For an annotated bibliography, see Austin and Calderón (1996).

In finalizing this section on model assessment, I wish to leave you with this important reminder—that global fit indices alone cannot possibly envelop all that needs to be known about a model in order to judge the adequacy of its fit to the sample data. As Sobel and Bohrnstedt (1985) so cogently stated over 2 decades ago, "Scientific progress could be impeded if fit coefficients (even appropriate ones) are used as the primary criterion for judging the adequacy of a model" (p. 158). They further posited that, despite the problematic nature of the χ^2 statistic, exclusive reliance on goodness-of-fit indices is unacceptable. Indeed, fit indices provide no guarantee whatsoever that a model is useful. In fact, it is entirely possible for a model to fit well and yet still be incorrectly specified (Wheaton, 1987). (For an excellent review of ways by which such a seemingly dichotomous event can happen, readers are referred to Bentler & Chou, 1987.) Fit indices yield information bearing only on the model's *lack of fit*. More importantly, they can in no way reflect the extent to which the model is plausible; *this judgment rests squarely on the shoulders of the researcher*. Thus, assessment of model adequacy must be based on multiple criteria that take into account theoretical, statistical, and practical considerations.

Thus far, on the basis of our goodness-of-fit results, we could very well conclude that our hypothesized four-factor CFA model fits the sample data well. However, in the interest of completeness, and for didactic purposes, I consider it instructive to walk you through the process involved in determining evidence of model misspecification. That is, we conduct an analysis of the data that serves in identifying any parameters that have been incorrectly specified. Let's turn now, then, to the process of determining evidence of model misspecification.

Model misspecification

AMOS yields two types of information that can be helpful in detecting model misspecification—the *standardized residuals* and the *modification indices*. Because this information was not provided as default output in our initial test of the model, we request this optional information now. To obtain this resource, we either click on the *Analysis Properties* icon, or pull down the *View* menu and select *Analysis Properties*. Both actions trigger a multiple-layered dialog box that offers a wide variety of options. Figure 3.10 shows this dialog box with the *Output* tab in a forward position. For our purposes here, we select only residuals and modification indices as our sole options, as indicated at the bottom left of the dialog box.

Residuals

Recall that the essence of SEM is to determine the fit between the restricted covariance matrix [$\Sigma(\theta)$], implied by the hypothesized model, and the sample covariance matrix (S); any discrepancy between the two is captured by the residual covariance matrix. Each element in this residual matrix, then, represents the discrepancy between the covariances in $\Sigma(\theta)$ and those in S [i.e., $\Sigma(\theta) - S$]; that is to say, there is one residual for each pair of observed variables (Jöreskog, 1993). In the case of our hypothesized model, for example, the residual matrix would contain ([16 × 17] / 2) = 136 elements. It may be worth noting that, as in conventional regression analysis, the

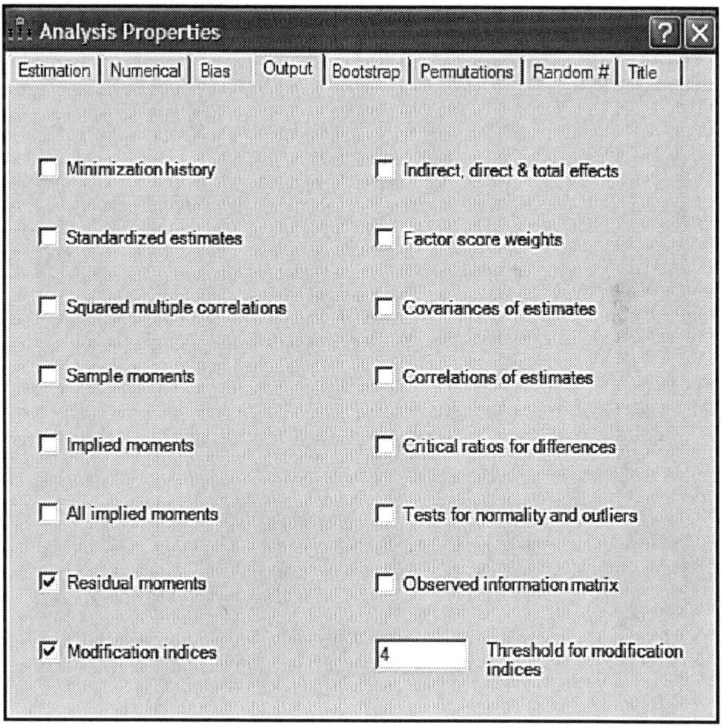

Figure 3.10 AMOS Graphics: Analysis properties dialog box with *output* tab selected.

residuals are not independent of one another. Thus, any attempts to test them (in the strict statistical sense) would be inappropriate. In essence, only their magnitude is of interest in alerting the researcher to possible areas of model misfit.

The matrices of both unstandardized and standardized residuals are presented in the optional AMOS output. (Recall that the unstandardized residuals were presented earlier.) However, because the fitted residuals are dependent on the unit of measurement of the observed variables, they can be difficult to interpret, and thus their standardized values are typically examined. As such, only the latter are presented in Table 3.6. Standardized residuals are fitted residuals divided by their asymptotically (large sample) standard errors (Jöreskog & Sörbom, 1993). As such, they are analogous to Z-scores and are therefore the easier of the two sets of residual values to interpret. In essence, they represent estimates of the number of standard deviations the observed residuals are from the zero residuals that would exist if model fit were perfect [i.e., $\Sigma(\theta) - S = 0.0$]. Values > 2.58 are considered to be large (Jöreskog & Sörbom, 1993). In examining the standardized residual values presented in Table 3.6, we observe only one that exceeds the cutpoint of 2.58. As such, the residual value of −2.942 represents the covariance between the observed variables SDQ2N07 and SDQ2N34. From this information, we can conclude that the only statistically significant discrepancy of note lies with the covariance between the two variables noted.

Modification indices

The second type of information related to misspecification reflects the extent to which the hypothesized model is appropriately described. Evidence of misfit in this regard is captured by the modification indices (MIs), which can be conceptualized as a χ^2 statistic with one degree of freedom (Jöreskog & Sörbom, 1993). Specifically, for each *fixed* parameter specified, AMOS provides an MI, the value of which represents the expected drop in overall χ^2 value if the parameter were to be freely estimated in a subsequent run; all freely estimated parameters automatically have MI values equal to zero. Although this decrease in χ^2 is expected to approximate the MI value, the actual differential can be larger. Associated with each MI is an expected parameter change (EPC) value (Saris, Satorra, & Sörbom, 1987), which is reported in the accompanying column labeled "Par Change." This latter statistic represents the predicted estimated change, in either a positive or negative direction, for each fixed parameter in the model and yields important information regarding the sensitivity of the evaluation of fit to any reparameterization of the model.[8] The MIs and accompanying EPC statistics related to our hypothesized model are presented in Table 3.7.

Table 3.6 Selected AMOS Output for Hypothesized 4-Factor CFA Model: Standardized Residual Covariances

	SDQ2N07	SDQ2N19	SDQ2N31	SDQ2N43	SDQ2N10	SDQ2N22	SDQ2N34
SDQ2N07	0.000						
SDQ2N19	0.251	0.000					
SDQ2N31	0.189	-0.457	0.000				
SDQ2N43	-0.458	1.013	-0.071	0.000			
SDQ2N10	-0.668	0.582	0.218	0.087	-0.000		
SDQ2N22	-0.408	1.027	0.845	-0.072	-0.121	0.000	
SDQ2N34	-2.942	-1.503	-2.030	-1.446	0.501	-0.440	0.000
SDQ2N46	-0.466	-0.548	0.514	1.457	-0.209	0.267	0.543
SDQ2N04	0.057	-0.061	0.333	-0.645	1.252	-0.442	-0.544
SDQ2N16	-0.645	0.422	0.059	0.100	-0.131	0.563	-1.589
SDQ2N28	-0.711	0.959	0.579	0.250	-0.609	-0.095	-2.184
SDQ2N40	-1.301	0.729	-0.227	0.909	0.516	0.574	-0.455
SDQ2N01	-0.496	-0.270	-0.229	-1.206	-0.052	-0.549	0.873
SDQ2N13	-1.141	-0.100	-0.037	0.175	0.248	0.001	1.423
SDQ2N25	0.011	-0.827	0.505	-0.220	-0.564	-0.135	0.621
SDQ2N37	-0.099	-0.190	1.285	-0.449	-0.099	0.060	0.756

(continued)

Table 3.6 Selected AMOS Output for Hypothesized 4-Factor CFA Model: Standardized Residual Covariances *(Continued)*

	SDQ2N46	SDQ2N04	SDQ2N16	SDQ2N28	SDQ2N40	SDQ2N01	SDQ2N13	SDQ2N25	SDQ2N37
SDQ2N46	0.000								
SDQ2N04	-0.382	0.001							
SDQ2N16	-0.276	0.272	0.000						
SDQ2N28	-0.350	-0.084	0.427	0.000					
SDQ2N40	0.983	-1.545	-0.240	0.358	0.000				
SDQ2N01	0.721	0.027	-0.620	-1.240	-0.611	-0.000			
SDQ2N13	0.443	1.777	-0.203	-0.719	-0.217	0.145	0.000		
SDQ2N25	-0.818	-0.493	-0.600	-0.894	-0.112	2.132	-0.588	0.000	
SDQ2N37	-0.598	0.796	0.884	0.568	1.727	-0.971	0.327	-0.645	0.000

As shown in Table 3.7, the MIs and EPCs are presented first for possible covariances, followed by those for the regression weights. Recall that the only model parameters for which the MIs are applicable are those that were fixed to a value of 0.0. Thus, no values appear under the heading "Variances" as all parameters representing variances (factors and measurement errors) were freely estimated.

In reviewing the parameters in the "Covariance" section, the only ones that make any substantive sense are those representing error covariances. In this regard, only the parameter representing a covariance between err25 and err01 appears to be of any interest. Nonetheless, an MI value of this size (13.487), with an EPC value of .285, particularly as these values relate to an error covariance, can be considered of little concern. Turning to the regression weights, I consider only two to make any substantive sense; these are SDQ2N07 <--- ESC, and SDQ2N34 <--- MSC. Both parameters represent cross-loadings. However, again, the MIs, and their associated EPC values, are not worthy of inclusion in a subsequently specified model. Of prime importance in determining whether or not to include additional parameters in the model is the extent to which (a) they are substantively meaningful, (b) the existing model exhibits adequate fit, and (c) the EPC value is substantial. Superimposed on this decision is the ever constant need for scientific parsimony. Because model respecification is commonly conducted in SEM in general, as well as in several applications highlighted in this book, I consider it important to provide you with a brief overview of the various issues related to these post hoc analyses.

Post hoc analyses

In the application of SEM in testing for the validity of various hypothesized models, the researcher will be faced, at some point, with the decision of whether or not to respecify and reestimate the model. If he or she elects to follow this route, it is important to realize that analyses then become framed within an *exploratory*, rather than a *confirmatory*, mode. In other words, once a hypothesized CFA model, for example, has been rejected, this spells the end of the confirmatory factor analytic approach, in its truest sense. Although CFA procedures continue to be used in any respecification and reestimation of the model, these analyses are exploratory in the sense that they focus on the detection of misfitting parameters in the originally hypothesized model. Such post hoc analyses are conventionally termed *specification searches* (see MacCallum, 1986). (The issue of post hoc model fitting is addressed further in Chapter 9 in the section dealing with cross-validation.)

The ultimate decision underscoring whether or not to proceed with a specification search is twofold. *First* and foremost, the researcher must determine whether the estimation of the targeted parameter is

Table 3.7 Selected AMOS Output for Hypothesized Four-Factor CFA Model: Modification Indices and Parameter Change Statistics

	M.I.	Par change
Covariances		
err31<-->err19	8.956	−.167
err43<-->err19	7.497	.201
err34<-->GSC	8.192	.225
err46<-->err43	4.827	.159
err04<-->err10	5.669	.162
err40<-->err43	5.688	.155
err40<-->err04	8.596	−.224
err13<-->err04	6.418	.217
err25<-->err01	13.487	.285
err37<-->ASC	6.873	.079
err37<-->err31	4.041	.097
err37<-->err40	5.331	.141
Variances		
Regression weights: (Group number 1—your model)		
SDQ2N07<---ESC	7.427	−.242
SDQ2N07<---SDQ2N34	4.897	−.083
SDQ2N07<---SDQ2N28	5.434	−.112
SDQ2N07<---SDQ2N40	6.323	−.119
SDQ2N31<---SDQ2N37	5.952	.107
SDQ2N10<---SDQ2N04	4.038	.081
SDQ2N34<---MSC	6.323	−.173
SDQ2N34<---SDQ2N07	7.695	−.157
SDQ2N34<---SDQ2N31	5.316	−.148
SDQ2N34<---SDQ2N28	4.887	−.167
SDQ2N04<---SDQ2N13	5.029	.123
SDQ2N40<---SDQ2N04	5.883	−.110
SDQ2N01<---SDQ2N25	8.653	.173
SDQ2N13<---SDQ2N04	4.233	.104
SDQ2N25<---SDQ2N01	7.926	.140
SDQ2N37<---SDQ2N40	5.509	.103

substantively meaningful. If, indeed, it makes no sound substantive sense to free up the parameter exhibiting the largest MI, then one may wish to consider the parameter having the next largest MI value (Jöreskog, 1993). *Second*, one needs to consider whether or not the respecified model would lead to an overfitted model. The issue here is tied to the idea of knowing when to stop fitting the model, or, as Wheaton (1987) phrased the problem, "knowing … how much fit is enough without being too much fit" (p. 123). In general, overfitting a model involves the specification of additional parameters in the model after having determined a criterion that reflects a minimally adequate fit. For example, an *overfitted model* can result from the inclusion of additional parameters that (a) are "fragile" in the sense of representing weak effects that are not likely replicable, (b) lead to a significant inflation of standard errors, and (c) influence primary parameters in the model, albeit their own substantive meaningfulness is somewhat equivocal (Wheaton, 1987). Although correlated errors often fall into this latter category,[9] there are many situations—particularly with respect to social psychological research—where these parameters can make strong substantive sense and therefore should be included in the model (Jöreskog & Sörbom, 1993).

Having laboriously worked our way through the process involved in evaluating the fit of a hypothesized model, what can we conclude regarding the CFA model under scrutiny in this chapter? In answering this question, we must necessarily pool all the information gleaned from our study of the AMOS output. Taking into account (a) the feasibility and statistical significance of all parameter estimates; (b) the substantially good fit of the model, with particular reference to the CFI (.962) and RMSEA (.048) values; and (c) the lack of any substantial evidence of model misfit, I conclude that any further incorporation of parameters into the model would result in an overfitted model. Indeed, MacCallum et al. (1992, p. 501) have cautioned that "when an initial model fits well, it is probably unwise to modify it to achieve even better fit because modifications may simply be fitting small idiosyncratic characteristics of the sample." Adhering to this caveat, I conclude that the four-factor model schematically portrayed in Figure 3.1 represents an adequate description of self-concept structure for grade 7 adolescents.

Hypothesis 2: Self-concept is a two-factor structure

The model to be tested here (Model 2) postulates a priori that SC is a two-factor structure consisting of GSC and ASC. As such, it argues against the viability of subject-specific academic SC factors. As with the four-factor model, the four GSC measures load onto the GSC factor; in contrast, all other measures load onto the ASC factor. This hypothesized model is represented schematically in Figure 3.11, which serves as the model specification for AMOS Graphics.

In reviewing the graphical specification of Model 2, two points pertinent to its modification are of interest. *First,* while the pattern of factor

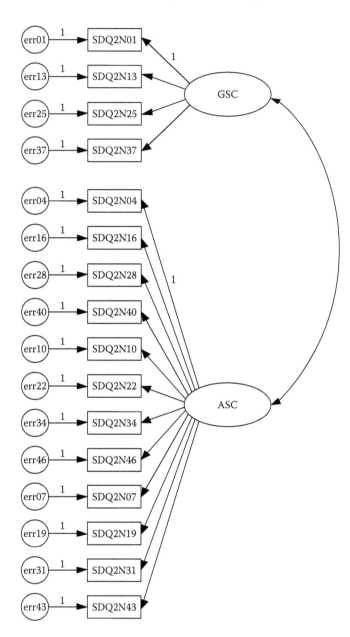

Figure 3.11 Hypothesized two-factor CFA model of self-concept.

loadings remains the same for the GSC and ASC measures, it changes for both the ESC and MSC measures in allowing them to load onto the ASC factor. *Second*, because only one of these eight ASC factor loadings needs to be fixed to 1.0, the two previously constrained parameters (SDQ2N10 ← ESC; SDQ2N07 ← MSC) are now freely estimated.

Selected AMOS text output: Hypothesized two-factor model

Only the goodness-of-fit statistics are relevant to the present application, and a selected group of these is presented in Table 3.8.

As indicated in the output, the $\chi^2_{(103)}$ value of 455.926 represents an extremely poor fit to the data, and a substantial decrement from the overall fit of the four-factor model ($\Delta\chi^2_{(5)} = 297.415$). The gain of 5 degrees of freedom can be explained by the estimation of two fewer factor variances and five fewer factor covariances, albeit the estimation of two additional factor loadings (formerly SDQ2N10 ← ESC and SDQ2N07 ← MSC). As expected, all other indices of fit reflect the fact that self-concept structure is not well represented by the hypothesized two-factor model. In particular, the CFI value of .776 and RMSEA value of .114, together with a PCLOSE value of 0.00, are strongly indicative of inferior goodness-of-fit between the hypothesized two-factor model and the sample data. Finally, the ECVI value of 1.977, compared with the substantially lower value of 0.888 for the hypothesized four-factor model, again confirms the inferior fit of Model 2.

Hypothesis 3: Self-concept is a one-factor structure

Although it now seems obvious that the structure of SC for grade 7 adolescents is best represented by a multidimensional model, there are still researchers who contend that SC is a unidimensional construct. Thus, for purposes of completeness, and to address the issue of unidimensionality, Byrne and Worth Gavin (1996) proceeded in testing the above hypothesis. However, because the one-factor model represents a restricted version of the two-factor model, and thus cannot possibly represent a better fitting model, in the interest of space, these analyses are not presented here.

In summary, it is evident from these analyses that both the two-factor and one-factor models of self-concept represent a misspecification of factorial structure for early adolescents. Based on these findings, then, Byrne and Worth Gavin (1996) concluded that SC is a multidimensional construct, which in their study comprised the four facets of general, academic, English, and math self-concepts.

Table 3.8 Selected AMOS Output for Hypothesized Two-Factor
CFA Model: Goodness-of-Fit Statistics

Model fit summary

CMIN

Model	NPAR	CMIN	DF	P	CMIN/ DF
Your model	33	455.926	103	.000	4.426
Saturated model	136	.000	0		
Independence model	16	1696.728	120	.000	14.139

RMR, GFI

Model	RMR	GFI	AGFI	PGFI
Your model	.182	.754	.675	.571
Saturated model	.000	1.000		
Independence model	.628	.379	.296	.334

Baseline comparisons

Model	NFI Delta 1	RFI rho 1	IFI Delta 2	TLI rho 2	CFI
Your model	.731	.687	.779	.739	.776
Saturated model	1.000		1.000		1.000
Independence model	.000	.000	.000	.000	.000

RMSEA

Model	RMSEA	LO 90	HI 90	PCLOSE
Your model	.114	.103	.124	.000
Independence model	.223	.214	.233	.000

ECVI

Model	ECVI	LO 90	HI 90	MECVI
Your model	1.977	1.741	2.242	1.994
Saturated model	1.030	1.030	1.030	1.101
Independence model	6.548	6.058	7.067	6.557

Endnotes

1. The term *uniqueness* is used here in the factor analytic sense to mean a composite of random measurement error and specific measurement error associated with a particular measuring instrument; in cross-sectional studies, the two cannot be separated (Gerbing & Anderson, 1984).

2. As noted in Chapter 2, a set of measures is said to be *congeneric* if each measure in the set purports to assess the same construct, except for errors of measurement (Jöreskog, 1971a).

3. Inaccurate standard errors are commonly found when analyses are based on the correlation matrix (Bollen, 1989a; Boomsma, 1985; Boomsma & Hoogland, 2001; Jöreskog, 1993).

4. Wheaton (1987) later advocated that this ratio not be used.

5. For alternate approaches to formulating baseline models, see Cudeck and Browne (1983), and Sobel and Bohrnstedt (1985).

6. The PCFI, in keeping with Bentler's recommended use of the CFI over the NFI, should be the index of choice. (see, e.g., Byrne, 1994a; Carlson & Mulaik, 1993; Williams & Holahan, 1994).

7. One possible limitation of the RMSEA, as noted by Mulaik (see Byrne, 1994a), is that it ignores the complexity of the model.

8. Bentler (2005) has noted, however, that because these parameter change statistics are sensitive to the way by which variables and factors are scaled or identified, their absolute value is sometimes difficult to interpret.

9. Typically, the misuse in this instance arises from the incorporation of correlated errors into the model purely on the basis of statistical fit and for the purpose of achieving a better fitting model.

chapter four

Testing for the factorial validity of scores from a measuring instrument
(First-order CFA model)

For our second application, we once again examine a first-order confirmatory factor analytic (CFA) model. However, this time we test hypotheses bearing on a single measuring instrument, the Maslach Burnout Inventory (MBI; Maslach & Jackson, 1981, 1986), designed to measure three dimensions of burnout, which the authors labeled emotional exhaustion (EE), depersonalization (DP), and reduced personal accomplishment (PA). The term *burnout* denotes the inability to function effectively in one's job as a consequence of prolonged and extensive job-related stress; *emotional exhaustion* represents feelings of fatigue that develop as one's energies become drained; *depersonalization*, the development of negative and uncaring attitudes toward others; and *reduced personal accomplishment*, a deterioration of self-confidence, and dissatisfaction in one's achievements.

Purposes of the original study (Byrne, 1994c) from which this example is taken were to test for the validity and invariance of factorial structure within and across gender for elementary and secondary teachers. For the purposes of this chapter, however, only analyses bearing on the factorial validity of the MBI for a calibration sample of elementary male teachers ($n = 372$) are of interest.

Confirmatory factor analysis of a measuring instrument is most appropriately applied to measures that have been fully developed, and their factor structures validated. The legitimacy of CFA use, of course, is tied to its conceptual rationale as a hypothesis-testing approach to data analysis. That is to say, based on theory, empirical research, or a combination of both, the researcher postulates a model and then tests for its validity given the sample data. Thus, application of CFA procedures to assessment instruments that are still in the initial stages of development represents a serious misuse of this analytic strategy. In testing for the validity of factorial structure for an assessment measure, the researcher seeks to determine the extent to which items designed to measure a particular factor (i.e., latent construct) actually do so. In general, subscales of a measuring instrument are considered to represent the factors; all items comprising a particular subscale are therefore expected to load onto their related factor.

Given that the MBI has been commercially marketed since 1981, is the most widely used measure of occupational burnout, and has undergone substantial testing of its psychometric properties over the years (see, e.g., Byrne 1991, 1993, 1994a), it most certainly qualifies as a candidate for CFA research. Interestingly, until my 1991 study of the MBI, virtually all previous factor analytic work had been based only on exploratory procedures. We turn now to a description of this assessment instrument.

The measuring instrument under study

The MBI is a 22-item instrument structured on a 7-point Likert-type scale that ranges from 0 (*feeling has never been experienced*) to 6 (*feeling experienced daily*). It is composed of three subscales, each measuring one facet of burnout; the EE subscale comprises nine items, the DP subscale five, and the PA subscale eight. The original version of the MBI (Maslach & Jackson, 1981) was constructed from data based on samples of workers from a wide range of human service organizations. Subsequently, however, Maslach and Jackson (1986), in collaboration with Schwab, developed the Educators' Survey (MBI Form Ed), a version of the instrument specifically designed for use with teachers. The MBI Form Ed parallels the original version of the MBI except for the modified wording of certain items to make them more appropriate to a teacher's work environment.

The hypothesized model

The CFA model of MBI structure hypothesizes a priori that (a) responses to the MBI can be explained by three factors, EE, DP, and PA; (b) each item has a nonzero loading on the burnout factor it was designed to measure, and zero loadings on all other factors; (c) the three factors are correlated; and (d) the error/uniqueness terms associated with the item measurements are uncorrelated. A schematic representation of this model is shown in Figure 4.1.[1]

Modeling with AMOS Graphics

The hypothesized three-factor model of MBI structure (see Figure 4.1) provided the specification input for analyses using AMOS Graphics. In Chapter 2, we reviewed the process involved in computing the number of degrees of freedom and, ultimately, in determining the identification

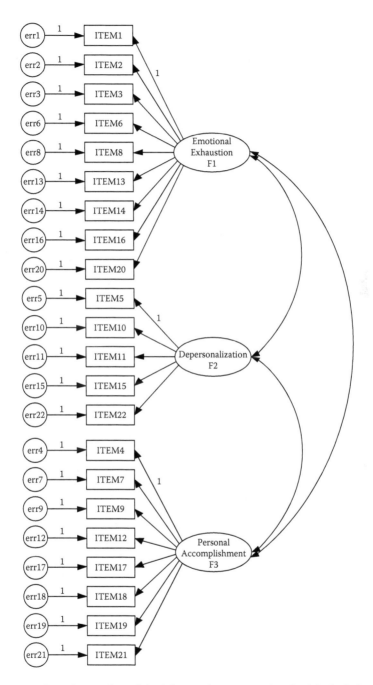

Figure 4.1 Hypothesized model of factorial structure for the Maslach Burnout inventory (Model 1).

status of a hypothesized model. Although all such information (esti-mated/fixed parameters; degrees of freedom) is provided in the *Model/Parameter Summary* dialog boxes of the AMOS output, I still encourage you to make this practice part of your routine as, I believe, it forces you to think through the specification of your model. In the present case, the sample covariance matrix comprises a total of 253 (23 × 22 / 2) pieces of information (or sample moments). Of the 72 parameters in the model, only 47 are to be freely estimated (19 factor loadings, 22 error variances, 3 factor variances, and 3 factor covariances); all others (25) are fixed param-eters in the model (i.e., they are constrained to equal zero or some nonzero value). As a consequence, the hypothesized model is overidentified with 206 (253 – 47) degrees of freedom.

Prior to submitting the model input to analysis, you will likely wish to review the *Analysis Properties* box (introduced in Chapter 3) in order to tailor the type of information to be provided on the AMOS output, on esti-mation procedures, and/or on many other aspects of the analyses. In the present case, we are only interested in output file information. Recall that clicking on the *Analysis Properties* icon ▦ yields the dialog box shown in Figure 4.2. For our purposes here, we request the modification indices (MIs), the standardized parameter estimates (provided in addition to the unstandardized estimates, which are default), and tests for normality and outliers, all of which are options you can choose when the *Output* tab is activated. In contrast to the MI specification in Chapter 3, however, we'll stipulate a threshold of 10. As such, only MI estimates equal to or greater than 10 will be included in the output file.

Having specified the hypothesized three-factor CFA model of MBI structure, located the data file to be used for this analysis (as illustrated in Chapter 3), and selected the information to be included in the report-ing of results, we are now ready to analyze the model. Surprisingly, after I clicked the *Calculation* icon, I was presented with the error message shown in Figure 4.3 in which the program is advising me that there is a prob-lem with Item 20. However, clearly this message does not make any sense as Item 20 is definitely an observed variable in the model. Thus, I knew the problem had to lie elsewhere. The question, of course, was "Where?" As it turned out, there was a discrepancy in the labeling of the observed variables. Specifically, whereas item labels on the model showed a space between *ITEM* and its related number in the instrument (e.g., ITEM 20), this was not the case for the item labels in the data set; that is, there was no space between the word *ITEM* and 1, 2, and so on (e.g., ITEM1). In fact, several labels in addition to Item 20 had to be modified so that any such spaces had to be deleted. Once I made the model item labels consistent with those of the data file, the analyses proceeded with no further problems. I consider it important to point this error message out to you as it is almost guaranteed

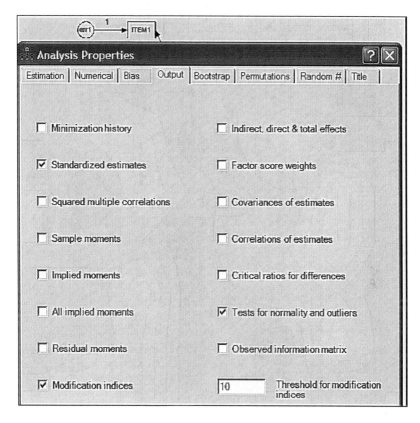

Figure 4.2 AMOS Graphics: Analysis properties dialog box with output tab open.

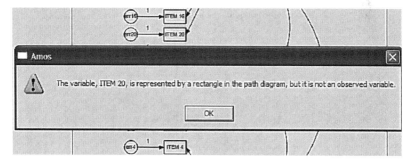

Figure 4.3 AMOS Graphics: Error message triggered by calculation command.

that you will encounter it at some time with respect to your own work. Now that you know what triggers this message, you can quickly resolve the situation. The moral of the story, then, is to always double check your input data before running the analyses! Let's now review the related output file.

Selected AMOS output: The hypothesized model

In contrast to Chapter 3, only selected portions of this file will be reviewed and discussed. We examine first the model summary, assessment of normality and outliers, indices of fit for the model as a whole, and, finally, MIs with a view to pinpointing areas of model misspecification.

Model summary

As shown in Figure 4.4, estimation of the hypothesized model resulted in an overall χ^2 value of 693.849 with 206 degrees of freedom and a probability value of .000. Of import also is the notation that the minimum was achieved. This latter statement indicates that AMOS was successful in estimating all model parameters, thereby resulting in a convergent solution. If, on the other hand, the program as not able to achieve this goal, it would mean that it was unsuccessful in being able to reach the minimum discrepancy value, as defined by the program in its comparison of the sample covariance and restricted covariance matrices. Typically, an outcome of this sort results from incorrectly specified models and/or data in which there are linear dependencies among certain variables.

Assessment of normality

A critically important assumption in the conduct of SEM analyses in general, and in the use of AMOS in particular (Arbuckle, 2007), is that the data are multivariate normal. This requirement is rooted in large sample theory from which the SEM methodology was spawned. Thus, before any analyses of data are undertaken, it is important to check that this criterion has been met. Particularly problematic to SEM analyses are data that

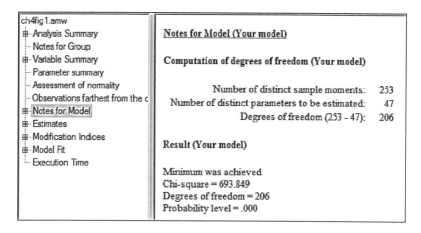

Figure 4.4 AMOS Graphics: Summary model statistics.

are multivariate kurtotic, the situation where the multivariate distribution of the observed variables has both tails and peaks that differ from those characteristic of a multivariate normal distribution (see Raykov & Marcoulides, 2000). More specifically, in the case of multivariate *positive* kurtosis, the distributions will exhibit peakedness together with heavy (or thick) tails; conversely, multivariate *negative* kurtosis will yield flat distributions with light tails (DeCarlo, 1997). To exemplify the most commonly found condition of multivariate kurtosis in SEM, let's take the case of a Likert-scaled questionnaire, for which responses to certain items result in the majority of respondents selecting the same scale point. For each of these items, the score distribution would be extremely peaked (i.e., leptokurtic); considered jointly, these particular items would reflect a multivariately positive kurtotic distribution. (For an elaboration of both univariate and multivariate kurtosis, readers are referred to DeCarlo.)

Prerequisite to the assessment of multivariate normality is the need to check for univariate normality as the latter is a necessary, although not sufficient, condition for multivariate normality (DeCarlo, 1997). Thus, we turn now to the results of our request on the *Analysis Properties* dialog box (see Figure 4.2) for an assessment of normality as it relates to the male teacher data used in this application. These results are presented in Figure 4.5.

Statistical research has shown that whereas skewness tends to impact tests of means, kurtosis severely affects tests of variances and covariances (DeCarlo, 1997). Given that SEM is based on the analysis of covariance structures, evidence of kurtosis is always of concern and, in particular, evidence of multivariate kurtosis, as it is known to be exceptionally detrimental in SEM analyses. With this in mind in turning first to the univariate statistics, we focus only on the last two columns of Figure 4.5, where we find the univariate kurtosis value and its critical ratio (i.e., z-value) listed for each of the 22 MBI items. As shown, positive values range from .007 to 5.100 and negative values from –.597 to –1.156, yielding an overall mean univariate kurtosis value of 1.00. The standardized kurtosis index (β_2) in a normal distribution has a value of 3, with larger values representing positive kurtosis and lesser values representing negative kurtosis. However, computer programs typically rescale this value by subtracting 3 from the β_2 value, thereby making zero the indicator of normal distribution and its sign the indicator of positive or negative kurtosis (DeCarlo; Kline, 2005; West, Finch, & Curran, 1995). Although there appears to be no clear consensus as to how large the nonzero values should be before conclusions of extreme kurtosis can be drawn (Kline, 2005), West et al. (1995) consider rescaled β_2 values equal to or greater than 7 to be indicative of early departure from normality. Using this value of 7 as a guide, a review of the kurtosis values reported in Figure 4.5 reveals no item to be substantially kurtotic.

ch4fig1.amw
⊞ Analysis Summary
  Notes for Group
⊞ Variable Summary
  Parameter summary
  Assessment of normality
  Observations farthest from th
⊞ Notes for Model
⊞ Estimates
⊞ Modification Indices
⊞ Model Fit
  Execution Time

Assessment of normality (Group number 1)

Variable	min	max	skew	c.r.	kurtosis	c.r.
ITEM4	2.000	7.000	-1.811	-14.261	3.666	14.435
ITEM7	2.000	7.000	-1.649	-12.984	3.802	14.969
ITEM9	1.000	7.000	-1.542	-12.144	1.869	7.360
ITEM12	1.000	7.000	-1.320	-10.390	1.867	7.350
ITEM17	2.000	7.000	-1.978	-15.577	5.100	20.079
ITEM18	1.000	7.000	-1.231	-9.692	1.364	5.370
ITEM19	1.000	7.000	-1.484	-11.684	2.241	8.822
ITEM21	2.000	7.000	-1.300	-10.236	1.182	4.655
ITEM5	1.000	7.000	1.328	10.459	.930	3.663
ITEM10	1.000	7.000	1.202	9.468	.583	2.294
ITEM11	1.000	7.000	1.273	10.024	.816	3.212
ITEM15	1.000	7.000	2.096	16.507	4.279	16.846
ITEM22	1.000	7.000	1.066	8.395	.199	.782
ITEM1	1.000	7.000	-.115	-.906	-1.156	-4.552
ITEM2	1.000	7.000	-.507	-3.992	-.693	-2.727
ITEM3	1.000	7.000	.317	2.496	-1.100	-4.330
ITEM6	1.000	7.000	.924	7.274	.007	.028
ITEM8	1.000	7.000	.741	5.832	-.597	-2.351
ITEM13	1.000	7.000	.347	2.734	-.780	-3.072
ITEM14	1.000	7.000	.031	.243	-.925	-3.643
ITEM16	1.000	7.000	.971	7.649	.174	.683
ITEM20	1.000	7.000	1.300	10.237	1.193	4.696
Multivariate					127.975	37.978

Figure 4.5 AMOS Graphics: Summary normality statistics.

Of import is the fact that although the presence of nonnormal observed variables precludes the possibility of a multivariate normal distribution, the converse is not necessarily true. That is, regardless of whether the distribution of observed variables is univariate normal, the multivariate distribution can still be multivariate nonnormal (West et al., 1995). Thus, we turn now to the index of multivariate kurtosis and its critical ratio, both of which appear at the bottom of the kurtosis and critical ratio (C.R.) columns, respectively. Of most import here is the C.R. value, which in essence represents Mardia's (1970, 1974) normalized estimate of multivariate kurtosis, although it is not explicitly labeled as such (J. L. Arbuckle, personal communication, March 2008). When the sample size is very large and multivariately normal, Mardia's normalized estimate is distributed as a unit normal variate such that large values reflect significant positive kurtosis and large negative values reflect significant negative kurtosis. Bentler (2005) has suggested that, in practice, values > 5.00 are indicative of data that are nonnormally distributed. In this application, the z-statistic of 37.978 is highly suggestive of nonnormality in the sample.

When data reveal evidence of multivariate kurtosis, interpretations based on the usual ML estimation may be problematic, and thus an alternative method of estimation is likely more appropriate. One approach to the analysis of nonnormal data is to base analyses on asymptotic distribution-free (ADF) estimation (Browne, 1984a), which is available in AMOS by selecting this estimator from those offered on the *Estimation* tab of the *Analysis Properties* icon or drop-down *View* menu. However, it is now well-known that unless sample sizes are extremely large (1,000 to 5,000 cases; West et al., 1995), the ADF estimator performs very poorly and can yield severely distorted estimated values and standard errors (Curran et al., 1996; Hu, Bentler, & Kano, 1992; West et al.). More recently, statistical research has suggested that, at the very least, sample sizes should be greater than 10 times the number of estimated parameters, otherwise the results from the ADF method generally cannot be trusted (Raykov & Marcoulides, 2000). (See Byrne, 1995, for an example of the extent to which estimates can become distorted using the ADF method with a less than adequate sample size.) As shown in Figure 4.4, the model under study in this chapter has 47 freely estimated parameters, thereby suggesting a minimal sample size of 470. Given that our current sample size is 372, we cannot realistically use the ADF method of estimation.

In contrast to the ADF method of estimation, Chou, Bentler, and Satorra (1991) and Hu et al. (1992) have argued that it may be more appropriate to correct the test statistic, rather than use a different mode of estimation. Satorra and Bentler (1988, 1994) developed such a statistic that incorporates a scaling correction for the χ^2 statistic (S–Bχ^2) when distributional assumptions are violated; its computation takes into account the model, the estimation method, and the sample kurtosis values. The S–Bχ^2 has been shown to be the most reliable test statistic for evaluating mean and covariance structure models under various distributions and sample sizes (Curran et al., 1996; Hu et al.). Although the Satorra-Bentler robust method works very well with smaller sample sizes such as ours (see, e.g., Byrne, 2006), this method unfortunately is not available in the AMOS program. Thus, we will continue to base our analyses on ML estimation. However, given that I have analyzed the same data using the Satorra-Bentler robust approach in the EQS program (Byrne, 2006), it will be instructive to see the extent to which the results deviate between the two estimation methods. Thus, a brief comparison of both the overall goodness-of-fit and selected parameter statistics for the final model will be presented at the end of the chapter.

Assessment of multivariate outliers

Outliers represent cases whose scores are substantially different from all the others in a particular set of data. A univariate outlier has an extreme score on a single variable, whereas a multivariate outlier has extreme scores on two or more variables (Kline, 2005). A common approach to the detection of multivariate outliers is the computation of the squared Mahalanobis distance (D^2) for each case. This statistic measures the distance in standard deviation units between a set of scores for one case and the sample means for all variables (centroids). Typically, an outlying case will have a D^2 value that stands distinctively apart from all the other D^2 values. A review of these values reported in Figure 4.6 shows minimal evidence of serious multivariate outliers.

Model evaluation

Goodness-of-fit summary

Because the various indices of model fit provided by the AMOS program were discussed in Chapter 3, model evaluation throughout the remaining

Observations farthest from the centroid (Mahalanobis distance) (Gr			
Observation number	Mahalanobis d-squared	p1	p2
30	73.502	.000	.000
84	68.146	.000	.000
26	67.485	.000	.000
171	66.016	.000	.000
200	64.512	.000	.000
76	62.927	.000	.000
65	62.673	.000	.000
32	61.483	.000	.000
227	60.898	.000	.000
284	60.708	.000	.000
4	51.828	.000	.000
235	50.054	.001	.000
351	49.441	.001	.000
147	48.890	.001	.000
18	48.744	.001	.000
7	48.686	.001	.000
72	48.143	.001	.000
326	48.087	.001	.000
325	48.061	.001	.000
202	46.466	.002	.000
255	45.510	.002	.000
151	45.497	.002	.000
52	44.862	.003	.000
269	44.672	.003	.000
310	44.566	.003	.000

Figure 4.6 AMOS Graphics: Summary outlier statistics.

chapters will be limited to those summarized in Table 4.1. These criteria were chosen on the basis of (a) their variant approaches to the assessment of model fit (see Hoyle, 1995b), and (b) their support in the literature as important indices of fit that should be reported.[2] This selection, of course, in no way implies that the remaining criteria are unimportant. Rather, it addresses the need for users to select a subset of goodness-of-fit indices from the generous quantity provided by the AMOS program.[3] These selected indices of fit are presented in Table 4.1.

In reviewing these criteria in terms of their optimal values (see Chapter 3), we can see that they are consistent in their reflection of an ill-fitting model. For example, the CFA value of .848 is indicative of a very poor fit of the model to the data. Thus, it is apparent that some modification in specification is needed in order to identify a model that better represents the sample data. To assist us in pinpointing possible areas of misfit, we examine the modification indices. Of course, as noted in Chapter 3, it is important to realize that once we have determined that the hypothesized model represents a poor fit to the data (i.e., the null hypothesis has been rejected), and then embark in post hoc model fitting to identify areas of misfit in the

Table 4.1 Selected AMOS Output for Hypothesized Model: Goodness-of-Fit Statistics

Model fit summary					
CMIN					
Model	NPAR	CMIN	DF	P	CMIN/ DF
Your model	47	693.849	206	.000	3.368
Saturated model	253	.000	0		
Independence model	22	3442.988	231	.000	14.905

Baseline comparisons					
Model	NFI Delta1	RFI rho1	IFI Delta2	TLI rho2	CFI
Your model	.798	.774	.849	.830	.848
Saturated model	1.000		1.000		1.000
Independence model	.000	.000	.000	.000	.000

RMSEA				
Model	RMSEA	LO 90	HI 90	PCLOSE
Your model	.080	.073	.086	.000
Independence model	.194	.188	.199	.000

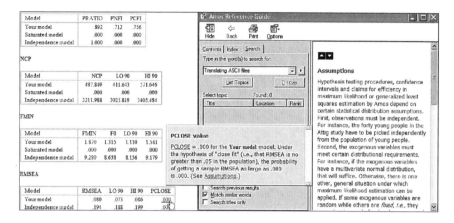

Figure 4.7 AMOS Graphics: AMOS reference guide dialog box.

model, we cease to operate in a confirmatory mode of analysis. All model specification and estimation henceforth represent exploratory analyses.

Before we examine the MIs as markers of possible model misspecification, however, let's divert briefly to review the *AMOS Reference Guide* dialog boxes pertinent to the PCLOSE statistic associated with the RMSEA, as shown in Figure 4.7. The initial box related to the PCLOSE statistic was generated by clicking on the .000 for *Your Model*. As is evident, information presented in this box explains the meaning of the PCLOSE statistic. Subsequently clicking on *Assumptions* then triggers a list of explanatory comments associated with various assumptions underlying SEM. These instructive *AMOS Reference Guide* dialog boxes are readily accessed for countless other statistics and other phenomena associated with the AMOS program.

Modification indices

We turn now to the MIs presented in Table 4.2. Based on the initially hypothesized model (Model 1), all factor loadings and error covariance terms that were fixed to a value of 0.0 are of substantial interest as they represent the only meaningful sources of misspecification in a CFA model. As such, large MIs argue for the presence of factor cross-loadings (i.e., a loading on more than one factor) and error covariances, respectively. However, consistent with other SEM programs, AMOS computes an MI for all parameters implicitly assumed to be zero, as well as for those that are explicitly fixed to zero or some other, nonzero value. In reviewing the list of MIs in Table 4.2, for example, you will see suggested regression paths between two observed variables (e.g., ITEM4 ← ITEM7) and suggested covariances between error terms and factors (e.g., err12 ↔ EMOTIONAL EXHAUSTION), neither of which makes any substantive sense. Given the

Table 4.2 Selected AMOS Output for Hypothesized Model:
Modification Indices

		M.I.	Par change
Covariances			
err7	<--> err4	31.870	.200
err12	<--> EMOTIONAL_EXHAUSTION	34.267	−.349
err18	<--> err7	10.386	−.128
err19	<--> err18	14.832	.200
err21	<--> err4	12.573	.193
err21	<--> err7	31.774	.250
err11	<--> err10	20.863	.319
err15	<--> err5	13.459	.271
err1	<--> PERSONAL_ACCOMPLISHMENT	24.032	.130
err2	**<--> err1**	**74.802**	**.557**
err3	<--> err12	15.462	−.255
err6	<--> err5	17.117	.354
err13	<--> PERSONAL_ACCOMPLISHMENT	11.203	−.089
err14	<--> err6	11.021	−.304
err16	**<--> err6**	**88.728**	**.714**
err20	<--> err8	12.451	.202
err20	<--> err13	12.114	.220
Regression weights			
ITEM4	<--- ITEM7	22.235	.267
ITEM7	<--- ITEM4	24.640	.193
ITEM7	<--- ITEM21	23.531	.149
ITEM12	**<--- EMOTIONAL_EXHAUSTION**	**33.856**	**−.256**
ITEM12	<--- ITEM1	23.705	−.158
ITEM12	<--- ITEM2	21.917	−.163
ITEM12	<--- ITEM3	44.109	−.206
ITEM12	<--- ITEM8	35.531	−.186
ITEM12	<--- ITEM14	11.569	−.106
ITEM12	<--- ITEM16	21.358	−.173
ITEM12	<--- ITEM20	13.784	−.141
ITEM21	<--- ITEM7	22.181	.334
ITEM5	<--- ITEM6	11.231	.142
ITEM11	<--- ITEM10	10.453	.137
ITEM1	<--- PERSONAL_ACCOMPLISHMENT	23.667	.720
ITEM1	<--- ITEM9	19.493	.197
ITEM1	<--- ITEM17	10.809	.227

(continued)

4.2 Selected AMOS Output for Hypothesized Model: Modification Indices (*Continued*)

		M.I.	Par change
Regression weights			
ITEM1 <--- ITEM18		16.058	.185
ITEM1 <--- ITEM19		14.688	.189
ITEM1 <--- ITEM2		31.830	.215
ITEM2 <--- PERSONAL_ACCOMPLISHMENT		10.507	.469
ITEM2 <--- ITEM9		13.645	.161
ITEM2 <--- ITEM1		27.403	.181
ITEM6 <--- ITEM5		15.020	.173
ITEM6 <--- ITEM16		*50.262*	*.327*
ITEM13 <--- PERSONAL_ACCOMPLISHMENT		10.418	−.481
ITEM13 <--- ITEM9		15.314	−.176
ITEM13 <--- ITEM19		11.414	−.168
ITEM16 <--- ITEM6		*52.454*	*.272*

meaninglessness of these MIs, then, we focus solely on those representing cross-loadings and error covariances.

Turning first to the MIs related to the *Covariances*, we see very clear evidence of misspecification associated with the pairing of error terms associated with Items 1 and 2 (err2↔err1; MI = 74.802) and those associated with Items 6 and 16 (err16↔err6; MI = 88.728). Although, admittedly, there are a few additionally quite large MI values shown, these two stand apart in that they are substantially larger than the others; they represent misspecified error covariances.[4] These measurement error covariances represent systematic, rather than random, measurement error in item responses, and they may derive from characteristics specific either to the items or to the respondents (Aish & Jöreskog, 1990). For example, if these parameters reflect item characteristics, they may represent a small omitted factor. If, on the other hand, they represent respondent characteristics, they may reflect bias such as yea-saying or nay-saying, social desirability, and the like (Aish & Jöreskog). Another type of method effect that can trigger error covariances is a high degree of overlap in item content. Such redundancy occurs when an item, although worded differently, essentially asks the same question. I believe the latter situation to be the case here. For example, Item 16 asks whether working with people directly puts too much stress on the respondent, while Item 6 asks whether working with people all day puts a real strain on him or her.[5]

Although a review of the MIs for the *Regression Weights* (i.e., factor loadings) reveals four parameters indicative of cross-loadings

(ITEM12 ← EMOTIONAL EXHAUSTION; ITEM1 ← PERSONAL ACCOMPLISHMENT; ITEM2 ← PERSONAL ACCOMPLISHMENT; ITEM13 ← PERSONAL ACCOMPLISHMENT), I draw your attention to the one with the highest value (MI = 33.856), which is highlighted in bold-face type.[6] This parameter, which represents the cross-loading of Item 12 on the EE factor, stands apart from the three other possible cross-loading misspecifications. Such misspecification, for example, could mean that Item 12, in addition to measuring personal accomplishment, also measures emotional exhaustion; alternatively, it could indicate that, although Item 12 was postulated to load on the PA factor, it may load more appropriately on the EE factor.

Post hoc analyses

Provided with information related both to model fit and to possible areas of model misspecification, a researcher may wish to consider respecifying an originally hypothesized model. As emphasized in Chapter 3, should this be the case, it is critically important to be cognizant of both the exploratory nature of, and the dangers associated with, the process of post hoc model fitting. Having determined (a) inadequate fit of the hypothesized model to the sample data, and (b) at least two misspecified parameters in the model (i.e., the two error covariances were specified as zero), it seems both reasonable and logical that we now move into exploratory mode and attempt to modify this model in a sound and responsible manner. Thus, for didactic purposes in illustrating the various aspects of post hoc model fitting, we'll proceed to respecify the initially hypothesized model of MBI structure taking this information into account.

Model respecification that includes correlated errors, as with other parameters, must be supported by a strong substantive and/or empirical rationale (Jöreskog, 1993), and I believe that this condition exists here. In light of (a) apparent item content overlap, (b) the replication of these same error covariances in previous MBI research (e.g., Byrne, 1991, 1993), and (c) Bentler and Chou's (1987) admonition that forcing large error terms to be uncorrelated is rarely appropriate with real data, I consider respecification of this initial model to be justified. Testing of this respecified model (Model 2) now falls within the framework of post hoc analyses.

Let's return now to AMOS Graphics and the respecification of Model 1 in structuring Model 2.

Model 2

Respecification of the hypothesized model of MBI structure involves the addition of freely estimated parameters to the model. However, because the estimation of MIs in AMOS is based on a univariate approach (cf. EQS and a multivariate approach), it is critical that we add only one parameter at a time to the model as the MI values can change substantially from one tested parameterization to another. Thus, in building Model 2, it seems most reasonable to proceed first in adding to the model the error covariance having the largest MI. As shown in Table 4.2, this parameter represents the error terms for Items 6 and 16 and, according to the *Parameter Change* statistic, should result in a parameter estimated value of approximately .714. Of related interest is the section in Table 4.2 labeled *Regression Weights*, where you see, highlighted in italics, two suggested regression paths. Although technically meaningless, because it makes no substantive sense to specify these two parameters (ITEM6 ← ITEM16; ITEM16 ← ITEM6), I draw your attention to them only as they reflect on the problematic link between Items 6 and 16. More realistically, this issue is addressed through the specification of an error covariance.

Turning to AMOS Graphics, we modify the initially hypothesized model by adding a covariance between these Item 16 and Item 6 error terms by first clicking on the *Covariance* icon ↔, then on err16, and, finally, on err6 as shown in Figure 4.8. The modified model structure for Model 2 is presented in Figure 4.9.

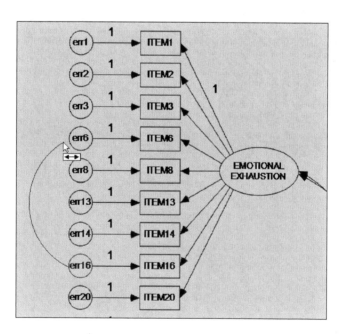

Figure 4.8 AMOS Graphics: Illustrated specification of covariance between error terms associated with items 16 and 6.

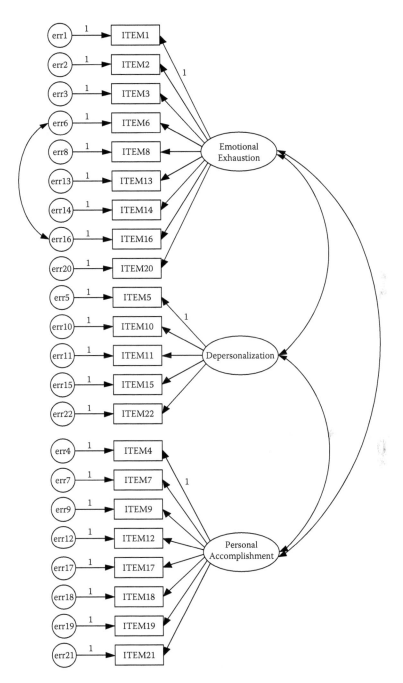

Figure 4.9 Respecified model of factorial structure for the Maslach Burnout Inventory (Model 2).

Selected AMOS output: Model 2

Goodness-of-fit statistics related to Model 2 revealed that incorporation of the error covariance between Items 6 and 16 made a substantially large improvement to model fit. In particular, the overall chi square value decreased from 693.849 to 596.124 and the RMSEA from .080 to .072, while the CFI value increased from .848 to .878. In assessing the extent to which a respecified model exhibits improvement in fit, it has become customary when using a univariate approach to determine if the difference in fit between the two models is statistically significant. As such, the researcher examines the difference in χ^2 ($\Delta\chi^2$) values between the two models. Doing so, however, presumes that the two models are nested.[7] The differential between the models represents a measurement of the overidentifying constraints and is itself χ^2 distributed, with degrees of freedom equal to the difference in degrees of freedom (Δdf); it can thus be tested statistically, with a significant $\Delta\chi^2$ indicating substantial improvement in model fit. Comparison of Model 2 ($\chi^2_{(205)} = 596.124$) with Model 1 ($\chi^2_{(205)} = 693.849$), for example, yields a difference in χ^2 value ($\Delta\chi^2_{(1)}$) of 97.725.[8]

The unstandardized estimate for this error covariance parameter is .733, which is highly significant (C.R. = 8.046) and even larger than the predicted value suggested by the *Parameter Change* statistic noted earlier; the standardized parameter estimate is .497, thereby reflecting a very strong error correlation!

Turning to the resulting MIs for Model 2 (see Table 4.3), we observe that the error covariance related to Items 1 and 2 remains a strongly misspecified parameter in the model, with the estimated parameter change statistic suggesting that if this parameter were incorporated into the model, it would result in an estimated value of approximately .527. As with the error covariance between Items 6 and 16, the one between Items 1 and 2 suggests redundancy due to content overlap. Item 1 asks if the respondent feels emotionally drained from his or her work, whereas Item 2 asks if the respondent feels used up at the end of the workday. Clearly, there appears to be an overlap of content between these two items.

Given the strength of this MI and, again, the obvious overlap of item content, I recommend that this error covariance parameter also be included in the model. This modified model (Model 3) is shown in Figure 4.10.

Model 3

Selected AMOS output: Model 3

Goodness-of-fit statistics related to Model 3 again revealed a statistically significant improvement in model fit between this model and Model 2

Table 4.3 Selected AMOS Output for Model 2: Modification Indices

		M.I.	Par change
Covariances			
err7	<--> err4	31.820	.200
err12	<--> *EMOTIONAL_EXHAUSTION*	*34.617*	*−.357*
err18	<--> err7	10.438	−.128
err19	<--> err18	14.832	.200
err21	<--> err4	12.536	.193
err21	<--> err7	31.737	.250
err11	<--> err10	20.105	.312
err15	<--> err5	13.899	.276
err1	<--> PERSONAL_ACCOMPLISHMENT	23.297	.127
err2	**<--> err1**	**69.604**	**.527**
err3	<--> err12	15.245	−.253
err6	<--> err5	10.677	.246
err13	<--> PERSONAL_ACCOMPLISHMENT	12.538	−.095
err13	<--> err1	10.786	−.217
err13	<--> err2	10.831	−.213
err20	<--> err2	11.083	−.203
err20	<--> err8	11.789	.196
err20	<--> err13	12.356	.224
Regression weights			
ITEM4	<--- ITEM7	22.192	.267
ITEM7	<--- ITEM4	24.589	.193
ITEM7	<--- ITEM21	23.495	.149
ITEM12	**<--- EMOTIONAL_EXHAUSTION**	**34.587**	**−.257**
ITEM12	<--- ITEM1	23.888	−.158
ITEM12	<--- ITEM2	22.092	−.164
ITEM12	<--- iTEM3	44.361	−.207
ITEM12	<--- ITEM8	35.809	−.187
ITEM12	<--- ITEM14	11.675	−.107
ITEM12	<--- ITEM16	21.653	−.174
ITEM12	<--- ITEM20	13.933	−.142
ITEM21	<--- ITEM7	22.148	.334
ITEM5	<--- ITEM6	12.189	.148
ITEM11	<--- ITEM10	10.025	.134
ITEM1	<--- PERSONAL_ACCOMPLISHMENT	23.397	.708
ITEM1	<--- ITEM9	19.875	.197
ITEM1	<--- ITEM17	10.128	.217

(continued)

Table 4.3 Selected AMOS Output for Model 2: Modification Indices (*Continued*)

			M.I.	Par change
	Regression weights			
ITEM1	<---	ITEM18	15.932	.182
ITEM1	<---	ITEM19	14.134	.184
ITEM1	<---	ITEM2	28.676	.202
ITEM2	<---	PERSONAL_ACCOMPLISHMENT	10.090	.455
ITEM2	<---	ITEM9	13.750	.160
ITEM2	<---	ITEM1	24.438	.169
ITEM13	<---	PERSONAL_ACCOMPLISHMENT	12.165	−.523
ITEM13	<---	ITEM9	16.039	−.182
ITEM13	<---	ITEM18	10.917	−.155
ITEM13	<---	ITEM19	12.992	−.181

($\chi^2_{(204)} = 519.082$; $\Delta\chi^2_{(1)} = 77.04$), and substantial differences in the CFI (.902 versus .878) and RMSEA (.065 versus .072) values.

Turning to the MIs, which are presented in Table 4.4, we see that there are still at least two error covariances with fairly large MIs (err7 ↔ err4 and err 21 ↔ err7). However, in reviewing the items associated with these two error parameters, I believe that the substantive rationale for their inclusion is very weak and therefore they should not be considered for addition to the model. On the other hand, I do see reason for considering the specification of a cross-loading with respect to Item 12 on Factor 1. In the initially hypothesized model, Item 12 was specified as loading on Factor 3 (Reduced Personal Accomplishment), yet the MI is telling us that this item should additionally load on Factor 1 (Emotional Exhaustion). In trying to understand why this cross-loading might be occurring, let's take a look at the essence of the item content, which asks for a level of agreement or disagreement with the statement that the respondent feels very energetic.

Although this item was deemed by Maslach and Jackson (1981, 1986) to measure a sense of personal accomplishment, it seems both evident and logical that it also taps into one's feelings of emotional exhaustion. Ideally, items on a measuring instrument should clearly target only one of its underlying constructs (or factors). The question related to our analysis of the MBI, however, is whether or not to include this parameter in a third respecified model. Provided with some justification for the double-loading effect, together with evidence from the literature that this same cross-loading has been noted in other research, I consider it appropriate to respecify the model (Model 4) with this parameter freely estimated.

In modifying Model 3 to include the cross-loading of Item 12 on Factor 1 (Emotional Exhaustion), we simply use the *Path* icon ⬅ to link the two. The resulting Model 4 is presented in Figure 4.11.

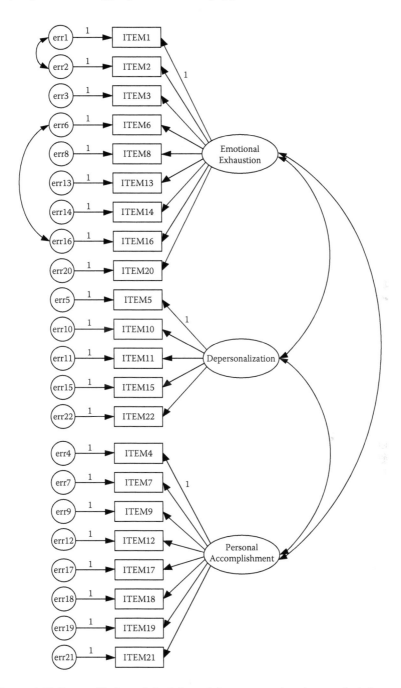

Figure 4.10 Respecified model of factorial structure for the maslach burnout inventory (Model 3).

Table 4.4 Selected AMOS Output for Model 3: Modification Indices

		M.I.	Par change
Covariances			
err7 <--> err4		31.968	.201
err12 <--> EMOTIONAL_EXHAUSTION		33.722	−.330
err18 <--> err7		10.252	−.127
err19 <--> err18		14.833	.200
err21 <--> err4		12.625	.193
err21 <--> err7		31.888	.251
err11 <--> err10		20.155	.312
err15 <--> err5		13.792	.275
err1 <--> PERSONAL_ACCOMPLISHMENT		14.382	.090
err3 <--> err12		16.376	−.265
err3 <--> err1		12.942	.231
err6 <--> err5		10.753	.247
Regression weights			
ITEM4 <--- ITEM7		22.336	.268
ITEM7 <--- ITEM4		24.730	.193
ITEM7 <--- ITEM21		23.633	.149
ITEM12 <--- EMOTIONAL_EXHAUSTION		**32.656**	**−.265**
ITEM12 <--- ITEM1		23.462	−.157
ITEM12 <--- ITEM2		21.722	−.162
ITEM12 <--- iTEM3		43.563	−.205
ITEM12 <--- ITEM8		34.864	−.184
ITEM12 <--- ITEM14		11.331	−.105
ITEM12 <--- ITEM16		21.145	−.172
ITEM12 <--- ITEM20		13.396	−.139
ITEM21 <--- ITEM7		22.294	.335
ITEM5 <--- ITEM6		11.953	.146
ITEM11 <--- ITEM10		10.063	.134
ITEM1 <--- PERSONAL_ACCOMPLISHMENT		11.766	.458
ITEM13 <--- ITEM9		11.958	−.154

Model 4

Selected AMOS output: Model 4

Not unexpectedly, goodness-of-fit indices related to Model 4 show a further statistically significant drop in the chi-square value from that of Model 3 ($\chi^2_{(203)} = 477.298$; $\Delta\chi^2_{(1)} = 41.784$). Likewise, there is evident improvement from Model 3 with respect to both the RMSEA (.060 versus .065) and the CFI (.915 versus .902).

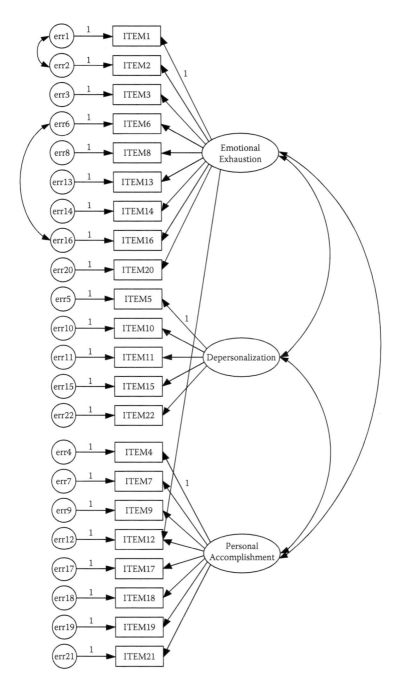

Figure 4.11 Final model of factorial structure for the Maslach Burnout Inventory (Model 4).

With respect to the MIs, which are shown in Table 4.5, I see no evidence of substantively reasonable misspecification in Model 4. Although, admittedly, the fit of .92 is not as high as I would like it to be, I am cognizant of the importance of modifying the model to include only those parameters that are substantively meaningful and relevant. Thus, on the basis of findings related to the test of validity for the MBI, I consider Model 4 to represent the final best-fitting and most parsimonious model to represent the data.

Finally, let's examine both the unstandardized and standardized factor loadings, factor covariances, and error covariances, which are presented in Tables 4.6 and 4.7, respectively. We note first that in reviewing the unstandardized estimates, all are statistically significant given C.R. values > 1.96.

Turning first to the unstandardized factor loadings, it is of particular interest to examine results for Item 12 for which its targeted loading was

Table 4.5 Selected AMOS Output for Model 4: Modification Indices

			M.I.	Par change
		Covariances		
err7	<-->	err4	30.516	.195
err18	<-->	err7	12.126	−.138
err19	<-->	err4	10.292	−.149
err19	<-->	err18	14.385	.197
err21	<-->	err4	11.866	.187
err21	<-->	err7	30.835	.245
err11	<-->	err10	19.730	.308
err15	<-->	err5	13.986	.277
err1	<-->	PERSONAL_ACCOMPLISHMENT	14.570	.094
err3	<-->	err12	10.790	−.202
err3	<-->	err1	12.005	.220
err6	<-->	err5	10.989	.250
err13	<-->	err12	13.020	.208
		Regression weights		
ITEM4	<---	ITEM7	20.986	.259
ITEM7	<---	ITEM4	23.327	.187
ITEM7	<---	ITEM21	22.702	.146
ITEM21	<---	ITEM7	21.218	.326
ITEM5	<---	ITEM6	12.141	.148
ITEM1	<---	PERSONAL_ACCOMPLISHMENT	12.559	.465
ITEM13	<---	ITEM9	12.332	−.158
ITEM13	<---	ITEM19	10.882	−.164

Table 4.6 Selected AMOS Output for Model 4: Unstandardized Parameter Estimates

			Estimate	S.E.	C.R.	P
Regression weights						
ITEM20	<---	EMOTIONAL_EXHAUSTION	.806	.062	13.092	***
ITEM16	<---	EMOTIONAL_EXHAUSTION	.726	.063	11.527	***
ITEM14	<---	EMOTIONAL_EXHAUSTION	.879	.075	11.644	***
ITEM13	<---	EMOTIONAL_EXHAUSTION	1.072	.073	14.714	***
ITEM8	<---	EMOTIONAL_EXHAUSTION	1.217	.075	16.300	***
ITEM6	<---	EMOTIONAL_EXHAUSTION	.761	.069	10.954	***
ITEM3	<---	EMOTIONAL_EXHAUSTION	1.074	.075	14.286	***
ITEM2	<---	EMOTIONAL_EXHAUSTION	.877	.049	17.942	***
ITEM1	<---	EMOTIONAL_EXHAUSTION	1.000			
ITEM22	<---	DEPERSONAL_IZATION	.769	.122	6.302	***
ITEM15	<---	DEPERSONAL_IZATION	.912	.110	8.258	***
ITEM11	<---	DEPERSONAL_IZATION	1.368	.145	9.446	***
ITEM10	<---	DEPERSONAL_IZATION	1.155	.129	8.936	***
ITEM5	<---	DEPERSONAL_IZATION	1.000			
ITEM21	<---	PERSONAL_ACCOMPLISHMENT	1.342	.213	6.288	***
ITEM19	<---	PERSONAL_ACCOMPLISHMENT	1.689	.232	7.285	***

(continued)

Table 4.6 Selected AMOS Output for Model 4: Unstandardized Parameter Estimates

			Estimate	S.E.	C.R.	P
Regression weights						
ITEM18	<---	PERSONAL_ACCOMPLISHMENT	1.892	.255	7.421	***
ITEM17	<---	PERSONAL_ACCOMPLISHMENT	1.328	.176	7.554	***
ITEM12	**<---**	**PERSONAL_ACCOMPLISHMENT**	**1.135**	**.188**	**6.035**	***
ITEM9	<---	PERSONAL_ACCOMPLISHMENT	1.762	.248	7.100	***
ITEM7	<---	PERSONAL_ACCOMPLISHMENT	.967	.147	6.585	***
ITEM4	<---	PERSONAL_ACCOMPLISHMENT	1.000			
ITEM12	<---	EMOTIONAL_EXHAUSTION	-.317	.050	-6.389	***
Covariances						
EMOTIONAL_EXHAUSTION	<-->	PERSONAL_ACCOMPLISHMENT	-.167	.040	-4.161	***
EMOTIONAL_EXHAUSTION	<-->	DEPERSONAL_IZATION	.669	.096	6.947	***
DEPERSONAL_IZATION	<-->	PERSONAL_ACCOMPLISHMENT	-.162	.034	-4.690	***
err16	**<-->**	**err6**	**.710**	**.090**	**7.884**	***
err2	**<-->**	**err1**	**.589**	**.083**	**7.129**	***

*** probability < .000

Table 4.7 Selected AMOS Output for Model 4: Standardized Parameter Estimates

			Estimate
Standardized regression weights			
ITEM20	<---	EMOTIONAL_EXHAUSTION	.695
ITEM16	<---	EMOTIONAL_EXHAUSTION	.616
ITEM14	<---	EMOTIONAL_EXHAUSTION	.621
ITEM13	<---	EMOTIONAL_EXHAUSTION	.778
ITEM8	<---	EMOTIONAL_EXHAUSTION	.860
ITEM6	<---	EMOTIONAL_EXHAUSTION	.586
iTEM3	<---	EMOTIONAL_EXHAUSTION	.756
ITEM2	<---	EMOTIONAL_EXHAUSTION	.693
ITEM1	<---	EMOTIONAL_EXHAUSTION	.735
ITEM22	<---	DEPERSONAL-_IZATION	.406
ITEM15	<---	DEPERSONAL-_IZATION	.585
ITEM11	<---	DEPERSONAL-_IZATION	.746
ITEM10	<---	DEPERSONAL-_IZATION	.666
ITEM5	<---	DEPERSONAL-_IZATION	.560
ITEM21	<---	PERSONAL_ACCOMPLISHMENT	.474

(continued)

Table 4.7 Selected AMOS Output for Model 4: Standardized Parameter Estimates (*Continued*)

			Estimate
Standardized regression weights			
ITEM19	<---	PERSONAL_ACCOMPLISHMENT	.635
ITEM18	<---	PERSONAL_ACCOMPLISHMENT	.665
ITEM17	<---	PERSONAL_ACCOMPLISHMENT	.697
ITEM12	**<---**	**PERSONAL_ACCOMPLISHMENT**	**.425**
ITEM9	<---	PERSONAL_ACCOMPLISHMENT	.599
ITEM7	<---	PERSONAL_ACCOMPLISHMENT	.515
ITEM4	<---	PERSONAL_ACCOMPLISHMENT	.448
ITEM12	**<---**	**EMOTIONAL_EXHAUSTION**	**-.324**
Correlations			
EMOTIONAL_EXHAUSTION	<-->	PERSONAL_ACCOMPLISHMENT	-.306
EMOTIONAL_EXHAUSTION	<-->	DEPERSONAL_IZATION	.660
DEPERSONAL_IZATION	<-->	PERSONAL_ACCOMPLISHMENT	-.435
err16	<-->	err6	**.489**
err2	<-->	err1	**.470**

on Personal Accomplishment (Factor 3) and its cross-loading on Emotional Exhaustion (Factor 1). As you will readily observe, the loading of this item on both factors not only is statistically significant but in addition is basically of the same degree of intensity. In checking its unstandardized estimate in Table 4.6, we see that the critical ratio for both parameters is almost identical (6.035 versus –6.389), although one has a positive sign and one a negative sign. Given that the item content states that the respondent feels very energetic, the negative path associated with the Emotional Exhaustion factor is perfectly reasonable. Turning to the related standardized estimates in Table 4.7, it is interesting to note that the estimated value for the targeted loading (.425) is only slightly higher than it is for the cross-loading (–.324), both being of moderate strength.

Presented with these findings and maintaining a watchful eye on parsimony, it behooves us at this point to test a model in which Item 12 is specified as loading onto the alternate factor (Emotional Exhaustion), rather than the one on which it was originally designed to load (Personal Accomplishment); as such, there is now no specified cross-loading. In the interest of space, however, I simply report the most important criteria determined from this alternate model (Model 3a) compared with Model 3 (see Figure 4.10) in which Item 12 was specified as loading on Factor 3, its original targeted factor. Accordingly, findings from the estimation of this alternative model (Model 3a) revealed (a) the model to be slightly less well fitting (CFI = .895) than for Model 3 (CFI = .902), and (b) the standardized estimate to be weaker (–.468) than for Model 3 (.554). As might be expected, a review of the MIs identified the loading of Item 12 on Factor 3 (MI = 49.661) to be the top candidate for considered respecification in a subsequent model; by comparison, the related MI in Model 3 was 32.656 and identified the loading of Item 12 on Factor 1 as the top candidate for respecification (see Table 4.4).

From these comparative results between Model 3 and Model 3a (the alternative model), it seems evident that Item 12 is problematic and definitely in need of content revision, a task that is definitely out of my hands. Thus, provided with evidence of no clear loading of this item, it seems most appropriate to leave the cross-loading in place, as in Model 4 (Figure 4.11).

Comparison with robust analyses based on the Satorra-Bentler scaled statistic

Given that the analyses in this chapter were based on the default ML method with no consideration of the multivariate nonnormality of the data noted earlier, I consider it both interesting and instructive to compare the overall goodness-of-fit pertinent to Model 4 as well as key statistics for a selected few of its estimated parameters. The major thrust of the S-B Robust ML approach in addressing nonnormality is that it provides

Table 4.8 Comparison of Model Fit and Parameter Statistics
Based on ML and Robust ML Estimation: Model 4

	ML estimation	DF	Robust ML estimation
Model fit statistics			
Chi-square	477.298	203	399.156
CFI	.915		.927
RMSEA	.060		.051
RMSEA 90% C.I.	.053, .067		.044, .058
Parameter statistics			
Err16 ↔ Err6			
Estimate	.710		.710
Standard error	.090		.122
Critical ratio	7.884		5.815
Err2 ↔ Err1			
Estimate	.589		.589
Standard error	.083		.086
Critical ratio	7.129		6.869
Item12 ← PA (Factor 3)			
Estimate	1.135		1.135
Standard error	.188		.202
Critical ratio	6.035		5.618
Item12 ← EE (Factor 1)			
Estimate	−.317		−.317
Standard error	.050		.054
Critical ratio	−6.389		−5.911

Note: DF = Degrees of freedom.

a scaled statistic (S-Bχ^2) which corrects the usual ML χ^2 value, as well as the standard errors (Bentler & Dijkstra, 1985; Satorra & Bentler, 1988, 1994). Although the ML estimates will remain the same for both programs, the standard errors of these estimates will differ in accordance with the extent to which the data are multivariate nonnormal. Because the critical ratio represents the estimate divided by its standard error, the corrected critical ratio for each parameter may ultimately lead to different conclusions regarding its statistical significance. This comparison of model fit as well as parameter statistics are presented in Table 4.8.

Turning first to the goodness-of-fit statistics, it is evident that the S-B corrected chi-square value is substantially lower than that of the uncorrected ML value (399.156 versus 477.298). Such a large difference between the two chi-square values provides evidence of substantial nonnormality of the data. Because calculation of the CFI necessarily involves the χ^2 value, you will note also a substantial increase in the robust CFI value (.927 versus .915). Finally, we note that the corrected RMSEA value is also lower (.044) than its related uncorrected value (.060).

In reviewing the parameter statistics, it is interesting to note that although the standard errors underwent correction to take nonnormality into account, thereby yielding critical ratios that differed across the AMOS and EQS programs, the final conclusion regarding the statistical significance of the estimated parameters remains the same. Importantly, however, it should be noted that the uncorrected ML approach tended to overestimate the degree to which the estimates were statistically significant. Based on this information, we can feel confident that, although we were unable to directly address the issue of nonnormality in the data for technical reasons, and despite the tendency of the uncorrected ML estimator to overestimate the statistical significance of these estimates, overall conclusions were consistent across CFA estimation approaches in suggesting Model 4 to most appropriately represent MBI factorial structure.

Endnotes

1. As was the case in Chapter 3, the first of each congeneric set of items was constrained to 1.00.
2. For example, Sugawara and MacCallum (1993) have recommended that the RMSEA always be reported when maximum likelihood estimation is the only method used because it has been found to yield consistent results across estimation procedures when the model is well specified; MacCallum, Browne, & Sugawara (1996) extended this caveat to include confidence intervals.
3. Although included here, due to the formatting of the output file, several fit indices provide basically the same information. For example, the AIC, CAIC, and ECVI each serve the same function in addressing parsimony. With respect to the NFI, Bentler (1990) has recommended that the CFI be the index of choice.
4. Although these misspecified parameters correctly represent error covariances, they are commonly termed *correlated errors*.
5. Unfortunately, refusal of copyright permission by the MBI test publisher prevents me from presenting the actual item statements for your perusal.
6. Although you will note larger MIs associated with the regression weights (e.g., 52.454; ITEM16 ← ITEM6), these values, as noted earlier, do not represent cross-loadings and are in essence meaningless.

7. Nested models are hierarchically related to one another in the sense that their parameter sets are subsets of one another (i.e., particular parameters are freely estimated in one model, but fixed to zero in a second model) (Bentler & Chou, 1987; Bollen, 1989a).

8. One parameter, previously specified as fixed in the initially hypothesized model (Model 1), was specified as free in Model 2, thereby using up one degree of freedom (i.e., one less degree of freedom).

chapter five

Testing for the factorial validity of scores from a measuring instrument
(Second-order CFA model)

In contrast to the two previous applications that focused on CFA first-order models, the present application examines a CFA model that comprises a second-order factor. As such, we test hypotheses related to the Chinese version (Chinese Behavioral Sciences Society, 2000) of the Beck Depression Inventory—II (BDI-II; Beck, Steer, & Brown, 1996) as it bears on a community sample of Hong Kong adolescents. The example is taken from a study by Byrne, Stewart, and Lee (2004). Although this particular study was based on an updated version of the original BDI (Beck, Ward, Mendelson, Mock, & Erbaugh, 1961), it nonetheless follows from a series of studies that have tested for the validity of second-order BDI factorial structure for high school adolescents in Canada (Byrne & Baron, 1993, 1994; Byrne, Baron, & Campbell, 1993, 1994), Sweden (Byrne, Baron, Larsson, & Melin, 1995, 1996), and Bulgaria (Byrne, Baron, & Balev, 1996, 1998). The purposes of the original Byrne et al. (2004) study were to test for the construct validity of the Chinese version of the BDI-II (C-BDI-II) structure based on three independent groups of students drawn from 11 Hong Kong high schools. In this example, we focus only on the Group 2 data ($N = 486$), which served as the calibration sample in testing for the factorial validity of the C-BDI-II. (For further details regarding the sample, analyses, and results, readers are referred to the original article, Byrne et al., 2004.)

The C-BDI-II is a 21-item scale that measures symptoms related to cognitive, behavioral, affective, and somatic components of depression. Specific to the Byrne et al. (2004) study, only 20 of the 21 C-BDI-II items were used in tapping depressive symptoms for Hong Kong high school adolescents. Item 21, designed to assess changes in sexual interest, was considered to be objectionable by several school principals, and the item was subsequently deleted from the inventory. For each item, respondents are presented with four statements rated from 0 to 3 in terms of intensity, and asked to select the one which most accurately describes their own feelings; higher scores represent a more severe level of reported depression. As noted in Chapter 4, the CFA of a measuring instrument is most appropriately conducted with fully developed assessment measures that have demonstrated satisfactory factorial validity. Justification for CFA procedures in the present instance is based on evidence provided by Tanaka and Huba (1984), and replicated studies by Byrne and associates (Byrne & Baron, 1993, 1994; Byrne et al., 1993, 1994, 1995, 1996; Byrne, Baron & Balev, 1996, 1998), that BDI score data are most adequately represented by a hierarchical factorial structure. That is to say, the first-order factors are explained by some higher order structure which, in the case of the C-BDI-II and its derivatives, is a single second-order factor of general depression.

Let's turn now, then, to a description of the C-BDI-II, and its postulated structure.

The hypothesized model

The CFA model to be tested in the present application hypothesizes a priori that (a) responses to the C-BDI-II can be explained by three first-order factors (Negative Attitude, Performance Difficulty, and Somatic Elements) and one second-order factor (General Depression); (b) each item has a nonzero loading on the first-order factor it was designed to measure, and zero loadings on the other two first-order factors; (c) error terms associated with each item are uncorrelated; and (d) covariation among the three first-order factors is explained fully by their regression on the second-order factor. A diagrammatic representation of this model is presented in Figure 5.1.

One additional point I need to make concerning this model is that, in contrast to the CFA models examined in Chapters 3 and 4, the factor-loading parameter fixed to a value of 1.00 for purposes of model identification here is not the first one of each congeneric group. Rather, these fixed values are specified for the factor loadings associated with BDI2_3 for Factor 1, BDI2_12 for Factor 2, and BDI2_16 for Factor 3. These assignments can be verified in a quick perusal of Table 5.6 in which the unstandardized estimates are presented.

Modeling with AMOS Graphics

As suggested in previous chapters, in an initial check of the hypothesized model, it is always wise to determine a priori the number of degrees of freedom associated with the model under test in order to ascertain its model identification status. Pertinent to the model shown in Figure 5.1,

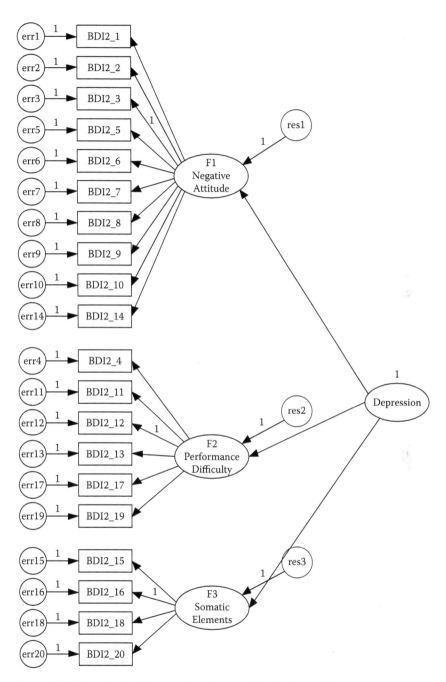

Figure 5.1 Hypothesized second-order model of factorial structure for the Chinese version of the Beck Depression Inventory—II.

there are 210 pieces of information contained in the covariance matrix (20 [items] × 21/2) and 43 parameters to be estimated, thereby leaving 167 degrees of freedom. As noted earlier, AMOS provides this information for each model tested (see Table 5.1). Included in the table also is a summary of the number of variables and parameters in the model.

To make sure that you fully comprehend the basis of the related numbers, I consider it important to detail this information as follows:

Variables (47): 20 observed and 27 unobserved
- **Observed variables** (20): 20 C-BDI-II items
- **Unobserved variables** (27): 20 error terms, 3 first-order factors, 1 second-order factor, and 3 residual terms
- **Exogenous variables** (24): 20 error terms, 1 second-order factor, and 3 residual terms
- **Endogenous variables** (23): 20 observed variables and 3 first-order factors

Parameters
- **Fixed**
  - **Weights** (26): 20 error term regression paths (fixed to 1.0), 3 factor loadings (fixed to 1.0), and 3 residual regression paths (fixed to 1.0)
  - **Variances**: Second-order factor
- **Unlabeled**
  - **Weights** (20): 20 factor loadings
  - **Variances** (23): 20 error variances and three residual variances

At first blush, one might feel confident that the specified model was overidentified and, thus, all should go well. However, as noted in Chapter 2, with hierarchical models, it is critical that one also check the identification status of the higher order portion of the model. In the present case, given the specification of only three first-order factors, the higher order structure will be just-identified unless a constraint is placed on at least one parameter in this upper level of the model (see, e.g., Bentler, 2005; Rindskopf & Rose, 1988). More specifically, with three first-order factors, we have six ([3 × 4] / 2) pieces of information; the number of estimable parameters is also six (three factor loadings; three residuals), thereby resulting in a just-identified model. Thus, prior to testing for the validity of the hypothesized structure shown in Figure 5.1, we need first to address this identification issue at the upper level of the model.

One approach to resolving the issue of just-identification in the present second-order model is to place equality constraints on particular

Table 5.1 Selected AMOS Output for Preliminary Model:
Summary Statistics, Variables, and Parameters

Computation of degrees of freedom

Number of distinct sample moments	210
Number of distinct parameters to be estimated	43
Degrees of freedom (210 – 43)	167

Results

Minimum was achieved.
Chi-square   = 385.358
Degrees of freedom = 167
Probability level   =   .000

Variables

Number of variables in your model: 47
Number of observed variables: 20
Number of unobserved variables: 27
Number of exogenous variables: 24
Number of endogenous variables: 23

Parameter summary

	Weights	Covariances	Variances	Means	Intercepts	Total
Fixed	26	0	1	0	0	27
Labeled	0	0	0	0	0	0
Unlabeled	20	0	23	0	0	43
Total	46	0	24	0	0	70

parameters at the upper level known to yield estimates that are approximately equal. Based on past work with the BDI and BDI-II, this constraint is typically placed on appropriate residual terms. The AMOS program provides a powerful and quite unique exploratory mechanism for separating promising from unlikely parameter candidates for the imposition of equality constraints. This strategy, termed the critical ratio difference (CRDIFF) method, produces a listing of critical ratios for the pairwise differences among all parameter estimates; in our case here, we would seek out these values as they relate to the residuals. A formal explanation of the CRDIFF as presented in the *AMOS Reference Guide* is shown in Figure 5.2. This information is readily accessed by first clicking on the *Help* menu and following these five steps: Click on *Contents*, which will then produce the *Search* dialog box; in the blank space, type in *critical ratio differences*; click on *List Topics*; select *Critical*

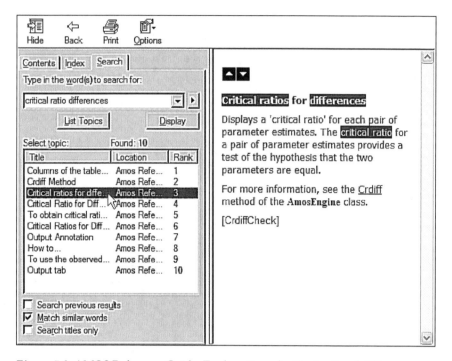

Figure 5.2 AMOS Reference Guide: Explanation of critical ratio of differences.

Ratios for Diffs (as shown highlighted in Figure 5.2); and click on *Display*. These actions will then yield the explanation presented on the right side of the dialog box.

Now that you know how to locate which residual parameters have values that are approximately of the same magnitude, the next step is to know how to obtain these CRDIFF values in the first place. This process, however, is easily accomplished by requesting that critical ratios for differences among parameters be included in the AMOS output which is specified on the *Analysis Properties* dialog box, as shown in Figure 5.3. All that is needed now is to calculate the estimates for this initial model (Figure 5.1). However, at this point, given that we have yet to finalize the identification issue at the upper level of the hypothesized structure, we'll refer to the model as the *preliminary model*.

Selected AMOS output: Preliminary model

In this initial output file, only labels assigned to the residual parameters and the CRDIFF values are of interest. This labeling action occurs as a consequence of having requested the CRDIFF values and, thus, has not

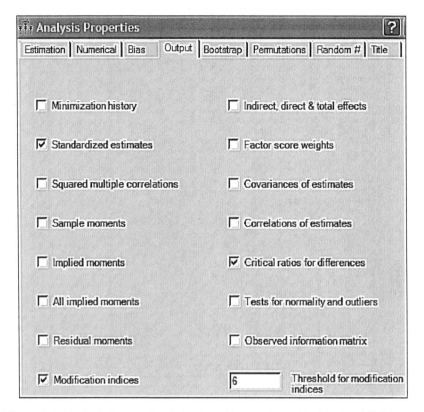

Figure 5.3 Analysis Properties dialog box: Requesting critical ratio of differences in the AMOS output.

been evident on the AMOS output related to the models in Chapters 3 and 4. Turning first to the content of Table 5.2, we note that the labels assigned to residuals 1, 2, and 3 are par_21, par_22, and par_23, respectively.

Let's turn now to the critical ratio differences among parameters, which are shown circled in Figure 5.4. The explanatory box to the right of the circle was triggered by clicking the cursor on the value of –2.797, the CRDIFF value between resid1 and resid2 (i.e., par_21 and par_22). The boxed area on the left of the matrix, as usual, represents labels for the various components of the output file; our focus has been on the "Pairwise Parameter Comparisons" section, which is shown highlighted. Turning again to the residual CRDIFF values, we can see that the two prime candidates for the imposition of equality constraints are the higher order residuals related to the Performance Difficulty and Somatic Elements factors, as their estimated values are very similar in magnitude (albeit their signs

Table 5.2 Selected AMOS Output for Preliminary Model:
Error Residual Variance Parameter Labels

	Estimate	S.E.	C.R.	P	Label
DEPRESSION	1.000				
res1	.055	.012	4.689	***	**par_21**
res2	.006	.010	.620	.535	**par_22**
res3	.030	.008	3.555	***	**par_23**
err14	.274	.020	13.399	***	par_24
err10	.647	.043	15.198	***	par_25
err9	.213	.014	14.873	***	par_26
err8	.373	.026	14.491	***	par_27
err7	.313	.023	13.540	***	par_28
err6	.698	.047	15.001	***	par_29
err5	.401	.027	14.772	***	par_30
err3	.510	.035	14.655	***	par_31
err2	.255	.018	13.848	***	par_32
err1	.406	.029	13.947	***	par_33
err19	.446	.031	14.467	***	par_34
err17	.310	.022	13.923	***	par_35
err13	.277	.020	13.825	***	par_36
err12	.258	.019	13.547	***	par_37
err11	.358	.026	13.795	***	par_38
err4	.311	.022	14.442	***	par_39
err16	.440	.030	14.534	***	par_40
err15	.260	.024	10.761	***	par_41
err18	.566	.038	15.012	***	par_42
err20	.248	.020	12.274	***	par_43

*** probability < .000

are different) and both are nonsignificant (<1.96). Given these findings, it seems reasonable to constrain variances of the residuals associated with Factors 2 (Performance Difficulty) and 3 (Somatic Elements) to be equal. As such, the higher order level of the model will be overidentified with one degree of freedom. That is to say, the variance will be estimated for resid2, and then the same value held constant for resid3. The degrees of freedom for the model as a whole should now increase from 167 to 168.

Now that we know which residual terms in the upper level of the model to constrain, we now need to include this information in the model to be tested. Such specification of equality constraints in AMOS is accomplished by assigning the same label to all parameters to be constrained equal. As per all processes conducted in AMOS, an elaboration of the

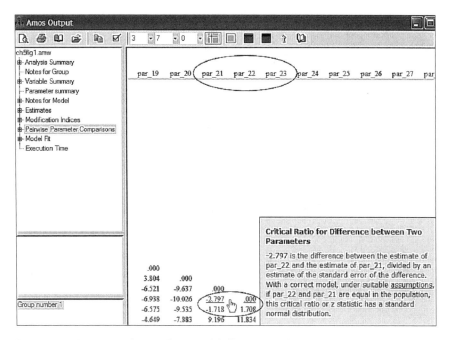

Figure 5.4 Location of critical ratio of differences values and parameter labels.

specification of equality constraints can be retrieved from the *AMOS Reference Guide* by clicking on the *Help* tab. The resulting information is shown in Figure 5.5.

Let's return, then, to our hypothesized model and assign these equality constraints to the two factor residuals associated with the first-order factors. Turning to the first residual (res2), a right-click on the outside perimeter of the circle will open the *Tools* menu, after which we click on the *Object Properties* tab and, once in that dialog box, click on the *Text* tab, where you should see the variable name *res2* already entered. In the empty space below marked *Variable Label*, we insert *var_a*. A representation of this completed box is illustrated in Figure 5.6. This process is then repeated for the residual term associated with Factor 3 (res3). The fully labeled hypothesized model showing the constraint between these two residual terms is schematically presented in Figure 5.7. Analyses are now based on this respecified model.

Selected AMOS output: The hypothesized model

Presented in Table 5.3 is a summary of both statistics and specified parameters related to the changes made to the original model of C-BDI-II

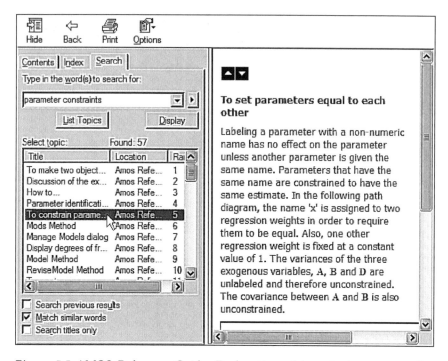

Figure 5.5 AMOS Reference Guide: Explanation of how to impose equality constraints.

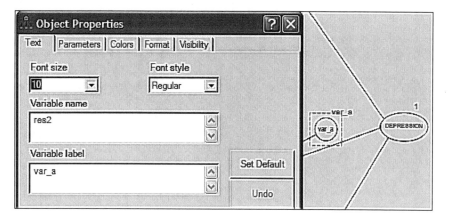

Figure 5.6 Object Properties dialog box: Creating a variable label.

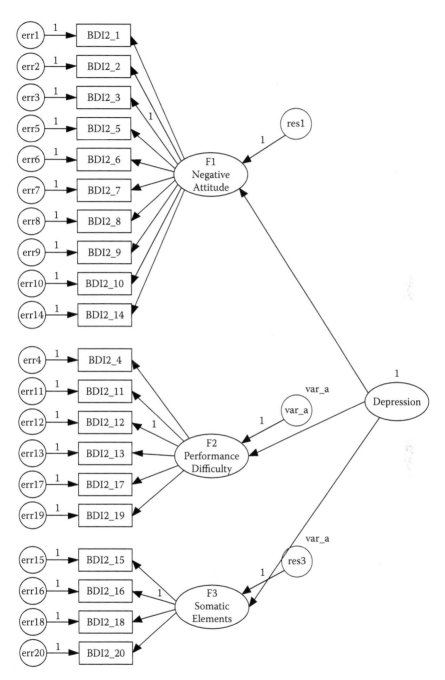

Figure 5.7 Hypothesized second-order model with residual variances for Factors 2 and 3 constrained equal.

Table 5.3 Selected AMOS Output for Hypothesized Model:
Summary Statistics and Parameters

Computation of degrees of freedom	
Number of distinct sample moments	210
Number of distinct parameters to be estimated	42
Degrees of freedom (210 – 42)	168

Results

Minimum was achieved.
Chi-square   = 388.427
Degrees of freedom = 168
Probability level   =   .000

Parameter summary

	Weights	Covariances	Variances	Means	Intercepts	Total
Fixed	26	0	1	0	0	27
Labeled	0	0	2	0	0	2
Unlabeled	20	0	21	0	0	41
Total	46	0	24	0	0	70

structure. As a consequence of the equality constraint imposed on the model, there are now two important differences from the preliminary model specification. First, as noted earlier, there are now 168, rather than 167, degrees of freedom. Second, there are now two labeled parameters (the var_a assigned to res2 and res3).

Model evaluation

Goodness-of-fit summary

In reviewing the goodness-of-fit statistics in Table 5.4, we can see that the hypothesized model fits the data very well as evidenced by the CFI of .936 and RMSEA of .052. As a consequence, we examine the modification indices purely in the interest of completeness. These values are presented in Table 5.5.

In reviewing the MIs related to the covariances, you will note two values that are substantially larger than the rest of the estimates. These relate to covariation between the error terms associated with Items 17 and 11, and with Items 9 and 10. However, as indicated by the reported parameter change statistics, incorporation of these two parameters into the model would result in parameter values of .083 and .080, respectively—clearly trivial estimates. Turning to the MIs related to regression weights, we see

Table 5.4 Selected AMOS Output for Hypothesized Model:
Goodness-of-Fit Statistics

		CMIN			
Model	NPAR	CMIN	DF	P	CMIN/DF
Your model	42	388.427	168	.000	2.312
Saturated model	210	.000	0		
Independence model	20	3649.228	190	.000	19.206

		Baseline comparisons			
	NFI	RFI	IFI	TLI	
Model	Delta1	rho1	Delta2	rho2	CFI
Your model	.894	.880	.937	.928	.936
Saturated model	1.000		1.000		1.000
Independence model	.000	.000	.000	.000	.000

		RMSEA		
Model	RMSEA	LO 90	HI 90	PCLOSE
Your model	.052	.045	.059	.304
Independence model	.194	.188	.199	.000

that they make no sense at all as they suggest the impact of one item loading on another. In light of the very good fit of the model, together with the trivial nature of the MIs, we can conclude that the second-order model shown in Figure 5.7 is the most optimal representing C-BDI-II structure for Hong Kong adolescents.

Model maximum likelihood (ML) estimates

As can be seen in Table 5.6, all estimates were found to have critical ratio values >1.96, thereby indicating their statistical significance. For clarification regarding terminology associated with the AMOS output, recall that the factor loadings are listed as *Regression Weights*. Listed first are the second-order factor loadings, followed by the first-order loadings. Note also that all parameters in the model have been assigned a label, which of course is due to our request for the calculation and reporting of CRDIFF values. Turning to the variance estimates, note that all values related to res2 and res3 (encircled) carry exactly the same values, which of course they should. Finally, the related standardized estimates are presented in Table 5.7.

In concluding this section of the chapter, I wish to note that, given the same number of estimable parameters, fit statistics related to a model parameterized either as a first-order structure or as a second-order structure will basically be equivalent. The difference between the two specifications

Table 5.5 Selected AMOS Output for
Hypothesized Model: Modification Indices

		M.I.	Par change
Covariances			
err11	<--> err4	9.632	–.051
err12	<--> err4	12.933	.051
err13	<--> err20	6.001	–.033
err17	<--> err18	6.694	.052
err17	**<--> err11**	**24.812**	**.083**
err17	<--> err12	9.399	–.044
err19	<--> res3	7.664	.025
err1	<--> err11	9.185	.058
err1	<--> err12	10.690	.054
err2	<--> err18	7.611	–.051
err2	<--> err4	7.337	.038
err3	<--> err12	7.787	–.050
err5	<--> res2	8.629	.031
err6	<--> res3	8.652	–.033
err6	<--> err15	8.570	–.066
err6	<--> err13	12.165	.075
err7	<--> err15	12.816	–.056
err9	<--> res2	7.800	–.021
err9	<--> err18	9.981	.052
err9	<--> err13	8.432	–.034
err10	<--> err16	6.194	.063
err10	<--> err8	11.107	–.077
err10	**<--> err9**	**21.479**	**.080**
err14	<--> err6	8.124	–.061
err14	<--> err7	9.280	.046
Regression weights			
BDI2_18 <--- BDI2_9		6.845	.167
BDI2_15 <--- BDI2_6		7.984	–.078
BDI2_15 <--- BDI2_7		7.754	–.091
BDI2_11 <--- BDI2_17		12.315	.134
BDI2_12 <--- BDI2_4		6.885	.092
BDI2_12 <--- BDI2_1		7.287	.076
BDI2_13 <--- BDI2_6		9.257	.080
BDI2_17 <--- BDI2_11		11.843	.111
BDI2_1 <--- BDI2_11		7.196	.099

(Continued)

Table 5.5 Selected AMOS Output for
Hypothesized Model: Modification
Indices (*Continued*)

	M.I.	Par change
Regression weights		
BDI2_1 <--- BDI2_12	7.682	.117
BDI2_2 <--- BDI2_18	6.543	−.075
BDI2_6 <--- BDI2_13	6.349	.135
BDI2_7 <--- BDI2_15	6.309	−.085
BDI2_8 <--- BDI2_10	9.040	−.097
BDI2_9 <--- BDI2_18	7.198	.070
BDI2_9 <--- BDI2_13	6.935	−.078
BDI2_9 <--- BDI2_10	17.471	.101
BDI2_10 <--- BDI2_16	6.739	.126
BDI2_10 <--- BDI2_8	6.568	−.123
BDI2_10 <--- BDI2_9	14.907	.263
BDI2_14 <--- BDI2_6	6.043	−.065

is that the second-order model is a special case of the first-order model, with the added restriction that structure be imposed on the correlational pattern among the first-order factors (Rindskopf & Rose, 1988). However, judgment as to whether or not a measuring instrument should be modeled as a first-order or as a second-order structure ultimately rests on substantive meaningfulness as dictated by the underlying theory.

Estimation of continuous versus categorical variables

Thus far in this book, analyses have been based on ML estimation. An important assumption underlying this estimation procedure is that the scale of the observed variables is continuous. In Chapters 3 and 4, as well as the present chapter, however, the observed variables were Likert-scaled items that realistically represent categorical data of an ordinal scale, albeit they have been treated as if they were continuous. Indeed, such practice has been the norm for many years now and applies to traditional statistical techniques (e.g., ANOVA; MANOVA) as well as SEM analyses. Paralleling this widespread practice of treating ordinal data as if they are continuous, however, has been an ongoing debate in the literature concerning the pros and cons of this practice. Given (a) the prevalence of this practice in the SEM field, (b) the importance of acquiring an understanding of the issues involved, and (c) my intent in this chapter to illustrate analysis of data that can address categorically coded

Table 5.6 Selected AMOS Output for Hypothesized Model: Unstandardized ML Parameter Estimates

			Estimate	S.E.	C.R.	P	Label
Regression weights							
PERFORMANCE_DIFFICULTY	<---	DEPRESSION	.495	.030	16.315	***	par_17
NEGATIVE_ATTITUDE	<---	DEPRESSION	.451	.036	12.363	***	par_18
SOMATIC_ELEMENTS	<---	DEPRESSION	.342	.034	10.209	***	par_19
BDI2_14	<---	NEGATIVE_ATTITUDE	1.125	.092	12.209	***	par_2
BDI2_10	<---	NEGATIVE_ATTITUDE	.720	.091	7.896	***	par_3
BDI2_9	<---	NEGATIVE_ATTITUDE	.566	.059	9.645	***	par_4
BDI2_8	<---	NEGATIVE_ATTITUDE	.928	.086	10.743	***	par_5
BDI2_7	<---	NEGATIVE_ATTITUDE	1.161	.096	12.072	***	par_6
BDI2_6	<---	NEGATIVE_ATTITUDE	.919	.102	9.034	***	par_7
BDI2_5	<---	NEGATIVE_ATTITUDE	.825	.083	9.958	***	par_8
BDI2_3	<---	NEGATIVE_ATTITUDE	1.000				
BDI2_2	<---	NEGATIVE_ATTITUDE	.966	.082	11.762	***	par_9
BDI2_1	<---	NEGATIVE_ATTITUDE	1.183	.102	11.634	***	par_10
BDI2_19	<---	PERFORMANCE_DIFFICULTY	.969	.078	12.385	***	par_11
BDI2_17	<---	PERFORMANCE_DIFFICULTY	.984	.071	13.925	***	par_12
BDI2_13	<---	PERFORMANCE_DIFFICULTY	.955	.068	14.110	***	par_13
BDI2_12	<---	PERFORMANCE_DIFFICULTY	1.000				
BDI2_11	<---	PERFORMANCE_DIFFICULTY	1.096	.077	14.173	***	par_14
BDI2_4	<---	PERFORMANCE_DIFFICULTY	.819	.066	12.479	***	par_15
BDI2_16	<---	SOMATIC_ELEMENTS	1.000				

		Estimate	S.E.	C.R.	P	Label
BDI2_15	<--- SOMATIC_ELEMENTS	1.651	.160	10.290	***	par_16
BDI2_18	<--- SOMATIC_ELEMENTS	.876	.125	6.984	***	par_20
BDI2_20	<--- SOMATIC_ELEMENTS	1.367	.137	10.017	***	par_21

***

Variances

	Estimate	S.E.	C.R.	P	Label
DEPRESSION	1.000				
res2	.021	.005	3.921	***	var_a
res3	.021	.005	3.921	***	var_a
res1	.051	.011	4.583	***	par_22
err14	.273	.020	13.375	***	par_23
err10	.647	.043	15.197	***	par_24
err9	.212	.014	14.865	***	par_25
err8	.372	.026	14.485	***	par_26
err7	.313	.023	13.539	***	par_27
err6	.700	.047	15.007	***	par_28
err5	.401	.027	14.776	***	par_29
err3	.510	.035	14.651	***	par_30
err2	.255	.018	13.845	***	par_31

(continued)

Table 5.6 Selected AMOS Output for Hypothesized Model: Unstandardized ML Parameter Estimates *(Continued)*

	Estimate	S.E.	C.R.	P	Label
Variances					
err1	.407	.029	13.951	***	par_32
err19	.444	.031	14.407	***	par_33
err17	.307	.022	13.822	***	par_34
err13	.275	.020	13.730	***	par_35
err12	.256	.019	13.433	***	par_36
err11	.356	.026	13.697	***	par_37
err4	.310	.022	14.378	***	par_38
err16	.444	.030	14.693	***	par_39
err15	.267	.024	11.118	***	par_40
err18	.566	.038	15.034	***	par_41
err20	.249	.020	12.398	***	par_42

Table 5.7 Selected AMOS Output for Hypothesized Model:
Standardized ML Parameter Estimates

Standardized regression weights			Estimate
PERFORMANCE_DIFFICULTY	<---	DEPRESSION	.960
NEGATIVE_ATTITUDE	<---	DEPRESSION	.894
SOMATIC_ELEMENTS	<---	DEPRESSION	.921
BDI2_14	<---	NEGATIVE_ATTITUDE	.736
BDI2_10	<---	NEGATIVE_ATTITUDE	.412
BDI2_9	<---	NEGATIVE_ATTITUDE	.527
BDI2_8	<---	NEGATIVE_ATTITUDE	.609
BDI2_7	<---	NEGATIVE_ATTITUDE	.723
BDI2_6	<---	NEGATIVE_ATTITUDE	.485
BDI2_5	<---	NEGATIVE_ATTITUDE	.549
BDI2_3	<---	NEGATIVE_ATTITUDE	.577
BDI2_2	<---	NEGATIVE_ATTITUDE	.695
BDI2_1	<---	NEGATIVE_ATTITUDE	.683
BDI2_19	<---	PERFORMANCE_DIFFICULTY	.600
BDI2_17	<---	PERFORMANCE_DIFFICULTY	.676
BDI2_13	<---	PERFORMANCE_DIFFICULTY	.685
BDI2_12	<---	PERFORMANCE_DIFFICULTY	.714
BDI2_11	<---	PERFORMANCE_DIFFICULTY	.688
BDI2_4	<---	PERFORMANCE_DIFFICULTY	.605
BDI2_16	<---	SOMATIC_ELEMENTS	.487
BDI2_15	<---	SOMATIC_ELEMENTS	.765
BDI2_18	<---	SOMATIC_ELEMENTS	.397
BDI2_20	<---	SOMATIC_ELEMENTS	.714

variables, I consider it important to address these issues before reanalyz-
ing the hypothesized model of C-BDI-II structure shown in Figure 5.7
via a different estimation approach. First, I present a brief review of the
literature that addresses the issues confronted in analyzing categorical
variables as continuous variables. Next, I briefly outline the theoretical
underpinning of, the assumptions associated with, and primary estimation approaches to the analysis of categorical variables when such
ordinality is taken into account. Finally, I outline the very different
approach to these analyses by the AMOS program and proceed to walk
you through a reanalysis of the hypothesized model previously tested
in this chapter.

Categorical variables analyzed as continuous variables

A review of SEM applications over the past 15 years (in the case of psychological research, at least) reveals most to be based on Likert-type scaled data with estimation of parameters using ML procedures (see, e.g., Breckler, 1990). Given the known limitations associated with available alternative estimation strategies (to be described below), however, this common finding is not surprising. We now review, briefly, the primary issues associated with this customary practice.

The issues

From a review of Monte Carlo studies that have addressed this issue of analyzing categorical data as continuous data (see, e.g., Babakus, Ferguson, & Jöreskog, 1987; Boomsma, 1982; Muthén & Kaplan, 1985), West, Finch, and Curran (1995) reported several important findings. *First*, Pearson correlation coefficients would appear to be higher when computed between two continuous variables than when computed between the same two variables restructured with an ordered categorical scale. However, the greatest attenuation occurs with variables having less than five categories and those exhibiting a high degree of skewness, the latter condition being made worse by variables that are skewed in opposite directions (i.e., one variable is positively skewed, and the other negatively skewed; see Bollen & Barb, 1981). *Second*, when categorical variables approximate a normal distribution, (a) the number of categories has little effect on the χ^2 likelihood ratio test of model fit, but increasing skewness, and particularly differential skewness (variables skewed in opposite directions), leads to increasingly inflated χ^2 values; (b) factor loadings and factor correlations are only modestly underestimated, although underestimation becomes more critical when there are fewer than three categories, skewness is greater than 1.0, and differential skewness occurs across variables; (c) error variance estimates, more so than other parameters, appear to be most sensitive to the categorical and skewness issues noted in (b); and (d) standard error estimates for all parameters tend to be too low, with this result being more so when the distributions are highly and differentially skewed (see also Finch, West, & MacKinnon, 1997).

In summary, the literature to date would appear to support the notion that when the number of categories is large and the data approximate a normal distribution, failure to address the ordinality of the data is likely negligible (Atkinson, 1988; Babakus et al., 1987; Muthén & Kaplan, 1985). Indeed, Bentler and Chou (1987) argued that, given normally distributed categorical variables, "continuous methods can be used with little worry when a variable has four or more categories" (p. 88). More recent findings support these earlier contentions and have further shown that the

χ^2 statistic is influenced most by the two-category response format and becomes less influenced as the number of categories increases (Green, Akey, Fleming, Hershberger, & Marquis, 1997).

Categorical variables analyzed as categorical variables

The theory

In addressing the categorical nature of observed variables, the researcher automatically assumes that each has an underlying continuous scale. As such, the categories can be regarded as only crude measurements of an unobserved variable that, in truth, has a continuous scale (Jöreskog & Sörbom, 1993), with each pair of thresholds (or initial scale points) representing a portion of the continuous scale. The crudeness of these measurements arises from the splitting of the continuous scale of the construct into a fixed number of ordered categories (DiStefano, 2002). Indeed, this categorization process led O'Brien (1985) to argue that the analysis of Likert-scaled data actually contributes to two types of error: (a) categorization error resulting from the splitting of the continuous scale into a categorical scale, and (b) transformation error resulting from categories of unequal widths.

For purposes of illustration, let's consider the measuring instrument under study in this current chapter, in which each item is structured on a four-point scale. I draw from the work of Jöreskog and Sörbom (1993) in describing the decomposition of these categorical variables. Let z represent the ordinal variable (the item), and z^* the unobserved continuous variable. The threshold values can then be conceptualized as follows:

$$\text{If } z^* < \text{ or } = \tau_1, z \text{ is scored 1;}$$

$$\text{If } \tau_1 < z^* < \text{ or } = \tau_2, z \text{ is scored 2;}$$

$$\text{If } \tau_2 < z^* < \text{ or } = \tau_3, z \text{ is scored 3; and}$$

$$\text{If } \tau_3 < z^*, z \text{ is scored 4;}$$

where $\tau_1 < \tau_2 < \tau_3$ represents threshold values for z^*.

In conducting SEM with categorical data, analyses must be based on the correct correlation matrix. Where the correlated variables are both of an ordinal scale, the resulting matrix will comprise polychoric correlations; where one variable is of an ordinal scale, while the other is of a continuous scale, the resulting matrix will comprise polyserial correlations. If two variables are dichotomous, this special case of a polychoric correlation is called a *tetrachoric correlation*. If a polyserial correlation involves a dichotomous, rather than a more general, ordinal variable, the polyserial correlation is also called a *biserial correlation*.

The assumptions

Applications involving the use of categorical data are based on three critically important assumptions: (a) Underlying each categorical observed variable is an unobserved latent counterpart, the scale of which is both continuous and normally distributed; (b) the sample size is sufficiently large to enable reliable estimation of the related correlation matrix; and (c) the number of observed variables is kept to a minimum. As Bentler (2005) cogently noted, however, it is this very set of assumptions that essentially epitomizes the primary weakness in this methodology. Let's now take a brief look at why this should be so.

That each categorical variable has an underlying continuous and normally distributed scale is undoubtedly a difficult criterion to meet and, in fact, may be totally unrealistic. For example, in the present chapter, we examine scores tapping aspects of depression for nonclinical adolescents. Clearly, we would expect such item scores for normal adolescents to be low, thereby reflecting no incidence of depressive symptoms. As a consequence, we can expect to find evidence of kurtosis, and possibly skewness, related to these variables, with this pattern being reflected in their presumed underlying continuous distribution. Consequently, in the event that the model under test is deemed to be less than adequate, it may well be that the normality assumption is unreasonable in this instance.

The rationale underlying the latter two assumptions stems from the fact that, in working with categorical variables, analyses must proceed *from* a frequency table comprising number of thresholds × number of observed variables, *to* an estimation of the correlation matrix. The problem here lies with the occurrence of cells having zero or near-zero cases, which can subsequently lead to estimation difficulties (Bentler, 2005). This problem can arise because (a) the sample size is small relative to the number of response categories (i.e., specific category scores across all categorical variables), (b) the number of variables is excessively large, and/or (c) the number of thresholds is large. Taken in combination, then, the larger the number of observed variables and/or number of thresholds for these variables, and the smaller the sample size, the greater the chance of having cells comprising zero to near-zero cases.

General analytic strategies

Until recently, two primary approaches to the analysis of categorical data (Jöreskog, 1990, 1994; Muthén, 1984) have dominated this area of research. Both methodologies use standard estimates of polychoric and polyserial correlations, followed by a type of asymptotic distribution-free (ADF) methodology for the structured model. Unfortunately, the positive aspects of these categorical variable methodologies have been offset by the ultra-restrictive assumptions noted above and which, for most practical researchers, are both impractical and difficult to meet. In particular, conducting ADF estimation here has the same problem of requiring huge sample sizes, as in Browne's (1984a) ADF method for continuous variables. Attempts to resolve these difficulties over the past few years have resulted in the development of several different approaches to modeling categorical data (see, e.g., Bentler, 2005; Coenders, Satorra, & Saris, 1997; Moustaki, 2001; Muthén & Muthén, 2004).

The AMOS approach to analysis of categorical variables

The methodological approach to analysis of categorical variables in AMOS differs substantially from that of the other SEM programs. In lieu of ML or ADF estimation, AMOS analyses are based on Bayesian estimation. Bayesian inference dates back as far as the 18th century, yet its application in social-psychological research has been rare. Although this statistical approach is still not widely practiced, there nevertheless has been some resurgence of interest in its application over the past few years. In light of this information, you no doubt will wonder why I am including a section on this methodology in the book. I do so for three primary reasons. *First,* I consider it important to keep my readers informed of this updated estimation approach when categorical variables are involved, which was not available in the program at my writing of the first edition of this book. *Second,* it enables me to walk you through the process of using this estimation method to analyze data with which you are already familiar. *Finally,* it allows the opportunity to compare estimated values derived from both the ML and Bayesian approaches to analyses of the same CFA model. I begin with a brief explanation of Bayesian estimation and then follow with a step-by-step walk through each component of the procedure. As with our first application in this chapter, we seek to test for the factorial validity of hypothesized C-BDI-II structure (see Figure 5.7) for Hong Kong adolescents.

What is Bayesian estimation?

In ML estimation and hypothesis testing, the true values of the model parameters are considered to be *fixed but unknown,* whereas their estimates (from a given sample) are considered to be *random but known* (Arbuckle, 2007). In contrast, Bayesian estimation considers any unknown quantity as a random variable and therefore assigns it a probability distribution. Thus, from the Bayesian perspective, true model parameters are unknown and therefore considered to be random. Within this context, then, these parameters are assigned a joint distribution—a *prior distribution* (probability distribution of the parameters before they are actually observed, also commonly termed the *priors*; Vogt, 1993), and a *posterior distribution* (probability distribution of parameters after they have been observed and combined with the prior distribution). This updated joint distribution is based on the formula known as Bayes' theorem and reflects a combination of prior belief (about the parameter estimates) and empirical evidence (Arbuckle, 2007; Bolstad, 2004). Two characteristics of this joint distribution are important to CFA analyses. *First*, the mean of this posterior distribution can be reported as the parameter estimate. *Second*, the standard deviation of the posterior distribution serves as an analog to the standard error in ML estimation.

Application of Bayesian estimation

Because Bayesian analyses require the estimation of all observed variable means and intercepts, the first step in the process is to request this information via the *Analysis Properties* dialog box as shown in Figure 5.8. Otherwise, in requesting that the analyses be based on this approach, you will receive an error message advising you of this fact.

Once you have the appropriately specified model (i.e., the means and intercepts are specified as freely estimated), to begin the Bayesian analyses, click on the ▲ icon in the toolbox. Alternatively, you can pull down

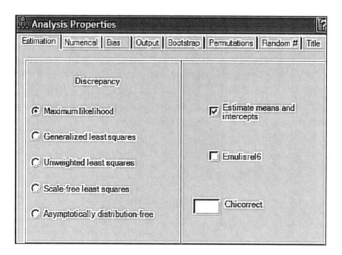

Figure 5.8 Analysis Properties dialog box: Requesting estimation of means and intercepts.

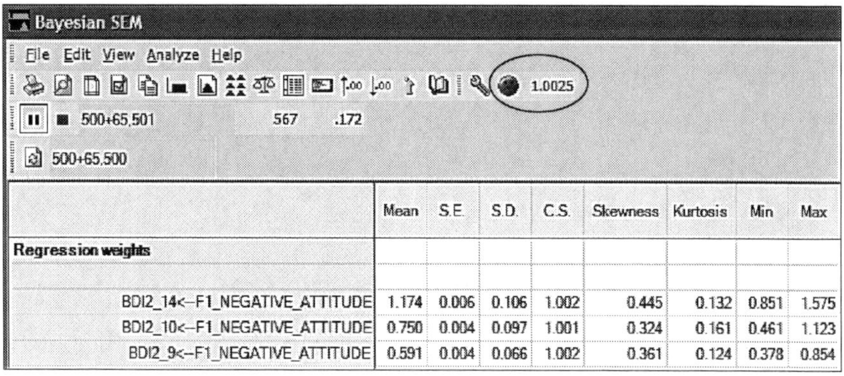

Bayesian SEM

File   Edit   View   Analyze   Help

1.0025

500+65,501   567   .172

500+65,500

	Mean	S.E.	S.D.	C.S.	Skewness	Kurtosis	Min	Max
Regression weights								
BDI2_14<--F1_NEGATIVE_ATTITUDE	1.174	0.006	0.106	1.002	0.445	0.132	0.851	1.575
BDI2_10<--F1_NEGATIVE_ATTITUDE	0.750	0.004	0.097	1.001	0.324	0.161	0.461	1.123
BDI2_9<--F1_NEGATIVE_ATTITUDE	0.591	0.004	0.066	1.002	0.361	0.124	0.378	0.854

Figure 5.9 Bayesian SEM window: Posterior distribution sampling and convergence status.

the *Analyze* menu and select *Bayesian Estimation*. Once you do this, you will be presented with the Bayesian SEM window shown partially in Figure 5.9, and fully in Figure 5.10. You will note also that the numbers in each of the columns are constantly changing. The reason for these ongoing number changes is because as soon as you request Bayesian estimation, the program immediately initiates the steady drawing of random samples based on the joint posterior distribution. This random sampling process is accomplished in AMOS via an algorithm termed the *Markov chain Monte Carlo (MCMC) algorithm*. The basic idea underlying this ever-changing number process is to identify, as closely as possible, the true value of each parameter in the model. This process will continue until you halt the process by clicking on the *Pause* button, shown within a square frame at the immediate left of the second line of the Toolbox in Figures 5.9 and 5.10.

Now, let's take a closer look at the numbers appearing in the upper section (the Toolbox) of the Bayesian SEM window. In Figure 5.9, note the numbers beside the *Pause* button, which read as 500 + 65.501 and indicate the point at which sampling was halted. This information conveys that AMOS generated and discarded 500 *burn-in samples* (the default value) prior to drawing the first one that was retained for the analysis. The reason for these burn-in samples is to allow the MCMC procedure to converge to the true joint posterior distribution (Arbuckle, 2007). After drawing and discarding the burn-in samples, the program then draws additional samples, the purpose of which is to provide the most precise picture of the values comprising the posterior distribution.

Clearly, a next logical question one might ask about this sampling process is how one knows when enough samples have been drawn to yield a posterior distribution that is sufficiently accurate. This question addresses the issue of convergence and the point at which enough samples have been

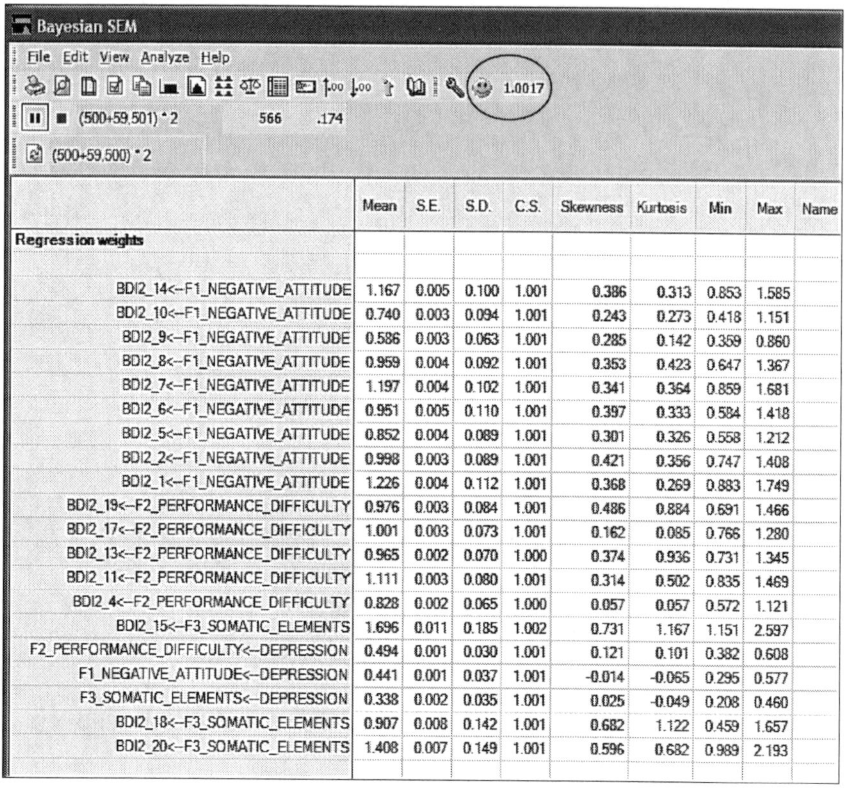

	Mean	S.E.	S.D.	C.S.	Skewness	Kurtosis	Min	Max	Name
Regression weights									
BDI2_14<--F1_NEGATIVE_ATTITUDE	1.167	0.005	0.100	1.001	0.386	0.313	0.853	1.585	
BDI2_10<--F1_NEGATIVE_ATTITUDE	0.740	0.003	0.094	1.001	0.243	0.273	0.418	1.151	
BDI2_9<--F1_NEGATIVE_ATTITUDE	0.586	0.003	0.063	1.001	0.285	0.142	0.359	0.860	
BDI2_8<--F1_NEGATIVE_ATTITUDE	0.959	0.004	0.092	1.001	0.353	0.423	0.647	1.367	
BDI2_7<--F1_NEGATIVE_ATTITUDE	1.197	0.004	0.102	1.001	0.341	0.364	0.859	1.681	
BDI2_6<--F1_NEGATIVE_ATTITUDE	0.951	0.005	0.110	1.001	0.397	0.333	0.584	1.418	
BDI2_5<--F1_NEGATIVE_ATTITUDE	0.852	0.004	0.089	1.001	0.301	0.326	0.558	1.212	
BDI2_2<--F1_NEGATIVE_ATTITUDE	0.998	0.003	0.089	1.001	0.421	0.356	0.747	1.408	
BDI2_1<--F1_NEGATIVE_ATTITUDE	1.226	0.004	0.112	1.001	0.368	0.269	0.883	1.749	
BDI2_19<--F2_PERFORMANCE_DIFFICULTY	0.976	0.003	0.084	1.001	0.486	0.884	0.691	1.466	
BDI2_17<--F2_PERFORMANCE_DIFFICULTY	1.001	0.003	0.073	1.001	0.162	0.085	0.766	1.280	
BDI2_13<--F2_PERFORMANCE_DIFFICULTY	0.965	0.002	0.070	1.000	0.374	0.936	0.731	1.345	
BDI2_11<--F2_PERFORMANCE_DIFFICULTY	1.111	0.003	0.080	1.001	0.314	0.502	0.835	1.469	
BDI2_4<--F2_PERFORMANCE_DIFFICULTY	0.828	0.002	0.065	1.000	0.057	0.057	0.572	1.121	
BDI2_15<--F3_SOMATIC_ELEMENTS	1.696	0.011	0.185	1.002	0.731	1.167	1.151	2.597	
F2_PERFORMANCE_DIFFICULTY<--DEPRESSION	0.494	0.001	0.030	1.001	0.121	0.101	0.382	0.608	
F1_NEGATIVE_ATTITUDE<--DEPRESSION	0.441	0.001	0.037	1.001	-0.014	-0.065	0.295	0.577	
F3_SOMATIC_ELEMENTS<--DEPRESSION	0.338	0.002	0.035	1.001	0.025	-0.049	0.208	0.460	
BDI2_18<--F3_SOMATIC_ELEMENTS	0.907	0.008	0.142	1.001	0.682	1.122	0.459	1.657	
BDI2_20<--F3_SOMATIC_ELEMENTS	1.408	0.007	0.149	1.001	0.596	0.682	0.989	2.193	

Figure 5.10 Bayesian SEM window: Posterior distribution sampling and convergence status, and related estimates and statistics.

drawn so as to generate stable parameter estimates. AMOS establishes this cutpoint on the basis of the convergence statistic (C.S.), which derives from the work of Gelman, Carlin, Stern, and Rubin (2004). By default, AMOS considers the sampling to have converged when the largest of the C.S. values is less than 1.002 (Arbuckle, 2007). Until this default C.S. value has been reached, AMOS displays an unhappy face (☹). Turning again to Figure 5.9, I draw your attention to the circled information in the Toolbar section of the window. Here you will note the "unhappy face" emoticon accompanied by the value of 1.0025, indicating that the sampling process has not yet attained the default cutpoint of 1.002; rather, it is ever so slightly higher than that value. Unfortunately, because this emoticon is colored red in the Bayesian toolbar, it is impossible to reproduce it in a lighter shade.

In contrast, turn now to Figure 5.10, in which you will find a happy face (☺) together with the C.S. value of 1.0017, thereby indicating convergence (in accordance with the AMOS default value). Moving down to the row that begins with the *Pause* icon, we see the numbers 500 + 59.501. This information conveys the notion that following the sampling and discarding of 500 burn-in samples, the MCMC algorithm has generated 59 additional samples and, as noted above, reached a convergent C.S. value of 1.0017.

Listed below the toolbar area are the resulting statistics pertinent to the model parameters; only the regression weights (i.e., factor loadings) are presented here. Each row in this section describes the posterior distribution value of a single parameter, while each column lists the related statistic. For example, in the first column (labeled *Mean*), each entry represents the average value of the posterior distribution and, as noted earlier, can be interpreted as the final parameter estimate. More specifically, these values represent the Bayesian point estimates of the parameters based on the data and the prior distribution. Arbuckle (2007) noted that with large sample sizes, these mean values will be close to the ML estimates. (We make this comparison later in the chapter.)

The second column, labeled *S.E.*, reports an estimated standard error that implies how far the estimated posterior mean may lie from the true posterior mean. As the MCMC procedures continue to generate more samples, the estimate of the posterior mean becomes more accurate and the S.E. will gradually drop. Certainly, in Figure 5.10, we can see that the S.E. values are very small thereby indicating that they are very close to the true values. The next column, labeled *S.D.*, can be interpreted as the likely distance between the posterior mean and the unknown true parameter; this number is analogous to the standard error in ML estimation. The remaining columns, as can be observed in Figure 5.10, represent the posterior distribution values related to the C.S., skewness, kurtosis, minimum value, and maximum value, respectively.

In addition to the C.S. value, AMOS makes several diagnostic plots available for you to check the convergence of the MCMC sampling method. To generate these plots, you need to click on the *Posterior* icon located on the *Bayesian SEM Toolbox* area, as shown encased in an ellipse in Figure 5.11. Just clicking this icon will trigger the dialog box shown in Figure 5.12. The essence of this message is that you must select one of the estimated parameters in the model. As can be seen in Figure 5.13, I selected the first model parameter (highlighted), the loading of C-BDI-II Item 14 onto Negative Attitude (Factor 1). Right-clicking the mouse generated the *Posterior Diagnostic* dialog box with the distribution shown within the framework of a polygon plot. Specifically, this frequency polygon displays the sampling distribution of Item 14 across 59 samples (the number sampled after the 500 burn-in samples were deleted).

AMOS produces an additional polygon plot that enables you to determine the likelihood that the MCMC samples have converged to the posterior distribution via a simultaneous distribution based on the first and last

Figure 5.11 Bayesian SEM window: Location of posterior icon.

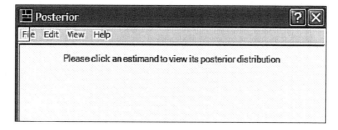

Figure 5.12 Bayesian SEM error message.

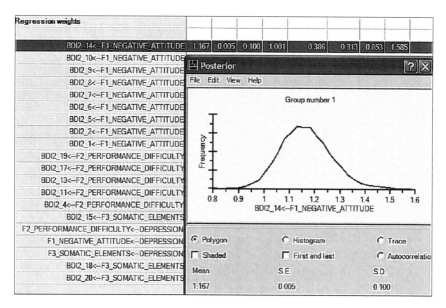

Figure 5.13 Bayesian SEM diagnostic polygon plot.

thirds of the accumulated samples. This polygon is accessed by selecting *First and Last*, as can be seen in Figure 5.14. From the display in this plot, we observe that the two distributions are almost identical, thereby suggesting that AMOS has successfully identified important features of the posterior distribution of Item 14. Notice that this posterior distribution appears to be centered at some value near 1.17, which is consistent with the mean value of 1.167 noted in Figure 5.10.

Two other available diagnostic plots are the histogram and trace plots illustrated in Figures 5.15 and 5.16, respectively. While the histogram is relatively self-explanatory, the trace plot requires some explanation. Sometimes termed the *time-series plot*, this diagnostic plot helps you to evaluate how quickly the MCMC sampling procedure converged in the posterior distribution. The plot shown in Figure 5.16 is considered to be very good as it exhibits rapid up-and-down variation with no long-term trends. Another way of looking at this plot is to imagine breaking up the distribution into sections. Results would show none of the sections to deviate much from the rest. This finding indicates that the convergence in distribution occurred rapidly, a clear indicator that the SEM model was specified correctly.

As one final analysis of the C-BDI-II, let's compare the unstandardized factor-loading estimates for the ML method versus the Bayesian posterior distribution estimates. A listing of both sets of estimates is presented in

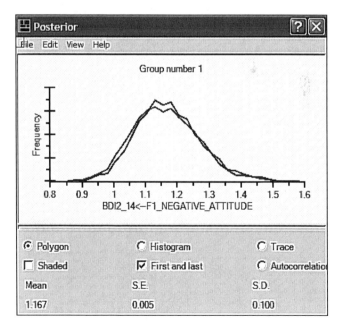

Figure 5.14 Bayesian SEM diagnostic first and last combined polygon plot.

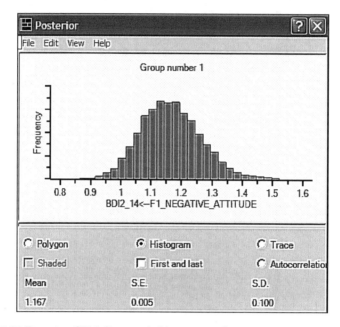

Figure 5.15 Bayesian SEM diagnostic histogram plot.

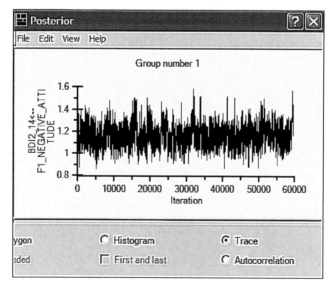

Figure 5.16 Bayesian SEM diagnostic trace plot.

Table 5.8. As might be expected, based on our review of the diagnostic plots, these estimates are very close pertinent to both the first- and second-factor loadings. These findings speak well for the validity of our hypothesized structure of the C-BDI-II for Hong Kong adolescents.

Table 5.8 Comparison of Factor Loading (i.e., Regression Weight) Unstandardized Parameter Estimates: Maximum Likelihood Versus Bayesian Estimation

Parameter			ML	Bayesian
BDI2_14	<---	NEGATIVE_ATTITUDE	1.125	1.167
BDI2_10	<---	NEGATIVE_ATTITUDE	.720	.740
BDI2_9	<---	NEGATIVE_ATTITUDE	.566	.586
BDI2_8	<---	NEGATIVE_ATTITUDE	.928	.959
BDI2_7	<---	NEGATIVE_ATTITUDE	1.161	1.197
BDI2_6	<---	NEGATIVE_ATTITUDE	.919	.951
BDI2_5	<---	NEGATIVE_ATTITUDE	.825	.852
BDI2_3	<---	NEGATIVE_ATTITUDE	1.000	1.000
BDI2_2	<---	NEGATIVE_ATTITUDE	.966	.998
BDI2_1	<---	NEGATIVE_ATTITUDE	1.183	1.226
BDI2_19	<---	PERFORMANCE_DIFFICULTY	.969	.979
BDI2_17	<---	PERFORMANCE_DIFFICULTY	.984	1.001
BDI2_13	<---	PERFORMANCE_DIFFICULTY	.955	.965
BDI2_12	<---	PERFORMANCE_DIFFICULTY	1.000	1.000
BDI2_11	<---	PERFORMANCE_DIFFICULTY	1.096	1.111
BDI2_4	<---	PERFORMANCE_DIFFICULTY	.819	.828
BDI2_16	<---	SOMATIC_ELEMENTS	1.000	1.000
BDI2_15	<---	SOMATIC_ELEMENTS	1.651	1.696
BDI2_18	<---	SOMATIC_ELEMENTS	.876	.907
BDI2_20	<---	SOMATIC_ELEMENTS	1.367	1.408
PERFORMANCE_DIFFICULTY	<---	DEPRESSION	.495	.494
NEGATIVE_ATTITUDE	<---	DEPRESSION	.451	.441
SOMATIC_ELEMENTS	<---	DEPRESSION	.342	.342

Estimation approach

In closing out this chapter, I wish to underscore the importance of our comparative analysis of C-BDI-II factorial structure from two perspectives: ML and Bayesian estimation. Given that items comprising this instrument are based on a four-point scale, the argument could be made that analyses should be based on a methodology that takes this ordinality into account. As noted earlier in this chapter, historically, these analyses have been based on the ML methodology, which assumes the data are of a continuous scale. Importantly, however, I also reviewed the literature with respect to (a) why researchers have tended to treat categorical variables as if they were continuous in SEM analyses, (b) the consequence of treating categorical variables as if they are of a continuous scale, and (c) identified scaling and other statistical features of the data that make it critical to take the ordinality of categorical variables into account as well as conditions that show this approach not to make much difference. At the very least, the researcher always has the freedom to conduct analyses based on both methodological approaches and then follow up with a comparison of the parameter estimates. In most cases, where the hypothesized model is well specified and the scaling based on more than three categories, it seems unlikely that there will be much difference between the findings.

One final comment regarding analysis of categorical data in AMOS relates to its alphanumeric capabilities. Although our analyses in this chapter were based on numerically scored data, the program can just as easily analyze categorical data based on a letter code. For details regarding this approach to SEM analyses of categorical data, as well as many more details related to the Bayesian statistical capabilities of AMOS, readers are referred to the manual (Arbuckle, 2007).

chapter six

Testing for the validity of a causal structure

In this chapter, we take our first look at a *full* structural equation model (SEM). The hypothesis to be tested relates to the pattern of causal structure linking several stressor variables that bear on the construct of burnout. The original study from which this application is taken (Byrne, 1994a) tested and cross-validated the impact of organizational and personality variables on three dimensions of burnout for elementary, intermediate, and secondary teachers. For purposes of illustration here, however, the application is limited to the calibration sample of elementary teachers only (N = 599).

As was the case with the factor analytic applications illustrated in Chapters 3 through 5, those structured as full SEMs are presumed to be of a confirmatory nature. That is to say, postulated causal relations among all variables in the hypothesized model must be grounded in theory and/or empirical research. Typically, the hypothesis to be tested argues for the validity of specified causal linkages among the variables of interest. Let's turn now to an in-depth examination of the hypothesized model under study in the current chapter.

The hypothesized model

Formulation of the hypothesized model shown in Figure 6.1 derived from the consensus of findings from a review of the burnout literature as it bears on the teaching profession. (Readers wishing a more detailed summary of this research are referred to Byrne, 1994a, 1999). In reviewing this model, you will note that burnout is represented as a multidimensional construct with Emotional Exhaustion (EE), Depersonalization (DP), and Personal Accomplishment (PA) operating as conceptually distinct factors. This part of the model is based on the work of Leiter (1991) in conceptualizing burnout as a cognitive-emotional reaction to chronic stress. The paradigm argues that EE holds the central position because it is considered to be the most responsive of the three facets to various stressors in the teacher's work environment. Depersonalization and reduced PA, on the other hand, represent the cognitive aspects of burnout in that they

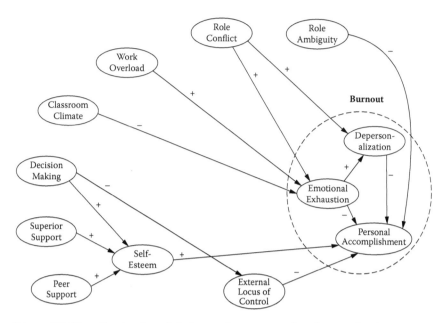

Figure 6.1 Hypothesized model of causal structure related to teacher burnout.

are indicative of the extent to which teachers' perceptions of their students, their colleagues, and themselves become diminished. As indicated by the signs associated with each path in the model, EE is hypothesized to impact positively on DP, but negatively on PA; DP is hypothesized to impact negatively on PA.

The paths (and their associated signs) leading from the organizational (role ambiguity, role conflict, work overload, classroom climate, decision making, superior support, peer support) and personality (self-esteem, external locus of control) variables to the three dimensions of burnout reflect findings in the literature.[1] For example, high levels of role conflict are expected to cause high levels of emotional exhaustion; in contrast, high (i.e., good) levels of classroom climate are expected to generate low levels of emotional exhaustion.

Modeling with AMOS Graphics

In viewing the model shown in Figure 6.1, we can see that it represents only the structural portion of the full SEM. Thus, before being able to test this model, we need to know the manner by which each of the constructs in this model is to be measured. In other words, we now need to specify the measurement portion of the model (see Chapter 1). In contrast to the CFA models studied previously, the task involved in developing the measurement model of a full SEM is twofold: (a) to determine the number of indicators to use in measuring each construct, and (b) to identify which items to use in formulating each indicator.

Formulation of indicator variables

In the applications examined in Chapters 3 through 5, the formulation of measurement indicators has been relatively straightforward; all examples have involved CFA models and, as such, comprised only measurement models. In the measurement of multidimensional facets of self-concept (see Chapter 3), each indicator represented a subscale score (i.e., the sum of all items designed to measure a particular self-concept facet). In Chapters 4 and 5, our interest focused on the factorial validity of a measuring instrument. As such, we were concerned with the extent to which items loaded onto their targeted factor. Adequate assessment of this specification demanded that each item be included in the model. Thus, the indicator variables in these cases each represented one item in the measuring instrument under study.

In contrast to these previous examples, formulation of the indicator variables in the present application is slightly more complex. Specifically, multiple indicators of each construct were formulated through the judicious combination of particular items to comprise item parcels. As such, items were carefully grouped according to content in order to equalize the measurement weighting across the set of indicators measuring the same construct (Hagtvet & Nasser, 2004). For example, the Classroom Environment Scale (Bacharach, Bauer, & Conley, 1986), used to measure Classroom Climate, consists of items that tap classroom size, ability and interest of students, and various types of abuse by students. Indicators of this construct were formed such that each item in the composite measured a different aspect of classroom climate. In the measurement of classroom climate, self-esteem, and external locus of control, indicator variables consisted of items from a single unidimensional scale; all other indicators comprised items from subscales of multidimensional scales. (For an extensive description of the measuring instruments, see Byrne, 1994a.) In total, 32 item–parcel indicator variables were used to measure the hypothesized structural model.

Since the current study was conducted, there has been a growing interest in the question of item parceling. Research has focused on such issues as method of parceling (Bandalos & Finney, 2001; Hagtvet & Nasser, 2004; Kim & Hagtvet, 2003; Kishton & Widaman, 1994; Little, Cunningham, Shahar, & Widaman, 2002; Rogers & Schmitt, 2004), number of items to include in a parcel (Marsh, Hau, Balla, & Grayson, 1998), extent to which item parcels affect model fit (Bandalos, 2002), and, more generally, whether or not researchers should even engage in item parceling at all (Little et al., 2002; Little, Lindenberger, & Nesselroade, 1999). Little et al. (2002) presented an excellent summary of the pros and cons of using item parceling, and the Bandalos and Finney (2001) chapter, a thorough review of the issues related to item parceling. (For details related to each of these aspects of item parceling, readers are advised to consult these references directly.)

A schematic presentation of the full SEM is presented in Figure 6.2. It is important to note that, in the interest of clarity, all double-headed arrows representing correlations among the independent (i.e., exogenous) factors, as well as error terms associated with the observed (i.e., indicator) variables, have been excluded from the figure. However, given that AMOS Graphics operates on the WYSIWYG (what you see is what you get) principle, these parameters must be included in the model before the program will perform the analyses. I revisit this issue after we fully establish the hypothesized model under test in this chapter.

The preliminary model (because we have not yet tested for the validity of the measurement model) in Figure 6.2 is most appropriately presented within the framework of the landscape layout. In AMOS Graphics, this is accomplished by pulling down the *View* menu and selecting the *Interface Properties* dialog box, as shown in Figure 6.3. Here you see the open *Paper Layout* tab that enables you to opt for landscape orientation.

Confirmatory factor analyses

Because (a) the structural portion of a full structural equation model involves relations among only latent variables, and (b) the primary concern in working with a full SEM model is to assess the extent to which these relations are valid, it is critical that the measurement of each latent variable is psychometrically sound. Thus, an important preliminary step in the analysis of full latent variable models is to test first for the validity of the measurement model before making any attempt to evaluate the structural model. Accordingly, CFA procedures are used in testing the validity of the indicator variables. Once it is known that the measurement model is operating adequately,[2] one can then have more confidence in findings related to the assessment of the hypothesized structural model.

In the present case, CFAs were conducted for indicator variables derived from each of the two multidimensional scales; these were the Teacher Stress Scale (TSS; Pettegrew & Wolf, 1982), which included all organizational indicator variables except Classroom Climate, and the

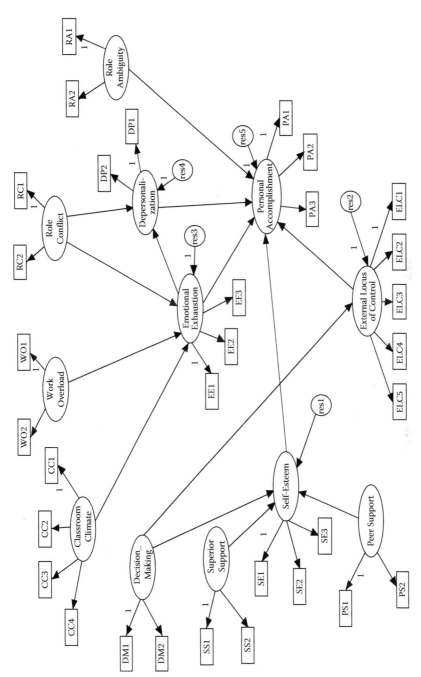

Figure 6.2 Hypothesized structural equation model of teacher burnout.

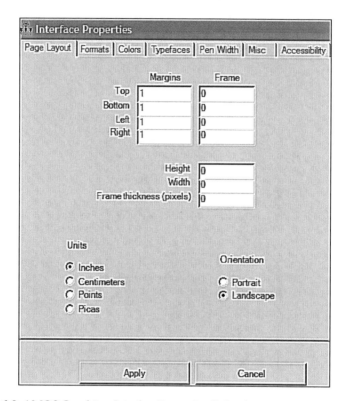

Figure 6.3 AMOS Graphics: *Interface Properties* dialog box.

Maslach Burnout Inventory (MBI; Maslach & Jackson, 1986), measuring the three facets of burnout. The hypothesized CFA model of the TSS is portrayed in Figure 6.4.

Of particular note here is the presence of double-headed arrows among all six factors. Recall from Chapter 2 and earlier in this chapter that AMOS Graphics assumes no correlations among the factors. Thus, should you wish to estimate these values in accordance with the related theory, they must be present in the model. However, rest assured that the program will definitely prompt you should you neglect to include one or more factor correlations in the model. Another error message that you are bound to receive at some time prompts that you forgot to identify the data file upon which the analyses are to be based. For example, Figure 6.5 presents the error message triggered by my failure to establish the data file a priori. However, this problem is quickly resolved by clicking on the *Data File* icon (▥); or select *Data Files* from the *File* drop-down menu, which then triggers the dialog box shown in Figure 6.6. Here you simply locate and click on the data file, and then click on *Open*. This action subsequently

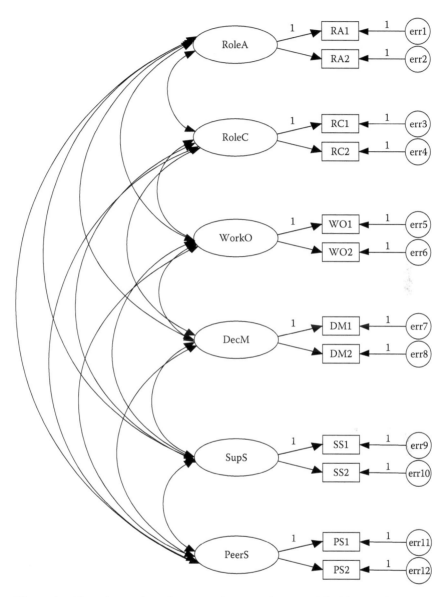

Figure 6.4 Hypothesized confirmatory factor analytic model of the Teacher Stress Scale.

produces the *Data Files* dialog box shown in Figure 6.7, where you will need to click on *OK*.

Although goodness-of-fit for both the MBI (CFI = .98) and TSS (CFI = .973) were found to be exceptionally good, the solution for the TSS was somewhat

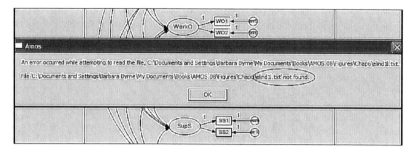

Figure 6.5 AMOS Graphics: Error message associated with failure to define data file.

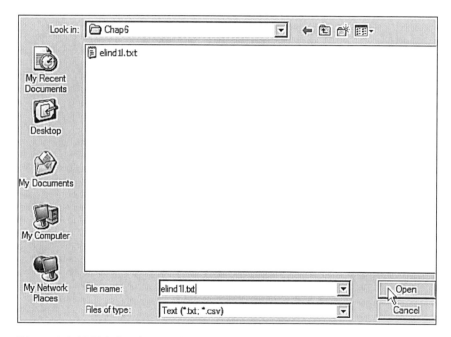

Figure 6.6 AMOS Graphics: Defining location and selection of data file.

problematic. More specifically, a review of the standardized estimates revealed a correlation value of 1.041 between the factors of Role Conflict and Work Overload, an indication of possible multicollinearity; these standardized estimates are presented in Table 6.1.

Multicollinearity arises from the situation where two or more variables are so highly correlated that they both essentially represent the same underlying construct. Substantively, this finding is not surprising as there appears to be substantial content overlap among TSS items measuring

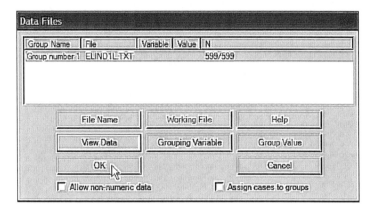

Figure 6.7 AMOS Graphics: Finalizing the data file.

Table 6.1 Selected AMOS Output
for CFA Model of the Teacher
Stress Scale: Factor Correlations

Factor correlations	Estimate
RoleA <--> RoleC	.841
RoleC <--> WorkO	1.041
WorkO <--> DecM	−.612
DecM <--> SupS	.924
WorkO <--> SupS	−.564
RoleA <--> WorkO	.771
RoleA <--> DecM	−.750
RoleC <--> SupS	−.592
RoleA <--> SupS	−.665
SupS <--> PeerS	.502
DecM <--> PeerS	.630
WorkO <--> PeerS	−.421
RoleC <--> PeerS	−.419
RoleA <--> PeerS	−.518
RoleC <--> DecM	−.622

role conflict and work overload. The very presence of a correlation > 1.00 is indicative of a solution that is clearly inadmissible. Of course, the flip side of the coin regarding inadmissible solutions is that they alert the researcher to serious model misspecifications. However, a review of the modification indices (see Table 6.2) provided no help whatsoever in this regard. All parameter change statistics related to the error covariances

Table 6.2 Selected AMOS Output for
Hypothesized Model of Teacher Stress
Survey: Modification Indices

	M.I.	Par change
Covariances		
err10 <--> err12	15.603	.056
err10 <--> err11	10.023	−.049
err9 <--> err12	17.875	−.066
err9 <--> err11	10.605	.056
err8 <--> err11	7.333	−.056
err8 <--> err10	13.400	.065
err8 <--> err9	6.878	−.053
err7 <--> err10	11.646	−.062
err3 <--> SupS	7.690	−.066
err3 <--> err11	7.086	−.061
err3 <--> err6	9.875	−.107
err2 <--> err12	6.446	.043
err2 <--> err11	7.646	−.051
err1 <--> err6	7.904	.083
Regression weights		
PS2 <--- RC1	7.439	.060
PS1 <--- RC1	9.661	−.074
SS1 <--- WO1	6.247	−.057
DM1 <--- WorkO	6.121	−.101
RC1 <--- SupS	7.125	−.088
RC1 <--- SS2	7.206	−.077
RC1 <--- SS1	7.970	−.080

revealed nonsignificant values less than, or close to, 0.1, and all modification indices (MIs) for the regression weights (or factor loadings) were
less than 10.00, again showing little to be gained by specifying any cross-
loadings. In light of the excellent fit of Model 2 of the TSS, together with
these nonthreatening MIs, I see no rational need to incorporate additional
parameters into the model. Thus, it seemed apparent that another tactic
was needed in addressing this multicollinearity issue.

One approach that can be taken in such instances is to combine the
measures as indicators of only one of the two factors involved. In the present case, a second CFA model of the TSS was specified in which the factor
of Work Overload was deleted, albeit its two observed indicator variables
were loaded onto the Role Conflict factor. Although goodness-of-fit related

to this five-factor model of the TSS ($\chi^2_{(48)}$ = 215.360; CFI = .958; RMSEA = .055) was somewhat less well fitting than for the initially hypothesized model, it nevertheless represented an exceptionally good fit to the data.

Table 6.3 Selected AMOS Output for CFA Model 2 of Teacher Stress Survey: Model Summary

Computation of degrees of freedom	
Number of distinct sample moments:	78
Number of distinct parameters to be estimated:	30
Degrees of freedom (78 – 30):	48

Result

Minimum was achieved.
Chi-square   = 215.360
Degrees of freedom =   48
Probability level   =   .000

Table 6.4 Selected AMOS Output for CFA Model 2 of Teacher Stress Survey: Unstandardized and Standardized Estimates

			Estimate	S.E.	C.R.	P
Regression weights						
RA1	<---	RoleA	1.000			
RA2	<---	RoleA	1.185	.071	16.729	***
DM2	<---	DecM	1.349	.074	18.247	***
PS1	<---	PeerS	1.000			
PS2	<---	PeerS	1.002	.064	15.709	***
RC1	<---	RoleC	1.000			
RC2	<---	RoleC	1.312	.079	16.648	***
DM1	<---	DecM	1.000			
WO1	<---	RoleC	1.079	.069	15.753	***
WO2	<---	RoleC	.995	.071	13.917	***
SS1	<---	DecM	1.478	.074	19.934	***
SS2	<---	DecM	1.550	.075	20.667	***
Standardized regression weights						
RA1	<---	RoleA	.718			
RA2	<---	RoleA	.824			
DM2	<---	DecM	.805			

(continued)

Table 6.4 Selected AMOS Output for CFA Model 2 of
Teacher Stress Survey: Unstandardized and Standardized
Estimates (*Continued*)

			Estimate	S.E.	C.R.	P
Standardized regression weights						
PS1	<---	PeerS	.831			
PS2	<---	PeerS	.879			
RC1	<---	RoleC	.700			
RC2	<---	RoleC	.793			
DM1	<---	DecM	.688			
WO1	<---	RoleC	.738			
WO2	<---	RoleC	.641			
SS1	<---	DecM	.889			
SS2	<---	DecM	.935			
Covariances						
RoleA <--> RoleC			.428	.041	10.421	***
RoleA <--> DecM			−.355	.035	−10.003	***
DecM <--> PeerS			.321	.036	8.997	***
RoleC <--> PeerS			−.263	.036	−7.338	***
RoleA <--> PeerS			−.288	.034	−8.388	***
DecM <--> RoleC			−.342	.037	−9.292	***
Correlations						
RoleA <--> RoleC			.800			
RoleA <--> DecM			−.698			
DecM <--> PeerS			.538			
RoleC <--> PeerS			−.419			
RoleA <--> PeerS			−.523			
DecM <--> RoleC			−.592			

*** probability < .000

The model summary and parameter estimates are shown in Tables 6.3 and 6.4, respectively.

This five-factor structure served as the measurement model for the TSS throughout analyses related to the full causal model. However, as a consequence of this measurement restructuring, the revised model of burnout shown in Figure 6.8 replaced the originally hypothesized model (see Figure 6.2) in serving as the hypothesized model to be tested. Once again, in the interest of clarity, the factor correlations and errors of measurement are not included.

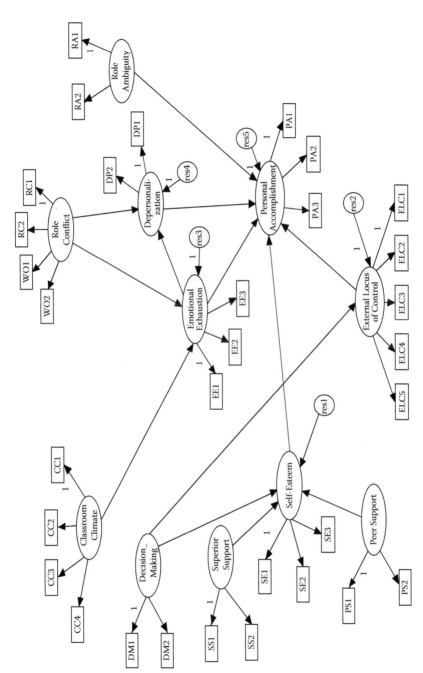

Figure 6.8 Revised hypothesized model of teacher burnout.

At the beginning of this chapter, I mentioned that AMOS Graphics operates on the WYSIWYG principle, and therefore unless regression paths and covariances are specified in the model, they will not be estimated. I promised to revisit this issue, and I do so here. In the case of full SEM structures failure to include double-headed arrows among the exogenous factors, as in Figure 6.8 (Role Ambiguity, Role Conflict, Classroom Climate, Decision Making, Superior Support, and Peer Support), prompts AMOS to alert you with a related error message. However, this omission is easily addressed. For every neatly drawn model that you submit for analysis, AMOS produces its own model behind the scenes. Thus, in revising any model for reanalyses, it is very easy and actually best simply to work on this backstage version, which can become very messy as increasingly more parameters are added to the model (see, e.g., Figure 6.9).

Selected AMOS output: Hypothesized model

Before examining test results for the hypothesized model, it is instructive to first review summary notes pertinent to this model, which are presented in four sections in Table 6.5. The initial information advises that (a) the

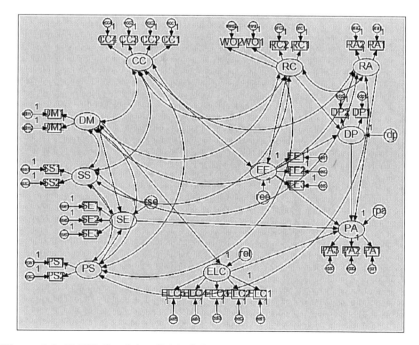

Figure 6.9 AMOS Graphics: Behind-the-scenes working file for hypothesized model of teacher burnout.

Table 6.5 Selected AMOS Output for Hypothesized
Model: Summary Notes

Computation of degrees of freedom

Number of distinct sample moments:	528
Number of distinct parameters to be estimated:	92
Degrees of freedom (528 – 92):	436

Result

Minimum was achieved.
Chi-square   = 1030.892
Degrees of freedom = 436
Probability level   =   .000

Dependent factors in the model

Unobserved, endogenous variables
DP
ELC
EE
PA
SE

Independent factors in the model

Unobserved, exogenous variables
RA
RC
DM
SS
PS
CC

analyses are based on 528 sample moments (32 [indicator measures] × 33 / 2), (b) there are 92 parameters to be estimated, and (c) by subtraction there are 436 degrees of freedom. The next section reports on the bottom-line information that the minimum was achieved in reaching a convergent solution, thereby yielding a χ^2 value of 1030.892 with 436 degrees of freedom.

Summarized in the lower part of the table are the dependent and independent factors in the model. Specifically, there are five dependent (or endogenous) factors in the model (DP; ELC; EE; PA; SE). Each of these factors has single-headed arrows pointing at it, thereby easily identifying it as a dependent factor in the model. The independent (or exogenous) factors are those hypothesized as exerting an influence on the dependent factors; these are RA, RC, DM, SS, PS, and CC.

Table 6.6 Selected AMOS Output for Hypothesized Model: Goodness-of-Fit Statistics

	Baseline comparisons				
	NFI	RFI	IFI	TLI	
Model	Delta1	rho1	Delta2	rho2	CFI
Default model	.903	.889	.941	.933	.941
Saturated model	1.000		1.000		1.000
Independence model	.000	.000	.000	.000	.000

		RMSEA		
Model	RMSEA	LO 90	HI 90	PCLOSE
Default model	.048	.044	.052	.833
Independence model	.184	.181	.188	.000

		ECVI		
Model	ECVI	LO 90	HI 90	MECVI
Default model	2.032	1.881	2.195	2.050
Saturated model	1.766	1.766	1.766	1.869
Independence model	17.817	17.263	18.382	17.823

Model assessment

Goodness-of-fit summary

Selected goodness-of-fit statistics related to the hypothesized model are presented in Table 6.6. In Table 6.5, we observed that the overall χ^2 value, with 436 degrees of freedom, is 1030.892. Given the known sensitivity of this statistic to sample size, however, use of the χ^2 index provides little guidance in determining the extent to which the model does not fit. Thus, it is more reasonable and appropriate to base decisions on other indices of fit. Primary among these in the AMOS Output are the CFI and RMSEA values.[3] Furthermore, given that we shall be comparing a series of models in our quest to obtain a final well-fitting model, the ECVI is also of interest.

In reviewing these fit indices, we see that the hypothesized model is relatively well fitting as indicated by a CFI of .941 and a RMSEA value of .048, which is well within the recommended range of acceptability (< .05 to .08). In addition, the ECVI for this initially hypothesized model is 2.032. This value, as noted earlier in the book, has no substantive meaning; rather, it is used within a relative framework. (For a review of these rule-of-thumb guidelines, you may wish to consult Chapter 3, where goodness-of-fit indices are described in more detail.)

Modification indices

Over and above the fit of the model as a whole, however, a review of the MIs reveals some evidence of misfit in the model. Because we are interested solely in the causal paths of the model at this point, only a subset of indices related to the regression weights is included in Table 6.7. Turning to this table, you will note that the first 10 MIs are enclosed in a rectangle. These parameters represent the structural (i.e., causal) paths in the model and are the only MIs of interest. The reason for this statement is because in working with full SEMs, any misfit to components of the measurement model should be addressed when that portion of the model is tested for its validity. Some of the remaining MIs in Table 6.7 represent the cross-loading of an indicator variable onto a factor other than the one it was designed to measure (EE3 <--- CC). Others represent the regression of one indicator variable on another; these MIs are substantively meaningless.[4]

In reviewing the information encased within the rectangle, we note that the maximum MI is associated with the regression path flowing from Classroom Climate to Depersonalization (DP<--- CC). The value of 24.776 indicates that, if this parameter were to be freely estimated in a subsequent model, the overall χ^2 value would drop by at least this

Table 6.7 Selected AMOS Output for
Hypothesized Model: Modification Indices

Regression weights	M.I.	Par Change
SE <---EE	10.039	–.047
SE <---ELC	9.253	–.138
SE <---DP	17.320	–.099
ELC <---RC	19.554	.108
ELC <---RA	6.905	.060
ELC <---EE	10.246	.047
ELC <---SE	20.273	–.184
ELC <---DP	8.513	.068
DP <---CC	24.776	–.351
DP <---SE	12.249	–.260
EE3 <---CC	9.711	–.220
EE3 <---DM	6.915	–.085
EE3 <---RA	10.453	.135
•		
•		
•		
•		

amount. If you turn now to the parameter change statistic related to this parameter, you will find a value of –0.351; this value represents the approximate value that the newly estimated parameter would assume. I draw your attention also to the four highlighted regression path MIs. The common link among these parameters is that the direction of the path runs counter to the general notion of the postulated causal model. That is, given that the primary focus is to identify determinants of teacher burnout, the flow of interest is from left to right; these high-lighted paths flow from right to left. Although, admittedly, there may be some legitimate reciprocal paths, they are not of substantive interest in the present study.

In data preparation, the TSS items measuring Classroom Climate were reflected such that low scores were indicative of a poor classroom milieu, and high scores, of a good classroom milieu. From a substantive perspective, it would seem perfectly reasonable that elementary school teachers whose responses yielded low scores for Classroom Climate should concomitantly display high levels of depersonalization. Given the meaningfulness of this influential flow, then, the model was reestimated with the path from Classroom Climate to Depersonalization specified as a freely estimated parameter; this model is subsequently labeled as Model 2. Results related to this respecified model are subsequently discussed within the framework of post hoc analyses.

Post Hoc analyses

Selected AMOS output: Model 2

In the interest of space, only the final model of burnout, as determined from the following post hoc model-fitting procedures, will be displayed. However, relevant portions of the AMOS output pertinent to each respecified model are presented and discussed.

Model assessment

Goodness-of-fit summary
The estimation of Model 2 yielded an overall $\chi^2_{(435)}$ value of 995.019, a CFI of .945, and a RMSEA of .046; the ECVI value was 1.975. Although the improvement in model fit for Model 2, compared with that of the originally hypothesized model, would appear to be trivial on the basis of the CFI and RMSEA values, the model difference nonetheless was statistically significant ($\Delta\chi^2_{(1)}$ = 35.873). Moreover, the parameter estimate for the path from Classroom Climate to Depersonalization was slightly higher than the one predicted by the expected parameter change statistic

Table 6.8 Selected AMOS Output for
Model 2: Modification Indices

Regression weights	M.I.	Par change
SE <--- EE	9.898	−.047
SE <--- ELC	9.156	−.138
SE <--- DP	14.692	−.092
ELC <--- RC	19.604	.108
ELC <--- RA	6.906	.060
ELC <--- EE	10.291	.047
ELC <--- SE	20.311	−.184
ELC <--- DP	7.774	.066
DP <--- SE	11.422	−.236
EE3 <--- CC	14.843	−.274
EE3 <--- DM	7.568	−.089
EE3 <--- RA	11.108	.140
•		
•		
•		
•		
DP2 <--- PA2	6.968	−.103

(−0.479 versus −0.351), and it was statistically significant (C.R. = −5.712). Modification indices related to the structural parameters for Model 2 are shown in Table 6.8.

Modification indices

In reviewing the boxed statistics presented in Table 6.8, we see that there are still nine MIs that can be taken into account in the determination of a well-fitting model of burnout, albeit four of these (highlighted and discussed earlier) are not considered in light of their reverse order of causal impact. The largest of these qualifying MIs (MI = 20.311) is associated with a path flowing from Self-Esteem to External Locus of Control (ELC <--- SE), and the expected value is estimated to be −.184. Substantively, this path again makes good sense as it seems likely that teachers who exhibit high levels of self-esteem are likely to exhibit low levels of external locus of control. On the basis of this rationale, we again focus on the path associated with the largest MI. Accordingly, the causal structure was again respecified—this time, with the path from Self-Esteem to External Locus of Control freely estimated (Model 3).

Selected AMOS output: Model 3

Model assessment

Goodness-of-fit summary   Model 3 yielded an overall $\chi^2_{(434)}$ value of 967.244, with CFI = .947 and RMSEA = .045; the ECVI was 1.932. Again, the χ^2 difference between Models 2 and 3 was statistically significant ($\Delta\chi^2_{(1)}$ = 27.775). Modification indices related to Model 3 are shown in Table 6.9. Of initial import here is the fact that the number of MIs has now dropped from nine to only four, with only one of the original four reverse-order causal links now highlighted. This discrepancy in the number of MI values between Model 2 and Model 3 serves as a perfect example of why the incorporation of additional parameters into the model must be done one at a time.

Modification indices

Reviewing the boxed statistics here, we see that the largest MI (17.074) is associated with a path from Self-Esteem to Emotional Exhaustion (EE <--- SE). However, it is important that you note that an MI (9.642) related to the reverse path involving these factors (SE <--- EE) is also included as an MI. As emphasized in Chapter 3, parameters identified by AMOS as belonging in a model are based on statistical criteria only; of more import, is the substantive meaningfulness of their inclusion. Within the context of the original study, the incorporation of this latter path (SE <--- EE) into the model would make no sense whatsoever since its primary purpose was to validate the impact of organizational and personality variables on burnout, and not the

Table 6.9 Selected AMOS Output for
Model 3: Modification Indices

Regression weights	M.I.	Par change
SE <--- EE	9.642	−.046
EE <--- SE	17.074	−.408
ELC <--- RC	14.322	.090
DP <--- SE	11.467	−.236
EE3 <--- CC	14.858	−.274
EE3 <--- DM	6.916	−.085
EE3 <--- RA	11.117	.140
•		
•		
•		
•		

reverse. Thus, again we ignore this suggested model modification.[5] Because it seems reasonable that teachers who exhibit high levels of self-esteem may, concomitantly, exhibit low levels of emotional exhaustion, the model was reestimated once again, with this path freely estimated (Model 4).

Selected AMOS output: Model 4

Model assessment

Goodness-of-fit summary The estimation of Model 4 yielded a χ^2 value of 943.243, with 433 degrees of freedom. Values related to the CFI and RMSEA were .949 and .044, respectively; the ECVI value was 1.895. Again, the difference in fit between this model (Model 4) and its predecessor (Model 3) was statistically significant ($\Delta\chi^2_{(1)} = 24.001$). Modification indices related to the estimation of Model 4 are presented in Table 6.10.

Modification indices

In reviewing these boxed statistics, note that the MI associated with the former regression path flowing from Emotional Exhaustion to Self-Esteem (SE <--- EE) is no longer present. We are left only with the paths leading from Role Conflict to External Locus of Control (ELC <--- RC), and from Self-Esteem to Depersonalization (DP <--- SE). Although the former is the larger of the two (MI = 15.170 versus 10.277), the latter exhibits the larger parameter change statistic (–.225 versus .093). Indeed, some methodologists (e.g., Kaplan, 1989) have suggested that it may be more appropriate to base respecification on size of the parameter change statistic, rather than on the MI (but recall Bentler's [2005] caveat noted in Chapter 3, footnote 8 that these values can be affected by both the scaling and identification of factors and variables). Given that this parameter is substantively meaningful, Model 4 was respecified to include the estimation of a regression path leading from Self-Esteem to Depersonalization in a model now labeled Model 5.

Table 6.10 Selected AMOS Output for Model 4: Modification Indices

Regression weights			M.I.	Par change
ELC	<---	RC	15.170	.093
DP	<---	SE	10.277	–.225
EE3	<---	CC	14.213	–.266
EE3	<---	DM	6.419	–.081
EE3	<---	RA	10.156	.133

Selected AMOS output: Model 5 assessment

Goodness-of-fit summary

Results from the estimation of Model 5 yielded a $\chi^2_{(432)}$ value of 928.843, a CFI of .951, and a RMSEA of .044; the ECVI value was 1.874. Again, the improvement in model fit was found to be statistically significant ($\Delta\chi^2_{(1)}$ = 14.400). Finally, the estimated parameter value (–.315), which exceeded the parameter change statistic estimated value, was also statistically significant (C.R. = –.3.800). Modification indices related to this model are presented in Table 6.11.

Modification indices

Not unexpectedly, a review of the output related to Model 5 reveals an MI associated with the path from Role Conflict to External Locus of Control (ELC <--- RC); note that the expected parameter change statistic has remained minimally unchanged (.092 versus .093). Once again, from a substantively meaningful perspective, we could expect that high levels of role conflict would generate high levels of external locus of control, thereby yielding a positive expected parameter change statistic value. Thus, Model 5 was respecified with the path (ELC <--- RC) freely estimated, and labeled as Model 6.

Selected AMOS output: Model 6

Up to this point in the post hoc modeling process, we have focused on only the addition of parameters to the model. Given that all additional structural paths, as identified by the MIs, were found to be justified, we need to look now at the flip side of the coin—those originally specified structural paths that are shown to be redundant to the model. This issue of model parsimony is addressed in this section.

Model assessment

Goodness-of-fit summary   Estimation of Model 6 yielded an overall $\chi^2_{(431)}$ value of 890.619; again, the χ^2 difference between Models 5 and 6 was statistically significant ($\Delta\chi^2_{(1)}$ = 38.224), as was the estimated parameter (.220, C.R. = 5.938), again much larger than the estimated parameter change statistic value of .092. Model fit statistics were as follows: CFI = .954 and RMSEA = .042; and the ECVI dropped a little further to 1.814, thereby indicating that Model 6 represented the best fit to the data thus far in the analyses. As expected, no MIs associated with structural paths were present in the output; only MIs related to the regression weights of factor loadings remained. Thus, no further consideration was given to the inclusion of additional parameters. Unstandardized estimates related to Model 6 are presented in Table 6.12.

The issue of model parsimony

Thus far, discussion related to model fit has focused solely on the addition of parameters to the model. However, another side to the question of fit, particularly as it pertains to a full model, is the extent to which

Table 6.11 Selected AMOS Output for
Model 5: Modification Indices

Regression weights	M.I.	Par change
ELC <--- RC	15.018	.092
EE3 <--- CC	14.167	−.266
EE3 <--- DM	6.738	−.084
EE3 <--- RA	10.655	.137
EE3 <--- SE	12.563	−.265
EE3 <--- ELC	10.180	.259
EE3 <--- DP	6.390	.108
EE3 <--- PA	22.520	−.265
EE3 <--- PA1	19.718	−.171
EE3 <--- ELC5	6.593	.117
EE3 <--- ELC3	6.245	.132
EE3 <--- CC1	8.821	−.166
EE3 <--- CC2	12.087	−.180
EE3 <--- CC4	12.397	−.156
EE3 <--- SE3	10.572	−.180
EE3 <--- SE1	11.125	−.221
EE3 <--- SE2	6.045	−.141
EE3 <--- PA3	14.149	−.135
EE3 <--- PA2	12.627	−.129
EE3 <--- ELC2	9.459	.157
EE3 <--- SS1	6.569	−.065
EE3 <--- RA2	12.402	.111
ELC5 <--- CC2	6.477	.084
ELC5 <--- SE2	6.345	−.092
ELC4 <--- CC	10.326	−.155
ELC4 <--- CC3	8.802	−.119
ELC4 <--- CC4	10.106	−.096
CC1 <--- RC	7.393	−.074

•
•
•
•

Table 6.12 Selected AMOS Output for Model 6: Unstandardized Estimates
Regression Weights: Structural Paths

			Estimate	S.E.	C.R.	P
SE	<---	DM	.734	.204	3.592	***
SE	<---	SS	−.475	.151	−3.147	.002
SE	**<---**	**PS**	**−.042**	**.071**	**−.595**	**.552**
EE	<---	RC	.782	.081	9.694	***
EE	<---	CC	−.361	.109	−3.309	***
EE	<---	SE	−.544	.111	−4.889	***
DP	<---	EE	.326	.040	8.217	***
DP	**<---**	**RC**	**−.051**	**.061**	**−.839**	**.402**
ELC	**<---**	**DM**	**−.035**	**.025**	**−1.400**	**.161**
DP	<---	CC	−.469	.083	−5.636	***
ELC	<---	SE	−.182	.045	−4.056	***
DP	<---	SE	−.310	.082	−3.766	***
ELC	<---	RC	.220	.037	5.938	***
PA	<---	DP	−.229	.051	−4.476	***
PA	**<---**	**EE**	**−.058**	**.033**	**−1.773**	**.076**
PA	<---	RA	−.096	.045	−2.145	.032
PA	<---	SE	.217	.071	3.042	.002
PA	**<---**	**ELC**	**−.068**	**.076**	**−.895**	**.371**
DP2	<---	DP	1.000			
DP1	<---	DP	1.166	.074	15.853	***
RA2	<---	RA	1.000			
RA1	<---	RA	.852	.050	16.949	***
RC2	<---	RC	1.346	.082	16.481	***
RC1	<---	RC	1.000			
			Factor covariances			
RA	<-->	RC	.486	.044	11.011	***
DM	<-->	CC	.183	.027	6.673	***
DM	<-->	SS	1.116	.077	14.507	***
SS	<-->	PS	.478	.049	9.756	***
DM	<-->	PS	.536	.049	10.827	***
PS	<-->	CC	.101	.021	4.856	***
RA	<-->	DM	−.627	.053	−11.777	***
RA	<-->	SS	−.630	.054	−11.570	***
RA	<-->	PS	−.345	.038	−9.159	***
RA	<-->	CC	−.150	.023	−6.539	***
RC	<-->	DM	−.508	.050	−10.092	***

(*continued*)

Table 6.12 Selected AMOS Output for Model 6: Unstandardized Estimates Regression Weights: Structural Paths (*Continued*)

		Estimate	S.E.	C.R.	P
		Factor Covariances			
RC	<-->SS	−.498	.051	−9.751	***
RC	<-->PS	−.262	.034	−7.644	***
RC	<-->CC	−.152	.022	−6.929	***
SS	<-->CC	.163	.029	5.629	***
		Factor Variances			
RA		.654	.060	10.879	***
RC		.575	.065	8.890	***
DM		.988	.085	11.566	***
SS		1.360	.090	15.103	***
PS		.668	.057	11.626	***
CC		.240	.028	8.717	***

*** probability < .000

certain initially hypothesized paths may be irrelevant to the model as evidenced from their statistical nonsignificance. In reviewing the structural parameter estimates for Model 6, we see highlighted five parameters that are nonsignificant; these parameters represent the paths from Peer Support to Self-Esteem (SE <--- PS; C.R.= −.595), from Role Conflict to Depersonalization (DP <--- RC; C.R.= −.839), from Decision Making to External Locus of Control (ELC <--- DM; −1.400), from Emotional Exhaustion to Personal Accomplishment (PA <--- EE; −1.773), and from External Locus of Control to Personal Accomplishment (PA <--- ELC; −.895). In the interest of parsimony, then, a final model of burnout needs to be estimated with these five structural paths deleted from the model. Importantly, as can be seen in Table 6.12, given that the factor of Peer Support (PS) neither has any influence on other factors nor is influenced by other factors in the model, it no longer has any meaningful relevance and thus needs also to be eliminated from the model. Finally, before leaving Model 6 and Table 6.12, note that all factor variances and covariances are found to be statistically significant.

Because standardized estimates are typically of interest in presenting results from structural equation models, it is usually of interest to request these statistics when you have determined your final model. Given that Model 7 will serve as our final model representing the determinants of teacher burnout, this request was made by clicking on the *Analysis Properties* icon (🖩), which, as demonstrated in Chapter 5, triggers the related dialog box and tabs. Select the *Output* tab and elect to have the standardized estimates included in the output file. In addition, it is also cogent to ask for the squared multiple correlations, an option made available on the same tab.

Selected AMOS output: Model 7 (final model)

As this revised model represents the final full SEM model to be tested in this chapter, several components of the AMOS output file are presented and discussed. We begin by reviewing results related to the model assessment, which are displayed in Table 6.13.

Model assessment

Goodness-of-fit summary As shown in Table 6.13, estimation of this final model resulted in an overall $\chi^2_{(382)}$ value of 803.875. At this point, you may wonder why there is such a big difference in this χ^2 value and its degrees of freedom compared with all previous models. The major reason, of course, is due to the deletion of one factor from the model (Peer Support).[6] Relatedly, this deletion changed the number of sample moments, which in turn substantially altered the number of degrees of freedom.

Table 6.13 Selected AMOS Output for Model 7 (Final Model): Goodness-of-Fit Statistics

Model	NPAR	CMIN	DF	P	CMIN/DF
Default model	83	803.875	382	.000	2.104
Saturated model	465	.000	0		
Independence model	30	9812.661	435	.000	22.558

| | **Baseline comparisons** | | | | |
| | NFI | RFI | IFI | TLI | |
Model	Delta1	rho1	Delta2	rho2	CFI
Default model	.918	.907	.955	.949	.955
Saturated model	1.000		1.000		1.000
Independence model	.000	.000	.000	.000	.000

| | **RMSEA** | | | |
Model	RMSEA	LO 90	HI 90	PCLOSE
Default model	.043	.039	.047	.998
Independence model	.190	.187	.193	.000

| | **ECVI** | | | |
Model	ECVI	LO 90	HI 90	MECVI
Default model	1.622	1.492	1.765	1.637
Saturated model	1.555	1.555	1.555	1.640
Independence model	16.509	15.976	17.054	16.515

To ensure that you completely understand how these large differences occurred, let's just review this process as outlined earlier in the book.

The Peer Support factor had two indicator variables, PS1 and PS2. Thus, following its deletion, the number of observed measures dropped from 32 to 30. Based on the formula (p × [p + 1]/2) discussed earlier in the book, this reduction resulted in 30 × 31/2 (465) distinct sample moments (or elements in the covariance matrix). Given the estimation of 83 parameters, the number of degrees of freedom is 382 (465 – 83). By comparison, had we retained the Peer Support factor, the number of sample moments would have been 32 × 33/2 (528). The number of estimated parameters would have increased by 9 (1 factor loading, 2 error variances, 1 factor variance, and 5 factor covariances), resulting in a total of 92, and 436 (528 – 92) degrees of freedom. However, in the interest of scientific parsimony, as noted earlier, given its presence as an isolated factor having no linkages with other factors in the model, I consider it most appropriate to exclude the factor of Peer Support from the model. Of import here is that this resulting change to the model now renders it no longer "nested" within the original model. As such, it would be inappropriate to calculate a chi-square difference value.

As evidenced from the remaining goodness-of-fit indices, this final model represented an excellent fit to the data (CFI = .955; RMSEA = .039). The ECVI value of 1.622 signals that this final, and most parsimonious, model represents the best fit to the data overall. We turn next to an examination of the parameter estimates, which are presented in Table 6.14.

Parameter estimates

Both the unstandardized and standardized estimates are presented in Table 6.14. However, in the interest of space, they are shown for only the structural paths and factor covariances; all factor and error variances (not shown), however, were found to be statistically significant. Turning first to the unstandardized estimates for the structural parameter paths, we see that all are statistically significant as indicated by the critical values and their related p-values. In a review of the standardized estimates, however, there are two values that are somewhat worrisome given their values greater than 1.00; these represent the paths flowing from Decision Making to Self-Esteem (SE <--- DM) and from Superior Support to Self-Esteem (SE <--- SS). Although all remaining standardized estimates are sound, the two aberrant estimates signal the need for further investigation.

A review of the factor covariances again shows all to be statistically significant. However, in reviewing the standardized estimates, we again see a disturbingly high correlation between the factors of Decision Making and Superior Support (DM <---> SS), which clearly ties in with the excessively high estimates for the related factors noted in the previous section.

Table 6.14 Selected AMOS Output for Model 7 (Final Model): Unstandardized and Standardized Estimates

	Estimate	S.E.	C.R.	P
Structural paths (regression weights)				
SE <--- DM	.614	.130	4.723	***
SE <--- SS	−.393	.110	−3.559	***
EE <--- RC	.777	.080	9.743	***
EE <--- CC	−.363	.109	−3.332	***
EE <--- SE	−.554	.110	−5.019	***
DP <--- EE	.317	.034	9.422	***
DP <--- CC	−.450	.080	−5.622	***
DP <--- SE	−.289	.081	−3.569	***
PA <--- DP	−.288	.044	−6.533	***
PA <--- RA	−.132	.040	−3.307	***
PA <--- SE	.240	.070	3.427	***
ELC <--- SE	−.193	.044	−4.390	***
ELC <--- RC	.252	.030	8.483	***
Standardized regression weights				
SE <--- DM	1.393			
SE <--- SS	−1.038			
EE <--- RC	.490			
EE <--- CC	−.147			
EE <--- SE	−.203			
DP <--- EE	.477			
DP <--- CC	−.275			
DP <--- SE	−.159			
PA <--- DP	−.377			
PA <--- RA	−.174			
PA <--- SE	.173			
ELC <--- SE	−.205			
ELC <--- RC	.463			
Factor covariances				
RA <--> RC	.490	.044	11.054	***
DM <--> CC	.187	.028	6.715	***
DM <--> SS	1.120	.077	14.529	***
RA <--> DM	−.634	.054	−11.811	***
RA <--> SS	−.629	.054	−11.555	***
RA <--> CC	−.149	.023	−6.523	***
RC <--> DM	−.517	.051	−10.185	***

(continued)

Table 6.14 Selected AMOS Output for Model 7 (Final Model): Unstandardized and Standardized Estimates (*Continued*)

	Estimate	S.E.	C.R.	P
Factor covariances				
RC <--> SS	−.504	.051	−9.825	***
RC <--> CC	−.152	.022	−6.913	***
SS <--> CC	.161	.029	5.575	***
Factor correlations				
RA <--> RC	.797			
DM <--> CC	.381			
DM <--> SS	.960			
RA <--> DM	−.784			
RA <--> SS	−.668			
RA <--> CC	−.378			
RC <--> DM	−.679			
RC <--> SS	−.568			
RC <--> CC	−.407			
SS <--> CC	.282			

*** probability < .000

Given these related atypical estimates, I consider it important to further probe the appropriateness of factors specified as determinants of teacher burnout. Before closing out this chapter, I return to this important and challenging issue, but first, let's complete our review of this final model by turning to results for the squared multiple correlations (SMCs), which are reported in Table 6.15.

The SMC is a useful statistic that is independent of all units of measurement. Once it is requested, AMOS provides an SMC for each endogenous variable in the model. Thus, in Table 6.15, you will see SMC values for each dependent factor in the model (SE, EE, DP, PA, ELC) and for each of the factor-loading regression paths (EE1 to RA2). The SMC value represents the proportion of variance that is explained by the predictors of the variable in question. For example, in order to interpret the SMC associated with Self-Esteem (SE; circled), we need first to review Figure 6.9 to ascertain which factors in the model serve as its predictors. Accordingly, we determine that 24.6% of the variance associated with Self-Esteem is accounted for by its two predictors—Decision Making (DM) and Superior Support (SS). Likewise, we can determine that the factor of Superior Support explains 90.2% of the variance associated with its second indicator variable (SS2; circled). The final version of this model of burnout for elementary teachers is schematically presented in Figure 6.10.

Table 6.15 Selected AMOS
Output for Model 7 (Final Model):
Squared Multiple Correlations

Parameter	Estimate
SE	.242
EE	.447
DP	.516
PA	.337
ELC	.324
EE1	.792
EE2	.840
EE3	.752
DP1	.696
DP2	.561
PA1	.732
PA2	.509
PA3	.515
ELC1	.480
ELC2	.332
ELC3	.540
ELC4	.442
ELC5	.632
CC1	.384
CC2	.590
CC3	.438
CC4	.485
SE1	.595
SE2	.667
SE3	.804
SS1	.794
SS2	.902
DM1	.505
DM2	.649
WO1	.574
WO2	.408
RC1	.465
RC2	.622
RA1	.520
RA2	.672

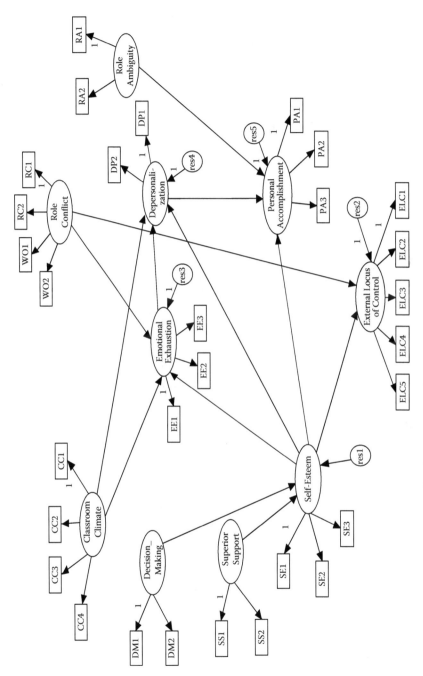

Figure 6.10 Final model of burnout for elementary teachers.

Let's return now to the problematic estimates noted earlier with respect to structural paths leading from Self-Esteem (SE) to Decision Making (DM), and to Superior Support (SS), and the factor correlation between DM and SS. Clearly the difficulty arises from an overlap of content in the items measuring these three constructs. Aside from a thorough investigation of the items involved, another approach might be to specify and test two alternative models of teacher burnout. In the first model (Model A), combine the factors of DM and SS by loading the two SS indicator variables onto the DM factor, as we did in the case of Role Conflict and Work Overload. In the second model (Model B), delete the factor of SS completely from the model. Schematic presentations of Models A and B are presented in Figures 6.11 and 6.12, respectively. Although restrictions of space prevent me from addressing these analyses here, I strongly encourage you to experiment yourself in testing these two alternative models using the same data that were used in testing the hypothesized model tested in this chapter, which can be found in the book's companion Web site.

In working with structural equation models, it is very important to know when to stop fitting a model. Although there are no firm rules or regulations to guide this decision, the researcher's best yardsticks include

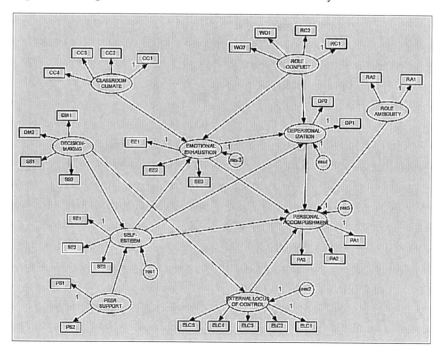

Figure 6.11 Alternative hypothesized model of teacher burnout: Combined decision making and superior support factors (Model A).

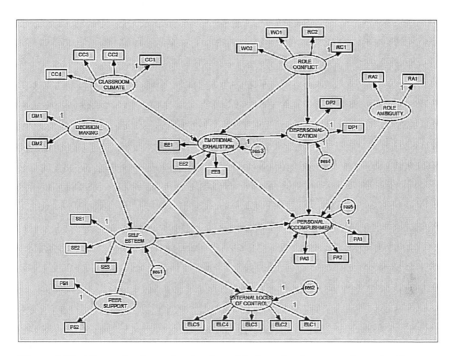

Figure 6.12 Alternative hypothesized model of teacher burnout: Superior Support factor deleted (Model B).

(a) a thorough knowledge of the substantive theory, (b) an adequate assessment of statistical criteria based on information pooled from various indices of fit, and (c) a watchful eye on parsimony. In this regard, the SEM researcher must walk a fine line between incorporating a sufficient number of parameters to yield a model that adequately represents the data, and falling prey to the temptation of incorporating too many parameters in a zealous attempt to attain the best-fitting model statistically. Two major problems with the latter tack are that (a) the model can comprise parameters that actually contribute only trivially to its structure, and (b) the more parameters there are in a model, the more difficult it is to replicate its structure should future validation research be conducted.

In bringing this chapter to a close, it may be instructive to summarize and review findings from the various models tested. *First*, of 13 causal paths specified in the revised hypothesized model (see Figure 6.8), eight were found to be statistically significant for elementary teachers. These paths reflected the impact of (a) classroom climate and role conflict on emotional exhaustion; (b) decision making and superior support on self-esteem; (c) self-esteem, role ambiguity, and depersonalization on perceived personal accomplishment; and (d) emotional exhaustion on depersonalization.

Second, five paths, not specified a priori (classroom climate → depersonalization; self-esteem → external locus of control; self-esteem → emotional exhaustion; role conflict → external locus of control; and self-esteem → depersonalization), proved to be essential components of the causal structure; given their substantive meaningfulness, they were subsequently added to the model. *Third,* five hypothesized paths (peer support → self-esteem; role conflict → depersonalization; decision making → external locus of control; emotional exhaustion → personal accomplishment; and external locus of control → personal accomplishment) were not statistically significant and were therefore deleted from the model. *Finally,* in light of the ineffectual impact of peer support on burnout for elementary teachers, this construct was also deleted from the model. In broad terms, based on our findings from this full SEM application, we can conclude that role ambiguity, role conflict, classroom climate, participation in the decision-making process, and the support of one's superiors are potent organizational determinants of burnout for elementary school teachers. The process, however, appears to be strongly tempered by one's sense of self-worth.

Endnotes

1. To facilitate interpretation, particular items were reflected such that high scores on Role Ambiguity, Role Conflict, Work Overload, EE, DP, and External Locus of Control represented negative perceptions, and high scores on the remaining constructs represented positive perceptions.
2. For example, it may be that to attain a more appropriate CFA model in representing the data at hand, the specification of a cross-loading or error covariance is needed.
3. Although my recommendation would be to include also the standardized root mean square residual (SRMR; see Byrne, 2006), the value of which should be < .10, this coefficient is not specifically included in the model fit section of the AMOS output file.
4. As previously noted, the present version of AMOS provides no mechanism for excluding MIs such as these from the output file.
5. Of course, had a nonrecursive model represented the hypothesized model, such feedback paths would be of interest.
6. Had we left that factor in, we would have gained five degrees of freedom due to the deletion of five structural paths, thereby changing the number of degrees of freedom to 436.

section three

Applications in multiple-group analyses

chapter seven

Testing for the factorial equivalence of scores from a measuring instrument
(First-order CFA model)

Up to this point, all applications have illustrated analyses based on single samples. In this section, however, we focus on applications involving more than one sample where the central concern is whether or not components of the measurement model and/or the structural model are equivalent (i.e., invariant) across particular groups of interest. Throughout this chapter and others involving multigroup applications, the terms *equivalence* and *invariance* are used synonymously (likewise, the adjectives *equivalent* and *invariant*); use of either term is merely a matter of preference.

In seeking evidence of multigroup equivalence, researchers are typically interested in finding the answer to one of five questions. *First*, do the items comprising a particular measuring instrument operate equivalently across different populations (e.g., gender, age, ability, and culture)? In other words, is the measurement model group-invariant? *Second*, is the factorial structure of a single instrument or of a theoretical construct equivalent across populations as measured either by items of a single assessment measure, or by subscale scores from multiple instruments? Typically, this approach exemplifies a construct validity focus. In such instances, equivalence of both the measurement and structural models are of interest. *Third*, are certain paths in a specified causal structure equivalent across populations? *Fourth*, are the latent means of particular constructs in a model different across populations? *Finally*, does the factorial structure of a measuring instrument replicate across independent samples drawn from the same population? This latter question, of course, addresses the issue of cross-validation. Applications presented in this chapter, as well as the next two chapters, provide you with specific examples of how each of these questions can be answered using structural equation modeling based on the AMOS graphical approach. The applications illustrated in Chapters 7 and 9 are based on the analysis of covariance structures (COVS), whereas the application in Chapter 8 is based on the analysis of mean and covariance structures (MACS). When analyses are based on COVS, only the variances and covariances of the observed variables are of interest; all single-group applications illustrated thus far in this book have been based on the analysis of COVS. However, when analyses are based on MACS, the modeled data include both sample means and covariances. Details related to the MACS approach to invariance are addressed in Chapter 8.

In this first multigroup application, we test hypotheses related to the invariance of a single measuring instrument across two different panels of teachers. Specifically, we test for equivalency of the factorial measurement (i.e., scale items) of the Maslach Burnout Inventory (MBI; Maslach & Jackson, 1986)[1] and its underlying latent structure (i.e., relations among dimensions of burnout) across elementary and secondary teachers. Purposes of the original study, from which this example is taken (Byrne, 1993), were (a) to test for the factorial validity of the MBI separately for each of three teacher groups, (b) given findings of inadequate fit, to propose and test an alternative factorial structure, (c) to cross-validate this structure over independent samples within each teacher group, and (d) to test for the equivalence of item measurements and theoretical structure across the three teaching panels. Only analyses bearing on tests for equivalence across total samples of elementary ($n = 1{,}159$) and secondary ($n = 1{,}384$) teachers are of interest in the present chapter.[2] Before reviewing the model under scrutiny, however, allow me first to provide you with a brief overview of the general procedure involved in tests for equivalence across groups.

Testing for multigroup invariance: The general notion

Development of a procedure capable of testing for multigroup invariance derives from the seminal work of Jöreskog (1971b). Accordingly, Jöreskog recommended that all tests for equivalence begin with a global test of the equality of covariance structures across the groups of interest. Expressed more formally, this initial step tests the null hypothesis (H_0), $\Sigma_1 = \Sigma_2 = \ldots \Sigma_G$, where Σ is the population variance–covariance matrix, and G is the number of groups. Rejection of the null hypothesis then argues for the nonequivalence of the groups and, thus, for the subsequent testing of increasingly restrictive hypotheses in order to identify the source of nonequivalence. On the other hand, if H_0 cannot be rejected, the groups are considered to have equivalent covariance structures, and, thus, tests for invariance are not needed. Presented with such findings, Jöreskog recommended that group data should be pooled and all subsequent investigative work based on single-group analyses.

Although this omnibus test appears to be reasonable and fairly straightforward, it often leads to contradictory findings with respect to equivalencies across groups. For example, sometimes the null hypothesis is found to be tenable, yet subsequent tests of hypotheses related to the equivalence of particular measurement or structural parameters must be rejected (see, e.g., Jöreskog, 1971b). Alternatively, the global null hypothesis may be rejected, yet tests for the equivalence of measurement and structural invariance hold (see, e.g., Byrne, 1988a). Such inconsistencies in the global test for equivalence stem from the fact that there is no baseline model for the test of invariant variance–covariance matrices, thereby making it substantially more restrictive than is the case for tests of invariance related to sets of model parameters. Indeed, any number of inequalities may possibly exist across the groups under study. Realistically, then, testing for the equality of specific sets of model parameters would appear to be the more informative and interesting approach to multigroup invariance.

In testing for equivalencies across groups, sets of parameters are put to the test in a logically ordered and increasingly restrictive fashion. Depending on the model and hypotheses to be tested, the following sets of parameters are most commonly of interest in answering questions related to multigroup equivalence: (a) factor loadings, (b) factor covariances, and (c) structural regression paths. Historically, the Jöreskog tradition of invariance testing held that the equality of error variances and their covariances should also be tested. However, it is now widely accepted that to do so represents an overly restrictive test of the data. Nonetheless, there may be particular instances where findings bearing on the equivalence or nonequivalence of these parameters can provide important information (e.g., scale items); we'll visit this circumstance in the present chapter.

The testing strategy

Testing for factorial equivalence encompasses a series of hierarchical steps that begins with the determination of a baseline model for each group separately. This model represents the one that best fits the data from the perspectives of both parsimony and substantive meaningfulness. Addressing the somewhat tricky combination of model fit and model parsimony, it ideally represents one for which fit to the data and minimal parameter specification are optimal. Following completion of this preliminary task, tests for the equivalence of parameters are conducted across groups at each of several increasingly stringent levels. Jöreskog (1971b) argued that these tests should most appropriately begin with scrutiny of the measurement model. In particular, the pattern of factor loadings for each observed measure is tested for its equivalence across the groups. Once it is known which measures are group-invariant, these parameters are constrained equal while subsequent tests of the structural parameters are conducted. As each new set of parameters is tested, those known to be group-invariant are cumulatively constrained equal. Thus, the process of determining nonequivalence of measurement and structural parameters across groups involves the testing of a series of increasingly restrictive hypotheses. We turn now to the invariance tests of interest in the present chapter.

The hypothesized model

In my preliminary single-group analyses reported in Byrne (1993), I found that, for each teacher group, MBI Items 12 and 16 were extremely problematic; these items were subsequently deleted, and a model proposed in which only the remaining 20 items were used to measure the underlying construct of burnout.[3] This 20-item version of the MBI provides the basis for the hypothesized model under test in the determination of the baseline model for each teacher group and is presented schematically in Figure 7.1. If this model fits the data well for both groups of teachers, it will remain the hypothesized model under test for equivalence across the two groups. On the other hand, should the hypothesized model of MBI structure exhibit a poor fit to the data for either elementary or secondary teachers, it will be modified accordingly and become the hypothesized multigroup model under test. We turn now to this requisite analysis.

Establishing baseline models: The general notion

Because the estimation of baseline models involves no between-group constraints, the data can be analyzed separately for each group. However, in testing for invariance, equality constraints are imposed on particular parameters and, thus, the data for all groups must be analyzed simultaneously to obtain efficient estimates (Bentler, 2005; Jöreskog & Sörbom, 1996a); the pattern of fixed and free parameters nonetheless remains consistent with the baseline model specification for each group.[4] However, it is important to note that because measuring instruments are often group specific in the way they operate, it is possible that these baseline models may not be completely identical across groups (see Bentler, 2005; Byrne, Shavelson, & Muthén, 1989). For example, it may be that the best-fitting model for one group includes an error covariance (see, e.g., Bentler, 2005) or a cross-loading (see, e.g., Byrne, 1988b, 2004; Reise, Widaman, & Pugh, 1993), whereas these parameters may not be specified for the other group. Presented with such findings, Byrne et al. (1989) showed that by implementing a condition of *partial measurement invariance*, multigroup analyses can still continue. As such, some but not all measurement parameters are constrained equal across groups in the testing for structural equivalence

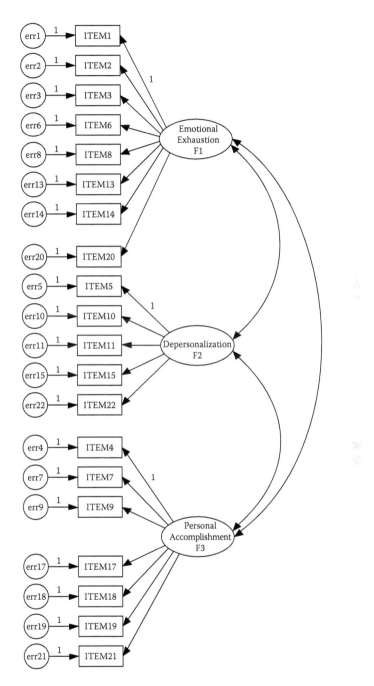

Figure 7.1 Initially hypothesized model of 20-item MBI structure for elementary and secondary teachers.

or latent factor mean differences. It is important to note, however, that over the intervening years, the concept of partial measurement equivalence has sparked a modest debate in the technical literature (see Millsap & Kwok, 2004; Widaman & Reise, 1997). Nonetheless, its application remains a popular strategy in testing for multigroup equivalence and is especially so in the area of cross-cultural research. The perspective taken in this book is consistent with our original postulation that a priori knowledge of major model specification differences is critical to the application of invariance-testing procedures.

Establishing the baseline models: Elementary and secondary teachers

In testing for the validity of scores related to the proposed 20-item MBI model for each teacher group, findings were consistent across panels in revealing exceptionally large error covariances between Items 1 and 2, and between Items 5 and 15. As was discussed in Chapter 4, these error covariances can reflect overlapping content between each item pair. Although overlap between Items 1 and 2 was also problematic with the narrower sample of elementary male teachers (see Chapter 4), its presence here with respect to the much larger samples of elementary and secondary teachers (no gender split) further substantiates the troublesome nature of these two MBI items, both of which are designed to measure emotional exhaustion. Item 1 expresses the notion of feeling emotionally drained from one's work; Item 2 talks about feeling used up at the end of the day. Clearly, these two items appear to be expressing the same idea, albeit the wording has been slightly modified. In a similar manner, Items 5 and 15, both designed to measure depersonalization, showed the same overlapping effects for the gender-free full sample of elementary and secondary teachers. Item 5 asks the respondent to reflect on the extent to which he or she treats some students as impersonal objects, while Item 15 taps into the feeling of not caring what happens to some students.[5]

Because many readers may wish to replicate these analyses based on the same data found on the book's companion Web site, I consider it worthwhile to discuss briefly the findings pertinent to each group of teachers. We turn first to the elementary teachers. With a modification index (MI) of 189.195 and an expected parameter change statistic (EPC) of .466, it is clear that the error covariance between Items 1 and 2 represents a major model misspecification. Likewise, the same situation holds for the error covariance involving Items 5 and 15 (MI = 56.361; EPC = .284),[6] albeit somewhat less dramatically. In addition, based on Model 3 in which the two previous error covariances were specified, results revealed an MI value of 44.766 and a EPC value of .337 related to an error covariance between Items 6 and 5.

Although these values are relatively high and close to those for the error covariance between Items 5 and 15, support for their specification is more difficult to defend substantively. Item 6, designed to measure Emotional Exhaustion, relates to stress incurred from working with people all day. In contrast, Item 5 is designed to measure Depersonalization and taps into the sense that the teacher feels he or she treats some students as if they are impersonal objects. Given an obvious lack of coherence between these two items, I consider it most appropriate not to add the error covariance between Items 5 and 6 to the model.

Let's turn now to the results for secondary teachers. Consistent with findings for elementary teachers, the initial test of the hypothesized model revealed excessively large MI (276.497) and EPC (.522) values representing an error covariance between Items 1 and 2. Likewise, results based on a test of Model 2 yielded evidence of substantial misspecification involving an error covariance between Items 5 and 15 (MI = 99.622; EPC = .414). In contrast to elementary teachers, however, results did not suggest any misspecification between the error terms related to Items 5 and 6. Nonetheless, an MI value of 45.104 related to an error covariance between Items 7 and 21 called for examination. Given the relatively small value of the EPC (.225), together with the incompatibility of item content, I dismissed the specification of this parameter in the model. Both items are designed to measure Personal Accomplishment. Whereas Item 7 suggests that the respondent deals effectively with student problems, Item 21 suggests that he or she deals effectively with emotional problems encountered in work. Although the content is somewhat similar from a general perspective, I contend that the specificity of Item 21 in targeting *emotional* problems argues against the specification of this parameter.

Although these modifications to the initially hypothesized model of MBI structure resulted in a much better fitting model for both elementary teachers ($\chi^2_{(165)}$ = 638.49; CFI = .92; RMSEA = .06) and secondary teachers ($\chi^2_{(165)}$ = 1083.39; CFI = .92; RMSEA = .06), the fit nonetheless was modestly good at best. However, in my judgment as explained above, it would be inappropriate to incorporate further changes to the model. As always, attention to parsimony is of utmost importance in SEM, and this is especially true in tests for multigroup equivalence. The more an originally hypothesized model is modified at this stage of the analyses, the more difficult it is to determine measurement and structural equivalence. Goodness-of-fit statistics related to the determination of the baseline models for each teacher group are summarized in Table 7.1.

Findings from this testing for a baseline model ultimately yielded one that was identically specified for elementary and secondary teachers. However, it is important to point out that just because the revised model was similarly specified for each teacher group, this fact in no

Table 7.1 Summary Goodness-of-Fit Statistics in Determination of Baseline Models

Model	χ^2	df	CFI	RMSEA	RMSEA 90% CI	ECVI
Elementary teachers						
1. Hypothesized three-factor model	1149.808	167	.893	.071	.067; .075	1.067
2. Model 1 with one error covariance specified (Items 1 and 2)	939.932	166	.916	.063	.060; .067	0.888
3. Model 2 with one error covariance specified (Items 5 and 15)	878.954	165	.922	.061	.057; .065	0.837
Secondary teachers						
1. Hypothesized three-factor model	1500.206	167	.877	.076	.072; .080	1.147
2. Model 1 with one error covariance specified (Items 1 and 2)	1190.005	166	.906	.067	.063; .070	0.924
3. Model 2 with one error covariance specified (Items 5 and 15)	1083.391	165	.916	.063	.060; .067	0.848

way guarantees the equivalence of item measurements and underlying theoretical structure; these hypotheses must be tested statistically. For example, despite an identically specified factor loading, it is possible that, with the imposition of equality constraints across groups, the tenability of invariance does not hold; that is, the link between the item and its target factor differs across the groups. Such postulated equivalencies, then, must be tested statistically.

As a consequence of modifications to the originally hypothesized 20-item MBI structure in the determination of baseline models, the hypothesized model under test in the present example is the revised 20-item MBI structure as schematically depicted in Figure 7.2. At issue is the extent to which its factorial structure is equivalent across elementary and secondary teachers. More specifically, we test for the equivalence of the factor loadings (measurement invariance) and factor correlations (structural invariance) across the teaching panels. In addition, it is instructive to test for cross-group equivalence of the two error covariances as this information reflects further on the validity of these particular items.

Modeling with AMOS Graphics

When working with analysis of covariance structures that involve multiple groups, the data related to each must of course be made known to the program. Typically, for most SEM programs, the data reside in some external file, the location of which is specified in an input file. In contrast, however, given that no input file is used with the graphical approach to AMOS analyses,[7] both the name of each group and the location of its data file must be communicated to the program prior to any analyses involving multiple groups. This procedure is easily accomplished via the *Manage Groups* dialog box, which, in turn, is made available by pulling down the *Model-Fit* menu and selecting the "Manage Groups" option as shown in Figure 7.3. Once you click on this option, you will be presented with the *Manage Groups* dialog box shown in Figure 7.4. However, when first presented, the text you will see in the dialog box will be *Group Number 1*. To indicate the name of the first group, click on *New* and replace the former text with the group name as shown for Elementary Teachers in Figure 7.4. Clicking on *New* again yields the text *Group Number 2*, which is replaced by the name *Secondary Teachers*. With more than two groups, each click produces the next group number and the process is repeated until all groups have been identified.

Once the group names have been established, the next task is to identify a data file for each. This procedure is the same as the one demonstrated earlier in the book for single groups, the only difference being that a filename for *each* group must be selected. The *Data File* dialog box for the

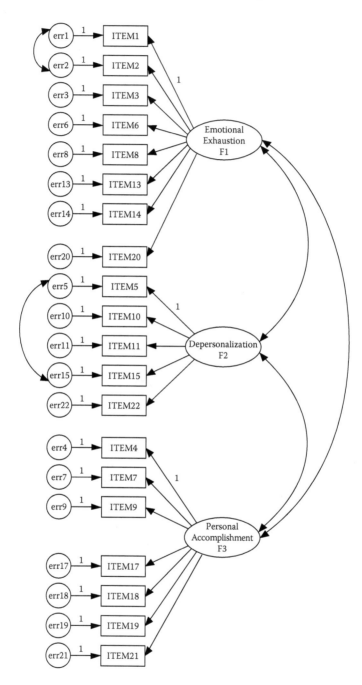

Figure 7.2 Hypothesized multigroup baseline model of MBI structure.

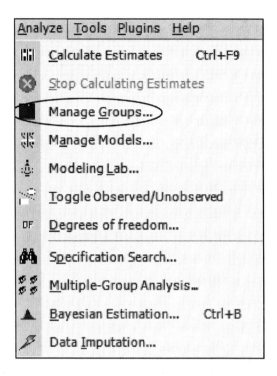

Figure 7.3 AMOS Graphics: Analyze drop-down menu showing selection of Manage Groups.

Figure 7.4 AMOS Graphics: Manage Groups dialog box showing labeling of a new group (Elementary Teachers).

present application that includes information related to both elementary (N = 1,159) and secondary (N = 1,384) teachers is shown in Figure 7.5.

Finally, specification of multigroup models in AMOS Graphics is guided by several basic default rules. One such default is that all groups

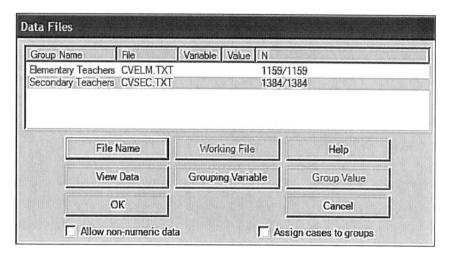

Figure 7.5 AMOS Graphics: Data Files dialog box: Identification of data files.

in the analysis will have the identical path diagram structure, unless explicitly declared otherwise. As a consequence, a model structure needs only to be drawn for the first group; all other groups will have the same structure by default. Thus, the hypothesized multigroup model shown in Figure 7.2 represents the one to be tested for its invariance across elementary and secondary teachers. On the other hand, should the baseline models be shown to differ in some way for each group, specific precautions that address this situation must be taken (for an example of this type of application, see Byrne, 2004).

Testing for multigroup invariance: The configural model

Having keyed in the name associated with each group, together with the related data files, we are now ready to proceed with the analyses. The initial step in testing for invariance requires only that the same number of factors and the factor-loading pattern be the same across groups. As such, no equality constraints are imposed on any of the parameters. Thus, the same parameters that were estimated in the baseline model for each group separately are again estimated in this multigroup model. In essence, then, you can think of the model being tested here as a multigroup representation of the baseline models. Accordingly, it incorporates the baseline models for elementary and secondary teachers within the same file. In the methodological literature, this model is commonly termed the *configural model;*

relatedly, we test for configural invariance. Of particular import in testing for configural invariance is that although the factor structure for each group is similar, it is *not* identical. Because no equality constraints are imposed on any parameters in the model, no determination of group differences related to either the items or the factor covariances can be made. Such claims derive from subsequent tests for invariance to be described shortly.

Given that we have already conducted this test in the establishment of baseline models, you are no doubt wondering why it is necessary to repeat the process. This multigroup model serves two important functions. *First*, it allows for invariance tests to be conducted across the two groups *simultaneously*. In other words, parameters are estimated for both groups at the same time. *Second*, in testing for invariance, the fit of this configural model provides the baseline value against which all subsequently specified invariance models are compared. Despite the multigroup structure of this and subsequent models, analyses yield only one set of fit statistics for overall model fit. When ML estimation is used, the χ^2 statistics are summative and, thus, the overall χ^2 value for the multigroup model should equal the sum of the χ^2 values obtained when the baseline model is tested separately for each group of teachers.[8] Consistent with single-group analyses, goodness-of-fit for this multigroup parameterization should exhibit a good fit to the data for both groups. Realistically, however, these multigroup fit statistics can never be better than those determined for each group separately. Thus, in light of only modestly good fit related to the baseline model for both elementary and secondary teachers, we cannot expect to see better results for this initial multigroup model.

Before testing for invariance related to the configural model, I addressed the caveat noted in note 8 (see end of chapter) and checked the *Emulisrel6* option listed on the *Estimation* tab of the *Analysis Properties* dialog box, illustrated in Figure 7.6. Because the AMOS output file for multigroup models may seem a little confusing at first, I now review selected portions as they relate to this initial model.

Selected AMOS output: The configural model (No equality constraints imposed)

Although this output definitely relates to the multigroup model, the program additionally provides separate information for each group under study. Because the basic output format for single-group analyses has been covered earlier in the book, I limit my review here to the *Parameter Summary* as it pertains only to elementary teachers. All other portions of the output focus on results for the two groups in combination. Let's turn first to Figure 7.7.

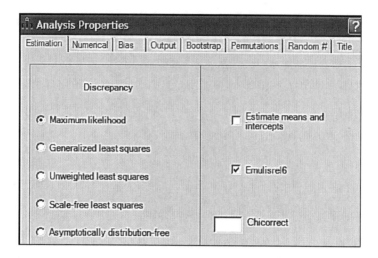

Figure 7.6 AMOS Graphics: Estimation tab of Output dialog box.

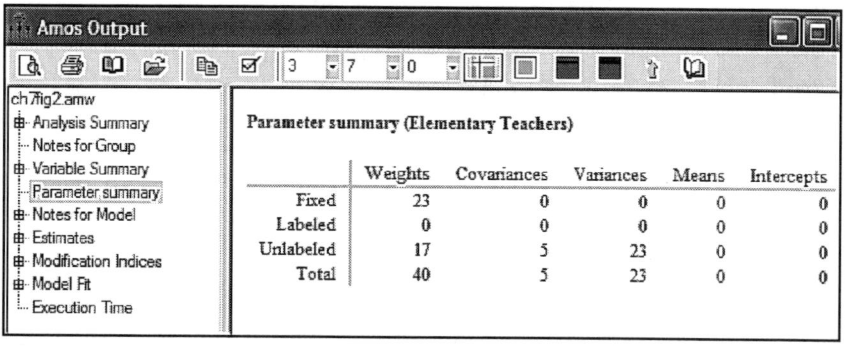

Figure 7.7 AMOS Graphics: Parameter summary for elementary teachers.

In reviewing Figure 7.7, you will see the usual text output tree in the narrow column on the left, from which you can select the portion of the output you wish to review. Not shown here due to space restrictions is the continuation of this vertical column where group names are listed. Given that I clicked on *Elementary Teachers* before selecting *Parameter Summary* from the output file tree, I was presented with the content shown in Figure 7.7; clicking on *Secondary Teachers*, of course, would yield results pertinent to that group. In this section of the output file, AMOS focuses on fixed and freely estimated parameters, the latter being further classified as *Labeled* and *Unlabeled*. Labeled parameters are those that are constrained equal to another group or parameter. Specifying equality constraints related to parameters was detailed in Chapter 5; specification for groups will be covered later in this chapter. Because no constraints have been imposed in this configural model, the output text shows zero labeled parameters. The only relevant parameters for this model are the regression paths representing the factor loadings (termed *Weights*), variances, and covariances, all of which are freely estimated.

Turning to results for the regression paths, we note that 23 are fixed, and 17 are freely estimated. The fixed parameters represent the 20 regression paths associated with the error terms, in addition to the three factor regression paths fixed to 1.00 for purposes of model identification; the 17 unlabeled parameters represent the estimated factor loadings. Continuing through the remainder of the table, the five covariances represent relations among the three factors plus the two error covariances. Finally, the 23 variances refer to the 20 error variances in addition to the 3 factor variances. In total, the number of parameters specified for the hypothesized multigroup model of MBI structure shown in Figure 7.2 is 68, of which 23 are fixed, and 45 freely estimated. However, recall that this number pertains only to one group—elementary teachers.

Let's turn now to Figure 7.8, where degrees of freedom information for the multigroup model is summarized. Under the heading *Computation of Degrees of Freedom (Your Model)*, we find three lines of information. The

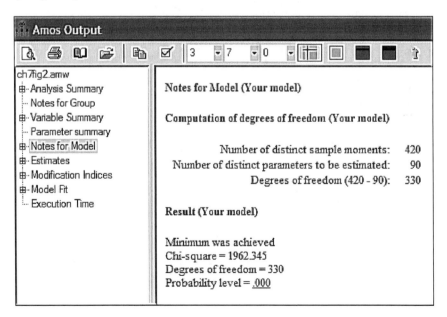

Figure 7.8 AMOS Graphics: Summary notes related to multigroup configural model.

first line relates to the number of sample moments (i.e., number of elements in the combined covariance matrices). In Chapter 2, you learned how to calculate this number for a single group. However, it may be helpful to review the computation relative to a multigroup application. Given that there are 20 observed variables (i.e., 20 items) in the hypothesized model, we know that, for one group, this would yield 210 (20 × 21 / 2) pieces of information (or, in other words, sample moments). Thus, for two groups, this number would be 420.

Line 2 in Figure 7.8 relates to the number of estimated parameters in the model. In Figure 7.7, we observed that this number (for elementary teachers) was 45 (17 + 5 + 23). Taking into account both groups, then, we have 90 estimated parameters. Degrees of freedom are reported on line 3 to be 330. Given 420 sample moments and 90 estimated parameters, this leaves us with 420 – 90 = 330 degrees of freedom. (For a review and explanation of these calculations, see Chapter 2.)

Model assessment

Let's turn now to Table 7.2, in which the goodness-of-fit statistics for this multigroup model are reported. The key values to note are those of the

Table 7.2 Goodness-of-Fit Statistics for Configural Model

Model	NPAR	CMIN	DF	P	CMIN/DF
Your model	90	1962.345	330	.000	5.946
Saturated model	420	.000	0		
Independence model	40	20445.418	380	.000	53.804

Baseline comparisons

Model	NFI Delta1	RFI rho1	IFI Delta2	TLI rho2	CFI
Your model	.904	.889	.919	.906	.919
Saturated model	1.000		1.000		1.000
Independence model	.000	.000	.000	.000	.000

RMSEA

Model	RMSEA	LO 90	HI 90	PCLOSE
Your model	.044	.042	.046	1.000
Independence model	.144	.142	.146	.000

χ^2 statistic, the CFI, and the RMSEA; the ECVI value is irrelevant in this context.

Results related to this first multigroup model testing for configural invariance reveal the χ^2 value to be 1,962.345 with 330 degrees of freedom. The CFI and RMSEA values, as expected, are .919 and .044, respectively. From this information, we can conclude that the hypothesized multigroup model of MBI structure is modestly well fitting across elementary and secondary teachers.

Having established goodness-of-fit for the configural model, we now proceed in testing for the invariance of factorial measurement and structure across groups. However, because you need to know how tests for invariance are specified using AMOS Graphics before trying to fully grasp an understanding of the invariance-testing process in and of itself, I present this material in two parts. First, I introduce you to two different approaches to testing for multigroup invariance in AMOS—*manual* versus *automated*—and then walk you through a test for invariance of the hypothesized multigroup model (see Figure 7.2) across elementary and secondary teachers within the framework of the manual approach. Application of the automated approach to testing for multigroup invariance is discussed and illustrated in Chapters 8 and 9.

Testing for measurement and structural invariance: The specification process

In testing for configural invariance, interest focused on the extent to which the number of factors and pattern of their structure were *similar* across elementary and secondary teachers. In contrast, in testing for measurement and structural invariance, interest focuses more specifically on the extent to which parameters in the measurement and structural components of the model are *equivalent* across the two groups. This testing process is accomplished by assigning equality constraints on particular parameters (i.e., the parameters are constrained equal across groups). The procedure operates in such a way that these parameters are estimated for the first group only; estimates for all remaining groups are constrained equal to those of the first group. In AMOS Graphics, constraints can be specified via two approaches: (a) individually assigning a label to each parameter to be held equal across groups, the approach taken in the earlier edition of this book (Byrne, 2001); and (b) using the automated models of parameter subsets contained in the *Multiple Group* dialog box. This latter approach was developed subsequent to the publication of the first edition. Although any parameters that are unlabeled will be freely estimated using the manual approach to invariance specification, this dictum does not hold for the automated approach. Despite the specification of selected parameters as freely estimated, their assigned labels remain on the graphical representation of the model albeit the related parameters are freely estimated (J. L. Arbuckle, personal communication, June 7, 2008). I begin by introducing you to the manual labeling approach to specification of equality constraints and then follow with the automated approach.

The manual multiple-group approach

In testing for invariance, my preference is to follow the classical approach, which entails first running a model in which only the factor loadings are constrained equal (i.e., a *measurement model*). Provided with evidence of group equivalence, these factor-loading parameters remain constrained and equality constraints are then placed on the factor variances and covariances (i.e., *structural model*). Although error variances associated with each of the observed variable items are also part of the measurement model, testing for their equality across groups is considered to be excessively stringent and therefore is rarely implemented. On the other hand, in our testing for the validity of the MBI, we determined two very strong and group-consistent error covariances. For both statistical and substantive reasons, I consider it important to include these particular error parameters in our test for invariance of the measurement model. *First*, each error covariance was found to be excessively large in both groups. *Second*, scrutiny of the related items revealed highly overlapping content across each aberrant pair of items. Such redundancy can reflect itself in the form of error covariation. Taking these two perspectives into account, it seems prudent to ascertain whether the two error covariance parameters hold across teaching panels as such evidence speaks to the problematic nature of the content related to these MBI items.

Specification of equality constraints using the manual approach entails two related steps. It begins by first clicking on the parameter you wish to label and then right-clicking on the mouse to produce the *Object Properties* dialog box (illustrated in previous chapters). Once this box is opened, the *Parameter* tab is activated, and then the label entered in the space provided in the bottom left corner. This process is graphically shown in Figure 7.9 as it relates to the labeling of the second factor regression path representing the loading of Item 2 on Factor 1 (Emotional Exhaustion). Once the cursor is clicked on the selected parameter, the latter takes on a red color. Right-clicking the mouse subsequently opens the *Object Properties* dialog box, where you can see that I have entered the label *L2* in the lower left corner under the heading *Regression Weight*. The second part of this initial step requires that you click on the *All Groups* box (shown within the ellipse in Figure 7.9). Checking this box tells the program that the parameter applies to both groups.[9]

Turning to Figure 7.10, you will see the factor loadings and two error covariances of the hypothesized model labeled and ready for a statistical

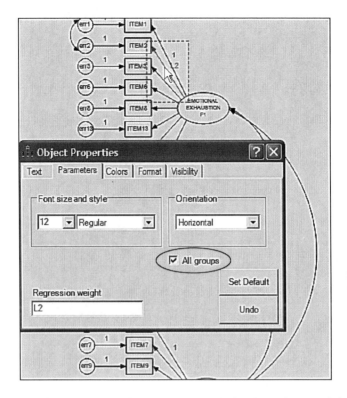

Figure 7.9 AMOS Graphics: Object Properties dialog box showing labeling of parameter.

testing of their invariance. However, three aspects of Figure 7.10 are note-worthy. *First,* selected labeling of parameters is purely arbitrary. In the present case, I chose to label the factor-loading regression paths as L. Thus, L2, for example, represents the loading of Item 2 on Factor 1. *Second,* you will note that the value of 1.00, assigned to the first of each congeneric set of indicator variables, remains as such and has not been relabeled with an "L"; given that this parameter is already constrained to equal 1.00, its value will be constant across the two groups. *Finally,* the somewhat erratic labeling of the factor-loading paths that may occur is a function of the automated label-ing process provided in AMOS. Although, technically, it should be possible to shift these labels to a more appropriate location using the *Move Parameter* tool ( ), this transition does not work well when there are several labeled parameters located in close proximity to one another, as is the case here. This malfunction appears to be related to the restricted space allotment assigned to each parameter. To use the *Move Parameters* tool, click either on

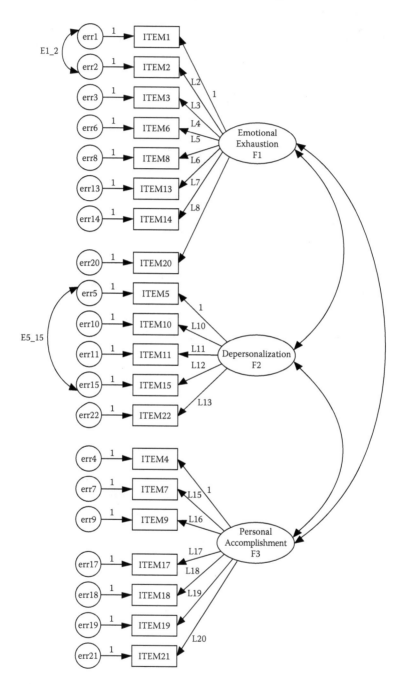

Figure 7.10 Baseline model with equality constraints specified for all factor loadings.

its icon in the toolbox, or on its name from the *Edit* drop-down menu. Once this tool is activated, point the cursor at the parameter you wish to relabel; the selected parameter will then take on a red color. Holding the left mouse button down will generate a broken line rectangle; continuing to hold this button enables you to move the rectangle to another location in close proximity to the selected parameter. This process is illustrated in Figure 7.11 as it relates to factor loading 8 (L8) representing Item 20.

As labeled, the hypothesized multigroup model in Figure 7.10 specifies the following parameters to be tested for group invariance: (a) 17 factor loadings, and (b) 2 error covariances (Items 1 and 2; Items 5 and 15).

Because the automated multiple approach to tests for invariance presents a fully labeled model by default (i.e., labeling associated with the factor loadings, variances, and covariances as well as the error variances), I additionally include here a model in which the factor variances and covariances, as well as the factor loadings and two error covariances, are postulated to be invariant (see Figure 7.12).

The automated multiple-group approach

This procedure is activated by either clicking on the *Multiple Group* icon ([::]), or by pulling down the *Analyze* menu and clicking on the *Multiple*

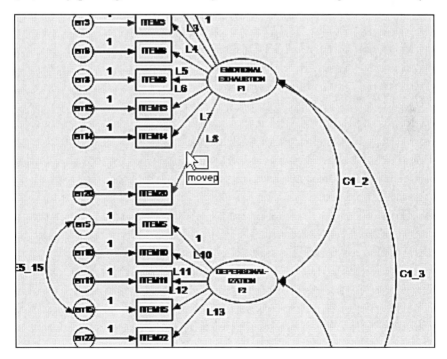

Figure 7.11 AMOS Graphics: Illustration of the Move Parameter tool in action.

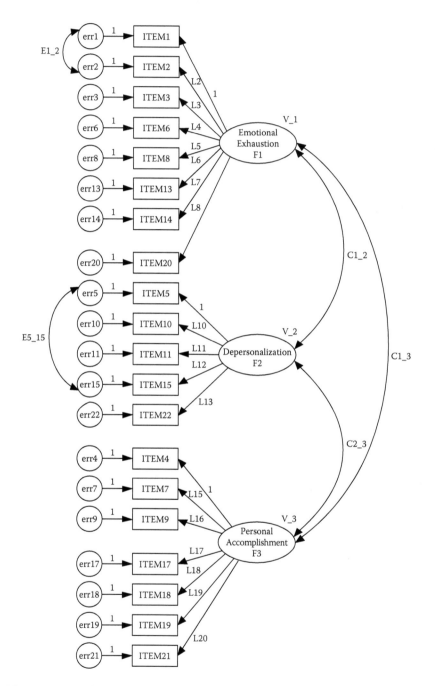

Figure 7.12 Baseline model with equality constraints specified for all factor load-ings, variances, and covariances.

Group tab as shown in Figure 7.13. Either action automatically produces the *Multiple Group Analysis* dialog box shown in Figure 7.14.

On the left side of this dialog box, you will see a list of parameter subsets, and along the top, a series of eight numbers, under each of which is a column of small squares. The darkest checkmarks that you see in the dialog box are default and represent particular models to be tested. When the dialog box is first opened, you will observe the three defaulted models shown in Figure 7.14. The checkmark in the first column (identified as "1") indicates a model in which only the factor loadings (i.e., measurement weights) are constrained equal across groups (Model 1). Turning to Columns 2 and 3, we see both dark and grayed checkmarks. The darkest checkmarks in Column 2 indicate a model in which all estimated factor loadings, as well as factor variances and covariances (i.e., structural covariances), are constrained equal across groups (Model 2); those in Column 3 represent a model having all estimated factor loadings, factor variances, factor covariances, and error variances (i.e., measurement residuals) constrained equal across groups

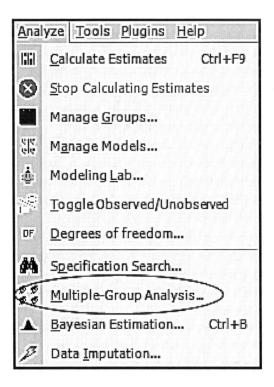

Figure 7.13 AMOS Graphics: Analyze drop-down menu showing selection of multiple-group analysis.

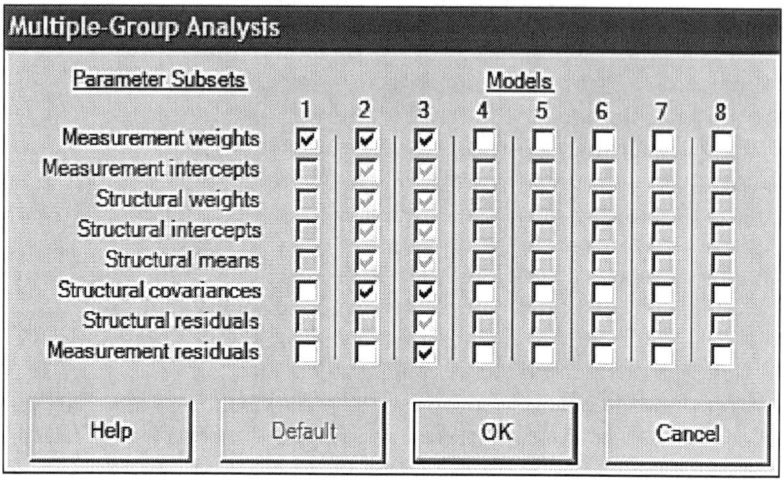

Figure 7.14 AMOS Graphics: Multiple Group dialog box showing specification of equality constraints on all factor loadings, factor variances and covariances, and error variances.

(Model 3). The grayed checkmarks in both columns represent parameter subsets that may be included in the testing of additional models.

Relating this approach to the checked dialog box shown in Figure 7.14 would be tantamount to testing Model 1 first, followed by a test of Model 2, as exemplified in Figures 7.10 and 7.12 for the manual approach to invariance. This process can continue with the addition of other parameter subsets, as deemed appropriate in testing any particular multigroup model. An important point to note in using AMOS Graphics, however, is the automated checkmarks related to Model 3. As noted earlier, measurement error variances are rarely constrained equal across groups as this parameterization is considered to be an excessively stringent test of multigroup invariance. Thus, the testing of Model 3 is relatively uncommon. However, one example of where Model 3 would be important is when a researcher is interested in testing for the equality of reliability related to an assessment scale across groups (see, e.g., Byrne, 1988a).

Although mentioned briefly in the introduction of this section, I consider it important to note again a major model specification aspect of this automated approach as currently implemented in AMOS (Version 17). Once you select the *Multiple Groups* option, AMOS automatically labels all parameters in the model whether or not you wish to constrain them equal across groups. For example, although we do not wish to test a multigroup model in which all error variances are postulated to be invariant across groups (Model 3), all labeling on the graphical model with respect to these parameters remains intact even though we wish not to have equality constraints on these parameters. Removal of these checkmarks (for Model 3) is easily accomplished by simply clicking on them. Although these error variances subsequently will not be estimated, the labeling of these parameters nonetheless remains on the "behind-the-scenes" working AMOS model.

Testing for measurement and structural invariance: Model assessment

As noted earlier, one major function of the configural model is that it provides the baseline against which all subsequent tests for invariance are compared. In the Jöreskog tradition, the classical approach in arguing for evidence of noninvariance is based on the χ^2 difference ($\Delta\chi^2$) test (see Chapter 4, note 7). The value related to this test represents the difference between the χ^2 values for the configural and other models in which equality constraints have been imposed on particular parameters. This difference value is distributed as χ^2 with degrees of freedom equal to the difference in degrees of freedom. Evidence of noninvariance is claimed if this χ^2 difference value is statistically significant. The researcher then follows up with additional tests aimed at targeting which parameters are accounting for these noninvariant findings. This procedure is demonstrated in the testing of both measurement and structural equivalence of the MBI in this chapter.

Over the past decade or so, applied researchers have argued that from a practical perspective, the χ^2 difference test represents an excessively stringent test of invariance and particularly in light of the fact that SEM models at best are only approximations of reality (Cudeck & Brown 1983; MacCallum, Roznowski, & Necowitz, 1992). Consistent with this perspective, Cheung and Rensvold (2002) reasoned that it may be more reasonable to base invariance decisions on a difference in CFI (ΔCFI) rather than on χ^2 values. Thus, based on a rigorous Monte Carlo study of several goodness-of-fit indices, Cheung and Rensvold proposed that evidence of noninvariance be based on a difference in CFI values exhibiting a probability < 0.01. Although this more recent and practical approach to testing for invariance has not been granted the official SEM stamp of approval to date, its use is increasingly reported in the literature—largely because it makes a lot of practical sense to do so. In reviewing results pertinent to tests for invariance of the MBI in this chapter, we will examine both the χ^2 difference and CFI difference results.

Testing for multigroup invariance: The measurement model

Now that you are familiar with the procedural steps conducted in testing for multigroup invariance, as well as with the two approaches to implementation of these procedures made available in AMOS Graphics, we now move on to actual implementation of these procedures as outlined earlier. In this chapter, we focus on only the manual approach to invariance testing; Chapters 8 and 9 address the automated approach.

Turning to the task at hand here, we examine results related to the labeled model shown in Figure 7.10. You will recall that this model, which we will call Model A to distinguish it from subsequently specified models and to simplify comparison of models, tests for the equivalence of all factor loadings plus two error covariances (Items 1 and 2; Items 5 and 15). Let's turn now to these results, which are summarized in Table 7.3.

Model assessment

A review of these results, as expected, reveals the fit of this model to be consistent with that of the configural model (CFI = .918; RMSEA = .043). However, of prime importance in testing for the invariance of the factor loadings and two error covariances are results related to the χ^2 difference and CFI difference tests. As noted earlier, computation of these results involves taking their differences from the χ^2 and CFI values reported for the configural model (see Table 7.2), which yields the following: $\Delta\chi^2_{(19)} = 35.912$ and ΔCFI = .001. Not surprisingly, given its statistical stringency, the χ^2 difference test argues for evidence of noninvariance, whereas the CFI difference test argues for invariance. That the $\Delta\chi^2$ test is said to argue for noninvariance is

Table 7.3 Goodness-of-Fit Statistics for Measurement Model

Model	NPAR	CMIN	DF	P	CMIN/DF
Your model	71	1998.257	349	.000	5.726
Saturated model	420	.000	0		
Independence model	40	20445.418	380	.000	53.804

Baseline comparisons

Model	NFI Delta1	RFI rho1	IFI Delta2	TLI rho2	CFI
Your model	.902	.894	.918	.911	.918
Saturated model	1.000		1.000		1.000
Independence model	.000	.000	.000	.000	.000

RMSEA

Model	RMSEA	LO 90	HI 90	PCLOSE
Your model	.043	.041	.045	1.000
Independence model	.144	.142	.146	.000

based on the finding that a χ^2 value of 35.912, with 19 degrees of freedom, is shown on the χ^2 distribution table to be statistically significant at a probability value < .01. On the other hand, the ΔCFI value of .001 contends that the measurement model is completely invariant in that this value is less than the .01 cutoff point proposed by Cheung and Rensvold (2002).

Presented with these divergent findings, the decision of which one to accept is purely an arbitrary one and rests solely with each individual researcher. It seems reasonable to assume that such decisions might be based on both the type of data under study and/or the circumstances at play. For our purposes here, however, I consider it worthwhile to focus on the $\Delta\chi^2$ results as it provides me with the opportunity to walk you through the subsequent steps involved in identifying which parameters in the model are contributing to these noninvariant findings; we press on then with the next set of analyses.

In testing for multigroup invariance, it is necessary to establish a logically organized strategy, the first step being a test for invariance of all factor loadings, which we have now been completed. Given findings of noninvariance at this level, we then proceed to test for the invariance of all factor loadings comprising each subscale (i.e., all loadings related to the one particular factor) separately. Given evidence of noninvariance at the subscale level, we then test for the invariance of each factor loading (related to the factor in question) separately. Of import in this process is that, as factor-loading parameters are found to be invariant across groups, their specified equality constraints are maintained, *cumulatively*, throughout the remainder of the invariance-testing process.

Having determined evidence of noninvariance when all factor loadings are held equal across groups, our next task is to test for the invariance of factor loadings relative to each subscale separately. This task is easily accomplished in AMOS Graphics through a simple modification of the existing labeled model shown in Figure 7.10. As such, we remove all factor-loading labels, except those associated with Emotional Exhaustion (Factor 1), simply by clicking on each label (to be deleted), right-clicking in order to trigger the *Object Properties* dialog box, and then deleting the label listed in the parameter rectangle of the dialog box (see Figure 7.9). Proceeding in this manner presents us with the labeled model (Model B) displayed in Figure 7.15; all unlabeled parameters will be freely estimated for both elementary and secondary teachers.

Turning to Table 7.4, we see that the testing of Model B yielded a χ^2 value of 1969.118 with 339 degrees of freedom. This differential of 9 degrees of freedom derives from the equality constraints placed on seven factor loadings (the first loading is already fixed to 1.0) plus the two error covariances. Comparison with the configural model yields a $\Delta\chi^2_{(9)}$ value of 6.173, which is not statistically significant.

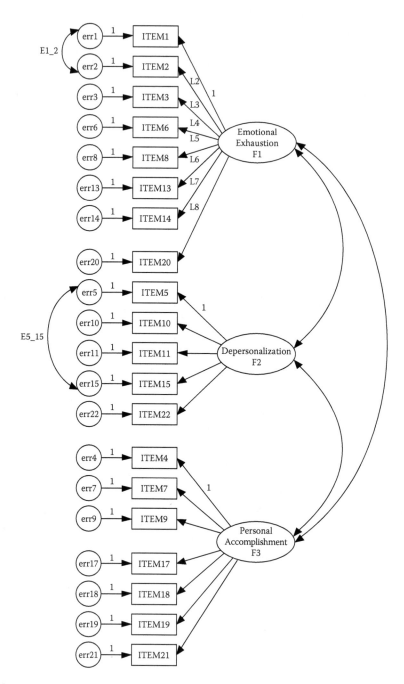

Figure 7.15 Baseline model with equality constraints specified for all factor loadings on EE only.

Table 7.4 Goodness-of-Fit Statistics for Measurement Model (Model 2)

		CMIN			
Model	NPAR	CMIN	DF	P	CMIN/DF
Your model	81	1969.118	339	.000	5.809
Saturated model	420	.000	0		
Independence model	40	20445.418	380	.000	53.804

		Baseline comparisons			
	NFI	RFI	IFI	TLI	
Model	Delta1	rho1	Delta2	rho2	CFI
Your model	.904	.892	.919	.909	.919
Saturated model	1.000		1.000		1.000
Independence model	.000	.000	.000	.000	.000

		RMSEA			
Model	RMSEA	LO 90	HI 90	PCLOSE	
Your model	.044	.042	.045	1.000	
Independence model	.144	.142	.146	.000	

These findings advise us that all items designed to measure Emotional Exhaustion are operating equivalently across the two groups of teachers. Our next task, then, is to test for the equivalence of items measuring Depersonalization. Accordingly, we place equality constraints on all freely estimated factor loadings associated with Factor 2, albeit at the same time, maintaining equality constraints for Factor 1 (Model C). Again, this specification simply means a modification of the model shown in Figure 7.15 in that labels are now added to the four estimated factor loadings for Depersonalization.

Because you are now familiar with the process involved in labeling these models and in the interest of space, no further figures or separate tables are presented for models yet to be tested. Results for these subsequent models are summarized in Table 7.5.

As reported in Table 7.5, the test of Model C yielded a χ^2 value of 1977.807 with 343 degrees of freedom; the additional 4 degrees of freedom derive from the equality constraints placed on the four estimated factor loadings for Factor 2. These results therefore yielded a $\Delta\chi^2_{(13)}$ value of 15.462, which once again is statistically nonsignificant. Provided with this information, we now know that the problematic items are housed in the subscale designed to measure Personal Accomplishment. Accordingly, we proceed

Table 7.5 Goodness-of-Fit Statistics for Tests of Multigroup Invariance: A Summary

Model description	Comparative model	χ^2	df	$\Delta\chi^2$	Δdf	Statistical significance	CFI	ΔCFI
1. Configural model; no equality constraints imposed	—	1962.345	330	—	—	—	.919	—
2. Measurement model								
(Model A) All factor loadings constrained equal.	2A versus 1	1998.257	349	35.912	19	$p < .001$	.918	.001
(Model B) Factor loadings for only EE constrained equal.	2B versus 1	1969.118	339	6.173	9	NS	.919	.000
(Model C) Factor loadings for only EE and DP constrained equal.	2C versus 1	1977.807	343	15.462	13	NS	.919	.000
(Model D) Model C with factor loading for Item 7 (PA) constrained equal.	2D versus 1	1980.466	344	18.121	14	NS	.918	.001
(Model E) Model C with factor loadings for Items 7 and 9 (on PA) constrained equal.	2E versus 1	1980.487	345	18.142	15	NS	.918	.001
(Model F) Model C with factor loadings for Items 7, 9, and 17 (on PA) constrained equal.	2F versus 1	1993.232	346	30.887	16	$p < .01$	.918	.001

		χ^2	df	$\Delta\chi^2$	Δdf	p	CFI	ΔCFI
(Model G) Model C with factor loadings for Items 7, 9, and 18 (on PA) constrained equal.	2G versus 1	1989.077	346	26.732	16	$p < .05$	.918	.001
(Model H) Model C with factor loadings for Items 7, 9, and 19 (on PA) constrained equal.	2H versus 1	1980.705	346	18.360	16	NS	.919	.000
(Model I) Model C with factor loadings for Items 7, 9, 19, and 21 (on PA) constrained equal.	2I versus 1	1980.956	347	18.611	17	NS	.919	.000
3. Structural model Model 2.I with covariances among EE, DP, and PA constrained equal.	3 versus 1	1986.048	350	23.703	20	NS	.918	.000

Note: $\Delta\chi^2$ = difference in χ^2 values between models; Δdf = difference in number of degrees of freedom between models; ΔCFI = difference in CFI values between models; EE = Emotional Exhaustion; DP= Depersonalization; PA = Personal Accomplishment.

by labeling (on the model) and testing one factor loading at a time within this subscale. Importantly, provided with evidence of nonsignificance related to a single factor loading, this invariant loading is held constrained during subsequent tests of the remaining items. Results related to these individual loadings are discussed as a group and reported in Table 7.5.

In reviewing these tests of individual factor loadings measuring Factor 3, Personal Accomplishment, findings reveal evidence of noninvariance related to two items—Item 17 ($p < .01$) and Item 18 ($p < .05$) (see results for measurement models F and G). Item 17 suggests that the respondent is able to create a relaxed atmosphere with his or her students, and Item 18 conveys the notion that a feeling of exhilaration follows from working closely with students. From these findings we learn that, for some reason, Items 17 and 18 are operating somewhat differently in their measurement of the intended content for elementary and secondary teachers. The task for the researcher confronted with these noninvariant findings is to provide possible explanations of this phenomenon.

Before moving on to a test of structural invariance, I consider it important to further clarify results reported in Table 7.5 with respect to measurement models F, G, and H. Specifically, it's important that I explain why each of these models has the same number of degrees of freedom. For Model F, of course, 16 degrees of freedom derives from the fact that we have added an equality constraint for Item 17 over and above the constraints specified in the previous model (Model E). Model G has 16 degrees of freedom because noninvariant Item 17 is now freely estimated with Item 18 constrained in its place. Likewise, Model H has 16 degrees of freedom as Item 19 replaced noninvariant Item 18, which is now freely estimated. Hopefully, this explanation should clear up any questions that you may have had concerning these results.

Testing for multigroup invariance: The structural model

Now that equivalence of the measurement model has been established, the next step in the process is to test for invariance related to the structural portion of the model. Although these tests can involve the factor variances as well as the factor covariances, many researchers consider the latter to be of most interest; I concur with this notion. In particular, testing for the invariance of factor covariances addresses concerns regarding the extent to which the theoretical structure underlying the MBI (in this case) is the same across groups.

In this part of the testing process, the model specifies all factor loadings except those for Items 17 and 18, in addition to the three factor covariances constrained equal across elementary and secondary teachers. This final model is presented in Figure 7.16. Given the rather poor labeling

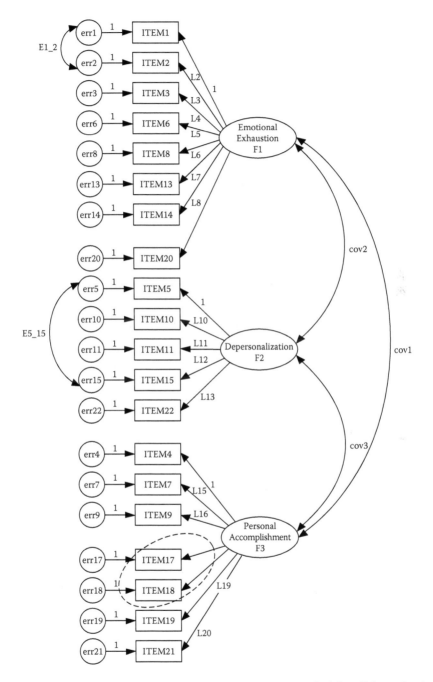

Figure 7.16 Baseline model with equality constraints specified for all factor loadings on EE and DP, and those representing Items 7, 9, 19, and 21 on PA.

mechanism for this model, I show the two noninvariant factor loadings for Items 17 and 18 encased in a broken-line oval; the fact that their factor loading regression paths are not labeled ensures that they are freely estimated. Results for this test of structural invariance, as reported in Table 7.5, revealed the factor covariances to be equivalent across elementary and secondary teachers.

Endnotes

1. For a detailed description of the MBI, readers are referred to Chapter 4 of the present volume.
2. Middle-school teachers comprised the third group.
3. For a more detailed account of analyses leading up to the 20-item model, readers are referred to the original article (Byrne, 1993).
4. In my experience of working with multigroup models in AMOS, I have found it best to establish three files—one for each of the single-group analyses in establishing the baseline models, and one multigroup file containing the final best fitting baseline model for each group.
5. As noted in Chapter 4, due to refusal of the MBI test publisher to grant copyright permission, I am unable to reprint the item here for your perusal.
6. Recall that in post hoc analyses, the specification of additional parameters in AMOS must be done one at a time. Accordingly, the error covariance between items 5 and 15 was determined on the basis of Model 2, in which only the error covariance between Items 1 and 2 was specified.
7. An input file is used in the case of modeling with VB.NET or C#, two analytic alternatives provided in the AMOS program for those who may prefer not to use the graphical approach (for details, see Arbuckle, 2007).
8. Although this fact is always exactly true with the LISREL and EQS programs, it is exactly true in AMOS if, and only if, a checkmark is placed next to *Emulisrel6* on the *Estimations* tab of the *Analysis Properties* dialog box; otherwise, it is almost, but not quite exactly, true (J. L. Arbuckle, personal communication, June 6, 2008).
9. Prior to AMOS 16, the *All Groups* box was checked by default, which meant that labeling a parameter in one group automatically assigned the same name to the corresponding parameter in another group. Since the advent of AMOS 16, however, the *All Groups* box is unchecked by default (J. L. Arbuckle, personal communication, June 20, 2008).

chapter eight

Testing for the equivalence of latent mean structures
(First-order CFA model)

In the years since the printing of my first AMOS book (Byrne, 2001), there has been a steady, yet moderate increase in reported findings from tests for multigroup equivalence. A review of the SEM literature, however, reveals most tests for invariance to have been based on the analysis of covariance structures (COVS), as exemplified in Chapters 7 and 9 of this volume. Despite Sörbom's (1974) introduction of the mean and covariance structures (MACS) strategy in testing for latent mean differences over 30 years ago, only a modicum of studies have been designed to test for latent mean differences across groups based on real (as opposed to simulated) data (see, e.g., Aikin, Stein, & Bentler, 1994; Byrne, 1988b; Cooke, Kosson, & Michie, 2001; Little, 1997; Marsh & Grayson, 1994; Reise, Widaman, & Pugh, 1993; Widaman & Reise, 1997). The aim of this chapter, then, is to introduce you to basic concepts associated with the analysis of latent mean structures, and to walk you through an application that tests for their invariance across two groups. Specifically, we test for differences in the latent means of general, academic, English, and mathematics self-concepts across high- and low-track secondary school students. The example presented here draws from two published papers—one that focuses on methodological issues related to testing for invariant covariance and mean structures (Byrne et al., 1989), and one oriented toward substantive issues related to social comparison theory (Byrne, 1988b).

Basic concepts underlying tests of latent mean structures

In the usual univariate or multivariate analyses involving multigroup comparisons, one is typically interested in testing whether the *observed* means representing the various groups are statistically significantly different from each other. Because these values are directly calculable from the raw data, they are considered to be *observed* values. In contrast, the means of latent variables (i.e., latent constructs) are *unobservable*; that is, they are not directly observed. Rather, these latent constructs derive their structure indirectly from their indicator variables, which, in turn, are directly observed and, hence, measurable. Testing for the invariance of mean structures, then, conveys the notion that we intend to test for the equivalence of means related to each underlying construct or factor. Another way of saying the same thing, of course, is that we intend to test for differences in the latent means (of factors for each group).

For all the examples that we have considered thus far, the analyses have been based on *covariance structures*. As such, only parameters representing regression coefficients, variances, and covariances have been of interest. Accordingly, the covariance structure of the observed variables constitutes the crucial parametric information; a hypothesized model can thus be estimated and tested via the sample covariance matrix. One limitation of this level of invariance is that while the unit of measurement for the underlying factors (i.e., the factor loading) is identical across groups, the origin of the scales (i.e., the intercepts) is not. As a consequence, comparison of latent factor means is not possible, thereby leading Meredith (1993) to categorize this level of invariance as "weak" factorial invariance. This limitation notwithstanding, evidence of invariant factor loadings nonetheless permits researchers to move on in testing further for the equivalence of factor variances, factor covariances, and the pattern of these factorial relations, a focus of substantial interest to researchers interested more in construct validity issues than in testing for latent mean differences. These subsequent tests would continue to be based on the analysis of COVS.

In the analysis of covariance structures, it is implicitly assumed that all observed variables are measured as deviations from their means; in other words, their means are equal to zero. As a consequence, the intercept terms generally associated with regression equations are not relevant to the analyses. However, when the observed means take on nonzero values, the intercept parameter must be considered, thereby necessitating a reparameterization of the hypothesized model. Such is the case when one is interested in testing for the invariance of latent *mean structures*. To help you in understanding the concept of mean structures, I draw on the work of Bentler (2005) in demonstrating the difference between covariance and mean structures as it relates to a simple bivariate regression equation. Consider, first, the following regression equation:

$$y = \alpha + \beta x + \varepsilon \tag{1}$$

where α is an intercept parameter. Although the intercept can assist in defining the mean of y, it does not generally equal the mean. Now, if we take expectations of both sides of this equation, and assume that the mean of ε is zero, the above expression yields:

$$\mu_y = \alpha + \beta\mu_x \tag{2}$$

where μ_y is the mean of y, and μ_x is the mean of x. As such, y and its mean can now be expressed in terms of the model parameters α, β, and μ_x. It is this decomposition of the mean of y, the dependent variable, that leads to the term *mean structures*. More specifically, it serves to characterize a model in which the means of the dependent variables can be expressed or "structured" in terms of structural coefficients and the means of the independent variables. The above equation serves to illustrate how the incorporation of a mean structure into a model necessarily includes the new parameters α and μ_x, the intercept and observed mean (of x), respectively. Thus, models with structured means merely extend the basic concepts associated with the analysis of covariance structures.

In summary, any model involving mean structures may include the following parameters:

- Regression coefficients
- Variances and covariances of the independent variables
- Intercepts of the dependent variables
- Means of the independent variables

As a consequence, these models involve the analysis of both covariance and mean structures.

Estimation of latent variable means

As with the invariance applications presented in Chapters 7 and 9, this application of a structured means model involves testing simultaneously across two groups.[1] The multigroup model illustrated in this chapter is used when one is interested in testing for group differences in the means of particular latent constructs. This approach to the estimation of latent mean structures was first brought to light in Sörbom's (1974) seminal extension of the classic model of factorial invariance. As such, testing for latent mean differences across groups is made possible through the implementation of two important strategies—*model identification* and *factor identification*.

Model identification

Given the necessary estimation of intercepts associated with the observed variables, in addition to those associated with the unobserved latent constructs, it is evident that the attainment of an overidentified model is possible only with the imposition of several specification constraints. Indeed, it is this very issue that complicates, and ultimately renders impossible, the estimation of latent means in single-group analyses. Multigroup analyses, on the other hand, provide the mechanism for imposing severe restrictions on the model such that the estimation of latent means is possible. More specifically, because two (or more) groups under study are tested simultaneously, evaluation of the identification criterion is considered across groups. As a consequence, although the structured means model may not be identified in one group, it can become so when analyzed within the framework of a multigroup model. This outcome occurs as a function of specified equality constraints across groups. More specifically, these equality constraints derive from the underlying assumption that both the observed variable intercepts and the factor loadings are invariant across groups.

Factor identification

This requirement imposes the restriction that the factor intercepts for one group be fixed to zero; this group then operates as a reference group against which latent means for the other group(s) are compared. The reason for this reconceptualization is that when the intercepts of the measured variables are constrained equal across groups, this leads to the latent factor intercepts having no definite origin (i.e., they are undefined in a statistical sense). A standard way of fixing the origin, then, is to set the factor intercepts of one group to zero (see Bentler, 2005; Jöreskog & Sörbom, 1996). As a consequence, factor intercepts are interpretable only in a relative sense. That is to say, one can test whether the latent variable means for one group *differ* from those of another, but one *cannot* estimate the mean of each factor in a model for each group. In other words, while it is possible to test for latent mean differences between, say, adolescent boys and girls, it is not possible to estimate, simultaneously, the mean of each factor for both boys and girls; the latent means for one group must be constrained to zero.

Having reviewed the conceptual and statistical underpinning of the mean structures model, I now introduce you to the hypothesized model under study in this chapter.

The hypothesized model

The application to be examined in this chapter addresses equivalency of the latent factor means related to four self-concept (SC) dimensions (general, academic, English, and mathematics) for high ($n = 582$) and low ($n = 248$) academically tracked high school students (Byrne, 1988b). The substantive focus of the initial study (Byrne, 1988b) was to test for latent mean differences in multidimensional SCs across these two ability groups. This

CFA model followed from an earlier study designed to test for the multidimensionality of SC (Byrne & Shavelson, 1986), as portrayed schematically in Figure 8.1.

As you will note in the figure, except for academic SC, the remaining dimensions are measured by three indicator variables, each of which represents a subscale score. Specifically, general SC is measured by subscale

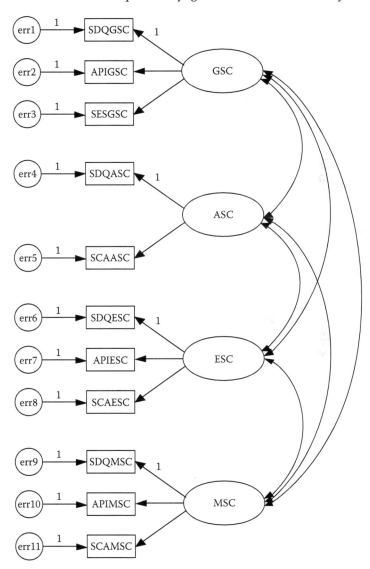

Figure 8.1 Hypothesized four-factor model of adolescent self-concept.

scores derived from the General SC subscale of the Self Description Questionnaire III (SDQIII; Marsh, 1992b), the Affective Perception Inventory (API; Soares & Soares, 1979), and the Self-Esteem Scale (SES; Rosenberg, 1965); these indicator variables are labeled as SDQGSC, APIGSC, and SESGSC, respectively. English SC is measured by subscale scores related to the SDQIII (SDQESC), the API (APIESC), and the Self-Concept of Ability Scale (SCAS; Brookover, 1962); the latter is labeled as SCAESC in Figure 8.1. Finally, math SC is measured by subscale scores derived from the SDQIII (SDQMSC), the API (APIMSC), and the SCAS (SCAMSC). In the case of academic SC, findings from a preliminary factor analysis of the API (see Byrne & Shavelson, 1986) revealed several inadequacies in its measurement of this SC dimension. Thus, it was deleted from all subsequent analyses in the Byrne and Shavelson (1986) study, and the same holds true here. Consequently then, Academic SC is measured by subscale scores from the SDQIII (SDQASC) and the SCAS (SCAASC).

In contrast to the CFA model discussed in Chapter 7 in which the items of a measuring instrument formed the units of measurement, the CFA model under study in this chapter entails subscale scores of measuring instruments as its units of measurement. It is hypothesized that each subscale measure will have a nonzero loading on the SC factor it is designed to measure, albeit a zero loading on all other factors, and that error and uniquenesses associated with each of the observed measures are uncorrelated. Consistent with theory and empirical research, the four SC factors are shown to be intercorrelated.

The baseline models

As with the example of multigroup invariance across independent samples in Chapter 7, goodness-of-fit related to the hypothesized model (Figure 8.1) was tested separately for high- and low-track students. Model fit statistics indicated only a modestly well-fitting model for both groups (high track, CFI = .923, RMSEA = .128; low track, CFI = .911, RMSEA = .114). Indeed, a review of the modification indices, for both groups, revealed substantial evidence of misspecification as a consequence of error covariances among subscales of both the API (ESC and MSC) and the SCAS. This finding of overlapping variance among the SCAS subscales is certainly not surprising and can be explained by the fact that items on the English and Math SC subscales were spawned from those comprising the Academic SC subscale. More specifically, the SCAS was originally designed to measure only Academic SC. However, in their attempt to measure the subject-specific facets of English and Math SCs, Byrne and Shavelson (1986) used the same items from the original SCAS, albeit modifying the content to tap into the more specific facets of English and Math SC.

Given both a substantively and psychometrically reasonable rationale for estimating these three additional parameters, the originally hypothesized model was respecified and reestimated accordingly for each group. Testing of these respecified models resulted in a substantially better fitting model for both high-track (CFI = .975; RMSEA = .076) and low-track (CFI = .974; RMSEA = .065) students. This final baseline model (which turns out to be the same for each group) serves as the model to be tested for its equivalence across high- and low-track students; it is schematically portrayed in Figure 8.2.

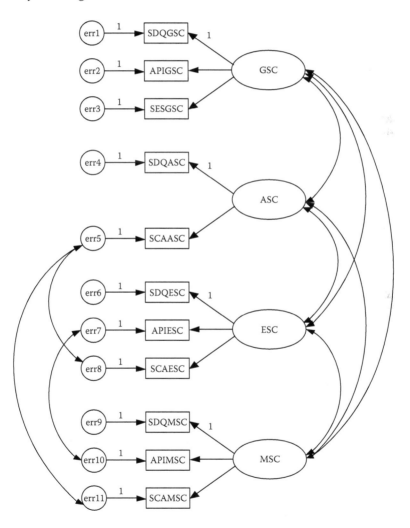

Figure 8.2 Hypothesized multigroup model of adolescent self-concept.

Modeling with AMOS Graphics
The structured means model

In working with AMOS Graphics, the estimation and testing of structured means models are not much different from those of testing for invariance based on the analysis of covariance structures. It does, however, require a few additional steps. As with the multigroup application presented in Chapter 7, the structured means model requires a system of labeling whereby certain parameters are constrained to be equal across groups, while others are free to take on any value. In testing for differences in factor latent means, for example, we would want to know that the measurement model is operating in exactly the same way for both high- and low-track students. In the structured means models, this requirement includes the observed variable intercepts in addition to the factor loadings (i.e., regression weights), and, thus, both are constrained equal across both groups. We turn now to a more detailed description of this process as it relates to testing for latent mean differences.

Testing for latent mean differences
The hypothesized multigroup model

In testing for latent mean differences using AMOS Graphics, the baseline model for each ability group must be made known to the program. However, in the case of our academically tracked groups in this chapter, the final model for each was the same. Thus, the multigroup model shown in Figure 8.2 represents both groups.[2]

Steps in the testing process

Once the multigroup model is established, the next step (illustrated in Chapter 7) is to identify the name of each group (via the *Manage Groups* dialog box), as well as the location of the related data (via the *Data Files* dialog box). For a review of these procedures, see Chapter 7, and in particular Figures 7.4 and 7.5. At this point, AMOS has all the information it requires with respect to both the model to be tested and the name and location of the data to be used. All that is needed now is to determine which analytic approach will be used in testing for differences in latent factor means across the two groups. In Chapter 7, procedures associated with only the selection of approach (manual versus automated) were illustrated. Details related to process once this choice has been made were necessarily limited to the manual multigroup strategy as it applied to tests for invariance. In this chapter, by contrast, I focus on details related to the automated multigroup approach.

Testing for configural invariance

Recall from Chapter 7 that all tests for invariance begin with the configural model for which interest focuses on the extent to which the same number of factors best represents the data for both groups. As such, no equality constraints are imposed and judgment is based on the adequacy of the goodness-of-fit statistics only. In this regard, the configural model was found to be exceptionally well fitting in its representation of the multigroup student data ($\chi^2_{(70)} = 225.298$; CFI = .975; RMSEA = .052).

To familiarize you with the AMOS output directory tree in multigroup analyses, I include here both the unstandardized and standardized factor-loading estimates for the configural model. Figure 8.3 is pertinent to the high-track group, while Figure 8.4 is pertinent to the low-track group. In reviewing both of these figures, I wish to direct your attention to four important pieces of information. *First,* turning to the directory tree shown in Figure 8.3, you will note that *High Track* is highlighted, thereby indicating that all results presented in this output file pertain only to this group. In contrast, if you were to click on *Low Track*, results pertinent to that group would be presented. *Second,* below this group identification section of the tree, you will see a list of four models (one unconstrained and three constrained). As indicated by the cursor, results presented here (and in Figure 8.4) relate to the unconstrained model. *Third,* because there are no constraints specified in this model, the parameters are freely estimated and, thus, vary across high- and low-track students. *Finally,* although equality constraints were not assigned to the factor loadings, the program automatically assigned labels that can be used to identify both the parameters and the groups in subsequent tests for invariance. These labels appear in the last column of the unstandardized estimate related to the regression weights. For example, the label assigned to the factor loading of SESGSC on GSC is a1_1 for high-track students and a1_2 for low-track students.[3]

Testing for measurement invariance

Subsequent to the configural model, all tests for invariance require the imposition of equality constraints across groups. Implementation of this process, using the automated approach, begins with the hypothesized model open followed by selection of the *Multiple Group Analysis* tab from the *Analysis* drop-down menu, as illustrated in Chapter 7 (Figure 7.13). Clicking on this selection will present you with the warning shown in Box 8.1.

Once you click on the *OK* tab, you will immediately be presented with the *Multiple Group Analysis* dialog box in which the default parameter subsets are checked (see Figure 7.14). However, as I emphasized in Chapter 7, in testing for invariance, I consider it prudent to test first for invariance related

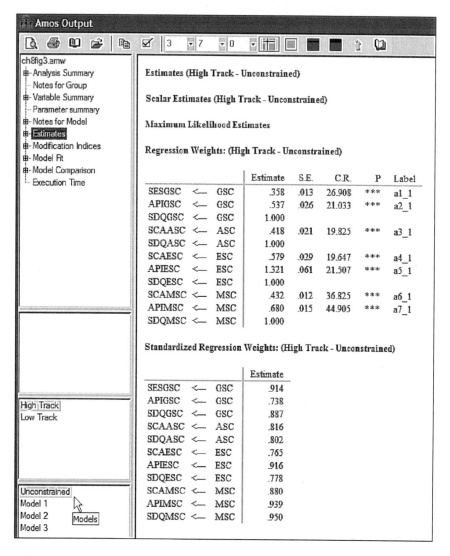

Figure 8.3 AMOS Graphics: Factor-loading estimates for the high-track group based on the unconstrained model.

to only the factor loadings. In this way, should the results yield evidence of noninvariance, you can then conduct follow-up analyses to determine which factor-loading parameters are not operating the same way across groups and can exclude them from further analyses. Thus, to test for invariance related only to the factor loadings, you will need to delete all checkmarks from the

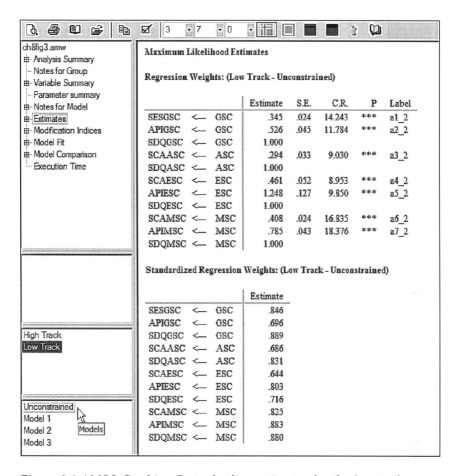

Figure 8.4 AMOS Graphics: Factor-loading estimates for the low-track group based on the unconstrained model.

BOX 8.1

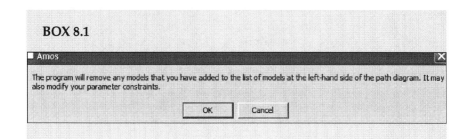

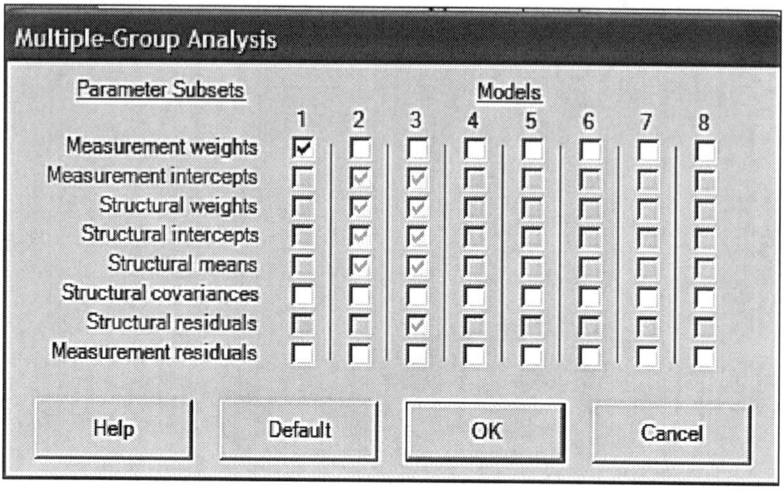

Figure 8.5 AMOS Graphics: *Multiple Group Analysis* dialog box with equality constraints indicated for only factor loadings.

Multiple Group Analysis dialog box, except the one in Column 1, which is shown in Figure 8.5 to represent only the "measurement weights."

Once you click on the *OK* tab of this dialog box, you will then see the assignment of constraint labels to your model. As noted in Chapter 7, one aberration of the current version of the program (AMOS 17) is that, regardless of which default checkmarks are removed from the *Multiple Group Analysis* dialog box (meaning the related parameters will be freely estimated), the program nonetheless adds the related labels to the model anyway. Displayed in Figure 8.6 is our hypothesized multigroup model with the appropriate factor-loading estimates labeled (a2_1 – a6_1), in addition to those representing the factor variances (vvv1_1 – vvv4_1), factor covariances (ccc1_1 – ccc6_1), and error variances (v1_1 – v11_1) as they pertain to Group 1, the high-track group. As noted earlier, clicking on the low-track group in the AMOS output directory tree would switch you to the same labeled model, albeit pertinent to the low-track group. As such, the labeling system uses the number "2" to indicate its relevance to this group of students (e.g., a2_2; a3_2).

Goodness-of-fit results from this test of invariant factor loadings again provided evidence of a well-fitting model ($\chi^2_{(77)} = 245.571$; CFI = .972; RMSEA = .051). Although the difference in χ^2 from the configural model was statically significant ($\Delta\chi^2_{(7)} = 20.273$), the difference between the CFI values met the recommended cutoff criterion of .01 (ΔCFI = .003). Using the CFI difference test as the criterion upon which to determine evidence of invariance, I concluded the factor loadings to be operating similarly across high-track and low-track students.

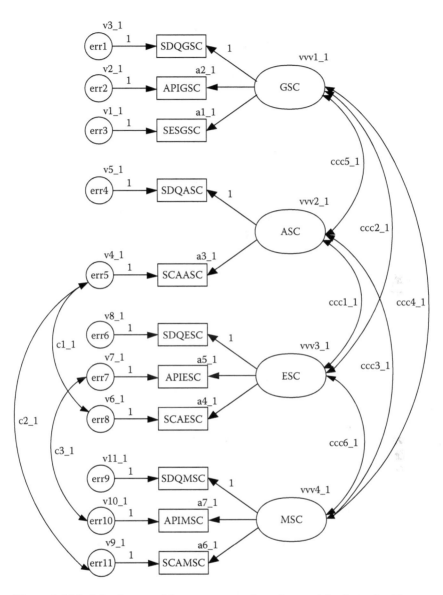

Figure 8.6 Model to be tested for cross-group invariance of the factor loadings.

Testing for latent mean differences

As noted earlier, in testing for differences in latent factor means, it is necessary to constrain both the factor loadings and the observed variable intercepts equal across the groups. However, in contrast to the case for factor loadings, which, if found to be noninvariant, are subsequently freely estimated, the intercepts must always be held constrained across the groups despite evidence of noninvariance. However, Cooke et al. (2001) contended that of the two, noninvariant factor loadings are by far the more serious. They further argued that group differences in intercepts need not preclude the usefulness of these items in measuring their underlying constructs.

Our first step in testing for latent mean differences, then, is to constrain the intercepts equal across groups. This task is easily accomplished by activating the *Analysis Properties* dialog box, either by clicking on its related icon or by selecting it from the *Analysis* drop-down menu. Once the *Analysis Properties* dialog box is open, we click on the *Estimation* tab and then select the *Estimate Means and Intercepts* option, as shown in Figure 8.7.

The next step in the process is to once again select the *Multiple Group Analysis* option from the *Analysis* drop-down menu. This time, however, in addition to placing a checkmark in Column 1 for only the measurement weights, we additionally check off Column 2, which incorporates both

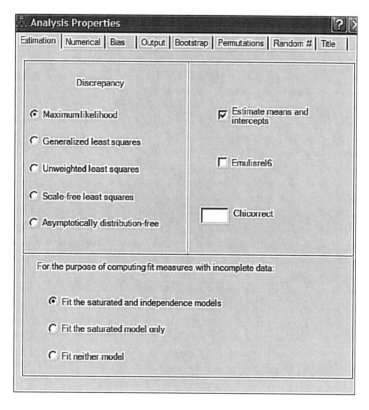

Figure 8.7 AMOS Graphics: *Analysis Properties* dialog box with means and intercept estimates requested.

the measurement weights and the measurement intercepts. Once these choices have been initiated, AMOS automatically assigns a zero followed by a comma (0,) to each factor. Figure 8.8 captures this labeling action by showing both the options checked in the *Multiple Group Analysis* dialog box, together with the resulting assignment of "0," to the general SC (GSC) and academic SC (ASC) factors.

The fixed zero values shown in Figure 8.8 are assigned to the model relevant to each group. However, as discussed at the beginning of this chapter, in testing for latent mean differences, one of the groups is freely estimated while the other is constrained equal to some fixed amount. In the case here, AMOS automatically fixes this zero value for *both* groups.

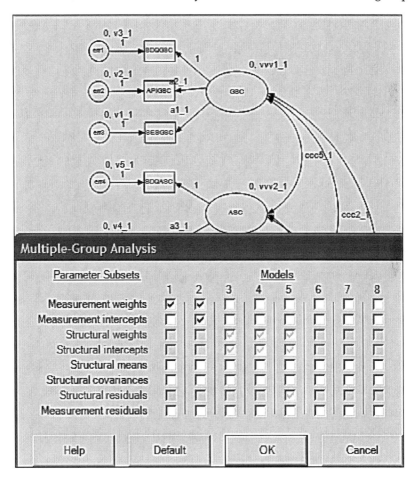

Figure 8.8 AMOS Graphics: *Multiple Group* dialog box with equality constraints indicated for factor loadings and intercepts.

Thus, the next step in the process is to remove these fixed factor values for one of the groups. The decision of which group will be fixed to zero is an arbitrary one and has no bearing on the final estimated mean values; regardless of which group is chosen, the results will be identical. In the present case, I elected to use the low-track group as the reference group (i.e., the latent means were fixed to a value of 0.0) and, thus, moved on to removing the mean constraints for the high-track group. With the model open, this process begins by first highlighting the factor to be relabeled by means of a left click of the mouse and then right-clicking on this factor, which will activate the *Object Properties* tab as shown in Figure 8.9.

Clicking on this tab opens the *Object Properties* dialog box, after which we click on the *Parameters* tab; this action enables us to relabel the mean parameters. Our interest here is in removing the fixed zero value assigned to each of the factor means and replacing them with a label that allows these parameters to be freely estimated for the high-track group; Figure 8.10 captures this process. More specifically, when the dialog box was first opened, the label seen in the space below "mean" was 0. I subsequently

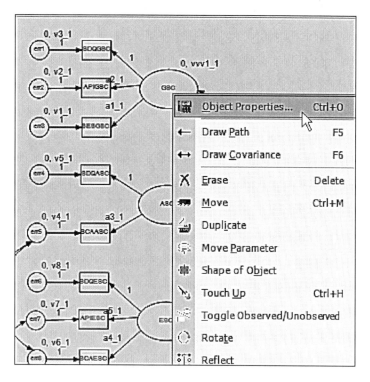

Figure 8.9 AMOS Graphics: Clicking on the *Object Properties* tab to open the dialog box.

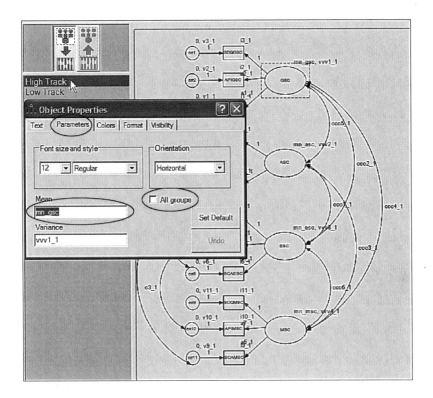

Figure 8.10 AMOS Graphics: *Object Properties* dialog box showing modification of the means-labeling protocol.

replaced this number with an appropriate label (e.g., mn_gsc) that could be modified in accordance with its related factor, as can be seen on the model behind. Circled within the dialog box, you can see assignment of the label to be assigned to the first factor (GSC). Note also that the square beside *All Groups* is empty and remains empty as we do not wish these relabeling changes to be applied to both groups.[4]

The final model to be tested for latent mean differences is shown in Figure 8.11 as it relates to the high-track group. However, clicking on the low-track label in the directory tree (see Figure 8.12) presents the same model, albeit with the zero values assigned to each of the factors. A mini version of both models is displayed in Figure 8.12.

Selected AMOS output: Model summary

Of primary interest in analyses related to structured means models are (a) the latent mean estimates, and (b) the goodness-of-fit between the

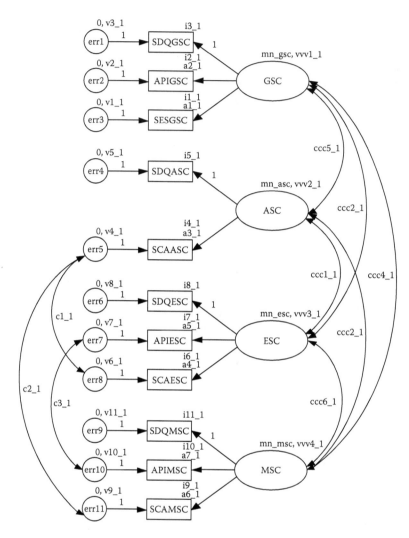

Figure 8.11 Structured means model as it represents the high-track group.

hypothesized model and the multigroup data. Before turning to these results for our analysis of high- and low-track students, let's once again take a few minutes to review a summary of the model in terms of the number of estimated parameters and resulting degrees of freedom. This summary is presented in Figure 8.13.

As you know by now, in order to calculate the degrees of freedom associated with the test of a model, you need to know two pieces of information: (a) the number of sample moments, and (b) the number of

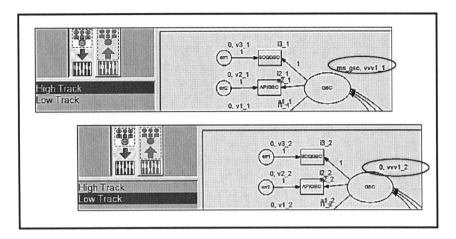

Figure 8.12 AMOS Graphics: Micro view of structured means model for high-track and low-track groups.

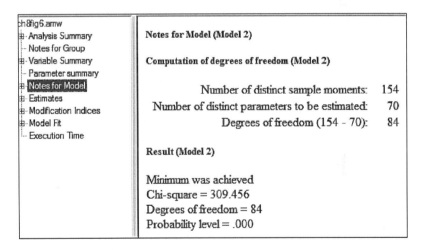

Figure 8.13 AMOS Graphics: Summary information related to structured means model.

estimated parameters. In Figure 8.13, we see that there are 154 distinct sample moments and 70 estimated parameters. Let's turn first to the number of sample moments. If you had calculated the number of moments in the same manner used with all other applications in this book, you would arrive at the number 132 ([11 × 12) / 2] = 66; given two groups, the total is 132). Why this discrepancy? The answer lies in the analysis of covariance versus means structures. All applications prior to the present chapter were based on covariance structures, and, thus, the only pieces of information needed for the analyses were the covariances among the observed variables. However, in the analysis of structured means models, information related to both the covariance matrix and the sample means is required. With 11 observed variables in the model, there will be 11 means, and 22 means for the two groups. The resulting number of moments, then, is 132 + 22 = 154.

Turning next to the reported 70 estimated parameters, let's look first at the number of parameters being estimated for the high-track group. As such, we have 7 factor loadings, 9 covariances (6 factor covariances; 3 error covariances), 15 variances (11 error variances; 4 factor variances), 11 intercepts, and 4 latent means, thereby yielding a total of 46 parameters to be estimated. For the low-track group, on the other hand, we have only 9 covariances and 15 variances, resulting in a total of 24 parameters to be estimated; all other parameters have been constrained equal to those of the high-track group. Across the two groups, then, there are 70 (46 + 24) parameters to be estimated. With 154 sample moments and 70 estimated parameters, the number of degrees of freedom will be 84.[5]

Selected AMOS output: Goodness-of-fit statistics

To provide you with a basis of comparison between the structured means model (Model 2 in the output) and both the configural model (i.e., unconstrained model) and measurement model in which only the factor loadings were group invariant (Model 1 in the output), goodness-of-fit statistics related to each are reported in Table 8.1. In each case, the fit statistics indicated well-fitting models. As reported earlier, although comparisons of Model 1 and 2 with the unconstrained model result in χ^2 difference tests that were statistically significant (p < .01 and p < .001, respectively), the CFI difference tests met the cutoff criteria of < .01 (with rounding in the case of Model 2). Indeed, despite the equality constraints imposed on both the factor loadings and the observed variable intercepts across the two groups, the structured means model fitted the data exceptionally well (e.g., CFI = .963) and demonstrated an adequate approximation to the two adolescent ability track populations (RMSEA = .057). Given these findings, then, we can feel confident in interpreting the estimates associated with the current solution.

Selected AMOS output: Parameter estimates

High-track students

We turn first to parameter estimates for the high-track students, which are reported in Table 8.2. In the interest of space, factor and error variances are not included. A brief perusal of the critical ratios (C.R.s) associated with these estimates reveals all, except the covariance between the factors ESC and MSC, to be statistically significant. This nonsignificant finding,

Table 8.1 Goodness-of-Fit Statistics for Configural and Measurement Models

Model	NPAR	CMIN	DF	P	CMIN/DF
Unconstrained	62	225.298	70	.000	3.219
Model 1	55	245.571	77	.000	3.189
Model 2	70	309.456	84	.000	3.684
Model 3	62	225.298	70	.000	3.219
Saturated model	132	.000	0		
Independence model	22	6213.470	110	.000	56.486

Baseline comparisons

	NFI	RFI	IFI	TLI	
Model	Delta1	rho1	Delta2	rho2	CFI
Unconstrained	.964	.943	.975	.960	.975
Model 1	.960	.944	.973	.961	.972
Model 2	.950	.935	.963	.952	.963
Model 3	.964	.943	.975	.960	.975
Saturated model	1.000		1.000		1.000
Independence model	.000	.000	.000	.000	.000

RMSEA

Model	RMSEA	LO 90	HI 90	PCLOSE
Unconstrained	.052	.044	.059	.338
Model 1	.051	.044	.059	.361
Model 2	.057	.050	.064	.045
Model 3	.052	.044	.059	.338
Independence model	.259	.253	.264	.000

however, is quite consistent with self-concept theory as it relates to these two academic dimensions and therefore is no cause for concern.

Of major interest here are the latent mean estimates reported for high-track students as they provide the key to the question of whether the latent factor means for this group are significantly different from those for low-track students. Given that the low-track group was designated as the reference group and thus their factor means were fixed to zero, the values reported here represent latent mean differences between the two groups. Reviewing these values, we see that whereas the latent factor means related to the more specific facets of academic, English, and mathematics self-concepts were statistically significant (as indicated by the critical ratio values > 1.96), this was not the case for general self-concept (C.R. = .304).

Given that the latent mean parameters were estimated for the high-track group, and that they represent positive values, we interpret these findings as indicating that high-track students in secondary school appear to have

Table 8.2 Selected AMOS Output: Parameter Estimates for
Means Structures Model—High-Track Students

	Estimate	S.E.	C.R.	P	Label
Regression weights					
SESGSC <--- GSC	.356	.012	30.458	***	a1_1
APIGSC <--- GSC	.535	.022	24.124	***	a2_1
SDQGSC <--- GSC	1.000				
SCAASC <--- ASC	.445	.018	25.030	***	a3_1
SDQASC <--- ASC	1.000				
SCAESC <--- ESC	.587	.026	22.252	***	a4_1
APIESC <--- ESC	1.307	.054	24.158	***	a5_1
SDQESC <--- ESC	1.000				
SCAMSC <--- MSC	.428	.010	41.502	***	a6_1
APIMSC <--- MSC	.698	.014	49.706	***	a7_1
SDQMSC <--- MSC	1.000				
*** probability < .000					
Standardized regression weights					
SESGSC <--- GSC	.913				
APIGSC <--- GSC	.738				
SDQGSC <--- GSC	.888				
SCAASC <--- ASC	.826				
SDQASC <--- ASC	.784				
SCAESC <--- ESC	.769				
APIESC <--- ESC	.913				
SDQESC <--- ESC	.781				
SCAMSC <--- MSC	.876				
APIMSC <--- MSC	.943				
SDQMSC <--- MSC	.947				
Means					
GSC	.296	.978	.302	.762	mn_gsc
ASC	10.397	.781	13.315	***	mn_asc
ESC	3.424	.571	6.001	***	mn_esc
MSC	7.639	1.062	7.193	***	mn_msc
*** probability < .000					
Intercepts					
SESGSC	31.317	.291	107.449	***	i1_1
APIGSC	76.653	.474	161.804	***	i2_1
SDQGSC	75.638	.813	93.086	***	i3_1

(continued)

Table 8.2 Selected AMOS Output: Parameter Estimates for
Means Structures Model—High-Track Students (*Continued*)

	Estimate	S.E.	C.R.	P	Label
Intercepts					
SCAASC	25.424	.283	89.745	***	i4_1
SDQASC	47.894	.675	70.991	***	i5_1
SCAESC	26.459	.289	91.679	***	i6_1
APIESC	57.401	.606	94.746	***	i7_1
SDQESC	54.382	.492	110.595	***	i8_1
SCAMSC	22.958	.364	63.034	***	i9_1
APIMSC	41.851	.585	71.518	***	i10_1
SDQMSC	41.444	.829	49.979	***	i11_1

*** probability < .000

	Estimate	S.E.	C.R.	P	Label
Covariances					
ASC <--> ESC	37.423	4.020	9.309	***	ccc1_1
GSC <--> ESC	23.971	4.773	5.022	***	ccc2_1
ASC <--> MSC	90.511	8.140	11.119	***	ccc3_1
GSC <--> MSC	54.373	9.556	5.690	***	ccc4_1
GSC <--> ASC	53.028	6.246	8.490	***	ccc5_1
ESC <--> MSC	.359	5.556	.065	.948	ccc6_1
err5 <--> err8	5.159	.588	8.773	***	c1_1
err5 <--> err11	4.546	.554	8.201	***	c2_1
err7 <--> err10	8.590	1.406	6.111	***	c3_1

*** probability < .000

	Estimate
Correlations	
ASC <--> ESC	.537
GSC <--> ESC	.240
ASC <--> MSC	.628
GSC <--> MSC	.263
GSC <--> ASC	.453
ESC <--> MSC	.003
err5 <--> err8	.499
err5 <--> err11	.439
err7 <--> err10	.487

significantly higher perceptions of self than their low-track peers with respect to perceived mathematics and English capabilities, as well as to school in general. On the other hand, when it comes to a global perception of self, there appears to be little difference between the two groups of students. Readers interested in a more detailed discussion of these results from a substantive perspective are referred to the original article (Byrne, 1988b).

Low-track students

Turning now to the results for low-track students reported in Table 8.3, we find that, consistent with the high-track group, all parameter estimates are statistically significant except for the factor covariance between English and Math SC. Upon further scrutiny, however, you may think that something is amiss with this table as both the factor loadings (i.e., regression weights) and the observed variable intercepts, as well as their related labels, are identical to those reported for the high-track group. These results are correct, of course, as these parameters (for the low-track group) were constrained equal to those estimated

Table 8.3 Selected AMOS Output: Parameter Estimates for Means Structure Model—Low-Track Students

	Regression weights				
	Estimate	S.E.	C.R.	P	Label
SESGSC <--- GSC	.356	.012	30.458	***	a1_1
APIGSC <--- GSC	.535	.022	24.124	***	a2_1
SDQGSC <--- GSC	1.000				
SCAASC <--- ASC	.445	.018	25.030	***	a3_1
SDQASC <--- ASC	1.000				
SCAESC <--- ESC	.587	.026	22.252	***	a4_1
APIESC <--- ESC	1.307	.054	24.158	***	a5_1
SDQESC <--- ESC	1.000				
SCAMSC <--- MSC	.428	.010	41.502	***	a6_1
APIMSC <--- MSC	.698	.014	49.706	***	a7_1
SDQMSC <--- MSC	1.000				
***					

Standardized regression weights	
SESGSC <--- GSC	.854
APIGSC <--- GSC	.698
SDQGSC <--- GSC	.880
SCAASC <--- ASC	.767
SDQASC <--- ASC	.694
SCAESC <--- ESC	.692
APIESC <--- ESC	.785
SDQESC <--- ESC	.684
SCAMSC <--- MSC	.851
APIMSC <--- MSC	.849
SDQMSC <--- MSC	.892

(continued)

Table 8.3 Selected AMOS Output: Parameter Estimates for
Means Structure Model—Low-Track Students (*Continued*)

	Estimate	S.E.	C.R.	P	Label
		Intercepts			
SESGSC	31.317	.291	107.449	***	i1_1
APIGSC	76.653	.474	161.804	***	i2_1
SDQGSC	75.638	.813	93.086	***	i3_1
SCAASC	25.424	.283	89.745	***	i4_1
SDQASC	47.894	.675	70.991	***	i5_1
SCAESC	26.459	.289	91.679	***	i6_1
APIESC	57.401	.606	94.746	***	i7_1
SDQESC	54.382	.492	110.595	***	i8_1
SCAMSC	22.958	.364	63.034	***	i9_1
APIMSC	41.851	.585	71.518	***	i10_1
SDQMSC	41.444	.829	49.979	***	i11_1
***					
		Covariances			
ASC <--> ESC	31.828	5.002	6.363	***	ccc1_2
GSC <--> ESC	23.400	5.860	3.993	***	ccc2_2
MSC <--> ASC	49.353	8.598	5.740	***	ccc3_2
MSC <--> GSC	49.941	10.717	4.660	***	ccc4_2
GSC <--> ASC	41.082	8.136	5.050	***	ccc5_2
MSC <--> ESC	3.018	5.764	.524	.601	ccc6_2
err5 <--> err8	5.051	1.050	4.808	***	c1_2
err5 <--> err11	3.882	.863	4.499	***	c2_2
err7 <--> err10	17.425	3.273	5.323	***	c3_2
***					
		Correlations			
ASC <--> ESC	.620				
GSC <--> ESC	.317				
MSC <--> ASC	.496				
MSC <--> GSC	.349				
GSC <--> ASC	.428				
MSC <--> ESC	.040				
Err5 <--> err8	.432				
Err5 <--> err11	.396				
Err7 <--> err10	.510				

for the high-track group. Finally, it is important to note that no estimates for the factor means are reported. Although these values were
constrained to zero, AMOS does not report these fixed values in the
output.

Endnotes

1. Of course, the procedure can also include more than two groups.
2. For an example of testing a multigroup model that involves two different baseline models, readers are referred to Byrne (2004).
3. Selection of which group serves as "Group 1" is purely arbitrary.
4. Although it was necessary to check this box when using the manual approach to invariance (see Chapter 7), this is not needed when the automated multi-group approach is used as AMOS programs these constraints automatically.
5. It is important to note a serious error in the *Parameter Summary* table for this model (not shown here), as it relates to the low-track group, in the current version of the program (AMOS 17). Turning first to the *Means* column, the correct values should report four *fixed* means, thus yielding a total of four means. Switching to a horizontal view of the *Parameter Summary* table, the *Fixed* row should show a total of 19 parameters, and the *Total* row, a grand total of 61 parameters. Calculation of these values will be corrected in Version 18 (J. L. Arbuckle, personal communication, December 10, 2008).

chapter nine

Testing for the equivalence of a causal structure

In Chapter 4, I highlighted several problematic aspects of post hoc model fitting in structural equation modeling. One approach to addressing problems associated with post hoc model fitting is to apply some mode of cross-validation analysis; this is the focus of the present chapter. In this chapter, we examine a full structural equation model and test for its equivalence across calibration and validation samples of secondary school teachers. Before walking you through this procedure, however, let's first review some of the issues related to cross-validation.

Cross-validation in covariance structure modeling

Typically, in applications of covariance structure modeling, the researcher tests a hypothesized model and then, from an assessment of various goodness-of-fit criteria, concludes that a statistically better fitting model could be attained by respecifying the model such that particular parameters previously constrained to zero are freely estimated (Breckler, 1990; MacCallum, Roznowski, Mar, & Reith, 1994; MacCallum, Roznowski, & Necowitz, 1992; MacCallum, Wegener, Uchino, & Fabrigar, 1993). Possibly as a consequence of considerable criticism of covariance structure modeling procedures during the 1980s and early 1990s (e.g., Biddle & Marlin, 1987; Breckler; Cliff, 1983), most researchers engaged in this respecification process are now generally familiar with the issues. In particular, they are cognizant of the exploratory nature of these follow-up procedures, as well as the fact that additionally specified parameters in the model must be theoretically substantiated.

The pros and cons of post hoc model fitting have been rigorously debated in the literature. Although some have severely criticized the practice (e.g., Cliff, 1983; Cudeck & Browne, 1983), others have argued that as long as the researcher is fully cognizant of the exploratory nature of his or her analyses, the process can be substantively meaningful because practical as well as statistical significance can be taken into account (Byrne, Shavelson, & Muthén, 1989; Tanaka & Huba, 1984). However, Jöreskog (1993) has been very clear in stating, "If the model is rejected by the data, the problem is to determine what is wrong with the model and how the model should be modified to fit the data better" (p. 298). The purists would argue that once a hypothesized model is rejected, that's the end of the story. More realistically, however, other researchers in this area of study recognize the obvious impracticality in the termination of all subsequent model analyses. Clearly, in the interest of future research, it behooves the investigator to probe deeper into the question of why the model is malfitting (see Tanaka, 1993). As a consequence of the concerted efforts of statistical experts in covariance structure modeling in addressing this issue, there are now several different approaches that can be used to increase the soundness of findings derived from these post hoc analyses.

Undoubtedly, post hoc model fitting in the analysis of covariance structures is problematic. With multiple model specifications, there is the risk of capitalization on chance factors because model modification may be driven by characteristics of the particular sample on which the model was tested (e.g., sample size, sample heterogeneity) (MacCallum et al., 1992). As a consequence of this sequential testing procedure, there is increased risk of making either a Type I or Type II error, and at this point in time, there is no direct way to adjust for the probability of such error. Because hypothesized covariance structure models represent only approximations of reality and, thus, are not expected to fit real-world phenomena exactly (Cudeck & Browne, 1983; MacCallum et al., 1992), most research applications are likely to require the specification of alternative models in the quest for one that fits the data well (Anderson & Gerbing, 1988; MacCallum, 1986). Indeed, this aspect of covariance structure modeling represents a serious limitation, and, to date, several alternative strategies for model testing have been proposed (see, e.g., Anderson & Gerbing, 1988; Cudeck & Henly, 1991; MacCallum, 1995; MacCallum et al., 1992, 1993).

One approach to addressing problems associated with post hoc model fitting is to employ a cross-validation strategy whereby the final model derived from the post hoc analyses is tested on a second (or more) independent sample(s) from the same population. Barring the availability of separate data samples, albeit a sufficiently large sample, one may wish to randomly split the data into two (or more) parts, thereby making it possible to cross-validate the findings (see Cudeck & Browne, 1983). As such, Sample A serves as the calibration sample on which the initially hypothesized model is tested, as well as any post hoc analyses conducted in the process of attaining a well-fitting model. Once this final model is determined, the validity of its structure can then be tested based on Sample B (the validation sample). In other words, the final best-fitting model for the calibration sample becomes the hypothesized model under test for the validation sample.

There are several ways by which the similarity of model structure can be tested (see, e.g., Anderson & Gerbing, 1988; Browne & Cudeck, 1989; Cudeck & Browne, 1983; MacCallum et al., 1994; Whittaker & Stapleton, 2006). For one example, Cudeck and Browne suggested the computation of a Cross-Validation Index (CVI) which measures the distance between the *restricted* (i.e., model-imposed) variance–covariance matrix for the calibration sample and the *unrestricted* variance–covariance matrix for the validation sample. Because the estimated predictive validity of the model is gauged by the smallness of the CVI value, evaluation is facilitated by their comparison based on a series of alternative models. It is important to note, however, that the CVI estimate reflects *overall* discrepancy between "the actual population covariance matrix, Σ, and the estimated population covariance matrix reconstructed from the parameter estimates obtained from fitting the model to the sample" (MacCallum et al., 1994, p. 4). More specifically, this global index of discrepancy represents combined effects arising from the discrepancy of approximation (e.g., nonlinear influences among variables) and the discrepancy of estimation (e.g., representative sample; sample size). (For a more extended discussion of these aspects of discrepancy, see Browne & Cudeck, 1989; Cudeck & Henly, 1991; MacCallum et al., 1994.)

More recently, Whittaker and Stapleton (2006), in a comprehensive Monte Carlo simulation study of eight cross-validation indices, determined that certain conditions played an important part in affecting their performance. Specifically, findings showed that whereas the performance of these indices generally improved with increasing factor loading and sample sizes, it tended to be less optimal in the presence of increasing non-normality. (For details related to these findings, as well as the eight cross-validation indices included in this study, see Whittaker & Stapleton.)

In the present chapter, we examine another approach to cross-validation. Specifically, we use an invariance-testing strategy to test for the replicability of a full structural equation model across groups. The selected application is straightforward in addressing the question of whether a model that has been respecified in one sample replicates over a second independent sample from the same population (for another approach, see Byrne & Baron, 1994).

Testing for invariance across calibration and validation samples

The example presented in this chapter comes from the same study briefly described in Chapter 6 (Byrne, 1994a), the intent of which was threefold: (a) to validate a causal structure involving the impact of organizational and personality factors on three facets of burnout for elementary, intermediate, and secondary teachers; (b) to cross-validate this model across a second independent sample within each teaching panel; and (c) to test for the invariance of common structural regression (or causal) paths across teaching panels. In contrast to Chapter 6, however, here we focus on (b) in testing for model replication across calibration and validation samples of secondary teachers. (For an in-depth examination of invariance-testing procedures within and between the three teacher groups, see Byrne, 1994a.)

It is perhaps important to note that although the present example of cross-validation is based on a full structural equation model, the practice is in no way limited to such applications. Indeed, cross-validation is equally as important for CFA models, and examples of such applications can be found across a variety of disciplines; for those relevant to psychology, see Byrne (1993, 1994b); Byrne and Baron (1994); Byrne, Baron, and Balev (1996, 1998); Byrne, Baron, and Campbell (1993, 1994); Byrne, Baron, Larsson, and Melin (1995); Byrne, Baron, Melin, and Larsson (1996); Byrne and Campbell (1999); and Byrne, Stewart, and Lee (2004). For those relevant to education, see Benson and Bandalos (1992) and Pomplun and Omar (2003). And for those relevant to medicine, see Francis, Fletcher, and Rourke (1988), as well as Wang, Wang, and Hoadley (2007). We turn now to the model under study.

The original study from which the present example is taken comprised a sample of 1,431 high school teachers. For purposes of cross-validation, this sample was randomly split into two; Sample A ($n = 716$) was used as the calibration group, and Sample B ($n = 715$) as the validation group. Preliminary analyses conducted for the original study determined two outlying cases which were deleted from all subsequent analyses, thereby rendering final sample sizes of 715 (Sample A) and 714 (Sample B).

The hypothesized model

The originally hypothesized model was tested and modified based on data from the calibration sample (Sample A) of high school teachers. The final best-fitting model for this sample is shown schematically in Figure 9.1. It is important to note that, for purposes of clarity, double-headed arrows representing correlations among the independent factors in the model and measurement error terms associated with each of the indicator variables are not included in this figure. Nonetheless, these specifications are essential to the model and must be added before being able to test the model; otherwise, AMOS will present you with the error message shown in Figure 9.2. Thus, in testing structural equation models using the AMOS program, I suggest that you keep two sets of matching model files—one in which you have a cleanly presented figure appropriate for publication purposes, and the other as a working file in which it doesn't matter how cluttered the figure might be (see, e.g., Figure 9.5).

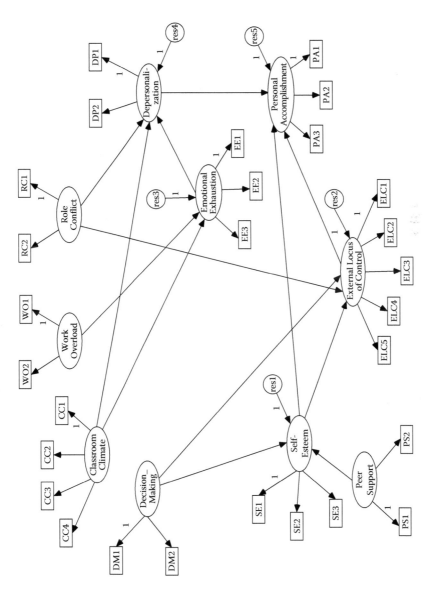

Figure 9.1 Hypothesized model of burnout for calibration sample of high school teachers.

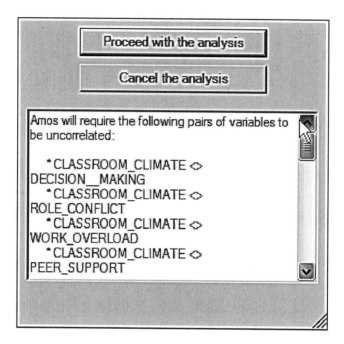

Figure 9.2 AMOS Graphics: Error message advising of need for double-headed arrows indicating correlation among independent factors in the model.

Establishing a baseline model

Because analysis of the hypothesized model in the original study was based on the EQS program (Bentler, 2005), for which the modification indices are derived multivariately rather than univariately (as in AMOS), I consider it important to test for its validity in establishing a baseline model here prior to conducting tests for its invariance across the calibration and validation samples. Initial testing of this model (see Figure 9.1) for the calibration sample yielded the goodness-of-fit statistics reported in Table 9.1. As indicated by a CFI value of .939 (RMSEA = .050), the postulated model of causal structure seems to fit these data well. Nonetheless, a review of both the modification indices and parameter estimates raises two concerns, which I believe need to be addressed. We turn first to the modification indices reported in Table 9.2, which represent only the structural paths of the model. Here you will quickly notice a large value of 43.899 indicative of an omitted path flowing from Self-Esteem to Emotional Exhaustion. As indicated by the Parameter Change Statistic, addition of this parameter to the model would yield an estimated value of –.568, which is substantial. The negative sign, of course, is substantively appropriate in that low levels

Table 9.1 Selected AMOS Output: Goodness-of-Fit Statistics for Hypothesized

		Causal structure			
Model	NPAR	CMIN	DF	P	CMIN/DF
Default model	79	910.697	327	.000	2.785
Saturated model	406	.000	0		
Independence model	28	9973.176	378	.000	26.384

		Baseline comparisons			
	NFI	RFI	IFI	TLI	
Model	Delta1	rho1	Delta2	rho2	CFI
Default model	.909	.894	.939	.930	.939
Saturated model	1.000		1.000		1.000
Independence model	.000	.000	.000	.000	.000

		RMSEA		
Model	RMSEA	LO 90	HI 90	PCLOSE
Default model	.050	.046	.054	.493
Independence model	.189	.185	.192	.000

Table 9.2 Selected AMOS Output: Modification Indices
for Structural Paths

Regression weights (calibration—default model)	M.I.	Par change
SE <--- WO	7.286	−.067
SE <--- EE	42.129	−.094
EE <--- SE	43.899	−.568
DP <--- SE	9.205	−.218
PA <--- PS	9.074	.099

of self-esteem are likely to precipitate high levels of emotional exhaustion and vice versa. In light of both the statistical results and the substantive meaningfulness of this structural regression path, I consider that this parameter should be included in the model, and the model reestimated.

Before taking a look at the parameter estimates, however, it is important that I make mention of the other large modification index (42.129), representing the same path noted above, albeit in reverse (from Emotional Exhaustion to Self-Esteem). Given the similar magnitude (relatively speaking) of these two indices, I'm certain that many readers will query why this parameter also is not considered for inclusion in the model. In this regard, I argue against its inclusion in the model for both statistical and substantive reasons. From a statistical perspective, I point to the related Parameter Change Statistic, which shows a negligible value of −.094, clearly indicative of its ineffectiveness as a parameter in the model. From a substantive perspective we need to remember the primary focus of the original study, which was to identify determinants of teacher burnout. Within this framework, specification of a path flowing from Emotional Exhaustion to Self-Esteem would be inappropriate as the direction of prediction (in this case) runs counter to the intent of the study.

Let's turn now to Table 9.3 in which estimates of the factor correlations are presented. Circled, you will observe an estimated value of .886 representing the correlation between Role Conflict and Work Overload, thereby indicating an overlap in variance of approximately 78%. Recall that we noted the same problematic correlation with respect to analyses for elementary teachers (see Chapter 6). As explained in Chapter 6, Role Conflict and Work Overload represent two subscales of the same measuring instrument (Teacher Stress Scale). Thus, it seems evident that the related item content is less than optimal in its measurement of behavioral characteristics that distinguish between these two factors.

Taking into account the large modification index representing a path from Self-Esteem to Emotional Exhaustion, together with the high correlation between the factors of Role Conflict and Work Overload and the similarity of results for elementary teachers, I consider it appropriate to respecify the hypothesized model such that it includes the new structural path (Self-Esteem ® Emotional Exhaustion) and the deletion of the Work Overload factor, thereby enabling its two indicators to load on the Role Conflict factor. This modified model is presented in Figure 9.3, with the additional regression path and reoriented indicators of Role Conflict encircled.

Table 9.3 Selected AMOS Output: Estimates for Factor Correlations

	Estimate
DM <--> CC	.387
DM <--> PS	.662
PS <--> CC	.216
RC <--> DM	−.746
RC <--> PS	−.406
RC <--> CC	−.284
CC <--> WO	−.205
DM <--> WO	−.682
RC <--> WO	.886
PS <--> WO	−.395

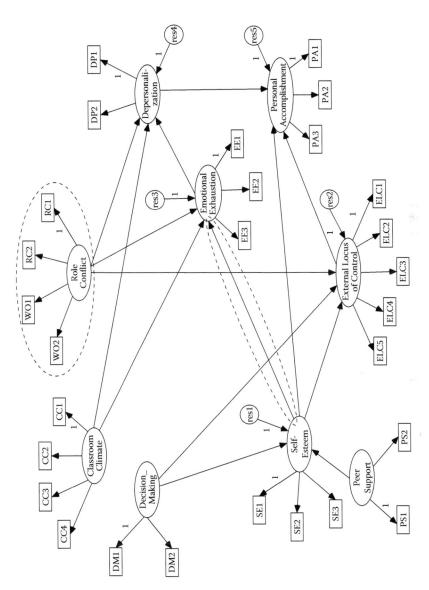

Figure 9.3 Revised model of burnout for calibration sample of high school teachers.

Results from the testing of this respecified model revealed an estimated value of −.719 (SE = .093; CR = −7.747) for the path from Self-Esteem to Emotional Exhaustion, which was somewhat higher than the expected value of −.568. Goodness-of-fit statistics results are reported in Table 9.4. Although the CFI value of .942 (RMSEA = .049) represents only a slight improvement in model fit over the initial CFI value of .939, it nonetheless represents a good fit to the data. Thus, the model shown in Figure 9.3 serves as the baseline model of causal structure that will now be tested for its invariance across calibration and validation samples.

Modeling with AMOS Graphics

Testing for the invariance of causal structure using the automated approach

In Chapter 7, I outlined the general approach to tests for invariance and introduced you to the specification procedures pertinent to both the manual and automated approaches available in the AMOS program. Whereas the application presented in Chapter 7 focused on the manual approach, the one illustrated in Chapter 8 centered on the automated approach. In this chapter, analyses again are based on the multiple-group automated procedure.

Table 9.4 Selected AMOS Output: Goodness-of-Fit Statistics for Revised

Causal structure				
Model	NPAR	CMIN	DF	P	CMIN/DF
Default model	76	884.384	330	.000	2.680
Saturated model	406	.000	0		
Independence model	28	9973.176	378	.000	26.384

Baseline comparisons				
	NFI	RFI	IFI	TLI	
Model	Delta1	rho1	Delta2	rho2	CFI
Default model	.911	.898	.943	.934	.942
Saturated model	1.000		1.000		1.000
Independence model	.000	.000	.000	.000	.000

RMSEA			
Model	RMSEA	LO 90	HI 90	PCLOSE
Default model	.049	.045	.052	.733
Independence model	.189	.185	.192	.000

Recall that in Chapter 7, we tested separately for the validity of the multigroup configural model, followed by tests for invariance related separately to each of the measurement and structural models. As noted in Chapter 7 and illustrated in Chapter 8, these tests can be tested simultaneously using the AMOS automated procedure. In the present chapter, we expand on this model-testing process by including both the structural residuals (i.e., error residual variances associated with the dependent factors in the model) and the measurement residuals (i.e., error variances associated with the observed variables). A review of the *Multiple Group Analysis* dialog box, shown in Figure 9.4, summarizes the parameters involved in testing for the invariance of these five models. As indicated by the gradual addition of constraints, these models are cumulative in the sense that each is more restrictive than its predecessor.

Although I noted in Chapter 7 that inclusion of these structural and measurement residuals in tests for invariance is somewhat rare and commonly considered to be excessively stringent, I include them here for two reasons. First, working with this set of five models provides an excellent vehicle for showing you how the automated approach to invariance works; and, second, it allows me to reinforce on you the importance of establishing invariance one step at a time (i.e., one set of constrained parameters at a time). Recall my previous notation that, regardless of which model(s) in which a researcher might be interested, AMOS automatically labels all parameters in the model. For example, although you may wish to activate only the measurement weight model (Model 1), the program will still label

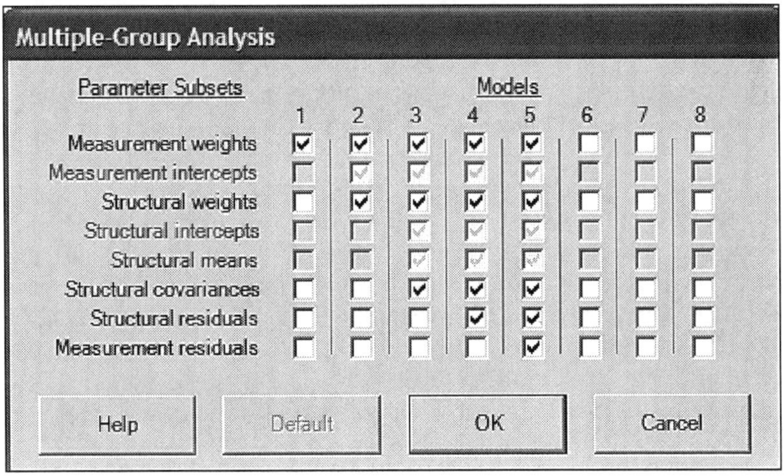

Figure 9.4 AMOS Graphics: *Multiple Group Analysis* dialog box showing default models to be tested for invariance.

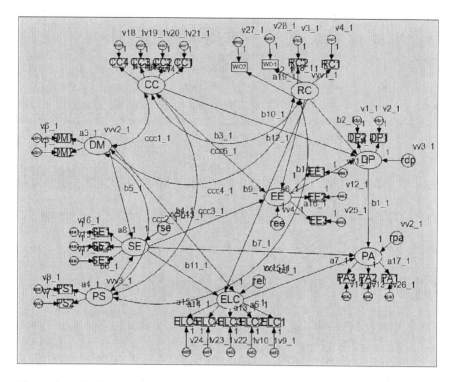

Figure 9.5 AMOS Graphics: Working behind-the-scenes model showing default labeling.

all parameters in the model, and not just the factor loadings. Figure 9.5, which represents the behind-the-scenes working multigroup model under test for invariance, provides a good example of this all-inclusive labeling action.

Turning next to Figure 9.6, we find the summary of parameters associated with the cumulative series of tests for these five models showing the breakdown pertinent to each model tested. In essence, the categorization of parameters presented in the summary is specific to Model 5. Let's now dissect this summary in order that you have a clear understanding of what each of these numbers represents and how each was derived; recall that a parameter categorized as *labeled* represents one that is constrained equal across groups. A breakdown of this parameter summary is as follows:

- Fixed weights (42): regression paths fixed to a value of 1.0 for 28 measurement error terms, 5 structural residuals, and 9 factor loadings
- Labeled weights (33): 19 factor loadings and 14 structural paths

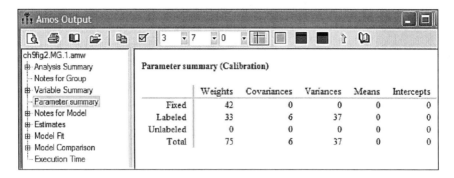

Figure 9.6 AMOS Graphics: Output summary of parameter status related to tests for invariance based on Model 5.

- Labeled covariances (6): 6 factor covariances associated with the 4 factors
- Labeled variances (37): 4 (independent) factor variances, 5 residual variances, and 28 error variances

Selected AMOS output: Goodness-of-fit statistics for comparative tests of multigroup invariance

Of primary interest in testing for multigroup invariance are the goodness-of-fit statistics but, most importantly, the χ^2 and CFI values as they enable us to determine the extent to which the parameters tested are operating equivalently across the groups. When several tests are conducted simultaneously, AMOS computes and reports these results as a set, which makes it easy to compare one model with another. Results for the χ^2 and CFI values related to the series of five models shown in Figure 9.4 are presented in Table 9.5. In light of the increasing number of multigroup studies of late reporting evidence of invariance based on CFI difference (ΔCFI) values versus the more traditional χ^2 difference ($\Delta\chi^2$) values, as noted in Chapter 7, I consider it instructive to present both sets of results here; each is reviewed separately.

The traditional χ^2 difference approach

We turn first to findings based on the χ^2 values as presented in Table 9.5. As can be expected, the first model in the group reported in the AMOS output is the configural model for which all parameters are estimated for the calibration and validation groups simultaneously; that is, no parameters are constrained equal across groups. This multigroup model yielded

Table 9.5 Selected AMOS Output: Model Comparisons of χ^2 and CFI Values

Model	CMIN	DF	P
Unconstrained	1671.998	660	.000
Measurement weights	1703.631	679	.000
Structural weights	1719.187	693	.000
Structural covariances	1730.585	703	.000
Structural residuals	1740.239	708	.000
Measurement residuals	1773.792	736	.000

Baseline comparisons

Model	NFI Delta1	RFI rho1	IFI Delta2	TLI rho2	CFI
Unconstrained	.913	.900	.946	.937	.945
Measurement weights	.911	.901	.945	.938	.945
Structural weights	.911	.903	.945	.939	.945
Structural covariances	.910	.903	.945	.940	.944
Structural residuals	.910	.903	.944	.940	.944
Measurement residuals	.908	.905	.944	.942	.944

a χ^2 value of 1671.998 with 660 degrees of freedom and serves as the base-line referent against which all subsequent models are compared. In the second model tested (measurement weights), all factor loadings of the indicator variables were constrained equal across groups. Analyses here reveal a χ^2 value of 1703.631 with 679 degrees of freedom. Computation of the $\Delta\chi^2$ value between this model and the configural model yields a difference of 31.633 with 19 degrees of freedom (because the 19 factor loadings for the validation group were constrained equal to those of the calibration group). This χ^2 difference value is statistically significant at a probability of less than .05. Based on these results, we conclude that one or more of the factor loadings is not operating equivalently across the two groups. Likewise, $\Delta\chi^2$ values related to each of the increasingly more restrictive models that follow show a steady augmentation of this differ-ential. Overall, then, if we use the traditional invariance-testing approach based on the χ^2 difference test as the basis for determining evidence of equivalence, we would conclude that the full structural equation model shown in Figure 9.3 is completely nonequivalent across the calibration and validation groups.

In Table 9.5, I presented findings related to the five models check-marked by default in AMOS 17 primarily for the educative purpose of showing you how this automated process works. Importantly, however, provided with evidence that the factor loadings (see Model 1 in Figure 9.4) are not equivalent across the two groups ($\Delta\chi^2_{(19)} = p < .05$), the next step, in practice, is to determine which factor loadings are contributing to these noninvariant findings. As such, you then need to conduct these steps in sequence using the labeling technique and procedure illustrated in Chapter 7. The model resulting from this series of tests (the one in which all estimated factor loadings are group-equivalent) then becomes the measurement model used in testing for Model 2. If results from the testing of Model 2 (all structural regression paths constrained equal across groups) are found also to yield evidence of noninvariance, the next task is to identify the paths contributing to these findings, and so the same process applied in the case of the factor loadings is once again implemented here for Model 2. Likewise, once a final model is established at this stage (one in which all factor loadings and structural regression paths are multigroup equivalent), the process is repeated for each subsequent model to be tested.

The practical CFI difference approach

We turn now to the alternative approach based on ΔCFI results. If we were to base our decision making regarding equivalence of the postulated pattern of causal structure on the more practical approach of the difference in CFI values (see Cheung & Rensvold, 2002; Chapter 7, this volume), we would draw a starkly different conclusion—that, indeed, the model is completely and totally invariant across the two groups. This conclusion, of course, is based on the fact that the ΔCFI never exceeded a value of .001. In summary, this conclusion advises that all factor loadings, structural paths, factor covariances, factor residual variances, and measurement error variances are operating equivalently across calibration and validation samples.

That researchers seeking evidence of multigroup equivalence related to assessment instruments, theoretical structures, and/or patterns of causal relations can be confronted with such diametrically opposed conclusions based solely on the statistical approach used in determining this information is extremely disconcerting to say the least. Indeed, it is to be hoped that statisticians engaged in Monte Carlo simulation research related to structural equation modeling will develop more efficient and useful alternative approaches to this decision-making process in the near future. Until such time, however, we must either choose the approach which we believe is most appropriate for the data under study, or report results related to both.

section four

Other important applications

chapter ten

Testing for construct validity
The multitrait-multimethod model

The application illustrated in this chapter uses CFA procedures to test hypotheses bearing on construct validity. Specifically, hypotheses are tested within the framework of a multitrait-multimethod (MTMM) design by which multiple traits are measured by multiple methods. Following from the seminal work of Campbell and Fiske (1959), construct validity research typically focuses on the extent to which data exhibit evidence of (a) convergent validity, the extent to which different assessment methods concur in their measurement of the same trait (i.e., construct; ideally, these values should be moderately high); (b) discriminant validity, the extent to which independent assessment methods diverge in their measurement of different traits (ideally, these values should demonstrate minimal convergence); and (c) method effects, an extension of the discriminant validity issue. Method effects represent bias that can derive from use of the same method in the assessment of different traits; correlations among these traits are typically higher than those measured by different methods.

In the time since its inception, the original MTMM design (Campbell & Fiske, 1959) has been the target of much criticism as methodologists uncovered a growing number of limitations in its basic analytic strategy (see, e.g., Marsh, 1988, 1989; Schmitt & Stults, 1986). Although several alternative MTMM approaches have been proposed in the interim (for an early review, see Schmitt & Stults), the analysis of MTMM data within the framework of covariance structure modeling has gained the most prominence. Within this analytic context, some argue for the superiority of the Correlated Uniqueness (CU) model (Kenny, 1976, 1979; Kenny & Kashy, 1992; Marsh, 1989), while others support the general CFA (Conway, Scullen, Lievens, & Lance, 2004; Lance, Noble, & Scullen, 2002) or composite direct product model (Browne, 1984b). Nonetheless, a review of the applied MTMM literature reveals that the general CFA model[1] has been, and continues to be, the method of choice (Kenny & Kashy; Marsh & Grayson, 1995), albeit with increasingly more and varied specifications of this model (see, e.g., Eid et al., 2008; Hox & Kleiboer, 2007; LaGrange & Cole, 2008). The popularity of this approach likely derives from Widaman's (1985) seminal paper in which he proposed a taxonomy of nested model comparisons. For diverse comparisons of the correlated uniqueness, composite direct product, and the general CFA models, readers are referred to Bagozzi (1993); Bagozzi and Yi (1990, 1993); Byrne and Goffin (1993); Coenders and Saris (2000); Hernández and González-Romá (2002); Lance et al. (2002); Marsh and Bailey (1991); Marsh, Byrne, and Craven (1992); Marsh and Grayson (1995); Tomás, Hontangas, and Oliver (2000); and Wothke (1996).

The present application is taken from a study by Byrne and Bazana (1996), which was based on the general CFA approach to MTMM analysis. However, given increasing interest in the CU model over the intervening years, I also work through an analysis based on this approach to MTMM data. The primary intent of the original study was to test for evidence of convergent validity, discriminant validity, and method effects related to four facets of perceived competence (social, academic, English, and mathematics) as measured by self, teacher, parent, and peer ratings for early and late preadolescents and adolescents in grades 3, 7, and 11, respectively. For our purposes here, however, we focus only on data for late preadolescents (grade 7; $n = 193$). (For further elaboration of the sample, instrumentation, and analytic strategy, see Byrne & Bazana.)

Rephrased within the context of a MTMM design, the model of interest in this chapter is composed of four traits (social competence, academic competence, English competence, and mathematics competence) and four methods (self-ratings, teacher ratings, parent ratings, and peer ratings). A schematic portrayal of this model is presented in Figure 10.1.

Before launching into a discussion of this model, I consider it worthwhile to make a slight diversion in order that I can show you an option in the AMOS Toolbar that can be very helpful when you are working with a complex model that occupies a lot of page space such as we have here. The difficulty with the building of this model is that the double-headed arrows extend beyond the drawing space allotted by the program. In Figure 10.2, however, I illustrate how you can get around that problem simply by clicking on the *Fit-to-Page Icon* identified with the cursor as shown to the left of the model. Clicking on this tool will immediately resize the model to fit within the page perimeter.

The general CFA approach to MTMM analyses

In testing for evidence of construct validity within the framework of the general CFA model, it has become customary to follow guidelines set forth by Widaman (1985). As such, the hypothesized MTMM model is compared with a nested series of more restrictive models in which specific parameters either are eliminated or are constrained equal to zero or 1.0. The difference in χ^2 ($\Delta\chi^2$) provides the yardstick by which to judge evidence of convergent and discriminant validity. Although these evaluative comparisons are

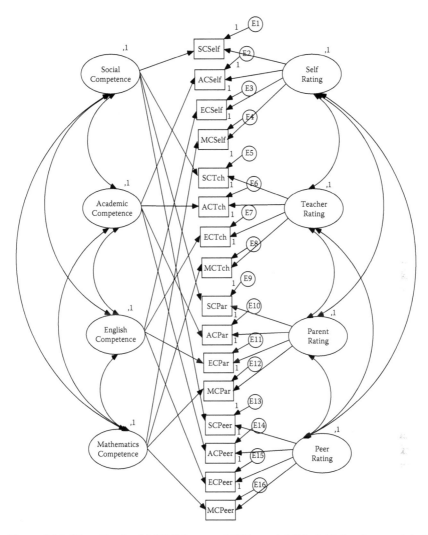

Figure 10.1 Hypothesized MTMM general CFA model (Model 1: freely correlated traits; freely correlated methods).

made solely at the matrix level, the CFA format allows for an assessment of construct validity at the individual parameter level. A review of the literature bearing on the CFA approach to MTMM analyses indicates that assessment is typically formulated at both the matrix and the individual parameter levels; we examine both in the present application.

The MTMM model portrayed in Figure 10.1 represents the hypothesized model and serves as the baseline against which all other alternatively nested

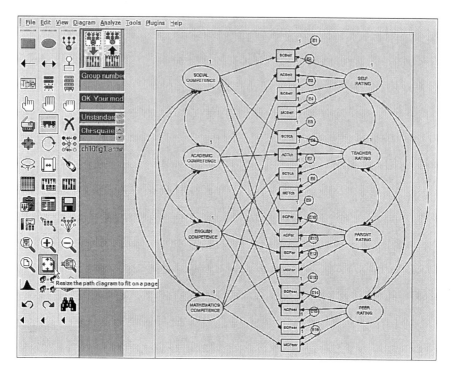

Figure 10.2 AMOS Graphics: *Resize* icon showing oversized MTMM model to the right.

models are compared in the process of assessing evidence of construct and discriminant validity. Clearly, this CFA model represents a much more complex structure than any of the CFA models examined thus far in this book. This complexity arises primarily from the loading of each observed variable onto *both* a trait and a method factor. In addition, the model postulates that, although the traits are correlated among themselves, as are the methods, any correlations between traits and methods are assumed to be zero.[2]

Testing for evidence of construct and discriminant validity involves comparisons between the hypothesized model (Model 1) and three alternative MTMM models. We turn now to a description of these four nested models; they represent those most commonly included in CFA MTMM analyses.

Model 1: Correlated traits/correlated methods

The first model to be tested (Model 1) represents the hypothesized model shown in Figure 10.1 and serves as the baseline against which all alternative

MTMM models are compared. As noted earlier, because its specification includes both trait and method factors, and allows for correlations among traits and among methods, this model is typically the least restrictive.[3]

Before working through the related analyses, I wish first to clarify the names of the variables, and then to point out two important and unique features regarding the specification of factor variances and covariances related to this first model. With respect to the labeling mechanism, the variables SCSELF to SCPEER represent general Social Competence (SC) scores as derived from self, teacher, parent, and peer ratings. Relatedly, for each of the remaining traits (Academic Competence [AC], English Competence [EC], and Math Competence [MC]), there are ratings by self, teacher, parents, and peers.

We turn now to the two critically important features of this model. *First*, in viewing Figure 10.1, you will see a comma, followed by a "1" (,1) above each of the six factors in the model. This specification indicates that the variance for each of these factors is fixed to 1.00. If either a number (indicating a fixed parameter) or a label (indicating an estimated parameter) were to precede the comma, these markings would refer to the factor mean (see, e.g., Figure 8.11); any like markings that instead follow the comma refer to the factor variance. The question now is: Why are these factor variances specified as fixed parameters in the model? In answering this question, recall from Chapter 5 that in the specification of model parameters, one can either estimate a factor loading, or estimate the variance of its related factor, but cannot estimate both, the rationale underlying this caveat being linked to the issue of model identification. In all previous examples thus far in the book, one factor loading in every set of congeneric measures has been fixed to 1.00 for this purpose. However, in MTMM models, interest focuses on the factor loadings and, thus, the alternative approach to model identification is implemented. The process of fixing the factor variance to a value of 1.0 is easily accomplished in AMOS Graphics by first right-clicking on the factor, selecting *Object Properties*, clicking on the *Parameter* tab, and then entering a "1" in the *Variance* box as shown in Figure 10.3.

Second, note in Figure 10.1 that all trait (Social Competence to Mathematics Competence) and method (Self-Rating to Peer Rating) covariances are freely estimated. Note, however, that covariances among traits and methods have *not* been specified (see note 2).

Let's turn now to the test of this correlated traits/correlated methods (CTCM) model. Immediately upon clicking on the *Calculate* icon (or drop-down menu), you will be presented with the dialog box shown in Figure 10.4, which lists a series of covariance parameters and warns that these pairs must remain uncorrelated. In fact, the parameters listed represent all covariances between trait and method factors, which as I noted

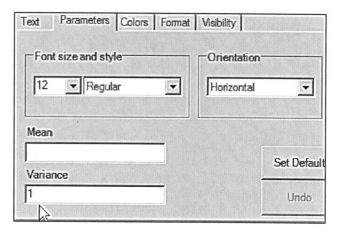

Figure 10.3 AMOS Graphics: *Object Properties* dialog box with parameter tab activated and showing a value of 1 assigned to a factor variance.

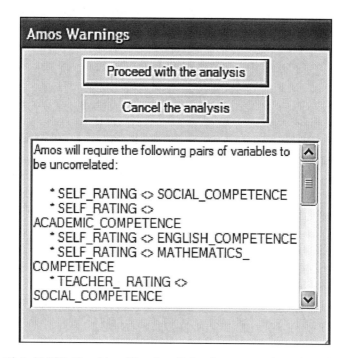

Figure 10.4 AMOS Graphics: *Warning* dialog box re: trait and method factor correlations.

earlier in this chapter cannot be estimated for statistical reasons. Thus, we can proceed by clicking on the *Proceed With the Analysis* tab.

In reviewing results for this initial analysis, we turn first to the "Parameter Summary" table, which is shown in Figure 10.5. Listed first in this summary are 48 weights (i.e., regression paths): 16 fixed weights associated with the error terms, and 32 estimated weights associated with the factor loadings. Next, we have 12 covariances (6 for each set of trait and method factors) and 24 variances (8 fixed factor variances; 16 estimated error variances).

The next critically important result reported in the output file is the message that the solution is not admissible, which is reported in Figure 10.6. A right-click of the mouse on this statement (which is highlighted in blue in the output) produced a pop-up dialog box suggesting why the solution might be inadmissible. A review of the estimates for this solution shows the variance associated with the error term E2 to be negative.

It is now widely known that the estimation of improper estimates, such as these, is a common occurrence with applications of the general CFA model to MTMM data. Indeed, so pervasive is this problem that the estimation of a proper solution may be regarded as a rare find (see, e.g., Kenny & Kashy, 1992; Marsh, 1989; Wothke, 1993). Although these results can be triggered by a number of factors, one likely cause in the case of MTMM models is the overparameterization of the model (see Wothke, 1993); this condition likely occurs as a function of the complexity of specification. In addressing this conundrum, early research has suggested a reparameterization of the model in the format of the correlated uniqueness (CU) model (see Kenny, 1976, 1979; Kenny & Kashy, 1992; Marsh, 1989; Marsh & Bailey, 1991; Marsh & Grayson, 1995). Alternative approaches have appeared in the more recent literature; these include the use of multiple indicators (Eid, Lischetzke, Nussbeck, & Trierweiler, 2003; Tomás et al., 2000), the specification of different models for different types of methods (Eid et al., 2008), and the specification of equality constraints in the CU model (Coenders & Saris, 2000; Corten et al., 2002). Because the CU model has become the topic of considerable interest and debate over the

Parameter summary (Group number 1)						
	Weights	Covariances	Variances	Means	Intercepts	Total
Fixed	16	0	8	0	0	24
Labeled	0	0	0	0	0	0
Unlabeled	32	12	16	0	0	60
Total	48	12	24	0	0	84

Figure 10.5 AMOS Graphics: Parameter summary for initially hypothesized model.

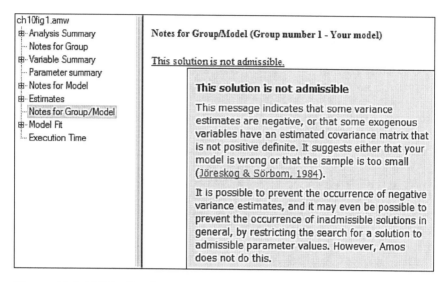

Figure 10.6 AMOS Graphics: *Warning* dialog box advising of inadmissible solution.

past few years, I considered it worthwhile to include this model also in the present chapter. However, given that (a) the CU model represents a special case of, rather than a nested model within, the general CFA framework, and (b) it is important first to work through the nested model comparisons proposed by Widaman (1985), I delay discussion and application of this model until later in the chapter.

Returning to our inadmissible solution, let's review the variance estimates (shown in Figure 10.7) where we find a negative variance associated error term E2. Important to this result is a study by Marsh et al. (1992) showing that when improper solutions occur in CFA modeling of MTMM data, one approach to resolution of the problem is to impose an equality constraint between parameters having similar estimates. Thus, in an attempt to resolve the inadmissible solution problem, Model 1 was respecified with the error variance for E2 constrained equal to that for E1, which represented a positive value of approximately the same size. Assignment of this constraint was implemented via the AMOS labeling process illustrated in Figure 10.8. (For a review of this process, see Chapters 5 and 7.)

This respecified model yielded a proper solution, the summary of which is reported in Figure 10.9; the estimates pertinent to the variances only are reported in Figure 10.10. As can be seen from the latter, this minor respecification resolved the negative error variance resulting in both parameters having an estimated value of .030.

Variances: (Group number 1 - Your model)					
	Estimate	S.E.	C.R.	P	Label
SELF_RATING	1.000				
TEACHER_RATING	1.000				
PARENT_RATING	1.000				
PEER_RATING	1.000				
SOCIAL_COMPETENCE	1.000				
ACADEMIC_COMPETENCE	1.000				
ENGLISH_COMPETENCE	1.000				
MATHEMATICS_COMPETENCE	1.000				
E6	.056	.025	2.233	.026	
E13	.911	.100	9.143	***	
E14	.103	.057	1.793	.073	
E16	.436	.057	7.717	***	
E1	.141	.060	2.328	.020	
E2	-.124	.135	-.916	.359	
E3	.099	.043	2.293	.022	
E4	.222	.043	5.099	***	
E5	.352	.039	8.987	***	
E8	.301	.038	7.878	***	
E7	.198	.031	6.433	***	
E9	.341	.054	6.329	***	
E10	.140	.026	5.411	***	
E11	.189	.038	4.937	***	
E12	.164	.042	3.920	***	
E15	.542	.064	8.412	***	

Figure 10.7 AMOS Graphics: Output file with problematic error variance circled.

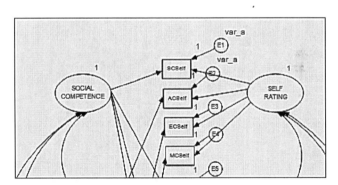

Figure 10.8 AMOS Graphics: Micro view of labeled error terms constrained equal.

Goodness-of-fit statistics related to this model are reported in Table 10.1. As evidenced from these results, the fit between this respecified CTCM model and the data was almost perfect (CFI = .999; RMSEA = .011; 90% C.I. .000, .043). Indeed, had additional parameters been added to

Notes for Model (Your model)

Computation of degrees of freedom (Your model)

Number of distinct sample moments:	136
Number of distinct parameters to be estimated:	59
Degrees of freedom (136 - 59):	77

Result (Your model)

Minimum was achieved
Chi-square = 78.721
Degrees of freedom = 77
Probability level = .424

Figure 10.9. AMOS Graphics: Model notation showing results of an admissible solution.

Variances: (Group number 1 - Your model)

	Estimate	S.E.	C.R.	P	Label
SELF_RATING	1.000				
TEACHER_RATING	1.000				
PARENT_RATING	1.000				
PEER_RATING	1.000				
SOCIAL_COMPETENCE	1.000				
ACADEMIC_COMPETENCE	1.000				
ENGLISH_COMPETENCE	1.000				
MATHEMATICS_COMPETENCE	1.000				
E1	.030	.023	1.295	.195	var_a
E2	.030	.023	1.295	.195	var_a
E6	.058	.025	2.321	.020	
E13	.949	.101	9.433	***	
E14	.126	.056	2.229	.026	
E16	.427	.057	7.475	***	
E3	.057	.045	1.262	.207	
E4	.160	.041	3.930	***	
E5	.371	.039	9.571	***	
E8	.311	.038	8.124	***	
E7	.191	.030	6.363	***	
E9	.378	.045	8.444	***	
E10	.119	.024	5.019	***	
E11	.214	.030	7.008	***	
E12	.158	.043	3.647	***	
E15	.526	.065	8.146	***	

Figure 10.10 AMOS Graphics: Output file with constrained estimates highlighted.

Table 10.1 Selected AMOS Output: Goodness-of-Fit Statistics for
Correlated Traits/Correlated Methods Model

Model	NPAR	CMIN	DF	P	CMIN/DF
Your model	59	78.721	77	.424	1.022
Saturated model	136	.000	0		
Independence model	16	1496.312	120	.000	12.469

Baseline comparisons

Model	NFI Delta1	RFI rho1	IFI Delta2	TLI rho2	CFI
Your model	.947	.918	.999	.998	.999
Saturated model	1.000		1.000		1.000
Independence model	.000	.000	.000	.000	.000

RMSEA

Model	RMSEA	LO 90	HI 90	PCLOSE
Your model	.011	.000	.043	.987
Independence model	.244	.233	.256	.000

the model as a result of post hoc analyses, I would have concluded that the results were indicative of an overfitted model. However, because this was not the case, I can only presume that the model fits the data exceptionally well.

We turn now to three additional MTMM models against which modified Model 1 will be compared.

Model 2: No traits/correlated methods

Specification of parameters for this model is portrayed schematically in Figure 10.11. Of major importance with this model is the total absence of trait factors. It is important to note that for purposes of comparison across all four MTMM models, the constraint of equality between the error terms E1 and E2 is maintained throughout. Goodness-of-fit for this model proved to be very poor ($\chi^2_{(99)} = 439.027$; CFI = .753; RMSEA = .134, 90% C.I. .121, .147). A summary of comparisons between this model and Model 1, as well as between all remaining models, is tabled following this review of each MTMM model.

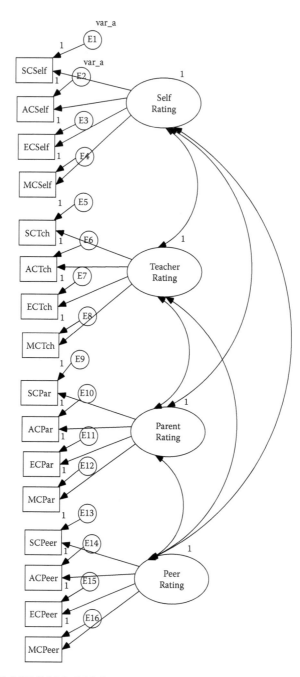

Figure 10.11 MTMM Model 2 (no traits; correlated methods).

Model 3: Perfectly correlated traits/freely correlated methods

In reviewing the specification for Model 3 shown in Figure 10.12, we can see that as with the hypothesized CTCM model (Model 1), each observed variable loads on both a trait and a method factor. However, in stark contrast to Model 1, this MTMM model argues for trait correlations that are

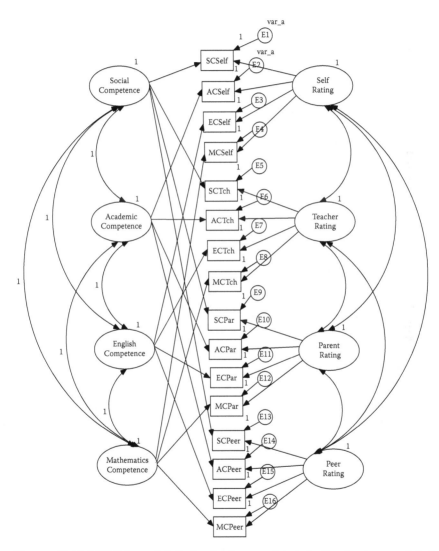

Figure 10.12 MTMM model 3 (perfectly correlated traits; freely correlated methods).

perfect (i.e., they are equal to 1.0); consistent with both Models 1 and 2, the method factors are freely estimated. Although goodness-of-fit results for this model were substantially better than for Model 2, they nonetheless were indicative of only a marginally well-fitting model and one that was somewhat less well-fitting than Model 1 ($\chi^2_{(83)}$ = 227.768; CFI = .895; RMSEA = .011, 90% C.I. .081, .110).

Model 4: Freely correlated traits/uncorrelated methods

This final MTMM model is portrayed in Figure 10.13 and differs from Model 1 only in the absence of specified correlations among the method factors. Goodness-of-fit results for this model revealed an exceptionally good fit to the data ($\chi^2_{(83)}$ = 120.291; CFI = .973; RMSEA = .048, 90% C.I. = .027, .067).

Testing for evidence of convergent and discriminant validity: MTMM matrix-level analyses

Comparison of models

Now that we have examined goodness-of-fit results for each of the MTMM models, we can turn to the task of determining evidence of construct and discriminant validity. In this section, we ascertain information at the matrix level only, through the comparison of particular pairs of models. A summary of fit related to all four MTMM models is presented in Table 10.2, and results of model comparisons are summarized in Table 10.3.

Evidence of convergent validity

As noted earlier, one criterion of construct validity bears on the issue of convergent validity, the extent to which *independent measures* of the *same trait* are correlated (e.g., teacher and self-ratings of social competence); these values should be substantial and statistically significant (Campbell & Fiske, 1959). Using Widaman's (1985) paradigm, evidence of convergent validity can be tested by comparing a model in which traits are specified (Model 1) with one in which they are not (Model 2), the difference in χ^2 between the two models ($\Delta\chi^2$) providing the basis for judgment; a significant difference in χ^2 supports evidence of convergent validity. In an effort to provide indicators of nested model comparisons that were more realistic than those based on the χ^2 statistic, Bagozzi and Yi (1990), Widaman (1985), and others have examined differences in CFI values. However, until the work of Cheung and Rensvold (2002), these ΔCFI values have served in only a heuristic sense as an evaluative base upon which to determine

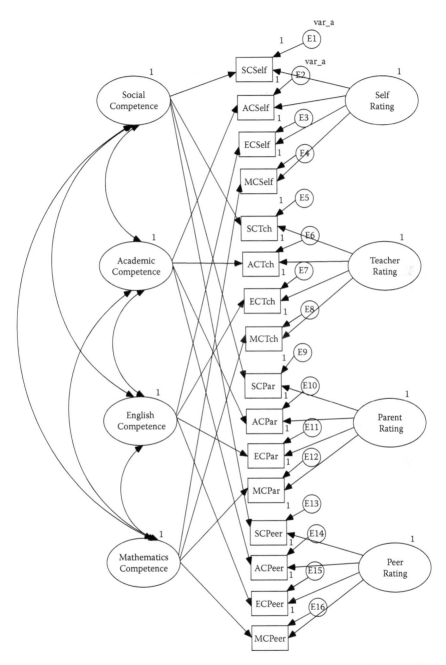

Figure 10.13 MTMM model 4 (freely correlated traits; uncorrelated methods).

Table 10.2 Summary of Goodness-of-Fit Indices for MTMM Models

Model	χ^2	df	CFI	RMSEA	RMSEA 90% C.I.	PCLOSE
1. Freely correlated traits;[a] freely correlated methods	78.721	77	.999	.011	.000, .043	.987
2. No traits; freely correlated methods	439.027	99	.753	.134	.121, .147	.000
3. Perfectly correlated traits; freely correlated methods	227.768	83	.895	.095	.081, .110	.000
4. Freely correlated traits; uncorrelated methods	120.291	83	.973	.048	.027, .067	.000

[a] Represents respecified model with an equality constraint imposed between E1 and E2.

Table 10.3 Differential Goodness-of-Fit Indices for MTMM Nested Model Comparisons

Model comparisons	Difference in χ^2	df	CFI
Test of Convergent Validity			
Model 1[a] versus Model 2 (traits)	360.306	22	.246
Test of Discriminant Validity			
Model 1[a] versus Model 3 (traits)	149.047	6	.104
Model 1[a] versus Model 4 (methods)	41.570	6	.026

[a] Represents respecified model with an equality constraint imposed between E1 and E2.

evidence of convergent and discriminant validity. Recently, Cheung and Rensvold examined the properties of 20 goodness-of-fit indices, within the context of invariance testing, and arbitrarily recommended that ΔCFI values should not exceed .01. Although the present application does not include tests for invariance, the same principle holds regarding the model comparisons. As shown in Table 10.3, the $\Delta\chi^2$ was highly significant ($\chi^2_{(22)} = 360.306$, $p < .001$), and the difference in practical fit (ΔCFI = .246) substantial, thereby arguing for the tenability of this criterion.

Evidence of discriminant validity

Discriminant validity is typically assessed in terms of both traits and methods. In testing for evidence of trait discriminant validity, one is interested in the extent to which *independent measures* of *different traits* are correlated; these values should be negligible. When the independent measures represent different methods, correlations bear on the discriminant validity of traits; when they represent the same method, correlations bear on the presence of method effects, another aspect of discriminant validity.

In testing for evidence of discriminant validity among traits, we compare a model in which traits correlate freely (Model 1) with one in which they are perfectly correlated (Model 3); the larger the discrepancy between the χ^2 and the CFI values, the stronger the support for evidence of discriminant validity. This comparison yielded a $\Delta\chi^2$ value that was statistically significant ($\chi^2_{(6)} = 149.047$, $p < .001$), and the difference in practical fit was fairly large (ΔCFI = .100), thereby suggesting only modest evidence of discriminant validity. As was noted for the traits (see endnote 3), we could alternatively specify a model in which perfectly correlated method factors are specified; as such, a minimal $\Delta\chi^2$ would argue *against* evidence of discriminant validity.

Based on the same logic, albeit in reverse, evidence of discriminant validity related to method effects can be tested by comparing a model in which method factors are freely correlated (Model 1) with one in which the method factors are specified as uncorrelated (Model 4). In this case, a large $\Delta\chi^2$ (or substantial ΔCFI) argues for the lack of discriminant validity and, thus, for common method bias across methods of measurement. On the strength of both statistical ($\Delta\chi^2_{(6)} = 41.570$) and nonstatistical ($\Delta$CFI = .026) criteria, as shown in Table 10.3, it seems reasonable to conclude that evidence of discriminant validity for the methods was substantially stronger than it was for the traits.

Testing for evidence of convergent and discriminant validity: MTMM parameter-level analyses

Examination of parameters

A more precise assessment of trait- and method-related variance can be ascertained by examining individual parameter estimates. Specifically, the factor loadings and factor correlations of the hypothesized model (Model 1) provide the focus here. Because it is difficult to envision the MTMM pattern of factor loadings and correlations from the output when more than six factors are involved, these values have been tabled to facilitate the assessment of convergent and discriminant validity; standardized estimates for the factor loadings are summarized in Table 10.4, and for the factor correlations in Table 10.5. (For a more extensive discussion of these MTMM findings, see Byrne & Bazana, 1996.)

Table 10.4 Trait and Method Loadings for MTMM Model 1
(Correlated Traits; Correlated Methods)[a]

	SC	AC	EC	MC	SR	TR	PAR	PER
Self-ratings (SR)								
Social competence	.969				.007[b]			
Academic competence		.805			.511			
English competence			.907		− .006[b]			
Mathematics competence				.773	.405			
Teacher ratings (TR)								
Social competence	.361					.274		
Academic competence		.312				.892		
English competence			.326			.758		
Mathematics competence				.478		.592		
Parent ratings (PAR)								
Social competence	.537						.376	
Academic competence		.512					.675	
English competence			.609				.441	
Mathematics competence				.726			.522	
Peer ratings (PER)								
Social competence	.281							.396
Academic competence		.312						.883
English competence			.276					.652
Mathematics competence				.372				.669

[a] Standardized estimates.
[b] Not statistically significant ($p < .05$).

Evidence of convergent validity

In examining individual parameters, convergent validity is reflected in the magnitude of the trait loadings. As indicated in Table 10.4, all trait loadings are statistically significant with magnitudes ranging from .276 (peer ratings of English competence) to .969 (self-ratings of social competence). However, in a comparison of factor loadings across traits and methods, we see that the proportion of method variance exceeds that of trait variance for all but one of the teacher ratings (social competence), only one of the parent ratings (academic competence), and all of the peer ratings.[4] Thus, although at first blush, evidence of convergent validity appeared to be fairly good at the matrix level, more in-depth examination at the individual parameter level reveals the attenuation of traits by method effects

Table 10.5 Trait and Method Correlations for MTMM Model 1 (Correlated Traits; Correlated Methods)[a]

| Measures | Traits | | | | | Methods | | | |
	SC	AC	EC	MC	SR	TR	PAR	PER
Social Competence (SC)	1.000							
Academic Competence (AC)	.370	1.000						
English Competence (EC)	.224	.834	1.000					
Mathematics Competence (MC)	.241	.758	.474	1.000				
Self-Ratings (SR)					1.000			
Teacher Ratings (TR)					.425	1.000		
Parent Ratings (PAR)					.224[b]	.562	1.000	
Peer Ratings (PER)					.263	.396	.160[b]	1.000

[a] Standardized estimates.
[b] Not statistically significant ($p < .05$).

related to teacher and peer ratings, thereby tempering evidence of convergent validity (see also Byrne & Goffin, 1993, with respect to adolescents).

Evidence of discriminant validity

Discriminant validity bearing on particular traits and methods is determined by examining the factor correlation matrices. Although, conceptually, correlations among traits should be negligible in order to satisfy evidence of discriminant validity, such findings are highly unlikely in general, and with respect to psychological data in particular. Although these findings, as shown in Table 10.5, suggest that relations between perceived academic competence (AC) and the subject-specific perceived competencies of English (EC) and mathematics (MC) are most detrimental to the attainment of trait discriminant validity, they are nonetheless consistent with construct validity research in this area as it relates to late preadolescent children (see Byrne & Worth Gavin, 1996).

Finally, an examination of method factor correlations in Table 10.5 reflects on their discriminability, and thus on the extent to which the methods are maximally dissimilar; this factor is an important underlying assumption of the MTMM strategy (see Campbell & Fiske, 1959). Given the obvious dissimilarity of self, teacher, parent, and peer ratings, it is somewhat surprising to find a correlation of .562 between teacher and parent ratings of competence. One possible explanation of this finding is that, except for minor editorial changes necessary in tailoring the instrument to either teacher or parent as respondents, the substantive content of all comparable items in the teacher and parent rating scales were identically worded, the rationale here being to maximize responses by different raters of the same student.

The correlated uniqueness approach to MTMM analyses

As noted earlier, the CU model represents a special case of the general CFA model. Building upon the early work of Kenny (1976, 1979), Marsh (1988, 1989) proposed this alternative MTMM model in answer to the numerous estimation and convergence problems encountered with analyses of general CFA models and, in particular, with the correlated traits/correlated methods model (Model 1 in this application). Recently, however, research has shown that the CU model, also, is not without its own problems, and researchers have proposed a number of specification alternatives to the general CU model (see, e.g., Conway et al., 2004; Corten et al., 2002; Lance et al., 2002). The hypothesized CU model tested here, however, is based on the originally postulated general CU model (see, e.g., Kenny, 1976, 1979; Kenny & Kashy, 1992; Marsh, 1989). A schematic representation of this model is shown in Figure 10.14.

In reviewing the model depicted in Figure 10.14, you will note that it embodies only the four correlated trait factors. In this aspect only, it is consistent with the model shown in Figure 10.1. The notably different feature about the CU model, however, is that although no method factors are specified per se, their effects are implied from the specification of correlated error terms (the uniquenesses)[5] associated with each set of observed variables embracing the same method. For example, as indicated in Figure 10.14, all error terms associated with the self-rating measures of social competence are intercorrelated; likewise, those associated with teacher, parent, and peer ratings are intercorrelated.

Consistent with the correlated traits/uncorrelated methods model (Model 4 in this application), the CU model assumes that effects associated with one method are uncorrelated with those associated with the other methods (Marsh & Grayson, 1995). However, one critically important difference between the CU model and both the correlated traits/correlated methods (Model 1) and correlated traits/no methods (Model 4) models involves the assumed unidimensionality of the method factors. Whereas Models 1 and 4 implicitly assume that the method effects associated with a particular method are unidimensional (i.e., they can be explained by a single latent method factor), the CU model carries no such assumption (Marsh & Grayson, 1995). These authors further noted (Marsh & Grayson, 1995, p. 185) that when an MTMM model includes *more than* three trait factors, this important distinction can be tested. However, when the number of traits equals three, the CU model is formally equivalent to the other two in the sense that the "number of estimated parameters and goodness-of-fit are the same, and parameter estimates from one can be transformed into the other" (Marsh & Grayson, 1995, p. 185).

Of course, from a practical perspective, the most important distinction between the CU model and Models 1 and 4 is that it typically results in a proper solution (Kenny & Kashy, 1992; Marsh, 1989; Marsh & Bailey, 1991). Model 1, on the other hand, is now notorious for its tendency to yield inadmissible solutions, as we observed in the present application. As a case in point, Marsh and Bailey (1991), in their analyses of 435 MTMM matrices based on both real and simulated data, reported that, whereas the correlated traits/correlated methods model resulted in improper solutions 77% of the time, the correlated uniqueness model yielded proper solutions nearly every time (98%). (For additional examples of the incidence of improper solutions with respect to Model 1, see Kenny & Kashy.) We turn now to the analyses based on the CU model (Model 5).

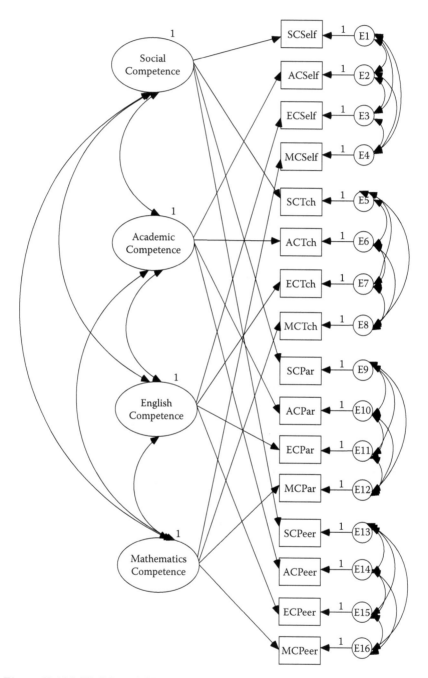

Figure 10.14 MTMM model 5 (correlated uniqueness model).

Model 5: Correlated uniqueness model

Reviewing, once again, the model depicted in Figure 10.14, we see that there are only four trait factors, and that these factors are hypothesized to correlate among themselves. In addition, we find the correlated error terms associated with each set of observed variables derived from the same measuring instrument (i.e., sharing the same method of measurement).

We turn now to selected sections of the AMOS output file pertinent to this correlated uniqueness model. In reviewing Table 10.6, we see that this model represents an excellent fit to the data ($\chi^2_{(74)} = 96.473$; CFI = .984; RMSEA = .040, 90%C.I. = .009, .060). Furthermore, consistent with past reported results (e.g., Kenny & Kashy, 1992; Marsh & Bailey, 1991), this solution resulted in no problematic parameter estimates.

Assessment of convergent and discriminant validity related to the CU model can be accomplished in the same way as it is for the general CFA model when focused at the individual parameter level. As can be seen in Table 10.7, evidence related to the convergent validity of the traits, not surprisingly, was substantial. Although all parameters were similar in terms of substantiality to those presented for Model 1 (see Table 10.4), there are interesting differences between the two models. In particular, these differences reveal all teacher and peer rating loadings to be higher for the CU model than for Model 1. Likewise, parent ratings, as they relate only to Social Competence, are also higher than for Model 1.

Table 10.6 Selected AMOS Output: Goodness-of-Fit Statistics for Correlated Uniqueness Model

Model	NPAR	CMIN	DF	P	CMIN/DF
Your model	62	96.473	74	.041	1.304
Saturated model	136	.000	0		
Independence model	16	1496.312	120	.000	12.469

Baseline comparisons

Model	NFI Delta1	RFI rho1	IFI Delta2	TLI rho2	CFI
Your model	.936	.895	.984	.974	.984
Saturated model	1.000		1.000		1.000
Independence model	.000	.000	.000	.000	.000

RMSEA

Model	RMSEA	LO 90	HI 90	PCLOSE
Your model	.040	.009	.060	.772
Independence model	.244	.233	.256	.000

Table 10.7 Trait and Method Loadings for MTMM
Model 5 (Correlated Uniqueness)[a]

	SC	AC	EC	MC
Self-ratings (SR)				
Social competence	.757			
Academic competence		.454		
English competence			.393	
Mathematics competence				.610
Teacher ratings (TR)				
Social competence	.464			
Academic competence		.424		
English competence			.447	
Mathematics competence				.537
Parent ratings (PAR)				
Social competence	.679			
Academic competence		.413		
English competence			.499	
Mathematics competence				.695
Peer ratings (PER)				
Social competence	.362			
Academic competence		.422		
English competence			.419	
Mathematics competence				.447

[a] Standardized estimates.

Let's look now at the factor correlations relevant to the traits; these estimates are presented in Table 10.8. In reviewing these values, we see that all but one estimated value is statistically significant and, for the most part, of similar magnitude across Model 1 and the CU model. The correlation between Social Competence and English Competence was found not to be statistically significant ($p < .05$) for the CU model.

Method effects in the CU model are determined by the degree to which the error terms are correlated with one another (Kenny & Kashy, 1992). In contrast to Model 1, there is no assumption that the method factor remains the same for all measures embracing the same method. Rather, as Kenny and Kashy explained, "In the Correlated Uniqueness model, each measure is assumed to have its own method effect, and the covariances between measures using the same method assess the extent to which there is a common method factor" (p. 169). In other words, as Kenny and

Table 10.8 Trait and Method Correlations for MTMM Model 5
(Correlated Uniqueness)[a]

Measures	Traits			
	SC	AC	EC	MC
Social competence (SC)	1.000			
Academic competence (AC)	.356	1.000		
English competence (EC)	.167[b]	.868	1.000	
Mathematics competence (MC)	.325	.800	.591	1.000

[a] Standardized estimates.
[b] Not statistically significant ($p < .05$).

Kashy further noted, whereas the general CFA MTMM model assumes that method effects are invariant across traits, the CU model allows for the multidimensionality of method effects. (For critiques of these effects, see Conway et al., 2004; Lance et al., 2002. For an attempt to understand the substance of these correlated error terms, see Saris & Aalberts, 2003.) It is interesting to see in Table 10.9 that the strongest method effects are clearly associated with teacher and peer ratings of the three academic competencies, and with parent ratings of only math competence. Indeed, from a substantive standpoint, these findings at least for the teacher and peer ratings certainly seem perfectly reasonable. On the other hand, the strong method effects shown for parent ratings involving relations between academic and math competencies are intriguing. One possible explanation may lie in the fact that when parents think "academic competence," their thoughts gravitate to "math competence." As such, academic competence appears to be defined in terms of how competent they perceive their son or daughter to be in math.

In concluding this chapter, it is worthwhile to underscore Marsh and Grayson's (1995, p. 198) recommendation regarding the analysis of MTMM data. As they emphasized, "MTMM data have an inherently complicated structure that will not be fully described in all cases by any of the models or approaches typically considered. There is, apparently, no 'right' way to analyze MTMM data that works in all situations" (Marsh & Grayson, 1995, p. 198). Consequently, Marsh and Grayson (1995), supported by Cudeck (1988), strongly advised that in the study of MTMM data, researchers should always consider alternative modeling strategies (see, e.g., Eid et al., 2009). In particular, Marsh and Grayson (1995) suggested an initial examination of data within the framework of the original Campbell-Fiske guidelines. This analysis should then be followed by the testing of a subset of at least four CFA models (including the CU model); for example, the five models considered in the present application would constitute an appropriate subset. Finally, given that the Composite Direct

Table 10.9 Error Correlations for MTMM Model 5 (Correlated Uniqueness)

	SC-Self	AC-Self	EC-Self	MC-Self	SC-Tchr	AC-Tchr	EC-Tchr	MC-Tch	SC-Par	AC-Par	EC-Par	MC-Par	SC-Peer	AC-Peer	EC-Peer	MC-Peer
SCSelf	1.000															
ACSelf	.338	1.000														
ECSelf	.375	.389	1.000													
MCSelf	.072[b]	.556	.173[b]	1.000												
SCTchr					1.000											
ACTchr					.238	1.000										
ECTchr					.132[b]	.684	1.000									
MCTchr					.046[b]	.511	.386	1.000								
SCPar									1.000							
ACPar									.220	1.000						
ECPar									.172[b]	.250	1.000					
MCPar									.176[b]	.467	.160[b]	1.000				
SCPeer													1.000			
ACPeer													.361	1.000		
ECPeer													.280	.579	1.000	
MCPeer													.206	.652	.434	1.000

[a] Standardized estimates.
[b] Not statistically significant ($p < .05$).

Product Model[6] is designed to test for the presence of multiplicative rather than additive effects, it should also be included in the MTMM analysis alternative approach strategy, but for a critique of this approach, readers are referred to Corten et al. (2002). In evaluating results from each of the covariance structure models noted here, Marsh and Grayson (1995) cautioned that, in addition to technical considerations such as convergence to proper solutions and goodness-of-fit, researchers should place a heavy emphasis on substantive interpretations and theoretical framework.

Endnotes

1. The term *general* is used to distinguish the generic CFA model from other special cases, such as the CU model (Marsh, 1989).
2. As a consequence of problems related to both the identification and estimation of CFA models, trait–method correlations cannot be freely estimated (see Schmitt & Stults, 1986; Widaman, 1985).
3. Alternatively, we could have specified a model in which the method factors were uncorrelated, indicating their zero correlation. Although both specifications provide the same yardstick by which to determine discriminant validity, the interpretation of results must necessarily be altered accordingly.
4. Trait and method variance, within the context of the general CFA MTMM model, equals the factor loading squared.
5. As noted in Chapter 3, the term *uniqueness* is used in the factor analytic sense to mean a composite of random measurement error and specific measurement error associated with a particular measuring instrument.
6. Whereas CFA models assume that test scores represent the sum of trait and method components (i.e., additive effects), the composite direct product model assumes that they derive from the product of the trait and method components (i.e., multiplicative effects).

chapter eleven

Testing for change over time
The latent growth curve model

Behavioral scientists have long been intrigued with the investigation of change. From a general perspective, questions of interest in such inquiry might be "Do the rates at which children learn differ in accordance with their interest in the subject matter?" From a more specific perspective, such questions might include "To what extent do perceptions of ability in particular school subjects change over time?" or "Does the rate at which self-perceived ability in math and/or science change differ for adolescent boys and girls?" Answers to questions of change such as these necessarily demand repeated measurements on a sample of individuals at multiple points in time. The focus of this chapter is directed toward addressing these types of change-related questions.

The application demonstrated here is based on a study by Byrne and Crombie (2003) in which self-ratings of perceived ability in math, language, and science were measured for 601 adolescents over a 3-year period that targeted grades 8, 9, and 10. In the present chapter, however, we focus on subscale scores related only to the subject areas of math and science. Consistent with most longitudinal research, some subject attrition occurred over the 3-year period; 101 cases were lost, thereby leaving 500 complete-data cases. In the original study, this issue of missingness was addressed by employing a multiple-sample missing-data model that involved three time-specific groups.[1] However, because the primary focus of this chapter is to walk you through a basic understanding and application of a simple latent growth curve (LGC) model, the present example is based on only the group having complete data across all three time points.[2] Nonetheless, I urge you to familiarize yourself with the pitfalls that might be encountered if you work with incomplete data in the analysis of LGC models (see Duncan & Duncan, 1994, 1995; Muthén, Kaplan, & Hollis, 1987) and to study the procedures involved in working with a missing data model (see Byrne & Crombie; Duncan & Duncan, 1994, 1995; Duncan, Duncan, Strycker, Li, & Alpert, 1999). For an elaboration of missing data issues in general, see Little and Rubin (1987), Muthén et al. (1987), and Chapter 13 of this volume; and related to longitudinal models in particular, see Duncan, Duncan, and Strycker (2006) and Hofer and Hoffman (2007).

Historically, researchers have typically based analyses of change on two-wave panel data, a strategy that Willett and Sayer (1994) deemed to be inadequate because of limited information. Addressing this weakness in longitudinal research, Willett (1988) and others (Bryk & Raudenbush, 1987; Rogosa, Brandt, & Zimowski, 1982; Rogosa & Willett, 1985) outlined methods of individual growth modeling that, in contrast, capitalized on the richness of multiwave data, thereby allowing for more effective testing of systematic interindividual differences in change. (For a comparative review of the many advantages of LGC modeling over the former approach to the study of longitudinal data, see Tomarken & Waller, 2005.)

In a unique extension of this earlier work, researchers (e.g., McArdle & Epstein, 1987; Meredith & Tisak, 1990; Muthén, 1997) have shown how individual growth models can be tested using the analysis of mean and covariance structures within the framework of structural equation modeling (SEM). Considered within this context, it has become customary to refer to such models as latent growth curve (LGC) models. Given its many appealing features (for an elaboration, see Willett and Sayer, 1994), together with the ease with which researchers can tailor its basic structure for use in innovative applications (see, e.g., Cheong, MacKinnon, & Khoo, 2003; Curran, Bauer, & Willoughby, 2004; Duncan, Duncan, Okut, Strycker, & Li, 2002; Hancock, Kuo, & Lawrence, 2001; Li et al., 2001), it seems evident that LGC modeling has the potential to revolutionize analyses of longitudinal research.

In this chapter, I introduce you to the topic of LGC modeling via three gradations of conceptual understanding. *First*, I present a general overview of measuring individual change in self-perceptions of math and science ability over a 3-year period from grade 8 through grade 10 (intraindividual change). *Next*, I illustrate the testing of an LGC model that measures differences in such change across all subjects (individual change). *Finally*, I demonstrate the addition of gender to the LGC model as a possible time-invariant predictor of change that may account for any heterogeneity in the individual growth trajectories (i.e., intercept, slope) of perceived ability in math and science.

Measuring change in individual growth over time: The general notion

In answering questions of individual change related to one or more domains of interest, a representative sample of individuals must be observed systematically over time, and their status in each domain measured on several temporally spaced occasions (Willett & Sayer, 1994). However, several conditions may also need to be met. *First*, the outcome variable representing the domain of interest must be of a continuous scale (but see Curran, Edwards, Wirth, Hussong, & Chassin, 2007, and Duncan et al., 2006, for more recent developments addressing this issue). *Second,* while the time lag between occasions can be either evenly or unevenly spaced, both the number and the spacing of these assessments must be the same for all individuals. *Third,* when the focus of individual change is structured as an LGC model, with analyses to be conducted using a SEM approach, data must be obtained for each individual on three or more occasions. *Finally,* the sample size must be large enough to allow for the detection of person-level effects (Willett & Sayer, 1994). Accordingly, one would expect minimum sample sizes of not less than 200 at each time point (see Boomsma, 1985; Boomsma & Hoogland, 2001).

The hypothesized dual-domain LGC model

Willett and Sayer (1994) have noted that the basic building blocks of the LGC model comprise two underpinning submodels which they have termed "Level 1" and "Level 2" models. The Level 1 model can be thought of as a "within-person" regression model that represents individual change over time with respect to (in the present instance) two single-outcome variables, *perceived ability in math* and *perceived ability in science.* The Level 2 model can be viewed as a "between-person" model that focuses on interindividual differences in change with respect to these outcome variables. We turn now to the first of these two submodels, which addresses the issue of intraindividual change.

Modeling intraindividual change

The first step in building an LGC model is to examine the within-person growth trajectory. In the present case, this task translates into determining, for each individual, the direction and extent to which his or her score in self-perceived ability in math and science changes from grade 8 through grade 10. Of critical import in most appropriately specifying and testing the LGC model, however, is that the shape of the growth trajectory be known a priori. If the trajectory of hypothesized change is considered to be linear (a typical assumption underlying LGC modeling in practice), then the specified model will include two growth parameters: (a) an intercept parameter representing an individual's score on the outcome variable at Time 1, and (b) a slope parameter representing the individual's rate of change over the time period of interest. Within the context of our work here, the intercept represents an adolescent's perceived ability in math and science at the end of grade 8; the slope represents the rate of change in this value over the 3-year transition from grade 8 through grade 10. As reported in Byrne and Crombie (2003), this assumption of linearity was tested and found to be tenable.[3] (For an elaboration of tests of underlying assumptions, see Byrne and Crombie; Willett & Sayer, 1994.)

Of the many advantages in testing for individual change within the framework of a structural equation model over other longitudinal strategies, two are of primary importance. *First,* this approach is based on the analysis of mean and covariance structures and, as such, can distinguish group effects observed in means from individual effects observed in covariances. *Second,* a distinction can be made between observed and unobserved (or latent) variables in the specification of models. This capability allows for both the modeling and estimation of measurement error. With these basic concepts in hand, let's turn now to Figure 11.1, where the hypothesized dual-domain model to be tested is schematically presented.

In reviewing this model, focus first on the six observed variables enclosed in rectangles at the top of the path diagram. Each variable constitutes a subscale score at one of three time points, with the first three representing *perceived math ability,* and the latter three, *perceived science ability.* Associated with each of these observed measures is their matching random measurement error term (E1–E6). Moving down to the bottom of the diagram, we see two latent factors associated with each of these math and science domains; these factors represent the intercept and slope for *perceived math ability* and *perceived science ability,* respectively.

Let's turn now to the modeled paths in the diagram. The arrows leading from each of the four factors to their related observed variables represent the regression of observed scores at each of three time points onto

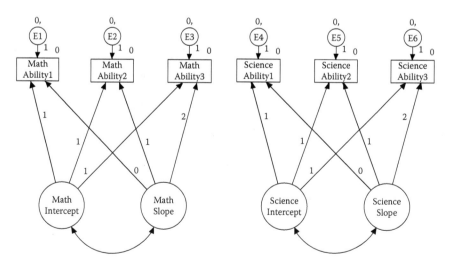

Figure 11.1 Hypothesized LGC model.

their appropriate Intercept and Slope factors. As usual, the arrows leading from the E's to the observed variables represent the influence of random measurement error. Finally, the modeled covariance between each pair of Intercept and Slope factors (for math and science ability) is assumed in the specification of an LGC model.

The numerical values assigned to the paths flow from the Intercept and Slope factors to the observed variables; these paths, of course, represent fixed parameters in the model. The 1's specified for the paths flowing from the Intercept factor to each of the observed variables indicate that each is constrained to a value of 1.0. This constraint reflects the fact that the intercept value remains constant across time for each individual (Duncan et al., 1999). The values of 0, 1, and 2 assigned to the slope parameters represent Years 1, 2, and 3, respectively. These constraints address the issue of model identification; they also ensure that the second factor can be interpreted as a slope. Three important points are of interest with respect to these fixed slope values: *First*, technically speaking, the first path (assigned a zero value) is really nonexistent and, therefore, has no effect. Although it would be less confusing to simply eliminate this parameter, it has become customary to include this path in the model, albeit with an assigned value of zero (Bentler, 2005). *Second*, these values represent equal time intervals (1 year) between measurements; had data collection taken place at unequal intervals, the values would need to be calculated accordingly (e.g., 6 months = .5). (For an example of needed adjustment to time points, see Byrne, Lam, & Fielding, 2008.) *Third*, the choice of fixed values assigned to the Intercept and Slope factor loadings is somewhat arbitrary, as any linear transformation of the time scale is usually permissible, and the specific coding of time chosen determines the interpretation of both factors. The Intercept factor is tied to a time scale (Duncan et al., 1999) because any shift in fixed loading values on the Slope factor will necessarily modify the scale of time bearing on the Intercept factor, which, in turn, will influence interpretations (Duncan et al., 1999). Relatedly, the variances and correlations among the factors in the model will change depending on the chosen coding (see, e.g., Bloxis & Cho, 2008).

In this section, our focus is on the modeling of intraindividual change. Within the framework of SEM, this focus is captured by the *measurement model*, the portion of a model that incorporates only linkages between the observed variables and their underlying unobserved factors. As you are well aware by now, of primary interest in any measurement model is the strength of the factor loadings or regression paths linking the observed and unobserved variables. As such, the only parts of the model in Figure 11.1 that are relevant in the modeling of intraindividual change are the regression paths linking the six observed variables to the four factors (two Intercepts, two Slopes), the factor variances and covariances, and the related measurement errors associated with these observed variables.

Essentially, we can think of this part of the model as an ordinary factor analysis model with two special features. *First,* all the loadings are fixed—there are no unknown factor loadings. *Second,* the particular pattern of fixed loadings plus the mean structure allows us to interpret the factors as Intercept and Slope factors. As in all factor models, the present case argues that each adolescent's perceived math and science ability scores, at each of three time points (Time 1 = 0; Time 2 = 1; Time 3 = 2), are a function of three distinct components: (a) a factor-loading matrix of constants (1; 1; 1) and known time values (0; 1; 2) that remain invariant across all individuals, multiplied by (b) a latent growth curve vector containing individual-specific and unknown factors, here called *individual growth parameters* (Intercept, Slope), plus (c) a vector of individual-specific and unknown errors of measurement. Whereas the latent growth curve vector represents the within-person *true* change in *perceived math ability* and *perceived science ability* over time, the error vector represents the within-person *noise* that serves to erode these true change values (Willett & Sayer, 1994).

In preparing for transition from the modeling of intraindividual change to the modeling of interindividual change, it is important that we review briefly the basic concepts underlying the analyses of mean and covariance structures in SEM. When population means are of no interest in a model, analysis is based on only covariance structure parameters. As such, all scores are considered to be deviations from their means, and, thus, the constant term (represented as α in a regression equation) equals zero. Given that mean values played no part in the specification of the Level 1 (or within-person) portion of our LGC model, only the analysis of covariance structures is involved. However, in moving to Level 2, the between-person portion of the model, interest focuses on mean values associated with the Intercept and Slope factors; these values in turn influence the means of the observed variables. Because both levels are involved in the modeling of interindividual differences in change, analyses are now based on both mean and covariance structures.

Modeling interindividual differences in change

Level 2 argues that, over and above hypothesized linear change in *perceived math ability* and *perceived science ability* over time, trajectories will necessarily vary across adolescents as a consequence of different intercepts and slopes. Within the framework of SEM, this portion of the model reflects the "structural model" component which, in general, portrays relations among unobserved factors and postulated relations among their associated residuals. Within the more specific LGC model, however, this structure is limited to the means of the Intercept and Slope factors, along with their related variances, which in essence represent deviations from the mean. The means carry information about average intercept and slope values, while the variances provide information on individual differences in intercept and slope values. The specification of these parameters, then, makes possible the estimation of interindividual differences in change.

Let's now reexamine Figure 11.1, albeit in more specific terms in order to clarify information bearing on possible differences in change across time. Within the context of the first construct, perceived ability in math, interest focuses on five parameters that are key to determining between-person differences in change: two factor means (Intercept; Slope), two factor variances, and one factor covariance. The factor means represent the average population values for the Intercept and Slope and answer the question "What is the population mean starting point and mean increment in *perceived math ability* from grades 8 through 10?" The factor variances represent deviations of the individual Intercepts and Slopes from their population means, thereby reflecting population interindividual differences in the initial (grade 8) *perceived math ability* scores, and the rate of change in these scores, respectively. Addressing the issue of variability, these key parameters answer the question "Are there interindividual differences in the starting point and growth trajectories of *perceived math ability* in the population?" Finally, the factor covariance represents the population covariance between any deviations in initial status and rate of change and answers the question "Do students who start higher (or lower) in *perceived math ability* tend to grow at higher (or lower) rates in that ability?"

Now that you have a basic understanding of LGC modeling, in general, and as it bears specifically on our hypothesized dual-domain model presented in Figure 11.1, let's direct our attention now on both the modeling and testing of this model within the framework of AMOS Graphics.

Testing latent growth curve models: A dual-domain model

The hypothesized model

In building an LGC model using AMOS Graphics, the program provides what it terms a *Plug-In,* an option that serves as a starter kit in providing the basic model and associated parameter specification. To use this

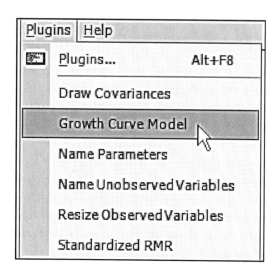

Figure 11.2 AMOS Graphics: Plug-in drop-down menu with LGC model selected.

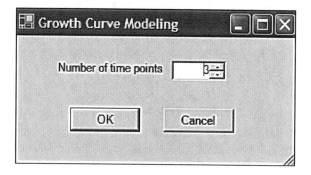

Figure 11.3 AMOS Graphics: *LGC Modeling* dialog box requesting information on number of time points involved.

Plug-In, click on the *Plug-In* menu and select *Growth Curve Model*, as shown in Figure 11.2. Once you make this selection, you will need to specify the number of time points pertinent to your data (see Figure 11.3). Of course, 3 is the default value as it represents the minimal appropriate number for LGC modeling.

Shown in Figure 11.4 is the automated LGC model that appears following the two previous steps. Simply duplicating this model allows for its application to the dual-domain model tested in this chapter. Importantly, however, there are several notations on this model that I consider to be

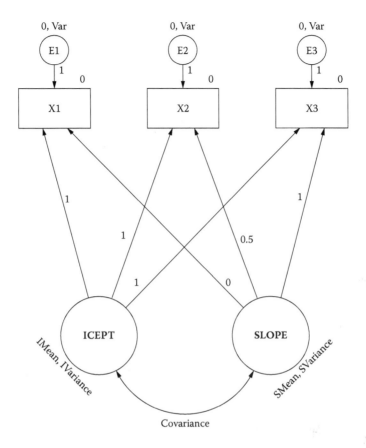

Figure 11.4 AMOS Graphics: Plug-in automated LGC model.

inappropriate specifications for our hypothesized model. As a result, you will note their absence from the model portrayed in Figure 11.1. (These modifications are easily implemented via the *Object Properties* dialog box, as has been demonstrated elsewhere in this volume, and are shown below in Figures 11.5 and 11.8.) *First,* associated with each of the three error terms you will see a zero value, followed by a comma and the letters *Var.* As you know from Chapter 8, the first of these represents the mean, and the second, the variance of each error term. As per AMOS Graphics notation, these labels indicate that the means of all error terms are constrained to zero and their variances are constrained equal across time. However, because specification of equivalent error variances would be inappropriate in the testing of our hypothesized model, these labels are not specified in Figure 11.1. Indeed, error variances contribute importantly to the interpretation of model parameters through correction for measurement error

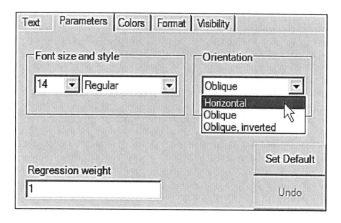

Figure 11.5 AMOS Graphics: *Object Properties* dialog box showing labeling orientation.

associated with the variances of the Intercept and Slope factors. In other words, specification of error variance allows for the same basic interpretation of model parameters, albeit with correction for random measurement error (Duncan et al., 2006). In all likelihood, the rationale underlying specification of the error variance equalities in the automated model is to offset an otherwise condition of model underidentification for the single-domain model generated by the Plug-In feature.

A second change between the model shown in Figure 11.1 and that of Figure 11.4 involves labels associated with the latent factors. On the automated model, you will note the labels *IMean*, *IVariance*, *SMean*, and *SVariance* associated with the Intercept and Slope factors, respectively. Again, these labels signal that these factor parameters are constrained equal across time. Because these constraint specifications are inappropriate for our analyses, they are not included in the hypothesized model. *Third*, note that the paths leading from the Slope factor to the observed variable for each time point are numbered 0, .50, and 1, whereas these path parameters in our hypothesized model are numbered 0, 1, and 2 in accordance with the time lag between data collections. Finally, of a relatively minor note is a change in orientation of the numbers assigned to the Intercept and Slope paths from oblique to horizontal (see Figure 11.5).

Before moving on to the analyses for this chapter, I consider it important to alert you to a couple of additional considerations related to the specification of LGC models. As is typical for these models, you will likely want to orient your page setup to landscape mode. Implementation of this reorientation is accomplished via the *Interface*

Properties dialog box as illustrated in Figure 11.6; its selection is made from the *View* drop-down menu.

In addition, I also want to draw your attention to an annoying error message which I have encountered on numerous occasions using AMOS Graphics. Hopefully, my notation here will prevent you from experiencing the same problem. Specifically, this error warning is triggered when a variable *name* in the data set differs in any way from the variable *name* noted in the *Object Properties* dialog box; even differences involving a space between characters can spark this error message! The variable *label* (i.e., shown on the model diagram), however, can be different. For example, the variable representing the Time 1 score for *perceived math ability* is shown as *m_abils* in the SPSS data file, but is labeled as *Math Ability* in the model (Figure 11.1). This error message and specification of name/label designation are illustrated in Figures 11.7 and 11.8, respectively.

Following this extended but nonetheless essential overview of the modeling and testing of LGC models using AMOS Graphics, we are now ready to examine their results. We turn first to results related to the initial test of our hypothesized model (see Figure 11.1).

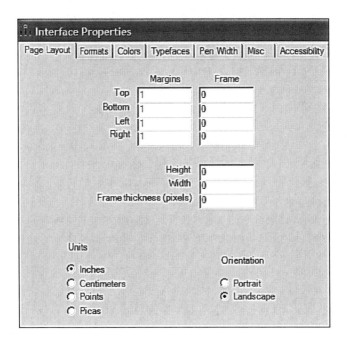

Figure 11.6 AMOS Graphics: *Interface Properties* dialog box showing page orientation with landscape mode selected.

Figure 11.7 AMOS Graphics: Error message advising of mismatch of variable name between data and program files.

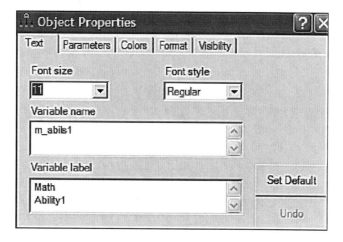

Figure 11.8 AMOS Graphics: *Object Properties* dialog box showing difference between variable name and label.

Selected AMOS output: Hypothesized model

Of prime importance in testing this first model are the extent to which it fits the data and the extent to which it may need some modification. We turn first to the goodness-of-fit statistics reported in Table 11.1. Of key concern here is the obviously poor fit of the model as indicated by the CFI value of .811 and the RMSEA value of .172. Clearly this model is misspecified in a very major way. For answers to this substantial misspecification, let's review the modification indices, which are reported in Table 11.2. Of primary interest are misspecification statistics associated with the two Intercept and two Slope Factors, which have been highlighted within the broken-line rectangle.

In reviewing these modification indices, we see that not including a covariance between the Math Ability and Science Ability Intercept factors is accounting for the bulk of the misspecification. Given the fairly

Table 11.1 Selected AMOS Output: Goodness-of-Fit Statistics Related to Hypothesized Model

Model fit summary

CMIN

Model	NPAR	CMIN	DF	P	CMIN/ DF
Default model	16	173.461	11	.000	15.769
Saturated model	27	.000	0		
Independence model	12	875.915	15	.000	58.394

Baseline comparisons

Model	NFIDelta1	RFI rho1	IFI Delta2	TLI rho2	CFI
Default model	.802	.730	.812	.743	.811
Saturated model	1.000		1.000		1.000
Independence model	.000	.000	.000	.000	.000

RMSEA

Model	RMSEA	LO 90	HI 90	PCLOSE
Default model	.172	.150	.195	.000
Independence model	.339	.320	.358	.000

substantial modification indices associated with the remaining three factor covariances, together with Willet and Sayer's (1996) caveat that, in multiple-domain LGC models, covariation among the growth parameters across domains should be considered, I respecified a second model (Model 2) in which all four factor covariances were specified; these results, as they relate to the parameter estimates, are reported in Table 11.3.

Although goodness-of-fit results pertinent to Model 2 were substantially improved ($\chi^2_{(7)} = 32.338$; CFI = .971; RMSEA = .085), a review of the estimates related to these factor covariances reveals only three to be statistically significant and, thus, worthy of incorporation into the final model. Specifically, results revealed the covariance between the Math and Science Ability Intercept factors and their related Slope factors to be important parameters in the model. In addition, given a probability value < .05 for the covariance between the Math Ability Intercept and the Science Ability Slope, I considered it important also to include this parameter in the final model. The remaining three statistically nonsignificant factor covariances were deleted from the model. This final model (Model 3) is shown schematically in Figure 11.9.

Of substantial interest in our review of results pertinent to this model is what a difference the incorporation of two additional factor covariances can make! As shown in Table 11.4, we now find a nice well-fitting model

Table 11.2 Selected AMOS Output: Modification Indices Related to Hypothesized Model

Covariances			M.I.	Par Change
Math_Slope	<-->	Science_Slope	30.836	.091
Math_Slope	<-->	Science Intercept	22.333	.131
Math_Intercept	<-->	Science_Slope	41.731	.182
Math_Intercept	<-->	Science Intercept	110.419	.503
E6	<-->	Math_Slope	8.320	.085
E6	<-->	Math_Intercept	10.448	.164
E5	<-->	Math_Slope	17.485	.122
E5	<-->	Math_Intercept	26.093	.256
E4	<-->	Math_Slope	4.634	−.065
E4	<-->	Math_Intercept	7.971	.147
E3	<-->	Science_Slope	20.103	.146
E3	<-->	Science Intercept	6.172	.137
E3	<-->	E6	13.781	.217
E2	<-->	Science Intercept	11.139	.139
E2	<-->	E5	28.126	.232
E1	<-->	Science Intercept	15.117	.160
E1	<-->	E4	18.549	.193

Table 11.3 Selected AMOS Output: Parameter Estimates Related to Model 2

			Estimate	S.E.	C.R.	P
Covariances						
Math_Intercept	<-->	Math_Slope	−.228	.073	−3.107	.002
Science Intercept	<-->	Science_Slope	−.055	.063	−.875	.382
Math_Slope	<-->	Science_Slope	.078	.022	3.544	***
Math_Slope	<-->	Science Intercept	−.070	.037	−1.877	.061
Math_Intercept	<-->	Science_Slope	−.028	.038	−.754	.451
Math_Intercept	<-->	Science Intercept	.536	.068	7.857	***
Correlations						
Math_Intercept	<-->	Math_Slope	−.442			
Science Intercept	<-->	Science_Slope	−.184			
Math_Slope	<-->	Science_Slope	.475			
Math_Slope	<-->	Science Intercept	−.181			
Math_Intercept	<-->	Science_Slope	−.071			
Math_Intercept	<-->	Science Intercept	.573			

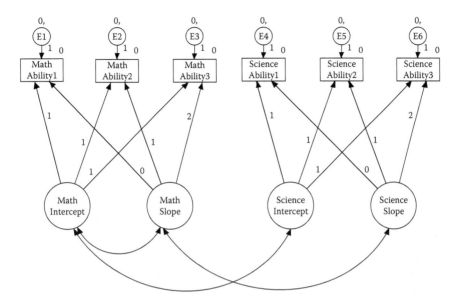

Figure 11.9 Final LGC model: No predictor.

Table 11.4 Selected AMOS Output: Goodness-of-Fit Statistics
Related to Model 3

Model fit summary				
CMIN				
Model	NPAR	CMIN	DF	P	CMIN/DF
Default model	17	36.265	10	.000	3.626
Saturated model	27	.000	0		
Independence model	12	875.915	15	.000	58.394

Baseline comparisons				
Model	NFI Delta1	RFI rho1	IFI Delta2	TLI rho2	CFI
Default model	.959	.938	.970	.954	.969
Saturated model	1.000		1.000		1.000
Independence model	.000	.000	.000	.000	.000

RMSEA			
Model	RMSEA	LO 90	HI 90	PCLOSE
Default model	.073	.048	.099	.064
Independence model	.339	.320	.358	.000

with related fit statistics of $\chi^2_{(10)} = 32.338$, CFI = .969, and RMSEA = .073. Having now determined a well-fitting model, we are ready to review the substantive results of the analysis. Both the unstandardized and standardized parameter estimates are reported in Table 11.5.

Table 11.5 Selected AMOS Output: Parameter Estimates Related to Model 3

	Estimate	S.E.	C.R.	P
Regression weights				
m_abils1 <--- Math_Intercept	1.000			
m_abils1 <--- Math_Slope	.000			
m_abils2 <--- Math_Intercept	1.000			
m_abils2 <--- Math_Slope	1.000			
m_abils3 <--- Math_Intercept	1.000			
m_abils3 <--- Math_Slope	2.000			
s_abils1 <--- Science Intercept	1.000			
s_abils1 <--- Science_Slope	.000			
s_abils2 <--- Science Intercept	1.000			
s_abils2 <--- Science_Slope	1.000			
s_abils3 <--- Science Intercept	1.000			
s_abils3 <--- Science_Slope	2.000			
Standardized regression weights				
m_abils1 <--- Math_Intercept	.897			
m_abils1 <--- Math_Slope	.000			
m_abils2 <--- Math_Intercept	.843			
m_abils2 <--- Math_Slope	.351			
m_abils3 <--- Math_Intercept	.729			
m_abils3 <--- Math_Slope	.606			
s_abils1 <--- Science Intercept	.656			
s_abils1 <--- Science_Slope	.000			
s_abils2 <--- Science Intercept	.648			
s_abils2 <--- Science_Slope	.245			
s_abils3 <--- Science Intercept	.625			
s_abils3 <--- Science_Slope	.474			
Means				
Math_Intercept	5.118	.055	93.529	***
Math_Slope	−.162	.032	−5.064	***
Science Intercept	4.763	.051	93.036	***
Science_Slope	.122	.030	4.073	***

(continued)

Table 11.5 Selected AMOS Output: Parameter Estimates Related to Model 3
(*Continued*)

	Estimate	S.E.	C.R.	P
Covariances				
Math_Intercept <--> Math_Slope	−.205	.072	−2.856	.004
Math_Slope <--> Science_Slope	.056	.017	3.217	.001
Math_Intercept <--> Science Intercept	.480	.054	8.814	***
Correlations				
Math_Intercept <--> Math_Slope	−.403			
Math_Slope <--> Science_Slope	.404			
Math_Intercept <--> Science Intercept	.548			
Variances				
Math_Intercept	1.220	.128	9.517	***
Math_Slope	.211	.058	3.638	***
Science Intercept	.628	.064	9.742	***
Science_Slope	.090	.031	2.909	.004
E2	.694	.062	11.124	***
E3	1.053	.135	7.820	***
E4	.831	.071	11.768	***
E5	.779	.064	12.185	***
E6	.619	.102	6.062	***
E1	.295	.104	2.851	.004

*** probability < .000

Given that the regression weights represented only fixed parameters, there is little of interest in this section. Of major importance, however, are the estimates reported in the remaining sections of the output file. Turning first to the Means estimates, we see that these parameters for both the Intercepts and Slopes were statistically significant. Specifically, findings reveal the average score for *perceived science ability* (4.763) to be slightly lower than for *perceived math ability* (5.118). However, whereas adolescents' average self-perceived Math Ability scores decreased over a 3-year period from grade 8 to grade 10 (as indicated by the a value of −0.162), those related to self-perceived Science Ability increased (0.122).

Let's turn now to the factor covariances, reviewing first the *within-domain* covariance, that is to say, the covariance between the intercept and slope related to the same construct. Here, we find the estimated covariance between the Intercept and Slope factors for Math Ability to be statistically significant (p < .05). The negative estimate of −.205 suggests that adolescents whose self-perceived scores in math ability were high in grade 8 demonstrated a lower rate of increase in these scores over the 3-year period from grade 8 through grade 10 than was the case for adolescents whose self-perceived math ability scores were lower at Time 1. In other words, grade 8 students who perceived themselves as being less able in math than their peers made the greater gains. A negative correlation between initial status and possible gain is an old phenomenon in psychology known as the law of initial values.

Turning to the first *between-domain* covariance shown in the output (Math Slope/Science Slope), we see that although statistically significant, this reported value is very small (.056). Nonetheless, a review of the standardized coefficients shows this correlation ($r = .404$), as for the other two covariances, to be moderately high. This result indicates that as growth in adolescents' perceptions of their math ability from grades 8 through 10 undergoes a moderate increase, so also do their perceptions of science ability. Finally, the fairly strong correlation between intercepts related to math and science ability ($r = .548$) indicate that for adolescents perceiving themselves as having high ability in math, they also view themselves as concomitantly as having high ability in science.

Finally, turning to the *Variance* section of the output file, we note that, importantly, all estimates related to the intercept and slope for each perceived ability domain are statistically significant ($p < .05$). These findings reveal strong interindividual differences in both the initial scores of perceived ability in math and science at Time 1, and in their change over time, as the adolescents progressed from grade 8 through grade 10. Such evidence of interindividual differences provides powerful support for further investigation of variability related to the growth trajectories. In particular, the incorporation of predictors into the model can serve to explain their variability. Of somewhat less importance substantively, albeit important methodologically, all random measurement error terms are also statistically significant ($p < .05$).

Testing latent growth curve models: Gender as a time-invariant predictor of change

As noted earlier, provided with evidence of interindividual differences, we can then ask whether, and to what extent, one or more predictors might explain this heterogeneity. For our purposes here, we ask whether statistically significant heterogeneity in the individual growth trajectories (i.e., intercept and slope) of perceived ability in math and science can be explained by gender as a time-invariant predictor of change. As such, two questions that we might ask are "Do self-perceptions of ability in math and science differ for adolescent boys and girls at Time 1 (grade 8)?" and "Does the rate at which self-perceived ability in math and science change over time differ for adolescent boys and girls?" To answer these questions, the predictor variable *gender* must be incorporated into the Level 2 (or structural) part of the model. This predictor model represents an extension of our final, best fitting multiple domain model (Model 3) and is shown schematically in Figure 11.10.

Of import regarding the path diagram displayed in Figure 11.10 is the addition of four new model components. *First,* note the four regression paths that flow from the variable of *gender* to the Intercept and Slope factors associated with each of the math and science ability domains. These regression paths are of primary interest in this predictor model as they hold the key in answering the question of whether the trajectory of Perceived Ability in Math and Perceived Ability in Science differs for adolescent boys and girls. *Second,* there is now a latent residual associated with each of the Intercept and Slope factors (D1 to D4). This addition is a necessary requirement as these factors are now dependent variables in the model due to the regression paths generated from the predictor variable of *gender.* Because the variance of dependent variables cannot be estimated in SEM, the latent factor residuals serve as proxies for the Intercept and Slope factors in capturing these variances. These residuals now represent variation remaining in the Intercepts and Slopes after all

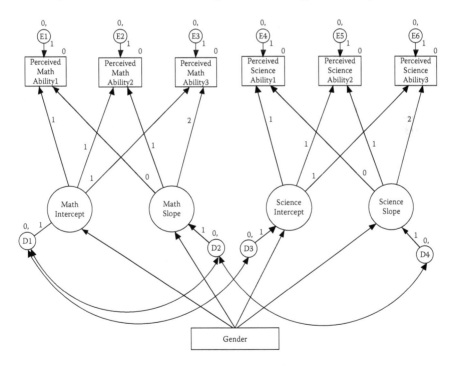

Figure 11.10 Hypothesized LGC model with gender as a predictor.

variability in their prediction by gender has been explained (Willett & Keiley, 2000). Rephrased within a comparative framework, we note that for the dual-domain model in which no predictors were specified, the residuals represented deviations between the factor Intercepts and Slopes, and their population means. In contrast, for this current model in which a predictor variable is specified, the residual variances represent deviations from their *conditional* population means. As such, these residuals represent the adjusted values of factor Intercepts and Slopes after partialing out the linear effect of the gender predictor variable (Willett & Keiley, 2000). *Third*, given that the four factors are now dependent variables in the model, they and their covariances are no longer estimable parameters in the model. Thus, the double-headed arrows representing the factor covariances are now shown linking their associated residuals rather than the factors themselves. *Finally*, the means of the residuals are fixed to 0.0, as indicated by the assigned 0 followed by a comma.

Let's turn now to the goodness-of-fit findings resulting from the test of this predictor model as summarized in Table 11.6. Interestingly, here we find evidence of an extremely well-fitting model that is even better fitting than the final LGC model having no predictor variable ($\chi^2_{(12)} = 35.887$; CFI = .973; RMSEA = .063).

Parameter estimates related to this predictor model are presented in Table 11.7. However, because the content of major import related to this

Table 11.6 Selected AMOS Output: Goodness-of-Fit Statistics Related to Predictor Model

Model	NPAR	CMIN	DF	P	CMIN/DF
Default model	23	35.877	12	.000	2.990
Saturated model	35	.000	0		
Independence model	14	903.439	21	.000	43.021

Baseline comparisons

Model	NFI Delta1	RFI rho1	IFI Delta2	TLI rho2	CFI
Default model	.960	.931	.973	.953	.973
Saturated model	1.000		1.000		1.000
Independence model	.000	.000	.000	.000	.000

RMSEA

Model	RMSEA	LO 90	HI 90	PCLOSE
Default model	.063	.040	.087	.162
Independence model	.290	.274	.307	.000

Table 11.7 Selected AMOS Output: Parameter
Estimates Related to Predictor Model

	Estimate	S.E.	C.R.	P
Regression weights				
Science Intercept <--- sex	.226	.102	2.222	.026
Science_Slope <--- sex	.017	.060	.287	.774
Math_Slope <--- sex	−.150	.064	−2.345	.019
Math_Intercept <--- sex	.563	.107	5.269	***
m_abils1 <--- Math_Slope	.000			
m_abils2 <--- Math_Intercept	1.000			
m_abils2 <--- Math_Slope	1.000			
m_abils3 <--- Math_Intercept	1.000			
m_abils3 <--- Math_Slope	2.000			
s_abils1 <--- Science Intercept	1.000			
s_abils1 <--- Science_Slope	.000			
s_abils2 <--- Science Intercept	1.000			
s_abils2 <--- Science_Slope	1.000			
s_abils3 <--- Science Intercept	1.000			
s_abils3 <--- Science_Slope	2.000			
m_abils1 <--- Math_Intercept	1.000			
Standardized regression weights				
Science Intercept <--- Sex	.143			
Science_Slope <--- Sex	.029			
Math_Slope <--- Sex	−.163			
Math_Intercept <--- Sex	.254			
m_abils1 <--- Math_Slope	.000			
m_abils2 <--- Math_Intercept	.845			
m_abils2 <--- Math_Slope	.350			
m_abils3 <--- Math_Intercept	.732			
m_abils3 <--- Math_Slope	.606			
s_abils1 <--- Science Intercept	.656			
s_abils1 <--- Science_Slope	.000			
s_abils2 <--- Science Intercept	.646			
s_abils2 <--- Science_Slope	.246			
s_abils3 <--- Science Intercept	.623			
s_abils3 <--- Science_Slope	.475			
m_abils1 <--- Math_Intercept	.897			

model focuses on the variable of *gender*, the results presented are pertinent only to the related regression paths and their weights.[4] Turning first to results for *perceived math ability*, we see that *gender* was found to be a statistically significant predictor of both initial status (.563) and rate of change (−.150) at $p < .05$. Given a coding of "0" for females and "1" for males, these findings suggest that, whereas self-perceived ability in math was, on average, higher for boys than for girls by a value of .563 at Time 1, the rate of change in this perception for boys, from grade 8 through grade 10, was slower than it was for girls by a value of .150. (The negative coefficient indicates that boys had the lower slope.)

Results related to *perceived science ability* again revealed *gender* to be a significant predictor of *perceived science ability* in grade 8, with boys showing higher scores on average than girls by a value of .226 ($p < .05$). On the other hand, rate of change was found to be indistinguishable between boys and girls as indicated by its nonsignificant estimate.

To conclude, I draw from the work of Willett and Sayer (1994, 1996) in highlighting several important features captured by the LGC modeling approach to the investigation of change. *First*, the methodology can accommodate anywhere from 3 to 30 waves of longitudinal data equally well. Willett (1988, 1989) has shown, however, that the more waves of data collected, the more precise will be the estimated growth trajectory and the higher will be the reliability for the measurement of change. *Second*, there is no requirement that the time lag between each wave of assessments be equivalent. Indeed, LGC modeling can easily accommodate irregularly spaced measurements, but with the caveat that all subjects are measured on the same set of occasions. *Third*, individual change can be represented by either a linear or a nonlinear growth trajectory. Although linear growth is typically assumed by default, this assumption is easily tested and the model respecified to address curvilinearity if need be. *Fourth*, in contrast to traditional methods used in measuring change, LGC models allow not only for the estimation of measurement error variances but also for their autocorrelation and fluctuation across time in the event that tests for the assumptions of independence and homoscedasticity are found to be untenable. *Fifth*, multiple predictors of change can be included in the LGC model. They may be fixed, as in the specification of gender in the present chapter, or they may be time varying (see, e.g., Byrne, 2008; Willett & Keiley, 2000). *Finally*, the three key statistical assumptions associated with our application of LGC modeling (linearity, independence of measurement error variances, and homoscedasticity of measurement error variances), although not demonstrated in this chapter, can be easily tested via a comparison of nested models (see Byrne & Crombie, 2003).

In closing out this chapter on LGC modeling, I wish to make you aware that multilevel models provide an alternative way to study change with structural models (see, e.g., Bovaird, 2007; Duncan et al., 2006; Singer & Willett, 2003).

Endnotes

1. Group 1 (n = 500) represented subjects for whom complete data were available across the 3-year time span, Group 2 (n = 543) represented subjects for whom data were available only for Years 2 and 3, and Group 3 (n = 601) represented subjects for whom data were available only for Year 1 of the study.
2. In the present case, however, the same pattern of results replicate those based on the multigroup missing data model.
3. If, on the other hand, the growth trajectory were considered to be nonlinear, the hypothesized model would then include a third parameter representing curvature (for an elaboration of this parameterization, see Byrne & Crombie, 2003; Duncan et al., 1999). Fitting a nonlinear model such as a polynomial model requires more time points of measurement (see Bentler, 2005).
4. As noted earlier in this chapter, it is essential that the variable names in the data set be consistent with those named for analysis by the AMOS program. Thus, although the variable was labeled *gender* in the figure, the name of the variable in the data set (and for the analysis) was *sex*.

section five

Other important topics

chapter twelve

Bootstrapping as an aid to nonnormal data

Two critically important assumptions associated with structural equation modeling (SEM), in the analysis of covariance and mean structures, is the requirement that the data are of a continuous scale and have a multivariate normal distribution. These underlying assumptions are linked to large-sample (i.e., asymptotic) theory within which SEM is embedded. More specifically, they derive from the approach taken in the estimation of parameters using the SEM methodology. Typically, either maximum likelihood (ML) or normal theory generalized least squares (GLS) estimation is used; both demand that the data be continuous and multivariate normal. This chapter focuses on the issue of multivariate nonnormality; readers interested in the issue of noncontinuous variables are referred to Bollen (1989a); Byrne (1998); Coenders, Satorra, and Saris (1997); and West, Finch, and Curran (1995).

Despite its import for all parametric statistical analyses, a review of the literature provides ample evidence of empirical research wherein the issue of distributional normality has been blatantly ignored. For example, in an analysis of 440 achievement and psychometric data sets, all of which exceeded a sample size of 400, Micceri (1989) reported that the majority of these data failed to follow either a univariate or multivariate normal distribution. Furthermore, he found that most researchers seemed to be totally oblivious to the fact that they had even violated this statistical assumption (see also Zhu, 1997). Within the more limited context of the SEM literature, it is easy to find evidence of the same phenomenon. As a case in point, we can turn to Breckler (1990), who identified 72 articles appearing in personality and social psychology journals between the years 1977 and 1987 that employed the SEM methodology. His review of these published studies revealed that only 19% actually acknowledged the normal theory assumptions, and fewer than 10% explicitly tested for their possible violation.

Following a review of empirical studies of nonnormality in SEM, West et al. (1995) summarized four important findings. *First*, as data become increasingly nonnormal, the χ^2 value derived from both ML and GLS estimation becomes excessively large. The consequence of this situation is that it encourages researchers to seek further modification of their hypothesized model in an effort to attain adequate fit to the data. However, given the spuriously high value of the χ^2 value, these efforts can lead to inappropriate and nonreplicable modifications to otherwise theoretically adequate models (see also Lei & Lomax, 2005; MacCallum, Roznowski, & Necowitz, 1992). *Second,* when sample sizes are small (even in the event of multivariate normality), both the ML and GLS estimators yield χ^2 values that are somewhat inflated. Furthermore, as sample size decreases; and nonnormality increases, researchers are faced with a growing proportion of analyses that fail to converge, or that result in an improper solution (see Anderson & Gerbing, 1984; Boomsma, 1982). *Third,* when data are nonnormal, fit indices such as the Tucker-Lewis Index (TLI; Tucker & Lewis, 1973) and the Comparative Fit Index (CFI; Bentler, 1990) yield values that are modestly underestimated (see also Marsh, Balla, & McDonald, 1988). *Finally,* nonnormality can lead to spuriously low standard errors, with degrees of underestimation ranging from moderate to severe. The consequences here are that, because the standard errors are underestimated, the regression paths and factor/error covariances will be statistically significant, although they may not be so in the population.

Given that, in practice, most data fail to meet the assumption of multivariate normality, West et al. (1995) noted increasing interest among SEM researchers in (a) establishing the robustness of SEM to violations of the normality assumption, and (b) developing alternative reparatory strategies when this assumption is violated. Particularly troublesome in SEM analyses is the presence of excessive kurtosis (see, e.g., Bollen & Stine, 1993; West et al.). In a very clearly presented review of both the problems encountered in working with multivariate nonnormal data in SEM, and the diverse remedial options proposed for their resolution, West and colleagues have provided the reader with a solid framework within which to comprehend the difficulties that arise. I highly recommend their book chapter to all SEM researchers, albeit with double emphasis for those who may be new to this methodology.

One approach to handling the presence of multivariate nonnormal data is to use a procedure known as "the bootstrap" (West et al., 1995; Yung & Bentler, 1996; Zhu, 1997). This technique was first brought to light by Efron (1979, 1982) and has been subsequently highlighted by Kotz and Johnson (1992) as having had a significant impact on the field of statistics. The term *bootstrap* derives from the expression "to pull oneself up by the bootstraps," thereby reflecting the notion that the original sample gives rise to multiple additional ones. As such, bootstrapping serves as a resampling procedure by which the original sample is considered to represent the population. Multiple subsamples of the same size as the parent sample are then drawn randomly, *with replacement,* from this population and provide the data for empirical investigation of the variability of parameter estimates and indices of fit. For very comprehensible introductions to the underlying rationale and operation of bootstrapping, readers are referred to Diaconis and Efron (1983), Stine (1990), and Zhu (1997).

Prior to the advent of high-speed computers, the technique of bootstrapping could not have existed (Efron, 1979). In fact, it is for this very reason that bootstrapping has been categorized as a computer-intensive statistical procedure in the literature (see, e.g., Diaconis & Efron, 1983; Noreen, 1989). Computer-intensive techniques share the appealing feature of being free from two constraining statistical assumptions generally associated with the analysis of data: (a) that the data are normally distributed, and (b) that the researcher is able to explore more complicated problems, using a wider array of statistical tools than was previously possible (Diaconis & Efron). Before turning to our example application in this chapter, let's review, first, the basic principles associated with the bootstrap technique, its major benefits and limitations, and, finally, some caveats bearing on its use in SEM.

Basic principles underlying the bootstrap procedure

The key idea underlying the bootstrap technique is that it enables the researcher to create multiple subsamples from an original database. The importance of this action is that one can then examine parameter distributions relative to each of these spawned samples. Considered cumulatively, these distributions serve as a bootstrap sampling distribution which technically operates in the same way as does the sampling distribution generally associated with parametric inferential statistics. In contrast to traditional statistical methods, however, the bootstrapping sampling distribution is concrete and allows for comparison of parametric values over repeated samples that have been drawn (with replacement) from the original sample. With traditional inferential procedures, on the other hand, comparison is based on an infinite number of samples drawn hypothetically from the population of interest. Of import here is the fact that the sampling distribution of the inferential approach is based on available analytic formulas which are linked to assumptions of normality, whereas the bootstrap sampling distribution is rendered free from such restrictions (Zhu, 1997).

To give you a general flavor of how the bootstrapping strategy operates in practice, let's examine a very simple example. Suppose that we have an original sample of 350 cases; the computed mean on variable X is found to be 8.0, with a standard error of 2.5. Then, suppose that we have the computer generate 200 samples consisting of 350 cases each by randomly selecting cases *with replacement* from the original sample. For each of these subsamples, the computer will record a mean value, compute the average mean value across the 200 samples, and calculate the standard error.

Within the framework of SEM, the same procedure holds, albeit one can evaluate the stability of model parameters, and a wide variety of other estimated quantities (Kline, 2005; Stine, 1990; Yung & Bentler, 1996). Furthermore, depending on the bootstrapping capabilities of the particular computer program in use, one may also test for the stability of goodness-of-fit indices relative to the model as a whole (Bollen & Stine, 1993; Kline, 2005); AMOS can provide this information. (For an evaluative review of the application and results of bootstrapping to SEM models, readers are referred to Yung and Bentler, 1996.)

Benefits and limitations of the bootstrap procedure

The primary advantage of bootstrapping, in general, is that it allows the researcher to assess the stability of parameter estimates and thereby report their values with a greater degree of accuracy. As Zhu (1997) noted, in implied reference to the traditional parametric approach, "[I]t may be better to draw conclusions about the parameters of a population strictly from the sample at hand... than to make perhaps unrealistic assumptions about the population" (p. 50). Within the more specific context of SEM, the bootstrap procedure provides a mechanism for addressing situations where the ponderous statistical assumptions of large sample size and multivariate normality may not hold (Yung & Bentler, 1996). Perhaps the strongest advantage of bootstrapping in SEM is "its 'automatic' refinement on standard asymptotic theories (e.g., higher-order accuracy) so that the bootstrap can be applied even for samples with moderate (but not extremely small) sizes" (Yung & Bentler, 1996, p. 223).

These benefits notwithstanding, the bootstrap procedure is not without its limitations and difficulties. Of primary interest are four such limitations. *First*, the bootstrap sampling distribution is generated from one "original" sample which is assumed to be representative of the population. In the event that such representation is not forthcoming, the bootstrap procedure will lead to misleading results (Zhu, 1997). *Second*, Yung and Bentler (1996) have noted that, in order for the bootstrap to work within the framework of covariance structure analysis, the assumption of independence and identical distribution of observations must be met. They contended that such an assumption is intrinsic to any justification of replacement sampling from the reproduced correlation matrix of the bootstrap. *Third*, the success of a bootstrap analysis depends on the degree to which the sampling behavior of the statistic of interest is consistent when the samples are drawn from the empirical distribution, and when they are drawn from the original population (Bollen & Stine, 1993). *Finally*, when data are multivariate normal, the bootstrap standard error estimates have been found to be more biased than those derived from the standard ML method (Ichikawa & Konishi, 1995). In contrast, when the underlying distribution is nonnormal, the bootstrap estimates are less biased than they are for the standard ML estimates.

Caveats regarding the use of bootstrapping in SEM

Although the bootstrap procedure is recommended for SEM as an approach to dealing with data that are multivariate nonnormal, it is important that researchers be cognizant of its limitations in this regard, as well as its use in addressing issues of small sample size and lack of independent samples for replication (Kline, 2005). Findings from Monte Carlo simulation studies of the bootstrap procedures have led researchers to issue several caveats regarding its use. Foremost among such caveats is Yung and Bentler's (1996) admonition that bootstrapping is *definitely not* a panacea for small samples. Because the bootstrap sample distributions depend heavily on the accuracy of estimates based on the parent distribution, it seems evident that such precision can only derive from a sample that is at least moderately large (see Ichikawa & Konishi, 1995; Yung & Bentler, 1994).

A second caveat addresses the adequacy of standard errors derived from bootstrapping. Yung and Bentler (1996) exhorted that, although the bootstrap procedure is helpful in estimating standard errors in the face of nonnormal data, it should not be regarded as the absolutely *only* and *best* method. They noted that researchers may wish to achieve particular statistical properties such as efficiency, robustness, and the like, and thus may prefer using an alternate estimation procedure.

As a third caveat, Yung and Bentler (1996) cautioned researchers against using the bootstrap procedure with the naïve belief that the results will be accurate and trustworthy. They pointed to the studies of Bollen and Stine (1988, 1993) in noting that, indeed, there are situations where bootstrapping simply will not work. The primary difficulty here, however, is that there is yet no way of pinpointing when and how the bootstrap procedure will fail. In the interim, we must await further developments in this area of SEM research.

Finally, Arbuckle (2007) admonished that when bootstrapping is used to generate empirical standard errors for parameters of interest in SEM, it is critical that the researcher constrain to some nonzero value, one factor loading path per factor, rather than the factor variance in the process of establishing model identification. Hancock and Nevitt (1999) have shown that constraining factor variances to a fixed value of 1.0, in lieu of one factor loading per congeneric set of indicators, leads to bootstrap standard errors that are highly inflated.

At this point, hopefully you have at least a good general idea of the use of bootstrapping within the framework of SEM analyses. With this background information in place, then, let's move on to an actual application of the bootstrap procedure.

Modeling with AMOS Graphics

When conducting the bootstrap procedure using AMOS Graphics, the researcher is provided with one set of parameter estimates, albeit two sets of their related standard errors. The first set of estimates is part of the regular AMOS output when ML or GLS estimation is requested. The calculation of these standard errors is based on formulas that assume a multivariate normal distribution of the data. The second set of estimates derives from the bootstrap samples and, thus, is empirically determined. The advantage of bootstrapping, as discussed above, is that it can be used to generate an approximate standard error for many statistics that AMOS computes, albeit without having to satisfy the assumption of multivariate normality. It is with this beneficial feature in mind that we review the present application.

The hypothesized model

The model to be used in demonstrating the bootstrap procedure represents a second-order CFA model akin to the one presented in Chapter 5 in that it also represents the Beck Depression Inventory (BDI). However, whereas analyses conducted in Chapter 5 were based on the revised version of the BDI (Beck, Steer, & Brown, 1996), those conducted in this chapter are based on the original version of the instrument (Beck, Ward, Mendelson, Mock, & Erbaugh, 1961). The sample data used in the current chapter represent item scores for 1,096 Swedish adolescents. The purpose of the original study from which this application is taken was to demonstrate the extent to which item score data can vary across culture despite baseline models that (except for two correlated errors) were structurally equivalent (see Byrne & Campbell, 1999). Although data pertinent to Canadian ($n = 658$) and Bulgarian ($n = 691$) adolescents were included in the original study, we focus our attention on only the Swedish group in the present chapter. In particular, we examine bootstrap samples related to the final baseline model for Swedish adolescents, which is displayed in Figure 12.1. Of particular note, over and above the factor-loading pattern of BDI items on Negative Attitude, Performance Difficulty, and Somatic Elements in formulating the originally hypothesized CFA model, are the additional parameterizations resulting from establishment of this baseline model presented here. These modifications include the two correlated

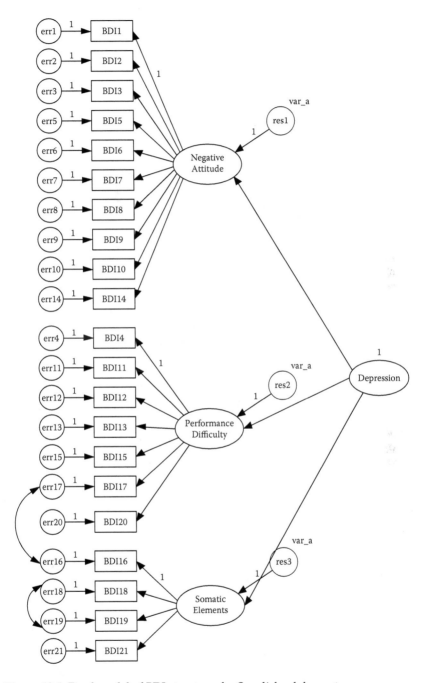

Figure 12.1 Final model of BDI structure for Swedish adolescents.

errors (Items 16/17; Items 18/19) and equality constraints on the three error residuals as indicated by assignment of the same label (var_a) to these parameters.

Characteristics of the sample

Of import in this bootstrapping example is that despite the adequately large size of the Swedish sample, the data are severely nonnormally distributed. Univariate skewness (SK) values ranged from 0.784 to 5.381, with a mean SK of 2.603; univariate kurtosis (KU) values ranged from 0.794 to 32.971, with a mean KU of 8.537. From a multivariate perspective, Mardia's (1970, 1974) normalized estimate of multivariate kurtosis was found to be 549.848. Based on a very large sample that is multivariate normal, this estimate is distributed as a unit normal variate (Bentler, 2005). Thus, when estimated values are large, they indicate significant positive kurtosis. Indeed, Bentler (2005) has suggested that in practice, values > 5.00 are indicative of data that are nonnormally distributed. Recall from the discussion of nonnormality in Chapter 4 that in AMOS, the critical ratio can be considered to represent Mardia's normalized estimate, although it is not explicitly labeled as such (J. L. Arbuckle, personal communication, March 2008). Given a normalized Mardia estimated value of 549.848, then, there is no question that the data clearly are not multivariate normal.

Applying the bootstrap procedure

Application of the bootstrap procedure, using AMOS, is very easy and straightforward. With the model shown in Figure 12.1 open, all that is needed is to access the *Analysis Properties* dialog box, either from the pull-down menu or by clicking on its related icon 🔠. Once this dialog box has been opened, you simply select the *Bootstrap* tab shown encircled in Figure 12.2. Noting the checked boxes, you will see that I have requested AMOS to perform a bootstrap on 500 samples using the ML estimator, and to provide bias-corrected confidence intervals for each of the parameter bootstrap estimates; the 90% level is default. As you can readily see in Figure 12.2, the program provides the researcher with several choices regarding estimators in addition to options related to (a) Monte Carlo bootstrapping, (b) details related to each bootstrap sample, (c) use of the Bollen-Stine bootstrap, and (d) adjusting the speed of the bootstrap algorithm via the Bootfactor.

Once you have made your selections on the *Bootstrap* tab, you are ready to execute the job. Selecting *Calculate Estimates* either from the *Model*

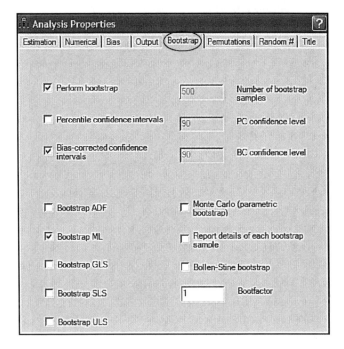

Figure 12.2 AMOS Graphics: Available bootstrap options within the *Analysis Properties* dialog box.

Fit pull-down menu or by clicking on the icon 🖩 sets the bootstrapping action in motion. Figure 12.3 shows the AMOS *Output* file directory tree that appears once the execution has been completed. In reviewing this set of output sections, it is worth noting the separation of the usual model information (upper section) and the bootstrap information (lower section). As can be seen in the summary notes presented in Figure 12.4, there were no estimation problems (minimum was achieved), and the χ^2 value is reported as 717.169, with 186 degrees of freedom.

Selected AMOS output

We now review various components of the AMOS text output, turning first to the parameter summary, which is presented in Figure 12.5.

Parameter summary

Although, by now, you will likely have no difficulty interpreting the *Summary of Parameters*, I would like to draw your attention to the three

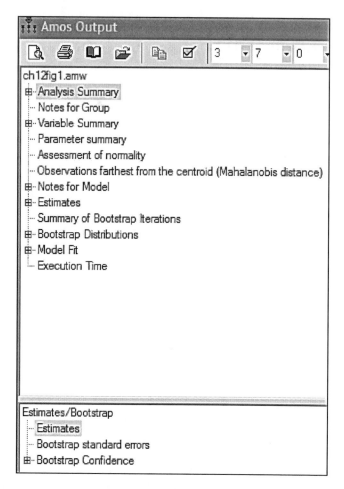

Figure 12.3 AMOS Graphics: *Output* directory tree.

labeled parameters listed in the *Variances* column. These variances pertain to the three residual errors which, as in Chapter 5, were constrained to be equal.[1] For safe measure, let's review the last column, which reports the total number of fixed, labeled, and unlabeled parameters in the model. Details related to the remainder of this summary are as follows:

- 28 fixed parameters: 21 regression paths (or weights) associated with the measurement error terms, 3 associated with the residual terms, and 3 associated with the first factor loading of each congeneric set of indicator measures; 1 variance fixed to 1.0 associated with the higher order factor

Notes for Model (Your model)

Computation of degrees of freedom (Your model)

Number of distinct sample moments: 231
Number of distinct parameters to be estimated: 45
Degrees of freedom (231 - 45): 186

Result (Your model)

Minimum was achieved
Chi-square = 717.169
Degrees of freedom = 186
Probability level = .000

Figure 12.4 AMOS Graphics: Summary notes related to CFA analysis of hypothesized model structure.

Parameter summary (Group number 1)

	Weights	Covariances	Variances	Means	Intercepts	Total
Fixed	27	0	1	0	0	28
Labeled	0	0	3	0	0	3
Unlabeled	21	2	21	0	0	44
Total	48	2	25	0	0	75

Figure 12.5 AMOS Graphics: Parameter summary related to hypothesized model of BDI structure.

- 44 unlabeled (estimated) parameters: 21 factor loadings (18 first order; 3 second order), 2 covariances (2 correlated errors), and 21 variances (measurement error terms)

Assessment of normality

Given the extreme nonnormality of these data, I consider it important that you have the opportunity to review this information as reported in the output file. This information is accessed by checking the *Normality/Outliers* option found on the *Estimation* tab of the *Analysis Properties* dialog box (see Chapter 4). As indicated by the labeling of this option, AMOS presents

information related to the normality of the data from two perspectives—
one indicative of the skewness and kurtosis of each parameter, the other of
the presence of outliers. We turn first to the skewness and kurtosis issue.

Statistical evidence of nonnormality

Although this information was summarized above, the output presented
in Table 12.1 enables you to review skewness and kurtosis values related
to each BDI item. As noted earlier, the multivariate value of 549.848 represents Mardia's (1970) coefficient of multivariate kurtosis, the critical ratio
of which is 292.839.

Statistical evidence of outliers

In addition to statistical information related to skewness and kurtosis,
AMOS provides information related to possible outliers in the data. This
option is labeled on the *Output* directory tree as "Observations farthest

Table 12.1 Selected AMOS Output: Assessment of Normality

Variable	Min	Max	Skew	C.R.	Kurtosis	C.R.
BDI16	1.000	4.000	1.177	15.903	1.898	12.823
BDI18	1.000	4.000	2.737	36.990	7.876	53.223
BDI19	1.000	4.000	4.139	55.940	19.876	134.313
BDI21	1.000	4.000	5.381	72.722	32.971	222.807
BDI4	1.000	4.000	2.081	28.128	4.939	33.379
BDI11	1.000	4.000	1.708	23.080	2.869	19.385
BDI12	1.000	4.000	4.270	57.710	20.302	137.193
BDI13	1.000	4.000	1.822	24.630	2.652	17.920
BDI15	1.000	4.000	.943	12.749	.794	5.363
BDI17	1.000	4.000	1.464	19.781	2.403	16.238
BDI20	1.000	4.000	3.921	52.989	16.567	111.956
BDI1	1.000	4.000	2.328	31.468	5.196	35.116
BDI2	1.000	4.000	2.597	35.099	6.003	40.569
BDI3	1.000	4.000	2.023	27.348	2.815	19.021
BDI5	1.000	4.000	3.340	45.137	11.620	78.527
BDI6	1.000	4.000	2.716	36.712	8.429	56.959
BDI7	1.000	4.000	2.209	29.861	6.238	42.152
BDI8	1.000	4.000	.784	10.590	−.838	−5.666
BDI9	1.000	4.000	3.240	43.785	11.504	77.744
BDI10	1.000	4.000	3.219	43.509	10.040	67.849
BDI14	1.000	4.000	2.569	34.722	5.127	34.646
Multivariate					549.848	292.839

Table 12.2 Selected AMOS Output: Detection of Outliers Among Cases

Observations farthest from the centroid (Mahalanobis distance) (Group number 1)			
Observation number	Mahalanobis d-squared	p1	p2
886	220.485	.000	.000
389	160.701	.000	.000
369	155.071	.000	.000
464	139.782	.000	.000
391	130.636	.000	.000
392	130.636	.000	.000
415	129.104	.000	.000
956	127.226	.000	.000
664	124.657	.000	.000
825	124.656	.000	.000
390	123.972	.000	.000
•	•	•	•
•	•	•	
•	•	•	•
•	•	•	•
603	52.101	.000	.000

from the centroid (Mahalanobis distance)" (see Figure 12.3). As such, the program identifies any case for which the observed scores differ markedly from the centroid of scores for all 1,096 cases; Mahalanobis d-squared values are used as the measure of distance, and they are reported in decreasing rank order. This information is presented in Table 12.2 for the first 11 and final ranked scores. Here we see that Case #886 is the furthest from the centroid with a Mahalanobis d^2 value of 220.485; this value is then followed by two columns, *p1* and *p2*. The *p1* column indicates that, *assuming normality*, the probability of d^2 (for Case #886) exceeding a value of 220.485 is < .000. The *p2* column, also *assuming normality*, reveals that the probability is still < .000 that the largest d^2 value for any individual case would exceed 220.485. Although small numbers appearing in the first column (*p1*) are to be expected, small numbers in the second column (*p2*) suggest observations that are improbably far from the centroid under the hypothesis of normality. Given the wide gap in Mahalanobis d^2 values between Case #886 and the second case (#389), relative to all other cases, I would judge Case #886 to be an outlier and would consider deleting this case from further analyses. Indeed, based on the same rationale of comparison, I would probably delete the next three cases as well.

Parameter estimates and standard errors

When bootstrapping is requested, AMOS provides two sets of information as could be seen in the *Output* tree directory (see Figure 12.3); these include the regular ML parameter estimates, along with their standard errors (shown in the upper section of the tree), together with related bootstrap information (shown in the lower section of the tree). We turn first to the regular ML estimates, which are presented in Table 12.3.

Sample ML estimates and standard errors

In the interest of space, the unstandardized and standardized estimates for only the factor loadings (i.e., first- and second-order regression weights) are presented here. Of primary interest are the standard errors (SEs) as they provide the basis for determining statistical significance related to the parameter estimates (i.e., estimate divided by standard error equals the critical ratio). Importantly, then, these initial standard errors subsequently can be compared with those reported for the bootstrapped samples (see Table 12.4). Sample ML estimates, standard errors, and critical ratios are reported in Table 12.3.

Bootstrap ML standard errors

Once the ML parameter estimates have been reported for the original sample of cases, the program then turns to results related to the bootstrap samples. AMOS provides a summary of the bootstrap iterations, which can be accessed from the *Output* directory tree. This option is visible in Figure 12.6, where it appears on the last line in the upper section of the tree. The summary reports two aspects of the iteration process: (a) minimization history of the number of iterations required to fit the hypothesized model to the bootstrap samples, and (b) the extent to which the process was successful. This information pertinent to the Swedish data is shown in Figure 12.7.

In reviewing Figure 12.7, you will note four columns. The first, labeled *Iterations*, reports that 19 iterations were needed to complete 500 bootstrap samples. The three method columns are ordered from left to right in terms of their speed and reliability. As such, minimization *Method 0* is the slowest and is not currently used in AMOS 17; thus, this column always contains 0's. *Method 1* is reported in AMOS documentation to be generally fast and reliable. *Method 2* represents the most reliable minimization algorithm and is used as a follow-up method if Method 1 fails during the bootstrapping process.

As evidenced from the information reported in Figure 12.7, Method 1 was completely successful in its task of bootstrapping 500 usable samples; none was found to be unusable. The numbers entered in the *Method 1*

Table 12.3 Selected AMOS Output: Maximum Likelihood Factor Loading Estimates

	Estimate	S.E.	C.R.	P
Unstandardized solution				
PERFORMANCE_DIFFICULTY <--- DEPRESSION	.288	.014	20.338	***
NEGATIVE_ATTITUDE <--- DEPRESSION	.303	.015	20.465	***
SOMATIC_ELEMENTS <--- DEPRESSION	.293	.021	14.017	***
BDI14 <--- NEGATIVE_ATTITUDE	1.228	.084	14.701	***
BDI10 <--- NEGATIVE_ATTITUDE	.928	.067	13.880	***
BDI9 <--- NEGATIVE_ATTITUDE	1.110	.057	19.573	***
BDI8 <--- NEGATIVE_ATTITUDE	1.389	.090	15.406	***
BDI7 <--- NEGATIVE_ATTITUDE	1.115	.057	19.440	***
BDI6 <--- NEGATIVE_ATTITUDE	.913	.056	16.329	***
BDI5 <--- NEGATIVE_ATTITUDE	1.104	.056	19.674	***
BDI3 <--- NEGATIVE_ATTITUDE	1.390	.073	18.958	***
BDI2 <--- NEGATIVE_ATTITUDE	1.101	.064	17.077	***
BDI1 <--- NEGATIVE_ATTITUDE	1.000			
BDI20 <--- PERFORMANCE_DIFFICULTY	.695	.054	12.975	***
BDI17 <--- PERFORMANCE_DIFFICULTY	1.269	.079	16.087	***
BDI15 <--- PERFORMANCE_DIFFICULTY	1.019	.068	14.995	***
BDI13 <--- PERFORMANCE_DIFFICULTY	.942	.068	13.898	***
BDI12 <--- PERFORMANCE_DIFFICULTY	.700	.049	14.277	***
BDI11 <--- PERFORMANCE_DIFFICULTY	.839	.084	10.008	***
BDI4 <--- PERFORMANCE_DIFFICULTY	1.000			
BDI21 <--- SOMATIC_ELEMENTS	.426	.046	9.355	***
BDI19 <--- SOMATIC_ELEMENTS	.358	.047	7.550	***
BDI18 <--- SOMATIC_ELEMENTS	.690	.073	9.479	***
BDI16 <--- SOMATIC_ELEMENTS	1.000			

*** probability < .000

(continued)

Table 12.3 Selected AMOS Output: Maximum Likelihood Factor Loading Estimates *(Continued)*

			Estimate	S.E.	C.R.	P
Standardized solution						
PERFORMANCE_DIFFICULTY	<---	DEPRESSION	.918			
NEGATIVE_ATTITUDE	<---	DEPRESSION	.925			
SOMATIC_ELEMENTS	<---	DEPRESSION	.921			
BDI14	<---	NEGATIVE_ATTITUDE	.497			
BDI10	<---	NEGATIVE_ATTITUDE	.467			
BDI9	<---	NEGATIVE_ATTITUDE	.692			
BDI8	<---	NEGATIVE_ATTITUDE	.524			
BDI7	<---	NEGATIVE_ATTITUDE	.687			
BDI6	<---	NEGATIVE_ATTITUDE	.559			
BDI5	<---	NEGATIVE_ATTITUDE	.697			
BDI3	<---	NEGATIVE_ATTITUDE	.666			
BDI2	<---	NEGATIVE_ATTITUDE	.589			
BDI1	<---	NEGATIVE_ATTITUDE	.646			
BDI20	<---	PERFORMANCE_DIFFICULTY	.454			
BDI17	<---	PERFORMANCE_DIFFICULTY	.576			
BDI15	<---	PERFORMANCE_DIFFICULTY	.533			
BDI13	<---	PERFORMANCE_DIFFICULTY	.490			
BDI12	<---	PERFORMANCE_DIFFICULTY	.505			
BDI11	<---	PERFORMANCE_DIFFICULTY	.343			
BDI4	<---	PERFORMANCE_DIFFICULTY	.660			
BDI21	<---	SOMATIC_ELEMENTS	.385			
BDI19	<---	SOMATIC_ELEMENTS	.294			
BDI18	<---	SOMATIC_ELEMENTS	.393			
BDI16	<---	SOMATIC_ELEMENTS	.480			

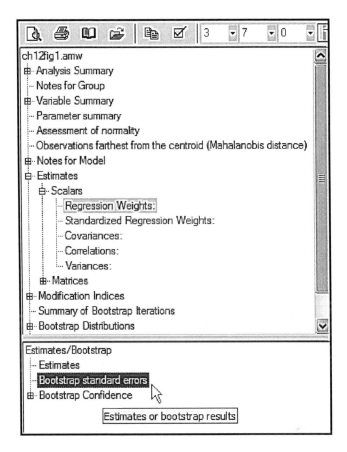

Figure 12.6 AMOS Graphics: *Output* directory tree detailing retrieval of bootstrap standard errors.

column represent the coordinate between number of bootstrap samples and number of iterations. For example, the number "65" on the fourth line indicates that for 65 bootstrap samples, Method 1 reached a minimum in four iterations.

It is important to note that, in the case of an original sample that either is small or is not continuously distributed (or both), it is quite conceivable that one or more of the bootstrap samples will have a singular covariance matrix. In such instances, AMOS may be unable to find a solution for some of the bootstrap samples. Given such findings, the program reports these failed bootstrap samples and excludes them from the bootstrap analysis (Arbuckle, 2007).

Before turning to the bootstrap results for our Swedish sample, I need first to explain how to obtain this information from the output tree as it

<u>Summary of Bootstrap Iterations (Your model)</u>

(Your model)

Iterations	Method 0	Method 1	Method 2
1	0	0	0
2	0	0	0
3	0	1	0
4	0	65	0
5	0	248	0
6	0	130	0
7	0	43	0
8	0	9	0
9	0	4	0
10	0	0	0
11	0	0	0
12	0	0	0
13	0	0	0
14	0	0	0
15	0	0	0
16	0	0	0
17	0	0	0
18	0	0	0
19	0	0	0
Total	0	500	0

0 bootstrap samples were unused because of a singular covariance matrix.
0 bootstrap samples were unused because a solution was not found.
500 usable bootstrap samples were obtained.

Figure 12.7 AMOS Graphics: Summary of bootstrap iterations.

is not exactly a straightforward retrieval process; that is, just clicking on the *Estimates* label listed in the bootstrap section will yield nothing. Let's review this procedure by returning to Figure 12.6, where a breakdown of the needed output is captured. To initiate the process, you will need to double-click on *Estimates* in the upper ML section of the tree, which yields the *Scalars* label. Double-clicking on *Scalars* then produces the five categories of estimates shown in Figure 12.6. It is imperative that you click on one of these five types of estimates, which will highlight the one of interest; regression weights are highlighted in the figure, although the highlighting is rather faded. Once you have identified the estimates of interest (in this case, the regression weights), the bootstrap section then becomes activated. Clicking on *Bootstrap Standard Errors* resulted in the standard error information presented in Table 12.4.

Table 12.4 Selected AMOS Output: Bootstrap Factor Loading Standard Errors

Parameter		S.E.	S.E-S.E	Mean	Bias	SE-Bias
Unstandardized solution						
PERFORMANCE_DIFFICULTY <---	DEPRESSION	.019	.001	.289	.001	.001
NEGATIVE_ATTITUDE <---	DEPRESSION	.032	.001	.303	.001	.001
SOMATIC_ELEMENTS <---	DEPRESSION	.023	.001	.291	−.002	.001
BDI14 <---	NEGATIVE_ATTITUDE	.150	.005	1.237	.009	.007
BDI10 <---	NEGATIVE_ATTITUDE	.102	.003	.915	−.013	.005
BDI9 <---	NEGATIVE_ATTITUDE	.111	.004	1.108	−.002	.005
BDI8 <---	NEGATIVE_ATTITUDE	.164	.005	1.398	.009	.007
BDI7 <---	NEGATIVE_ATTITUDE	.117	.004	1.118	.003	.005
BDI6 <---	NEGATIVE_ATTITUDE	.088	.003	.913	−.001	.004
BDI5 <---	NEGATIVE_ATTITUDE	.103	.003	1.101	−.003	.005
BDI3 <---	NEGATIVE_ATTITUDE	.145	.005	1.392	.002	.006
BDI2 <---	NEGATIVE_ATTITUDE	.105	.003	1.106	.005	.005
BDI1 <---	NEGATIVE_ATTITUDE	.000	.000	1.000	.000	.000
BDI20 <---	PERFORMANCE_DIFFICULTY	.099	.003	.690	−.005	.004
BDI17 <---	PERFORMANCE_DIFFICULTY	.103	.003	1.273	.004	.005
BDI15 <---	PERFORMANCE_DIFFICULTY	.120	.004	1.027	.008	.005
BDI13 <---	PERFORMANCE_DIFFICULTY	.106	.003	.943	.001	.005
BDI12 <---	PERFORMANCE_DIFFICULTY	.097	.003	.707	.007	.004
BDI11 <---	PERFORMANCE_DIFFICULTY	.088	.003	.832	−.007	.004
BDI4 <---	PERFORMANCE_DIFFICULTY	.000	.000	1.000	.000	.000
BDI21 <---	SOMATIC_ELEMENTS	.094	.003	.422	−.004	.004
BDI19 <---	SOMATIC_ELEMENTS	.095	.003	.362	.003	.004
BDI18 <---	SOMATIC_ELEMENTS	.110	.003	.681	−.008	.005
BDI16 <---	SOMATIC_ELEMENTS	.000	.000	1.000	.000	.000

(continued)

Table 12.4 Selected AMOS Output: Bootstrap Factor Loading Standard Errors *(Continued)*

Parameter			S.E.	S.E-S.E	Mean	Bias	SE-Bias
Standardized solution							
PERFORMANCE_DIFFICULTY	<---	DEPRESSION	.013	.000	.919	.000	.001
NEGATIVE_ATTITUDE	<---	DEPRESSION	.019	.001	.924	−.001	.001
SOMATIC_ELEMENTS	<---	DEPRESSION	.016	.000	.919	−.001	.001
BDI14	<---	NEGATIVE_ATTITUDE	.036	.001	.498	.001	.002
BDI10	<---	NEGATIVE_ATTITUDE	.043	.001	.461	−.006	.002
BDI9	<---	NEGATIVE_ATTITUDE	.033	.001	.691	−.001	.001
BDI8	<---	NEGATIVE_ATTITUDE	.029	.001	.524	.000	.001
BDI7	<---	NEGATIVE_ATTITUDE	.032	.001	.687	.000	.001
BDI6	<---	NEGATIVE_ATTITUDE	.039	.001	.558	−.001	.002
BDI5	<---	NEGATIVE_ATTITUDE	.029	.001	.695	−.002	.001
BDI3	<---	NEGATIVE_ATTITUDE	.027	.001	.663	−.003	.001
BDI2	<---	NEGATIVE_ATTITUDE	.034	.001	.589	.000	.002
BDI1	<---	NEGATIVE_ATTITUDE	.039	.001	.647	.001	.002
BDI20	<---	PERFORMANCE_DIFFICULTY	.047	.001	.451	−.003	.002
BDI17	<---	PERFORMANCE_DIFFICULTY	.030	.001	.576	.000	.001
BDI15	<---	PERFORMANCE_DIFFICULTY	.042	.001	.534	.001	.002
BDI13	<---	PERFORMANCE_DIFFICULTY	.035	.001	.490	.000	.002
BDI12	<---	PERFORMANCE_DIFFICULTY	.050	.002	.508	.003	.002
BDI11	<---	PERFORMANCE_DIFFICULTY	.036	.001	.340	−.003	.002
BDI4	<---	PERFORMANCE_DIFFICULTY	.029	.001	.659	.000	.001
BDI21	<---	SOMATIC_ELEMENTS	.065	.002	.378	−.007	.003
BDI19	<---	SOMATIC_ELEMENTS	.068	.002	.292	−.002	.003
BDI18	<---	SOMATIC_ELEMENTS	.054	.002	.387	−.007	.002
BDI16	<---	SOMATIC_ELEMENTS	.029	.001	.478	−.002	.001

Table 12.5 Selected AMOS Output: Bias-Corrected Percentile Method Factor Loading Confidence Intervals

Parameter		Estimate	Lower	Upper	P
Unstandardized solution					
PERFORMANCE_DIFFICULTY	<--- DEPRESSION	.288	.259	.323	.004
NEGATIVE_ATTITUDE	<--- DEPRESSION	.303	.251	.352	.004
SOMATIC_ELEMENTS	<--- DEPRESSION	.293	.260	.333	.002
BDI14	<--- NEGATIVE_ATTITUDE	1.228	1.021	1.494	.003
BDI10	<--- NEGATIVE_ATTITUDE	.928	.778	1.132	.002
BDI9	<--- NEGATIVE_ATTITUDE	1.110	.940	1.303	.003
BDI8	<--- NEGATIVE_ATTITUDE	1.389	1.168	1.697	.003
BDI7	<--- NEGATIVE_ATTITUDE	1.115	.944	1.315	.004
BDI6	<--- NEGATIVE_ATTITUDE	.913	.770	1.081	.003
BDI5	<--- NEGATIVE_ATTITUDE	1.104	.957	1.304	.002
BDI3	<--- NEGATIVE_ATTITUDE	1.390	1.200	1.733	.002
BDI2	<--- NEGATIVE_ATTITUDE	1.101	.947	1.295	.003
BDI1	<--- NEGATIVE_ATTITUDE	1.000	1.000	1.000	...
BDI20	<--- PERFORMANCE_DIFFICULTY	.695	.542	.864	.003
BDI17	<--- PERFORMANCE_DIFFICULTY	1.269	1.107	1.446	.004
BDI15	<--- PERFORMANCE_DIFFICULTY	1.019	.814	1.215	.006
BDI13	<--- PERFORMANCE_DIFFICULTY	.942	.765	1.119	.004
BDI12	<--- PERFORMANCE_DIFFICULTY	.700	.541	.865	.004
BDI11	<--- PERFORMANCE_DIFFICULTY	.839	.703	.994	.002
BDI4	<--- PERFORMANCE_DIFFICULTY	1.000	1.000	1.000	...
BDI21	<--- SOMATIC_ELEMENTS	.426	.283	.600	.003
BDI19	<--- SOMATIC_ELEMENTS	.358	.213	.508	.005
BDI18	<--- SOMATIC_ELEMENTS	.690	.524	.899	.002
BDI16	<--- SOMATIC_ELEMENTS	1.000	1.000	1.000	...

(continued)

Table 12.5 Selected AMOS Output: Bias-Corrected Percentile Method Factor Loading Confidence Intervals (*Continued*)

Parameter	Estimate	Lower	Upper	P
Standardized solution				
PERFORMANCE_DIFFICULTY <--- DEPRESSION	.918	.894	.939	.006
NEGATIVE_ATTITUDE <--- DEPRESSION	.925	.885	.950	.005
SOMATIC_ELEMENTS <--- DEPRESSION	.921	.894	.943	.004
BDI14 <--- NEGATIVE_ATTITUDE	.497	.442	.555	.005
BDI10 <--- NEGATIVE_ATTITUDE	.467	.390	.538	.003
BDI9 <--- NEGATIVE_ATTITUDE	.692	.633	.744	.004
BDI8 <--- NEGATIVE_ATTITUDE	.524	.477	.574	.004
BDI7 <--- NEGATIVE_ATTITUDE	.687	.634	.737	.004
BDI6 <--- NEGATIVE_ATTITUDE	.559	.493	.618	.004
BDI5 <--- NEGATIVE_ATTITUDE	.697	.648	.743	.003
BDI3 <--- NEGATIVE_ATTITUDE	.666	.620	.710	.003
BDI2 <--- NEGATIVE_ATTITUDE	.589	.531	.639	.005
BDI1 <--- NEGATIVE_ATTITUDE	.646	.571	.700	.008
BDI20 <--- PERFORMANCE_DIFFICULTY	.454	.370	.536	.003
BDI17 <--- PERFORMANCE_DIFFICULTY	.576	.519	.622	.005
BDI15 <--- PERFORMANCE_DIFFICULTY	.533	.448	.596	.007
BDI13 <--- PERFORMANCE_DIFFICULTY	.490	.423	.542	.006
BDI12 <--- PERFORMANCE_DIFFICULTY	.505	.404	.575	.008
BDI11 <--- PERFORMANCE_DIFFICULTY	.343	.286	.404	.003
BDI4 <--- PERFORMANCE_DIFFICULTY	.660	.607	.703	.006
BDI21 <--- SOMATIC_ELEMENTS	.385	.287	.498	.002
BDI19 <--- SOMATIC_ELEMENTS	.294	.186	.406	.003
BDI18 <--- SOMATIC_ELEMENTS	.393	.310	.493	.002
BDI16 <--- SOMATIC_ELEMENTS	.480	.433	.530	.003

The first column (*S.E.*) in the table lists the bootstrap estimate of the standard error for each factor-loading parameter in the model. This value represents the standard deviation of the parameter estimates computed across the 500 bootstrap samples. These values should be compared with the approximate ML standard error estimates presented in Table 12.3. In doing so, you will note several large discrepancies between the two sets of standard error estimates. For example, in a comparison of the standard error for the loading of BDI Item 9 (BDI9) on the Negative Attitude factor across the original (S.E. = .057) and bootstrap (S.E. = .111) samples, we see a differential of 0.054, which represents a 95% increase in the bootstrap standard error over that of the ML error. Likewise, the bootstrap standard error for the loading of Item 3 (BDI3) on the same factor is 99% larger than the ML estimate. These findings suggest that the distribution of these parameter estimates appears to be wider than would be expected under normal theory assumptions. No doubt, these results reflect the presence of outliers, as well as the extremely kurtotic nature of these data.

The second column, labeled *S.E. S.E.*, provides the approximate standard error of the bootstrap standard error itself. As you will see, these values are all very small, and so they should be. Column 3, labeled *Mean*, lists the mean parameter estimate computed across the 500 bootstrap samples. It is important to note that this bootstrap mean is not necessarily identical to the original estimate, and Arbuckle and Wothke (1999) have cautioned that, in fact, it can often be quite different. The information provided in Column 4 (*Bias*) represents the difference between the bootstrap mean estimate and the original estimate. In the event that the mean estimate of the bootstrap samples is higher than the original estimate, then the resulting bias will be positive. Finally, the last column, labeled *S.E. Bias*, reports the approximate standard error of the bias estimate.

Bootstrap bias-corrected confidence intervals

The last set of information to be presented here relates the 90% (default) bias-corrected confidence intervals for both the unstandardized and standardized factor-loading estimates, which are reported in Table 12.5. Although AMOS has the capability to produce percentile as well as bias-corrected confidence intervals, the latter are considered to yield the more accurate values (Efron & Tibshirani, 1993). Values for BDI items 1, 4, and 16 are replaced with dots (...) as these parameters were constrained to a non-zero value for purposes of model identification. Bias-corrected confidence intervals are interpreted in the usual manner. For example, the loading of BDI14 on the factor of Negative Attitude has a confidence interval ranging from 1.021 to 1.494. Because this range does not include zero, the hypothesis that the BDI14 factor loading is equal to zero in the population can be rejected. This information can also be derived from the *p* values, which indicate how small the confidence level must be to yield a confidence interval that would include zero. Turning again to the BDI14 parameter, then, a p-value of .003 implies that the confidence interval would have to be at the 99.7% level before the lower bound value would be zero.

In this chapter, I have endeavored to give you a flavor of how AMOS enables you to conduct the bootstrap procedure. Due to space limitations, I have not attempted to provide you with details or examples related to the use of bootstrapping for comparisons of models and/or estimation methods. However, for readers who may have an interest in these types of applications, this information is well presented in the manual (Arbuckle, 2007).

Endnote

1. In Chapter 5, however, only two of the three residual variances were constrained equal.

chapter thirteen

Addressing the issue of missing data

Missing (or incomplete) data, an almost inevitable occurrence in social science research, may be viewed either as a curse or as a gold mine of untapped resources. As with other life events, the extent to which they are viewed either positively or negatively is a matter of perspective. For example, McArdle (1994) has noted that although the term "missing data" typically conjures up images of negative consequences and problems, such missingness can provide a wealth of information in its own right and, indeed, often serves as a useful part of experimental analyses. (For an interesting example in support of this statement, see Rosén, 1998.) In reality, of course, the issue of terminology is moot. Of import is the extent to which, and pattern by which, data are incomplete, missing, or otherwise unobserved, and the steps taken in addressing the situation.

The presence of missing data can occur for a wide variety of reasons that are usually beyond the researcher's control. Some examples are as follows: absence on the day of data collection, failure to answer certain items in the questionnaire, refusal to answer sensitive items related to one's age and/or income, equipment failure or malfunction, attrition of subjects (e.g., the family moved away, the individual no longer wishes to participate, or the subject dies), and so on. In contrast, data may be incomplete by design, a situation in which the researcher is in total control. Two examples suggested by Kline (1998) include the case where (a) a questionnaire is excessively long and the researcher decides to administer only a subset of items to each of several different subsamples, and (b) a relatively inexpensive measure is administered to the entire sample, whereas another more expensive test is administered to a smaller set of randomly selected subjects. Needless to say, there may be many more examples that are not cited here.

Because missing data can seriously bias conclusions drawn from an empirical study, they must be addressed, regardless of the reason for their missingness. The extent to which such conclusions can be biased depends on both the amount and pattern of missing values. Unfortunately, to the best of my knowledge, there are currently no clear guidelines regarding what constitutes a "large" amount of missing data, although Kline (1998, p. 75) has suggested that they should probably constitute less than 10% of the data. On the other hand, guidelines related to the pattern of incomplete data are now widely cited and derive from the seminal works of Rubin (1976), Allison (1987), and Little and Rubin (1987). In order for you to more fully comprehend the AMOS approach to handling incomplete data, it behooves us to review, first, the differential patterns of missingness proposed by Rubin and by Little and Rubin.

Basic patterns of incomplete data

Rubin (1976) and Little and Rubin (1987) distinguished between three primary patterns of missing data: those missing *completely* at random (MCAR), those missing at random (MAR), and those considered to be nonignorable (i.e., systematic; NMAR). A brief description of each is now given.

- MCAR represents the most restrictive assumption and argues that the missingness is independent of both the unobserved values and the observed values of all other variables in the data. Conceptualizing the MCAR condition from a different perspective, Enders (2001) suggested considering these unobserved values as representing a random subsample of the hypothetically complete data. Indeed, Muthén, Kaplan, and Hollis (1987) noted that MCAR is typically what is meant when researchers use the expression, albeit imprecisely, "missing at random."

- MAR is a somewhat less restrictive condition than MCAR and argues that the missingness is independent only of the missing values and *not* of the observed values of other variables in the data. That is to say, although the occurrence of the missing values, themselves, may be random, their missingness can be linked to the observed values of other variables in the data.

- NMAR is the least restrictive condition and refers to missingness that is nonrandom, or of a systematic nature. In other words, there is an existing dependency between the variables for which the values are missing and those for which the values are present. This condition is particularly serious because (a) there is no known statistical means to alleviate the problem, and (b) it can seriously impede the generalizability of findings.

Before reviewing various approaches to the handling of incomplete data, I consider it worthwhile to detour momentarily, in order to provide you with a simple fictitious example that can help in distinguishing between the two major patterns of missingness—MCAR and MAR. Indeed, Muthén et al. (1987) noted that most researchers, when confronted with incomplete data, typically assume that the missingness is MCAR when, in fact, they are often MAR. Drawing on the works of Allison (1987) and Little and Rubin (1987), and paraphrasing Arbuckle (1996), suppose a questionnaire is composed of two items. One item taps into years of schooling; the other taps into income. Suppose, further, that while all respondents answer the education question, not everyone answers the income question. Within the framework of the missingness issue, the question is whether the incomplete data on the income variable are MCAR or MAR. Rubin reasoned that if a respondent's answer to the income question is independent of both income and education, then the missing data can be regarded as MCAR. If, on the other hand, those with higher education are either more or less likely than others to reveal their income, but among those with the same level of education, the probability of reporting income is unrelated to income, the missing data are MAR. Finally, given that, even among people with the same level of education, high-income individuals are either more or less likely to report their income, the missing data are not even MAR; the systematic pattern of this type of missingness makes them NMAR (see Enders, 2001; Jamshidian & Bentler, 1999). (For a thorough explanation and discussion of these three forms of missingness, readers are referred to Schafer & Graham, 2002.)

Once again, to give you a more complete understanding of the AMOS approach to the treatment of incomplete data, I consider it worthwhile to review strategies which, historically, have been those most commonly applied in dealing with missing data; these include listwise deletion, pairwise deletion, and single imputation. These methods are categorized as *indirect* approaches to the resolution of missing data.

Common approaches to handling incomplete data

Listwise deletion

By far, the most popular method for dealing with incomplete data is that of listwise deletion. Such popularity likely got its jumpstart in the 1980s, when numerous articles appeared in the SEM literature detailing various problems that can occur when the analysis of covariance structures is based on incomplete data (see, e.g., Bentler & Chou, 1987; Boomsma, 1985). Because SEM models are based on the premise that the covariance matrix follows a Wishart distribution (Brown, 1994; Jöreskog, 1969), complete data are required for the probability density. In meeting this requirement, researchers have therefore sought to modify incomplete data sets, through either removal of cases or the substitution of values for those that are unobserved. The fact that listwise deletion of missing data is by far the fastest and simplest answer to the problem likely has led to the popularity of its use.

Implementation of listwise deletion simply means that all cases having a missing value for any of the variables in the data are excluded from all computations. As a consequence, the final sample to be used in the analyses includes only cases with complete records. The obvious disadvantage of the listwise deletion approach, then, is the loss of information resulting from the reduced sample size. As a result, two related problems subsequently emerge: (a) the decrease in statistical power (Raaijmakers, 1999), and (b) the risk of nonconvergent solutions, incorrect standard errors, and other difficulties encountered in SEM when sample sizes are small (see, e.g., Anderson & Gerbing, 1984; Boomsma, 1982; Marsh & Balla, 1994; Marsh, Balla, & McDonald, 1988). Of course, the extent to which these problems manifest themselves is a function of both the size of the original sample and the amount of incomplete data. For example, if only a few cases have missing values, and the sample size is adequately large, then the deletion of these cases is likely a good choice. Finally, use of listwise deletion assumes that the incomplete data are MCAR (Arbuckle, 1996; Brown, 1994). Given the validity of this assumption, there will be consistent estimation of model parameters (Bollen, 1989a; Brown, 1994); failing such validity, the estimates will be severely biased, regardless of sample size (Schafer & Graham, 2002).

Pairwise deletion

In the application of pairwise deletion, only cases having missing values on variables tagged for a particular computation are excluded from the analysis. In contrast to listwise deletion, then, a case is not totally deleted from the entire set of analyses but, rather, only from particular analyses involving variables for which there are unobserved scores. The critical result of this approach is that the sample size necessarily varies across variables in the data set. This phenomenon subsequently leads to at least five major problems. *First*, the sample covariance matrix can fail to be nonpositive definite, thereby impeding the attainment of a convergent solution (Arbuckle, 1996; Bollen, 1989a; Brown, 1994; Wothke, 1993; but see Marsh, 1998). *Second*, the choice of which sample size to use in obtaining appropriate parameter estimates is equivocal (Bollen, 1989a; Brown, 1994). *Third*, goodness-of fit indices, based on the χ^2 statistic, can be substantially biased as a result of interaction between the percentage of missing data and the sample size (Marsh, 1998). *Fourth*, given that parameters are estimated from different sets of units, computation of standard errors is problematic (Schafer & Graham, 2002). *Finally*, consistent with listwise deletion of missing data, pairwise deletion assumes all missing values to be MCAR.

Single imputation

A third method for dealing with incomplete data is to simply impute, or, in other words, replace the unobserved score with some estimated value. Typically, one of three strategies is used to provide these estimates. Probably the most common of these is *mean imputation*, whereby the arithmetic mean is substituted for a missing value. Despite the relative simplicity of this procedure, however, it can be problematic in at least two ways. *First*, because the arithmetic mean represents the most likely score value for any variable, the variance of the variable will necessarily shrink; as a consequence, the correlation between the variable in question and other variables in the model will also be reduced (Brown, 1994). The overall net effect is that the standard errors will be biased, as will the other reported statistics. *Second*, if the mean imputation of missing values is substantial, the frequency distribution of the imputed variable may be misleading because too many centrally located values will invoke a leptokurtic distribution (Rovine & Delaney, 1990). In summary, Arbuckle and Wothke (1999) cautioned that, because structural equation modeling is based on variance and covariance information, "means imputation is not a recommended approach" (see also Brown, 1994). In addition to this caveat, Schafer and Graham (2002) noted that mean substitution produces biased estimates under any type of missingness.

A second type of imputation is based on multiple regression procedures. With *regression imputation*, the incomplete data serve as the dependent variables, while the complete data serve as the predictors. In other words, cases having complete data are used to generate the regression equation that is subsequently used to postulate missing values for the cases having incomplete data. At least three difficulties have been linked to regression imputation. *First*, although this approach provides for greater variability than is the case with mean imputation, it nevertheless suffers from the same limitation of inappropriately restricting variance. *Second*, substitution of the regression-predicted scores will spuriously inflate the covariances (Schafer & Olsen, 1998). *Finally*, Kline (1998) cautioned that this procedure may not be feasible in the case where the variable having the missing value does not covary, at least moderately, with other variables in the data.

The third procedure for imputing values may be termed *pattern-matching imputation*. Although application of this approach is less common than the others noted above, it is included here because the SEM statistical package within which it is embedded is so widely used (LISREL 8; Jöreskog & Sörbom, 1996a).[1] With pattern-matching imputation, a missing variable is replaced with an observed score from another case in the data for which the response pattern across all variables is similar (Byrne, 1998). One limitation of this procedure is that, in the event that no matching case is determined, no imputation is performed. As a consequence, the researcher is still left with a proportion of the data that is incomplete. To date, however, I am not aware of any scholarly articles that have evaluated pattern-matching imputation. As a consequence, little is yet known about the strengths and/or weaknesses associated with this approach within the context of SEM (Brown, 1994).

More recently, and certainly since publication of the first edition of this book, there has been substantial interest on the part of statistical researchers to establish sound methodological approaches to dealing with missing data. Indeed, much progress has been made in the development of model-based methods capable of addressing many of the limitations associated with the earlier techniques described above. These methods seek to replace the missing scores with estimated values based on a predictive distribution of scores that models the underlying pattern of missing data. As such, two models are defined—one representing the complete data and one representing the missing data. Based on the full sample, the software program subsequently computes estimates of the mean and variances such that they satisfy a statistical criterion (Kline, 2005). In SEM, the most widely used criterion is the maximum likelihood (ML) algorithm.

At the present time, there appear to be two dominant model-based strategies—the full information maximum likelihood (FIML) estimation and expectation maximization (EM) estimation, both of which are based on the ML algorithm (Enders, 2001). EM differs from the FIML approach in that it involves two steps in achieving the criterion; the latter may involve multiple imputations before a satisfactory criterion is reached. (For a general breakdown of these procedures, readers are referred to Kline, 2005; for a more extensive explanation and discussion of missing data as they bear on SEM analyses, see Enders, 2001; Schafer & Graham, 2002).

Beyond this work, there is now substantial interest in resolving many problematic issues related to the conduct of SEM based on incomplete data. To name just a few, these issues include (a) the presence of nonnormality (Savalei & Bentler, 2005; Yuan & Bentler, 2000; Yuan, Lambert, & Fouladi, 2004), (b) the number of imputations needed to achieve an established statistical criterion (Bodner, 2008; Hershberger & Fisher, 2003), and (c) the loss of data in longitudinal studies (Raykov, 2005).

The AMOS approach to handling missing data

AMOS does not provide for the application of any of the older *indirect* methods described earlier (listwise and pairwise deletion, and single imputation). Rather, the method used in AMOS represents a *direct* approach based on ML estimation and, thus, is theoretically based (Arbuckle, 1996). In contrast, the *indirect* methods lack any kind of theoretical rationale and must therefore be considered as ad hoc procedures.

Arbuckle (1996) has described the extent to which ML estimation, in the presence of incomplete data, offers several important advantages over both the listwise and pairwise deletion approaches. *First*, where the unobserved values are MCAR, listwise and pairwise estimates are consistent, but *not* efficient (in the statistical sense); ML estimates are *both* consistent and efficient. *Second*, where the unobserved values are only MAR, both listwise and pairwise estimates can be biased; ML estimates are asymptotically unbiased. In fact, it has been suggested that ML estimation will reduce bias even when the MAR condition is not completely satisfied (Muthén et al., 1987; Little & Rubin, 1989). *Third*, pairwise estimation, in contrast to ML estimation, is unable to yield standard error estimates or provide a method for testing hypotheses. *Finally*, when missing values are NMAR, all procedures can yield biased results. However, compared with the other options, ML estimates will exhibit the least bias (Little & Rubin, 1989; Muthén et al., 1987; Schafer, 1997). (For more extensive discussion and illustration of the comparative advantages and disadvantages across the listwise, pairwise, and ML approaches to incomplete data, see Arbuckle, 1996.)

With this background on the major issues related to missing data, let's move on to an actual application of ML estimation of data that are incomplete.

Modeling with AMOS Graphics

The basic strategy used by AMOS in fitting structural equation models with *missing* data differs in at least two ways from the procedure followed when data are *complete* (Arbuckle & Wothke, 1999). *First*, in addition to fitting a hypothesized model, the program needs also to fit the completely saturated model in order to compute the χ^2 value, as well as derived statistics such as the AIC and RMSEA; the independence model, as for *complete* data, must also be computed. *Second*, because substantially more computations are required in the determination of parameter estimates when data are missing, the execution time can be more extensive (although my experience with the present application revealed this additional time to be minimal).

The hypothesized model

Because the primary interest in this application focuses on the extent to which estimates and goodness-of-fit indices vary between an analysis based on *complete* data and one for which the data are *missing*, I have chosen to use the same hypothesized CFA model as the one presented in

Chapter 3. Thus, rather than reproduce the schematic representation of this model again here, readers are referred to Figure 3.1.

Although the same sample of 265 grade 7 adolescents provides the base for both chapters, the data used in testing the hypothesized model in Chapter 3 were *complete*, whereas the data to be used in this chapter have 25% of the data points missing. These artificially derived missing data points were deleted randomly. AMOS automatically recognizes missing data designations from many different formats. In the case of the current data, which are in ASCII format with comma delimiters, two adjacent delimiters indicate missing data. In this case, then, two adjacent commas (, ,) are indicative of missing data. For illustrative purposes, the first five lines of the *incomplete* data set used in the current chapter are shown here.

```
SDQ2N01,SDQ2N13,SDQ2N25,SDQ2N37,SDQ2N04,
SDQ2N16,SDQ2N28,SDQ2N40,SDQ2N10,SDQ2N22,
SDQ2N34,SDQ2N46,SDQ2N07,SDQ2N19,SDQ2N31,SDQ2
N436,,4,,3,4,,6,2,6,,5,,,,66,6,6,,6,6,6,6,5,,6,6,6,6,6,6
4,6,6,2,6,4,6,3,6,5,4,5,6,6,3,1
5,5,5,6,5,6,5,,5,6,3,5,6,6,6,5
6,5,,4,3,4,4,4,4,6,5,6,3,4,4,5
```

ML estimation of the hypothesized model incurs only one basic difference when data are *incomplete* rather than when they are *complete*. That is, in specifying the model for analyses based on *incomplete* data, it is necessary to activate the *Analysis Properties* dialog box and then check off *Means and Intercepts* on the *Estimation* tab. Although this dialog box was illustrated in Chapter 8 with respect to structured means models, it is reproduced again here in Figure 13.1.

Once this input information has been specified, the originally hypothesized model shown in Figure 3.1 becomes transformed into the one shown in Figure 13.2. You will quickly recognize at least one similarity with the model shown in Figure 8.11 (but for the low-track group) and the brief comparative display in Figure 8.12 with respect to the assignment of the 0. to each of the factors. Recall that these 0. values represent the latent factor means and indicate their constraint to zero. In both Figures 8.11 and 13.2, the means of the factors, as well as those for the error terms, are shown constrained to zero. Although the intercept terms were estimated for both the latent means model and the missing data model, their related labels do not appear in Figure 13.2. The reason for this important difference is twofold: (a) In testing for latent mean differences, the intercepts must be constrained equal across groups; and

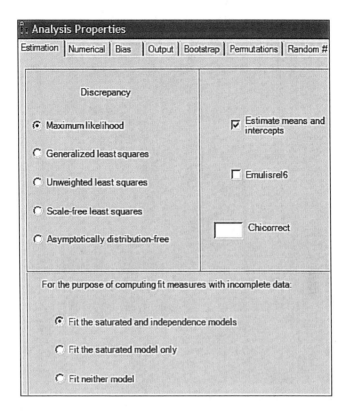

Figure 13.1 Selection of the *Estimate Means and Intercepts* option on the *Estimation* tab of the *Analysis Properties* dialog box.

(b) in order to specify these constraints in AMOS Graphics, it is necessary to attach matching labels to the constrained parameters. Because we are working with only a single group in this chapter, the intercept labels are not necessary.

Selected AMOS output: Parameter and model summary information

Presented in Table 13.1, you will see both the parameter summary and model summary information pertinent to our current *incomplete* data sample. In the interest of pinpointing any differences between the *incomplete* and *complete* (see Table 3.3 and Figure 3.7) data samples, let's now compare this information with respect to these same sections of the output file.

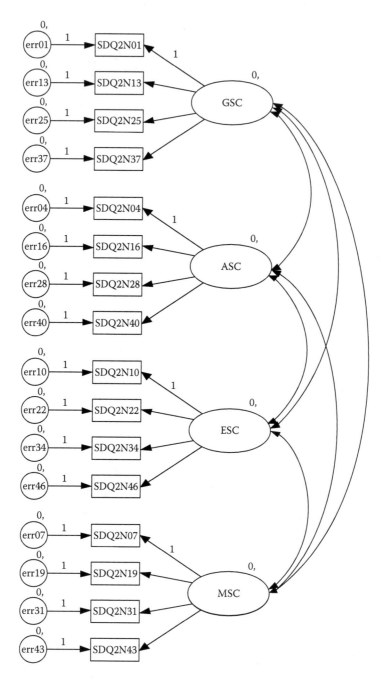

Figure 13.2 Hypothesized model of self-concept structure tested for sample with incomplete data.

Table 13.1 Selected AMOS Output: Parameter and Model Summary
Information (Incomplete Data)

	Parameter summary					
	Weights	Covariances	Variances	Means	Intercepts	Total
Fixed	20	0	0	0	0	20
Labeled	0	0	0	0	0	0
Unlabeled	12	6	20	0	16	54
Total	32	6	20	0	16	74

Model summary

Number of distinct sample moments	152
Number of distinct parameters to be estimated	54
Degrees of freedom (152 – 54)	98

Minimum was achieved.
Chi-square   = 159.650
Degrees of freedom = 98
Probability level   =   .000

First, notice that, although the number of fixed parameters in the model is the same (20) for the two samples, the number of unlabeled parameters (i.e., estimated parameters) varies, with the *incomplete* data group having 54 estimated parameters, and the *complete* data sample having 38. The explanation of this discrepancy lies with the estimation of 16 intercepts for the *incomplete* data sample (but not for the complete data sample). *Second*, observe that although the number of degrees of freedom (98) remains the same across complete and incomplete data samples, its calculation is based upon a different number of sample moments (152 versus 136), as well as a different number of estimated parameters (54 versus 38). Finally, note that, despite the loss of 25% of the data for the one sample, the overall χ^2 value remains relatively close to that for the complete data sample (159.650 versus 158.511).

Selected AMOS output: Parameter estimates

Let's turn our attention now to a comparison of parameter estimates between the *incomplete* and *complete* data samples. In reviewing these estimates for the *incomplete* data sample (Table 13.2) and for the *complete* data sample (Table 3.4), you will see that the values are relatively close. Although the estimates for the *incomplete* data sample are sometimes a little higher but also a little lower than those for the *complete* data sample, overall, they are not very much different. Indeed, considering the substantial depletion

Table 13.2 Selected AMOS Output: Parameter Estimates (Incomplete Data)

	Estimate	S.E.	C.R.	P
Regression weights				
SDQ2N37 <--- GSC	.843	.152	5.549	***
SDQ2N25 <--- GSC	.950	.171	5.565	***
SDQ2N13 <--- GSC	1.103	.192	5.741	***
SDQ2N01 <--- GSC	1.000			
SDQ2N40 <--- ASC	1.218	.197	6.191	***
SDQ2N28 <--- ASC	1.439	.212	6.774	***
SDQ2N16 <--- ASC	1.340	.195	6.883	***
SDQ2N04 <--- ASC	1.000			
SDQ2N46 <--- ESC	.837	.149	5.632	***
SDQ2N34 <--- ESC	.609	.180	3.381	***
SDQ2N22 <--- ESC	.817	.127	6.440	***
SDQ2N10 <--- ESC	1.000			
SDQ2N43 <--- MSC	.728	.064	11.358	***
SDQ2N31 <--- MSC	1.037	.071	14.513	***
SDQ2N19 <--- MSC	.795	.079	10.104	***
SDQ2N07 <--- MSC	1.000			
***				
Covariances				
ASC <--> ESC	.463	.089	5.182	***
GSC <--> ESC	.373	.084	4.418	***
MSC <--> ASC	.789	.140	5.638	***
MSC <--> GSC	.633	.127	4.975	***
GSC <--> ASC	.352	.080	4.406	***
MSC <--> ESC	.403	.108	3.732	***
***				

of data for the sample used in this chapter, it seems quite amazing that the estimates are as close as they are!

Selected AMOS output: Goodness-of-fit statistics

In comparing the goodness-of-fit statistics in Table 13.3 for the *incomplete* data sample, with those reported in Table 3.5 for the *complete* data sample, you will note some values that are almost the same (e.g., χ^2 [as noted above]; RMSEA: .049 versus .048), while others vary slightly at the second or third decimal point (e.g., CFI: .941 versus .962). Generally speaking, however, the

Table 13.3 Selected AMOS Output: Goodness-of-Fit Statistics
(Incomplete Data)

CMIN

Model	NPAR	CMIN	DF	P	CMIN/DF
Your model	54	159.650	98	.000	1.629
Saturated model	152	.000	0		
Independence model	16	1188.843	136	.000	8.741

Baseline comparisons

Model	NFI Delta1	RFI rho1	IFI Delta2	TLI rho2	CFI
Your model	.866	.814	.943	.919	.941
Saturated model	1.000		1.000		1.000
Independence model	.000	.000	.000	.000	.000

RMSEA

Model	RMSEA	LO 90	HI 90	PCLOSE
Your model	.049	.035	.062	.541
Independence model	.171	.162	.180	.000

goodness-of-fit statistics are very similar across the two samples. Given the extent to which both the parameter estimates and the goodness-of-fit statistics are similar, despite the 25% data loss for one sample, these findings provide strong supportive evidence for the effectiveness of the direct ML approach to addressing the problem of missing data values.

Endnote

1. The imputation is actually performed using the companion preprocessing package PRELIS (Jöreskog & Sörbom, 1996b).

References

Aikin, L. S., Stein, J. A., & Bentler, P. M. (1994). Structural equation analyses of clinical sub-population differences and comparative treatment outcomes: Characterizing the daily lives of drug addicts. *Journal of Consulting and Clinical Psychology, 62*, 488–499.

Aish, A. M., & Jöreskog, K. G. (1990). A panel model for political efficacy and responsiveness: An application of LISREL 7 with weighted least squares. *Quality and Quantity, 19*, 716–723.

Akaike, H. (1987). Factor analysis and AIC. *Psychometrika, 52*, 317–332.

Allison, P. D. (1987). Estimation of linear models with incomplete data. In C. Clogg (Ed.), *Sociological methodology 1987* (pp. 71–103). San Francisco: Jossey-Bass.

American Psychologist. (1995). [Replies to Cohen (1994)]. *American Psychologist, 50*, 1098–1103.

Anderson, J. C., & Gerbing, D. W. (1984). The effect of sampling error on convergence, improper solutions, and goodness-of-fit indices for maximum likelihood confirmatory factor analysis. *Psychometrika, 49*, 155–173.

Anderson, J.C., & Gerbing, D.W. (1988). Structural equation modeling in practice: A review and recommended two-step approach. *Psychological Bulletin, 103*, 411–423.

Arbuckle, J. L. (1996). Full information estimation in the presence of incomplete data. In G. A. Marcoulides & R. E. Schumacker (Eds.), *Advanced structural equation modeling: Issues and techniques* (pp. 243–277). Mahwah, NJ: Erlbaum.

Arbuckle, J. L. (2007). *Amos™ 16 user's guide.* Chicago: SPSS.

Arbuckle, J. L., & Wothke, W. (1999). *AMOS 4.0 user's guide.* Chicago: Smallwaters.

Atkinson, L. (1988). The measurement-statistics controversy: Factor analysis and subinterval data. *Bulletin of the Psychonomic Society, 26*, 361–364.

Austin, J. T., & Calderón, R. F. (1996). Theoretical and technical contributions to structural equation modeling: An updated bibliography. *Structural Equation Modeling, 3*, 105–175.

Babakus, E., Ferguson, C. E., Jr., & Jöreskog, K. G. (1987). The sensitivity of confirmatory maximum likelihood factor analysis to violations of measurement scale and distributional assumptions. *Journal of Marketing Research, 24*, 222–228.

Bacharach, S. B., Bauer, S. C., & Conley, S. (1986). Organizational analysis of stress: The case of elementary and secondary schools. *Work and Occupations, 13*, 7–32.

Bagozzi, R. P. (1993). Assessing construct validity in personality research: Applications to measures of self-esteem. *Journal of Research in Personality, 27*, 49–87.

Bagozzi, R. P., & Yi, Y. (1990). Assessing method variance in multitrait-multimethod matrices: The case of self-reported affect and perceptions at work. *Journal of Applied Psychology, 75*, 547–560.

Bagozzi, R. P., & Yi, Y. (1993). Multitrait-multimethod matrices in consumer research: Critique and new developments. *Journal of Consumer Psychology, 2*, 143–170.

Bandalos, D. L. (1993). Factors influencing cross-validation of confirmatory factor analysis models. *Multivariate Behavioral Research, 28*, 351–374.

Bandalos, D. L. (2002). The effects of item parceling on goodness-of-fit and parameter estimate bias in structural equation modeling. *Structural Equation Modeling Journal, 9*, 78–102.

Bandalos, D. L., & Finney S. J. (2001). Item parceling issues in structural equation modeling. In G. A. Marcoulides & R. E. Schumacker (Eds.), *New developments and techniques in structural equation modeling* (pp. 269–296). Mahwah, NJ: Erlbaum.

Beauducel, A., & Wittmann, W. W. (2005). Simulation study on fit indexes in CFA based on data with slightly distorted simple structure. *Structural Equation Modeling, 12*, 41–75.

Beck, A., Steer, R., & Brown, G. (1996). *Beck Depression Inventory manual* (2nd ed.). San Antonio, TX: Psychological Association.

Beck, A. T., Ward, C. H., Mendelson, M., Mock, J., & Erbaugh, J. (1961). An inventory for measuring depression. *Archives of General Psychiatry, 4*, 561–571.

Benson, J., & Bandalos, D.L. (1992). Second-order confirmatory factor analysis of the Reactions to Tests Scale with cross-validation. *Multivariate Behavioral Research, 27*, 459–487.

Bentler, P. M. (1980). Multivariate analysis with latent variables: Causal modeling. *Annual Review of Psychology, 31*, 419–456.

Bentler, P. M. (1988). Causal modeling via structural equation systems. In J. R. Nesselroade & R. B. Cattell (Eds.), *Handbook of multivariate experimental psychology* (2nd ed., pp. 317–335). New York: Plenum.

Bentler, P. M. (1990). Comparative fit indexes in structural models. *Psychological Bulletin, 107*, 238–246.

Bentler, P. M. (1992). On the fit of models to covariances and methodology to the *Bulletin. Psychological Bulletin, 112*, 400–404.

Bentler, P. M. (2005). *EQS 6 Structural equations program manual.* Encino, CA: Multivariate Software.

Bentler, P. M., & Bonett, D. G. (1980). Significance tests and goodness of fit in the analysis of covariance structures. *Psychological Bulletin, 88*, 588–606.

Bentler, P. M., & Bonett, D. G. (1987). This week's citation classic. *Current Contents, 19*, 16.

Bentler, P. M., & Chou, C-P. (1987). Practical issues in structural modeling. *Sociological Methods & Research, 16*, 78–117.

Bentler, P. M., & Dijkstra, T. (1985). Efficient estimation via linearization in structural model. In P. R. Krishnaiah (Ed.), *Multivariate analysis VI* (pp. 9–42). Amsterdam: North-Holland.

Bentler, P. M., & Yuan, K-H. (1999). Structural equation modeling with small samples: Test statistics. *Multivariate Behavioral Research, 34*, 181–197.

Biddle, B. J., & Marlin, M.M. (1987). Causality, confirmation, credulity, and structural equation modeling. *Child Development, 58*, 4–17.

Bloxis, S. A., & Cho, Y. I. (2008). Coding and centering of time in latent curve models in the presence of interindividual time heterogeneity. *Structural Equation Modeling, 15,* 413–433.

Bodner, T. E. (2008). What improves with increasing missing data imputations? *Structural Equation Modeling, 15,* 651–675.

Bollen, K. A. (1986). Sample size and Bentler and Bonett's nonnormed fit index. *Psychometrika, 51,* 375–377.

Bollen, K. A. (1989a). *Structural equations with latent variables.* New York: Wiley.

Bollen, K. A. (1989b). A new incremental fit index for general structural models. *Sociological Methods & Research, 17,* 303–316.

Bollen, K. A., & Barb, K. H. (1981). Pearson's *r* and coursely categorized measures. *American Sociological Review, 46,* 232–239.

Bollen, K. A., & Long, J. S. (Eds.). (1993). *Testing structural equation models.* Newbury Park, CA: Sage.

Bollen, K. A., & Stine, R. A. (1988, August). Bootstrapping structural equation models: Variability of indirect effects and goodness-of-fit measures. Paper presented at the American Sociological Association annual meeting, Atlanta, GA.

Bollen, K. A., & Stine, R. A. (1993). Bootstrapping goodness-of-fit measures in structural equation modeling. In K. A. Bollen & J. S. Long (Eds.), *Testing structural equation models* (pp. 111–135). Newbury Park, CA: Sage.

Bolstad, W. M. (2004). *Introduction to Bayesian statistics.* Hoboken, NJ: Wiley.

Boomsma, A. (1982). The robustness of LISREL against small sample sizes in factor analysis models. In H. Wold & K. Jöreskog (Eds.), *Systems under indirect observation* (pp. 149–173). New York: Elsevier-North-Holland.

Boomsma, A. (1985). Nonconvergence, improper solutions, and starting values in LISREL maximum likelihood estimation. *Psychometrika, 50,* 229–242.

Boomsma, A., & Hoogland, J. J. (2001). The robustness of LISREL modeling revisited. In R. Cudeck, S. DuToit, & D. Sörbom (Eds.), *Structural equation modeling: Present and future.* Lincolnwood, IL: Scientific Software International.

Bovaird, J. A. (2007). Multilevel structural equation models for contextual factors. In T. D. Little, J. A. Bovaird, & N. A. Card (Eds.), *Modeling contextual effects in longitudinal studies* (pp. 149–182). Mahwah, NJ: Erlbaum.

Bozdogan, H. (1987). Model selection and Akaike's information criteria (AIC): The general theory and its analytical extensions. *Psychometrika, 52,* 345–370.

Breckler, S. J. (1990). Applications of covariance structure modeling in psychology: Cause for concern? *Psychological Bulletin, 107,* 260–271.

Brookover, W. B. (1962). *Self-Concept of Ability Scale.* East Lansing, MI: Educational Publication Services.

Brown, R. L. (1994). Efficacy of the indirect approach for estimating structural equation models with missing data: A comparison of five methods. *Structural Equation Modeling, 1,* 287–316.

Browne, M. W. (1984a). Asymptotically distribution-free methods for the analysis of covariance structures. *British Journal of Mathematical and Statistical Psychology, 37,* 62–83.

Browne, M. W. (1984b). The decomposition of multitrait-multimethod matrices. *British Journal of Mathematical and Statistical Psychology, 37,* 1–21.

Browne, M. W., & Cudeck, R. (1989). Single sample cross-validation indices for covariance structures. *Multivariate Behavioral Research, 24,* 445–455.

Browne, M. W., & Cudeck, R. (1993). Alternative ways of assessing model fit. In K. A. Bollen & J. S. Long (Eds.), *Testing structural equation models* (136–162). Newbury Park, CA: Sage.

Bryk, A. S., & Raudenbush, S. W. (1987). Applications of hierarchical linear models to assessing change. *Psychological Bulletin, 101,* 147–158.

Byrne, B. M. (1988a). The Self Description Questionnaire III: Testing for equivalent factorial validity across ability. *Educational and Psychological Measurement, 48,* 397–406.

Byrne, B. M. (1988b). Adolescent self-concept, ability grouping, and social comparison: Reexamining academic track differences in high school. *Youth and Society, 20,* 46–67.

Byrne, B. M. (1989). *A primer of LISREL: Basic applications and programming for confirmatory factor analytic model.* New York: Springer-Verlag.

Byrne, B. M. (1991). The Maslach Inventory: Validating factorial structure and invariance across intermediate, secondary, and university educators. *Multivariate Behavioral Research, 26,* 583–605.

Byrne, B. M. (1993). The Maslach Inventory: Testing for factorial validity and invariance across elementary, intermediate, and secondary teachers. *Journal of Occupational and Organizational Psychology, 66,* 197–212.

Byrne, B. M. (1994a). Burnout: Testing for the validity, replication, and invariance of causal structure across elementary, intermediate, and secondary teachers. *American Educational Research Journal, 31,* 645–673.

Byrne, B. M. (1994b). *Structural equation modeling with EQS and EQS/Windows: Basic concepts, applications, and programming.* Thousand Oaks, CA: Sage.

Byrne, B. M. (1994c). Testing for the factorial validity, replication, and invariance of a measuring instrument: A paradigmatic application based on the Maslach Burnout Inventory. *Multivariate Behavioral Research, 29,* 289–311.

Byrne, B. M. (1995). Strategies in testing for an invariant second-order factor structure: A comparison of EQS and LISREL. *Structural Equation Modeling, 2,* 53–72.

Byrne, B. M. (1996). *Measuring self-concept across the lifespan: Issues and instrumentation.* Washington, DC: American Psychological Association.

Byrne, B. M. (1998). *Structural equation modeling with LISREL, PRELIS, and SIMPLIS: Basic concepts, applications, and programming.* Mahwah, NJ: Erlbaum.

Byrne, B. M. (1999). The nomological network of teacher burnout: A literature review and empirically validated model. In M. Huberman & R. Vandenberghe (Eds.), *Understanding and preventing teacher burnout: A sourcebook of international research and practice* (pp. 15–37). London: Cambridge University Press.

Byrne, B. M. (2001). *Structural equation modeling with AMOS: Basic concepts, applications, and programming.* Mahwah, NJ: Erlbaum.

Byrne, B. M. (2003). Confirmatory factor analysis. In R. Fernández-Ballesteros (Ed.), *Encyclopedia of psychological assessment* (Vol. 1, pp. 399–402). Thousand Oaks, CA: Sage.

Byrne, B. M. (2004). Testing for multigroup invariance using AMOS Graphics: A road less traveled. *Structural Equation Modeling, 11,* 272–300.

Byrne, B. M. (2005a). Factor analytic models: Viewing the structure of an assessment instrument from three perspectives. *Journal of Personality Assessment, 85,* 17–30.

Byrne, B. M. (2005b). Factor analysis: Confirmatory. In B. S. Everitt & D. C. Howell (Eds.), *Encyclopedia of statistics in behavioural science* (pp. 599–606). London: Wiley.

Byrne, B. M. (2006). *Structural equation modeling with EQS: Basic concepts, applications, and programming* (2nd ed.). Mahwah, NJ: Erlbaum.

Byrne, B. M. (2008). Testing for time-invariant and time-varying predictors of self-perceived ability in math, language, and science: A look at the gender factor. In H. M. G. Watt & J. S. Eccles (Eds.), *Gender and occupational outcomes: Longitudinal assessments of individual, social, and cultural influences* (pp. 145–169). Washington, DC: American Psychological Association.

Byrne, B. M., & Baron P. (1993). The Beck Depression Inventory: Testing and cross-validating an hierarchical factor structure for nonclinical adolescents. *Measurement and Evaluation in Counseling and Development, 26,* 164–178.

Byrne, B. M., & Baron, P. (1994). Measuring adolescent depression: Tests of equivalent factorial structure for English and French versions of the Beck Depression Inventory. *Applied Psychology: An International Review, 43,* 33–47.

Byrne, B. M., Baron, P., & Balev, J. (1996). The Beck Depression Inventory: Testing for its factorial validity and invariance across gender for Bulgarian adolescents. *Personality and Individual Differences, 21,* 641–651.

Byrne, B. M., Baron, P., & Balev, J. (1998). The Beck Depression Inventory: A cross-validated test of second-order structure for Bulgarian adolescents. *Educational and Psychological Measurement, 58,* 241–251.

Byrne, B. M., Baron, P., & Campbell, T. L. (1993). Measuring adolescent depression: Factorial validity and invariance of the Beck Depression Inventory across gender. *Journal of Research on Adolescence, 3,* 127–143.

Byrne, B. M., Baron, P., & Campbell, T. L. (1994). The Beck Depression Inventory (French version): Testing for gender-invariant factorial structure for nonclinical adolescents. *Journal of Adolescent Research, 9,* 166–179.

Byrne, B. M., Baron, P., Larsson, B., & Melin, L. (1995). The Beck Depression Inventory: Testing and cross-validating a second-order factorial structure for Swedish nonclinical adolescents. *Behaviour Research and Therapy, 33,* 345–356.

Byrne, B. M., Baron, P., Larsson, B., & Melin, L. (1996). Measuring depression for Swedish nonclinical adolescents: Factorial validity and equivalence of the Beck Depression Inventory. *Scandinavian Journal of Psychology, 37,* 37–45.

Byrne, B. M., & Bazana, P. G. (1996). Investigating the measurement of social and academic competencies for early/late preadolescents and adolescents: A multitrait-multimethod analysis. *Applied Measurement in Education, 9,* 113–132.

Byrne, B. M., & Campbell, T. L. (1999). Cross-cultural comparisons and the presumption of equivalent measurement and theoretical structure: A look beneath the surface. *Journal of Cross-Cultural Psychology, 30,* 557–576.

Byrne, B. M., & Crombie, G. (2003). Modeling and testing change over time: An introduction to the latent growth curve model. *Understanding Statistics: Statistical Issues in Psychology, Education, and the Social Sciences, 2,* 177–203.

Byrne, B. M., & Goffin, R. D. (1993). Modeling MTMM data from additive and multiplicative covariance structures: An audit of construct validity concordance. *Multivariate Behavioral Research, 28,* 67–96.

Byrne, B. M., Lam, W. W. T., & Fielding, R. (2008). Measuring patterns of change in personality assessments: An annotated application of latent growth curve modeling. *Journal of Personality Assessment, 90*, 1–11.

Byrne, B. M., & Shavelson, R. J. (1986). On the structure of adolescent self-concept. *Journal of Educational Psychology, 78*, 474–481.

Byrne, B. M., & Shavelson, R. J. (1996). On the structure of social self-concept for pre-, early, and late adolescents. *Journal of Personality and Social Psychology, 70*, 599–613.

Byrne, B. M., Shavelson, R. J., & Muthén, B. (1989). Testing for the equivalence of factor covariance and mean structures: The issue of partial measurement invariance. *Psychological Bulletin, 105*, 456–466.

Byrne, B. M., Stewart, S. M., & Lee, P. W. H. (2004). Validating the Beck Depression Inventory—II for Hong Kong community adolescents. *International Journal of Testing, 4*, 199–216.

Byrne, B. M., & Worth Gavin, D. A. (1996). The Shavelson model revisited: Testing for the structure of academic self-concept across pre-, early, and late adolescents. *Journal of Educational Psychology, 88*, 215–228.

Campbell, D. T., & Fiske, D.W. (1959). Convergent and discriminant validation by the multitrait-multimethod matrix. *Psychological Bulletin, 56*, 81–105.

Carlson, M., & Mulaik, S.A. (1993). Trait ratings from descriptions of behavior as mediated by components of meaning. *Multivariate Behavioral Research, 28*, 111–159.

Cheong, J. W., MacKinnon, D. P., & Khoo, S. T. (2003). Investigation of mediational processes using parallel process latent growth curve modeling. *Structural Equation Modeling, 10*, 238–262.

Cheung, G. W., & Rensvold, R. B. (2002). Evaluating goodness-of-fit indexes for testing measurement invariance. *Structural Equation Modeling: A Multidisciplinary Journal, 9*, 233–255.

Chinese Behavioral Sciences Society. (2000). *The Chinese version of the Beck Depression Inventory* (2nd ed., licensed Chinese translation, The Psychological Corporation). New York: Harcourt Brace.

Chou, C-P., Bentler, P. M., & Satorra, A. (1991). Scaled test statistics and robust standard errors for non-normal data in covariance structure analysis: A Monte Carlo study. *British Journal of Mathematical and Statistical Psychology, 44*, 347–357.

Cliff, N. (1983). Some cautions concerning the application of causal modeling methods. *Multivariate Behavioral Research, 18*, 115–126.

Coenders, G., & Saris, W. E. (2000). Testing nested additive, multiplicative, and general multitrait-multimethod models. *Structural Equation Modeling, 7*, 219–250.

Coenders, G., Satorra, A., & Saris, W. E. (1997). Alternative approaches to structural modeling of ordinal data: A Monte Carlo study. *Structural Equation Modeling, 4*, 261–282.

Cohen, J. (1994). The earth is round (*p*<.05). *American Psychologist, 49*, 997–1003.

Comrey, A. L. (1992). *A first course in factor analysis*. Hillsdale, NJ: Erlbaum.

Conway, J. M., Scullen, S. E., Lievens, F., & Lance, C. E. (2004). Bias in the correlated uniqueness model for MTMM data. *Structural Equation Modeling, 11*, 535–559.

Cooke, D. J., Kosson, D. S., & Michie, C. (2001). Psychopathy and ethnicity: Structural, item, and test generalizability of the Psychopathy Checklist—Revised (PCL-R) in Caucasian and African American participants. *Psychological Assessment, 13,* 531–542.

Corten, I. W., Saris, W. E., Coenders, G., van der Veld, W., Aalberts, C. E., & Kornelis, C. (2002). Fit of different models for multitrait-multimethod experiments. *Structural Equation Modeling, 9,* 213–232.

Cudeck, R. (1989). Analysis of correlation matrices using covariance structure models. *Psychological Bulletin, 105,* 317–327.

Cudeck, R., & Browne, M. W. (1983). Cross-validation of covariance structures. *Multivariate Behavioral Research, 18,* 147–167.

Cudeck, R., du Toit, S., & Sörbom, D. (2001). *Structural equation modeling: Present and future.* Lincolnwood, IL: Scientific Software International.

Cudeck, R., & Henly, S. J. (1991). Model selection in covariance structures analysis and the "problem" of sample size: A clarification. *Psychological Bulletin, 109,* 512–519.

Curran, P. J., Bauer, D. J., & Willoughby, M. T. (2004). Testing main effects and interactions in latent curve analysis. *Psychological Methods, 9,* 220–237.

Curran, P. J., Edwards, M. C., Wirth, R. J., Hussong, A. M., & Chassin, L. (2007). The incorporation of categorical measurement models in the analysis of individual growth. In T. D. Little, J. A. Bovaird, & N. A. Card (Eds.), *Modeling contextual effects in longitudinal studies* (pp. 89–120). Mahwah, NJ: Erlbaum.

Curran, P. J., West, S. G., & Finch, J. F. (1996). The robustness of test statistics to nonnormality and specification error in confirmatory factor analysis. *Psychological Methods, 1,* 16–29.

Davey, A., Savla, J., & Luo, Z. (2005). Issues in evaluating model fit with missing data. *Structural Equation Modeling, 12,* 578–597.

DeCarlo, L. T. (1997). On the meaning and use of kurtosis. *Psychological Methods, 2,* 292–307.

Diaconis, P., & Efron, B. (1983). Computer-intensive methods in statistics. *Scientific American, 248,* 116–130.

DiStefano, C. (2002). The impact of categorization with confirmatory factor analysis. *Structural Equation Modeling, 9,* 327–346.

Duncan, T. E., & Duncan, S. C. (1994). Modeling incomplete longitudinal substance use data using latent variable growth curve methodology. *Multivariate Behavioral Research, 29,* 313–338.

Duncan, T. E., & Duncan, S. C. (1995). Modeling the processes of development via latent growth curve methodology. *Structural Equation Modeling, 3,* 187–205.

Duncan, T. E., Duncan, S. C., Okut, H., Stryker, L. A., & Li, F. (2002). An extension of the general latent variable growth modeling framework to four levels of the hierarchy. *Structural Equation Modeling, 9,* 303–326.

Duncan, T. E., Duncan, S. C., & Stryker, L. A. (2006). *An introduction to latent variable growth curve modeling: Concepts, issues, and applications* (2nd ed.). Mahwah, NJ: Erlbaum.

Duncan, T. E., Duncan, S. C., Stryker, L. A., Li, F., & Alpert, A. (1999). *An introduction to latent variable growth curve modeling.* Mahwah, NJ: Erlbaum.

Efron, B. (1979). Bootstrap methods: Another look at the jackknife. *Annals of Statistics, 7,* 1–26.

Efron, B. (1982). *The jackknife, the bootstrap and other resampling plans*. Philadelphia: SIAM.

Efron, B., & Tibshirani, R. J. (1993). *An introduction to the bootstrap*. New York: Chapman and Hall.

Eid, M., Lischetzke, T., Nussbeck, F. W., & Trierweiler, L. I. (2003). Separating trait effects from trait-specific method effects in multitrait-multimethod models: A multiple-indicator CT-C(M-1) model. *Psychological Methods, 8*, 38–60.

Eid, M., Nussbeck, F. W., Geiser, C., Cole, D. A., Gollwitzer, M., & Lischetzke, T. (2008). Structural equation modeling of multitrait-multimethod data: Different models for different types of methods. *Psychological Methods, 13*, 230–253.

Enders, C. K. (2001). A primer on maximum likelihood algorithms available for use with missing data. *Structural Equation Modeling, 8*, 128–141.

Fabrigar, L. R., Wegener, D. T., MacCallum, R. C., & Strahan, E. J. (1999). Evaluating the use of exploratory factor analysis in psychological research. *Psychological Methods, 4*, 272–299.

Fan, X., & Sivo, S. A. (2005). Sensitivity of fit indexes to misspecified structural or measurement model components: Rationale of two-index strategy revisited. *Structural Equation Modeling, 12*, 343–367.

Fan, X., Thompson, B., & Wang, L. (1999). Effects of sample size, estimation methods, and model specification on structural equation modeling fit indexes. *Structural Equation Modeling, 6*, 56–83.

Finch, J. F., West, S. G., & MacKinnon, D. P. (1997). Effects of sample size and nonnormality on the estimation of mediated effects in latent variable models. *Structural Equation Modeling, 4*, 87–107.

Francis, D.J., Fletcher, J.M., & Rourke, B.P. (1988). Discriminant validity of lateral sensorimotor tests in children. *Journal of Clinical and Experimental Neuropsychology, 10*, 779-799.

Gelman, A., Carlin, J. B., Stern, H. S., & Rubin, D. B. (2004). *Bayesian data analysis* (2nd ed.). Boca Raton, FL: Chapman & Hall/CRC.

Gerbing, D. W., & Anderson, J. C. (1984). On the meaning of within-factor correlated measurement errors. *Journal of Consumer Research, 11*, 572–580.

Gerbing, D. W., & Anderson, J. C. (1993). Monte Carlo evaluations of goodness-of-fit indices for structural equation models. In K. A. Bollen & J. S. Long (Eds.), *Testing structural equation models* (pp. 40–65). Newbury Park, CA: Sage.

Gorsuch, R. L. (1983). *Factor analysis*. Hillsdale, NJ: Erlbaum.

Green, S. B., Akey, T. M., Fleming, K. K., Hershberger, S. L., & Marquis, J. G. (1997). Effect of the number of scale points on chi-square fit indices in confirmatory factor analysis. *Structural Equation Modeling, 4*, 108–120.

Hagtvet, K. A., & Nasser, F. M. (2004). How well do item parcels represent conceptually defined latent constructs? A two-facet approach. *Structural Equation Modeling, 11*, 168–193.

Hancock, G. R., Kuo, W-L., & Lawrence, F. R. (2001). An illustration of second-order latent growth models. *Structural Equation Modeling, 8*, 470–489.

Hancock, G. R., & Nevitt, J. (1999). Bootstrapping and the identification of exogenous latent variables within structural equation models. *Structural Equation Modeling, 6*, 394–399.

Harlow, L. L., Mulaik, S. A., & Steiger, J. H. (Eds.). (1997). *What if there were no significance tests?* Mahwah, NJ: Erlbaum.

Harter, S. (1990). Causes, correlates, and the functional role of global self-worth; A lifespan perspective. In R. J. Sternberg & J. Kolligian (Eds.), *Competence considered* (pp. 67–97). New Haven, CT: Yale University Press.

Hayashi, K., & Marcoulides, G. A. (2006). Examining identification issues in factor analysis. *Structural Equation Modeling, 13,* 631–645.

Hernández, A., & González-Romá, V. (2002). Analysis of multitrait-multioccasion data: Additive versus multiplicative models. *Multivariate Behavioral Research, 37,* 59–87.

Hershberger, S. L., & Fisher, D. G. (2003). A note on determining the number of imputations for missing data. *Structural Equation Modeling, 10,* 648–650.

Hoelter, J. W. (1983). The analysis of covariance structures: Goodness-of-fit indices. *Sociological Methods & Research, 11,* 325–344.

Hofer, S. M., & Hoffman, L. (2007). Statistical analysis with incomplete data: A developmental perspective. In T. D. Little, J. A. Bovaird, & N. A. Card (Eds.), *Modeling contextual effects in longitudinal studies* (pp. 13–32). Mahwah, NJ: Erlbaum.

Hox, J. J., & Kleiboer, A. M. (2007). Retrospective questions or a diary method? A two-level multitrait-multimethod analysis. *Structural Equation Modeling, 14,* 311–325.

Hoyle, R. H. (1995a). The structural equation modeling approach: Basic concepts and fundamental issues. In R. H. Hoyle (Ed.), *Structural equation modeling: Concepts, issues, and applications* (pp. 1–15). Thousand Oaks, CA: Sage.

Hoyle, R. H. (Ed.). (1995b). *Structural equation modeling: Concepts, issues, and applications.* Thousand Oaks, CA: Sage.

Hu, L-T., & Bentler, P. M. (1995). Evaluating model fit. In R. H. Hoyle (Ed.), *Structural equation modeling: Concepts, issues, and applications* (pp. 76–99). Thousand Oaks, CA: Sage.

Hu, L-T., & Bentler, P. M. (1998). Fit indices in covariance structure modeling: Sensitivity to underparameterized model misspecification. *Psychological Methods, 3,* 424–453.

Hu, L-T., & Bentler, P. M. (1999). Cutoff criteria for fit indexes in covariance structure analysis: Conventional criteria versus new alternatives. *Structural Equation Modeling, 6,* 1–55.

Hu, L-T., Bentler, P. M., & Kano, Y. (1992). Can test statistics in covariance structure analysis be trusted? *Psychological Bulletin, 112,* 351–362.

Ichikawa, M., & Konishi, S. (1995). Application of the bootstrap methods in factor analysis. *Psychometrika, 60,* 77–93.

James, L. R., Mulaik, S. A., & Brett, J. M. (1982). *Causal analysis: Assumptions, models, and data.* Beverly Hills, CA: Sage.

Jamshidian, M., & Bentler, P. M. (1999). ML estimation of mean and covariance structures with missing data using complete data routines. *Journal of Educational and Behavioral Statistics, 24,* 21–41.

Jöreskog, K. G. (1969). A general approach to confirmatory maximum likelihood factor analysis. *Psychometrika, 34,* 183–202.

Jöreskog, K. G. (1971a). Statistical analysis of sets of congeneric tests. *Psychometrika, 36,* 109–133.

Jöreskog, K. G. (1971b). Simultaneous factor analysis in several populations. *Psychometrika, 36,* 409–426.

Jöreskog, K. G. (1990). New developments in LISREL: Analysis of ordinal variables using polychoric correlations and weighted least squares. *Quality and Quantity, 24,* 387–404.

Jöreskog, K. G. (1993). Testing structural equation models. In K. A. Bollen & J. S. Long (Eds.), *Testing structural equation models* (pp. 294–316). Newbury Park, CA: Sage.

Jöreskog, K. G. (1994). On the estimation of polychoric correlations and their asymptotic covariance matrix. *Psychometrika, 59,* 381–389.

Jöreskog, K. G., & Sörbom, D. (1989). *LISREL 7 user's reference guide.* Chicago: Scientific Software.

Jöreskog, K. G., & Sörbom, D. (1993). *LISREL 8: Structural equation modeling with the SIMPLIS command language.* Chicago: Scientific Software International.

Jöreskog, K. G., & Sörbom, D. (1996a). *LISREL 8: User's reference guide.* Chicago: Scientific Software International.

Jöreskog, K. G., & Sörbom, D. (1996b). *PRELIS: User's reference guide.* Chicago: Scientific Software International.

Kaplan, D. (1989). Model modification in covariance structure analysis: Application of the expected parameter change statistic. *Multivariate Behavioral Research, 24,* 285–305.

Kenny, D. A. (1976). An empirical application of confirmatory factor analysis to the multitrait-multimethod matrix. *Journal of Experimental Social Psychology, 12,* 247–252.

Kenny, D. A. (1979). *Correlation and causality.* New York: Wiley.

Kenny, D. A., & Kashy, D. A. (1992). Analysis of the multitrait-multimethod matrix by confirmatory factor analysis. *Psychological Bulletin, 112,* 165–172.

Kerlinger, F. N. (1984). *Liberalism and conservatism: The nature and structure of social attitudes.* Hillsdale, NJ: Erlbaum.

Kim, S., & Hagtvet, K. A. (2003). The impact of misspecified item parceling on representing latent variables in covariance structure modeling: A simulation study. *Structural Equation Modeling, 10,* 101–127.

Kirk, R. E. (1996). Practical significance: A concept whose time has come. *Educational and Psychological Measurement, 56,* 746–759.

Kishton, J. M., & Widaman, K. F. (1994). Unidimensional versus domain representative parcelling of questionnaire items: An empirical example. *Educational and Psychological Measurement, 54,* 757–765.

Kline, R. B. (1998). *Principles and practice of structural equation modeling.* New York: Guilford.

Kline, R. B. (2005). *Principles and practice of structural equation modeling* (2nd ed.). New York: Guilford.

Kotz, S., & Johnson, N. I. (1992). *Breakthrough in statistics* (Vols. 1 and 2). New York: Springer-Verlag.

La Du, T. J., & Tanaka, J. S. (1989). Influence of sample size, estimation method, and model specification on goodness-of-fit assessments in structural equation modeling. *Journal of Applied Psychology, 74,* 625–636.

LaGrange, B., & Cole, D. A. (2008). An expansion of the trait-state-occasion model: Accounting for shared method variance. *Structural Equation Modeling, 15,* 241–271.

Lance, C. E., Noble, C. L., & Scullen, S. E. (2002). A critique of the correlated trait-correlated method and correlated uniqueness models for multitrait-multimethod data. *Psychological Methods, 7,* 228–244.

Lei, M., & Lomax, R. G. (2005). The effect of varying degrees of nonnormality in structural equation modeling. *Structural Equation Modeling, 12,* 1–17.

Leiter, M. P. (1991). Coping patterns as predictors of burnout: The function of control and escapist coping patterns. *Journal of Organizational Behavior, 12,* 123–144.

Li, F., Duncan, T. E., Duncan, S. C., McAuley, E., Chaumeton, N. R., & Harmer, P. (2001). Enhancing the psychological well-being of elderly individuals through tai chi exercise: A latent growth curve analysis. *Structural Equation Modeling, 8,* 493–530.

Little, R. J. A., & Rubin, D. B. (1987). *Statistical analysis with missing data.* New York: Wiley.

Little, R. J. A., & Rubin, D. B. (1989). The analysis of social science data with missing values. *Sociological Methods and Research, 18,* 292–326.

Little, T. D. (1997). Mean and covariance structures (MACS) analyses of cross-cultural data: Practical and theoretical issues. *Multivariate Behavioral Research, 32,* 53–76.

Little, T. D., Cunningham, W. A., Shahar, G., & Widaman, K. F. (2002). To parcel or not to parcel: Exploring the question, weighing the merits. *Structural Equation Modeling, 9,* 151–173.

Little, T. D., Lindenberger, U., & Nesselroade, J. R. (1999). On selecting indicators for multivariate measurement and modeling with latent variables: When "good" indicators are bad and "bad" indicators are good. *Psychological Methods, 4,* 192–211.

Loehlin, J. C. (1992). *Latent variable models: An introduction to factor, path, & structural analyses.* Hillsdale, NJ: Erlbaum.

Long, J. S. (1983a). *Confirmatory factor analysis.* Beverly Hills, CA: Sage.

Long, J. S. (1983b). *Covariance structure models: An introduction to LISREL.* Beverly Hills, CA: Sage.

MacCallum, R. C. (1986). Specification searches in covariance structure modeling. *Psychological Bulletin, 100,* 107–120.

MacCallum, R. C. (1995). Model specification: Procedures, strategies, and related issues. In R. H. Hoyle (Ed.), *Structural equation modeling: Concepts, issues, and applications* (pp. 76–99). Newbury Park, CA: Sage.

MacCallum, R. C., & Austin, J. T. (2000). Applications of structural equation modeling in psychological research. *Annual Review of Psychology, 51,* 201–226.

MacCallum, R. C., Browne, M. W., & Sugawara, H. M. (1996). Power analysis and determination of sample size for covariance structure modeling. *Psychological Methods, 1,* 130–149.

MacCallum, R. C., Roznowski, M., Mar, M., & Reith, J. V. (1994). Alternative strategies for cross-validation of covariance structure models. *Multivariate Behavioral Research, 29,* 1–32.

MacCallum, R. C., Roznowski, M., & Necowitz, L. B. (1992). Model modifications in covariance structure analysis: The problem of capitalization on chance. *Psychological Bulletin, 111,* 490–504.

MacCallum, R. C., Wegener, D. T., Uchino, B. N., & Fabrigar, L. R. (1993). The problem of equivalent models in applications of covariance structure analysis. *Psychological Bulletin, 114,* 185–199.

MacCallum, R. C., Widaman, K. F., Zhang, S., & Hong, S. (1999). Sample size in factor analysis. *Psychological Methods, 4,* 84–99.

Marcoulides, G. A., & Schumacker, R. E. (Eds.). (1996). *Advanced structural equation modeling: Issues and techniques.* Mahwah, NJ: Erlbaum.

Mardia, K. V. (1970). Measures of multivariate skewness and kurtosis with applications. *Biometrika, 57,* 519–530.

Mardia, K. V. (1974). Applications of some measures of multivariate skewness and kurtosis in testing normality and robustness studies. *Sankhya, B36,* 115–128.

Marsh, H. W. (1988). Multitrait-multimethod analyses. In J. P. Keeves (Ed.), *Educational research methodology, measurement, and evaluation: An international handbook* (pp. 570–578). Oxford: Pergamon.

Marsh, H. W. (1989). Confirmatory factor analyses of multitrait-multimethod data: Many problems and a few solutions. *Applied Psychological Measurement, 15,* 47–70.

Marsh, H. W. (1992a). *Self Description Questionnaire (SDQ) II: A theoretical and empirical basis for the measurement of multiple dimensions of adolescent self-concept: An interim test manual and research monograph.* Macarthur, NSW, Australia: Faculty of Education, University of Western Sydney.

Marsh, H. W. (1992b). *Self Description Questionnaire (SDQ) III: A theoretical and empirical basis for the measurement of multiple dimensions of late adolescent self-concept: An interim test manual and research monograph.* Macarthur, NSW, Australia: Faculty of Education, University of Western Sydney.

Marsh, H. W. (1998). Pairwise deletion for missing data in structural equation models: Nonpositive definite matrices, parameter estimates, goodness of fit, and adjusted sample sizes. *Structural Equation Modeling, 5,* 22–36.

Marsh, H. W., & Bailey, M. (1991). Confirmatory factor analyses of multitrait-multimethod data: A comparison of alternative models. *Applied Psychological Measurement, 15,* 47–70.

Marsh, H. W., & Balla, J. R. (1994). Goodness-of-fit indices in confirmatory factor analysis: The effect of sample size and model complexity. *Quality and Quantity, 28,* 185–217.

Marsh, H. W., Balla, J. R., & McDonald, R. P. (1988). Goodness-of-fit indexes in confirmatory factor analysis: The effect of sample size. *Psychological Bulletin, 103,* 391–410.

Marsh, H. W., Byrne, B. M., & Craven, R. (1992). Overcoming problems in confirmatory factor analyses of MTMM data: The correlated uniqueness model and factorial invariance. *Multivariate Behavioral Research, 27,* 489–507.

Marsh, H. W., & Grayson, D. (1994). Longitudinal stability of means and individual differences: A unified approach. *Structural Equation Modeling, 1,* 317–359.

Marsh, H. W., & Grayson, D. (1995). Latent variable models of multitrait-multimethod data. In R. H. Hoyle (Ed.), *Structural equation modeling: Concepts, issues, and applications* (pp. 177–198). Thousand Oaks, CA: Sage.

Marsh, H. W., Hau, K-T., Balla, J. R., & Grayson, D. (1998). Is more ever too much? The number of indicators per factor in confirmatory factor analysis. *Multivariate Behavioral Research, 33,* 181–220.

Maslach, C., & Jackson, S. E. (1981). *Maslach Burnout Inventory manual.* Palo Alto, CA: Consulting Psychologists Press.

Maslach, C., & Jackson, S. E. (1986). *Maslach Burnout Inventory manual* (2nd ed.). Palo Alto, CA: Consulting Psychologists Press.

McArdle, J. J. (1994). Structural factor analysis experiments with incomplete data. *Multivariate Behavioral Research, 29*, 409–454.

McArdle, J. J., & Epstein, D. (1987). Latent growth curves within developmental structural equation models. *Child Development, 58*, 110–133.

McDonald, R. P. (1985). *Factor analysis and related methods.* Hillsdale, NJ: Erlbaum.

Meredith, W. (1993). Measurement invariance, factor analysis, and factorial invariance. *Psychometrika, 58*, 525–543.

Meredith, W., & Tisak, J. (1990). Latent curve analysis. *Psychometrika, 55*, 107–122.

Micceri, T. (1989). The unicorn, the normal curve, and other improbable creatures. *Psychological Bulletin, 105*, 156–166.

Millsap, R. E., & Kwok, O-M. (2004). Evaluating the impact of partial factorial equivalence on selection in two populations. *Psychological Methods, 9*, 93–115.

Moustaki, I. (2001). A review of exploratory factor analysis for ordinal categorical data. In R. Cudeck, S. du Toit, & D. Sörbom (Eds.), *Structural equation modeling: Present and future* (pp. 461–480). Lincolnwood, IL: Scientific Software.

Mulaik, S. A. (1972). *The foundations of factor analysis.* New York: McGraw-Hill.

Mulaik, S. A., James, L. R., Van Altine, J., Bennett, N., Lind, S., & Stilwell, C. D. (1989). Evaluation of goodness-of-fit indices for structural equation models. *Psychological Bulletin, 105*, 430–445.

Muthén, B. O. (1984). A general structural equation model with dichotomous, ordered categorical, and continuous latent variable indicators. *Psychometrika, 49*, 115–132.

Muthén, B. O. (1997). Latent variable modeling of longitudinal and multilevel data. In A. E. Raftery (Ed.), *Sociological methodology 1997* (pp. 453–481). Washington, DC: American Sociological Association.

Muthén, B., & Kaplan, D. (1985). A comparison of some methodologies for the factor analysis of non-normal Likert variables. *British Journal of Mathematical and Statistical Psychology, 38*, 171–189.

Muthén, B., Kaplan, D., & Hollis, M. (1987). On structural equation modeling with data that are not missing completely at random. *Psychometrika, 52*, 431–462.

Muthén, B.O., & Muthén, L.K. (2004). *Mplus user's guide.* Muthén & Muthén.

Noreen, E. W. (1989). *Computer-intensive methods for testing hypotheses.* New York: Wiley.

O'Brien, R. M. (1985). The relationship between ordinal measures and their underlying values: Why all the disagreement? *Quality and Quantity, 19*, 265–277.

Pettegrew, L. S., & Wolf, G. E. (1982). Validating measures of teacher stress. *American Educational Research Journal, 19*, 373–396.

Pomplun, M., & Omar, M.H. (2003). Do minority representative reading passages provide factorially invariant scores for all students? *Structural Equation Modeling, 10*, 276–288.

Preacher, K. J., & MacCallum, R. C. (2003). Repairing Tom Swift's electric factor analysis machine. *Understanding Statistics, 2*, 13–43.

Raaijmakers, Q. A. (1999). Effectiveness of different missing data treatments in surveys with Likert-type data: Introducing the relative mean substitution approach. *Educational and Psychological Measurement, 59*, 725–748.

Raftery, A. E. (1993). Baysian model selection in structural equation models. In K. A. Bollen & J. S. Long (Eds.), *Testing structural equation models* (pp. 163–180). Newbury Park, CA: Sage.

Raykov, T. (2005). Analysis of longitudinal studies with missing data using covariance structure modeling with full-information maximum likelihood. *Structural Equation Modeling, 12,* 493–505.

Raykov, T., & Marcoulides, G. A. (2000). *A first course in structural equation modeling.* Mahwah, NJ: Erlbaum.

Raykov, T., & Widaman, K. F. (1995). Issues in structural equation modeling research. *Structural Equation Modeling, 2,* 289–318.

Reise, S. P., Widaman, K. F., & Pugh, P. H. (1993). Confirmatory factor analysis and item response theory: Two approaches for exploring measurement invariance. *Psychological Bulletin, 114,* 552–566.

Rindskopf, D., & Rose, T. (1988). Some theory and applications of confirmatory second-order factor analysis. *Multivariate Behavioral Research, 23,* 51–67.

Rogers, W. M., & Schmitt, N. (2004). Parameter recovery and model fit using multidimensional composites: A comparison of four empirical parcelling algorithms. *Multivariate Behavioral Research, 39,* 379–412.

Rogosa, D. R., Brandt, D., & Zimowski, M. (1982). A growth curve approach to the measurement of change. *Psychological Bulletin, 90,* 726–748.

Rogosa, D. R., & Willett, J. B. (1985). Understanding correlates of change by modeling individual differences in growth. *Psychometrika, 50,* 203–228.

Rosén, M. (1998). Gender differences in hierarchically ordered ability dimensions: The impact of missing data. *Structural Equation Modeling, 5,* 37–62.

Rosenberg, M. (1965). *Society and the adolescent self-image.* Princeton, NJ: Princeton University Press.

Rovine, M. J., & Delaney, M. (1990). Missing data estimation in developmental research. In A. Von Eye (Ed.), *Statistical methods in longitudinal research: Vol. I. Principles and structuring change* (pp. 35–79). New York: Academic Press.

Rozeboom, W. W. (1960). The fallacy of the null hypothesis significance test. *Psychological Bulletin, 57,* 416–428.

Rubin, D. B. (1976). Inference and missing data. *Biometrika, 63,* 581–592.

Saris, W. E., & Aalberts, C. (2003). Different explanations for correlated disturbance terms in MTMM studies. *Structural Equation Modeling, 10,* 193–213.

Saris, W. E., Satorra, A., & Sörbom, D. (1987). The detection and correction of specification errors in structural equation models. In C. Clogg (Ed.), *Sociological methodology 1987* (pp. 105–130). San Francisco: Jossey-Bass.

Saris, W., & Stronkhorst, H. (1984). *Causal modeling: Nonexperimental research: An introduction to the LISREL approach.* Amsterdam: Sociometric Research Foundation.

Satorra, A., & Bentler, P. M. (1988). Scaling corrections for chi-square statistics in covariance structure analysis. In *American Statistical Association 1988 proceedings of the business and economics section* (pp. 308–313). Alexandria, VA: American Statistical Association.

Satorra, A., & Bentler, P. M. (1994). Corrections to test statistics and standard errors in covariance structure analysis. In A. von Eye & C. C. Clogg (Eds.), *Latent variables analysis: Applications for developmental research* (pp. 399–419). Thousand Oaks, CA: Sage.

Satorra, A., & Saris, W. E. (1985). Power of the likelihood ratio test in covariance structure analysis. *Psychometrika, 50,* 83–90.

Savalei, V., & Bentler, P. M. (2005). A statistically justified pairwise ML method for incomplete nonnormal data: A comparison with direct ML and pairwise ADF. *Structural Equation Modeling, 12,* 183–214.

Schafer, J. L. (1997). *Analysis of incomplete multivariate data*. London: Chapman Hall.

Schafer, J. L., & Graham, J. W. (2002). Missing data: Our view of the state of the art. *Psychological Methods, 7*, 147–177.

Schafer, J. L., & Olsen, M. K. (1998). Multiple imputation for multivariate missing-data problems: A data analyst's perspective. *Multivariate Behavioral Research, 33*, 545–571.

Schmidt, F. L. (1996). Statistical significance testing and cumulative knowledge in psychology: Implications for training of researchers. *Psychological Methods, 1*, 115–129.

Schmitt, N., & Stults, D. M. (1986). Methodology review: Analysis of multitrait-multimethod matrices. *Applied Psychological Measurement, 10*, 1–22.

Schumacker, R. E., & Lomax, R. G. (2004). *A beginner's guide to structural equation modeling* (2nd ed.). Mahwah, NJ: Erlbaum.

Schwartz, G. (1978). Estimating the dimension of a model. *Annals of Statistics, 6*, 461–464.

Shavelson, R. J., Hubner, J. J., & Stanton, G. C. (1976). Self-concept: Validation of construct interpretations. *Review of Educational Research, 46*, 407–441.

Singer, J. D., & Willett, J. D. (2003). *Applied longitudinal data analysis: Modeling change and event occurrence*. New York: Oxford.

Soares, A. T., & Soares, L. M. (1979). *The Affective Perception Inventory: Advanced level*. Trumbell, CT: ALSO.

Sobel, M. F., & Bohrnstedt, G. W. (1985). Use of null models in evaluating the fit of covariance structure models. In N. B. Tuma (Ed.), *Sociological methodology 1985* (pp. 152–178). San Francisco: Jossey-Bass.

Sörbom, D. (1974). A general method for studying differences in factor means and factor structures between groups. *British Journal of Mathematical and Statistical Psychology, 27*, 229–239.

Steiger, J. H. (1990). Structural model evaluation and modification: An interval estimation approach. *Multivariate Behavioral Research, 25*, 173–180.

Steiger, J. H. (1998). A note on multiple sample extensions of the RMSEA fit index. *Structural Equation Modeling, 5*, 411–419.

Steiger, J. H., & Lind, J. C. (1980, June). Statistically based tests for the number of common factors. Paper presented at the Psychometric Society annual meeting, Iowa City, IA.

Stine, R. A. (1990). An introduction to bootstrap methods: Examples and ideas. *Sociological Methods and Research, 8*, 243–291.

Stoel, R. D., Garre, F. G., Dolan, C., & van den Wittenboer, W. W. (2006). On the Likelihood Ratio test in structural equation modeling when parameters are subject to boundary constraints. *Psychological Methods, 11*, 439–455.

Sugawara, H. M., & MacCallum, R. C. (1993). Effect of estimation method on incremental fit indexes for covariance structure models. *Applied Psychological Measurement, 17*, 365–377.

Tanaka, J. S. (1993). Multifaceted conceptions of fit in structural equation models. In J. A. Bollen & J. S. Long (Eds.), *Testing structural equation models* (pp. 10–39). Newbury Park, CA: Sage.

Tanaka, J. S., & Huba, G. J. (1984). Confirmatory hierarchical factor analyses of psychological distress measures. *Journal of Personality and Social Psychology, 46*, 621–635.

Thompson, B. (1996). AERA editorial policies regarding statistical significance testing: Three suggested reforms. *Educational Researcher, 25*, 26–30.

Tomarken, A. J., & Waller, N. G. (2005). Structural equation modeling: Strengths, limitations, and misconceptions. *Annual Review of Clinical Psychology, 1*, 2.1–2.35.

Tomás, J. M., Hontangas, P. M., & Oliver, A. (2000). Linear confirmatory factor models to evaluate multitrait-multimethod matrices: The effects of number of indicators and correlation among methods. *Multivariate Behavioral Research, 35*, 469–499.

Tucker, L. R., & Lewis, C. (1973). A reliability coefficient for maximum likelihood factor analysis. *Psychometrika, 38*, 1–10.

Vogt, W. P. (1993). *Dictionary of statistics and methodology: A nontechnical guide for the social sciences.* Newbury Park, CA: Sage.

Wang, S., Wang, N., & Hoadley, D. (2007). Construct equivalence of a national certification examination that uses dual languages and audio assistance. *International Journal of Testing, 7*, 255–268.

Weng, L-J., & Cheng, C-P (1997). Why might relative fit indices differ between estimators? *Structural Equation Modeling, 4*, 121–128.

West, S. G., Finch, J. F., & Curran, P. J. (1995). Structural equation models with non-normal variables: Problems and remedies. In R. H. Hoyle (Ed.), *Structural equation modeling: Concepts, issues, and applications* (pp. 56–75). Thousand Oaks, CA: Sage.

Wheaton, B. (1987). Assessment of fit in overidentified models with latent variables. *Sociological Methods & Research, 16*, 118–154.

Wheaton, B., Muthén, B., Alwin, D. F., & Summers, G. F. (1977). Assessing reliability and stability in panel models. In D. R. Heise (Ed.), *Sociological methodology 1977* (pp. 84–136). San Francisco: Jossey-Bass.

Widaman, K. F. (1985). Hierarchically tested covariance structure models for multitrait-multimethod data. *Applied Psychological Measurement, 9*, 1–26.

Whittaker, T.A., & Stapleton, L.M. (2006). The performance of cross-validation indices used to select among competing covariance structure models under multivariate nonnormality conditions. *Multivariate Behavioral Research, 41*, 295–335.

Widaman, K. F., & Reise, S. P. (1997). Exploring the measurement equivalence of psychological instruments: Applications in the substance use domain. In K. J. Bryant, M. Windle, & S. G. West (Eds.), *The science of prevention* (pp. 281–324). Washington, DC: American Psychological Association.

Willett, J. B. (1988). Questions and answers in the measurement of change. In E. Z. Rothkopf (Ed.), *Review of research in education* (Vol. 15, pp. 345–422). Washington, DC: American Educational Research Association.

Willett, J. B. (1989). Some results on reliability for the longitudinal measurement of change: Implications for the design of studies of individual growth. *Educational and Psychological Measurement, 49*, 587–602.

Willett, J. B., & Keiley, M. K. (2000). Using covariance structure analysis to model change over time. In H. E. A. Tinsley & S. D. Brown (Eds.), *Handbook of applied multivariate statistics and mathematical modeling* (pp. 665–694). San Diego, CA: Academic Press.

Willett, J. B., & Sayer, A. G. (1994). Using covariance structure analysis to detect correlates and predictors of individual change over time. *Psychological Bulletin, 116*, 363–381.

Willett, J. B., & Sayer, A. G. (1996). Cross-domain analyses of change over time: Combining growth modeling and covariance structure analysis. In G. A. Marcoulides & R. E. Schumacker (Eds.), *Advanced structural equation modeling: Issues and techniques* (pp. 125–157). Mahwah, NJ: Erlbaum.

Williams, L. J., & Holahan, P. J. (1994). Parsimony-based fit indices for multiple-indicator models: Do they work? *Structural Equation Modeling, 1,* 161–189.

Wood, J. M., Tataryn, D. J., & Gorsuch, R. L. (1996). Effects of under- and overextraction on principal axis factor analysis with varimax rotation. *Psychological Methods, 1,* 354–365.

Wothke, W. (1993). Nonpositive definite matrices in structural modeling. In K. A. Bollen & J. S. Long (Eds.), *Testing structural equation models* (pp. 256–293). Newbury Park, CA: Sage.

Wothke, W. (1996). Models for multitrait-multimethod matrix analysis. In G. A. Marcoulides & R. E. Schumacker (Eds.), *Advanced structural equation modeling: Issues and techniques* (pp. 7–56). Mahwah, NJ: Erlbaum.

Yuan, K.-H., & Bentler, P. M. (2000). Three likelihood-based methods for mean and covariance structure analysis with nonnormal missing data. In *Sociological methodology* (pp. 165–200). Washington, DC: American Sociological Association.

Yuan, K.-H., Lambert, P. L., & Fouladi, R .T. (2004). Mardia's multivariate kurtosis with missing data. *Multivariate Behavioural Research, 39,* 413–437.

Yung, Y-F., & Bentler, P. M. (1994). Bootstrap-corrected ADF test statistics in covariance structure analysis. *British Journal of Mathematical and Statistical Psychology, 47,* 63–84.

Yung, Y-F., & Bentler, P. M. (1996). Bootstrapping techniques in analysis of mean and covariance structures. In G. A. Marcoulides & R. E. Schumacker (Eds.), *Advanced structural equation modeling: Issues and techniques* (pp. 195–226). Mahwah, NJ: Erlbaum.

Zhu, W. (1997). Making bootstrap statistical inferences: A tutorial. *Research Quarterly for Exercise and Sport, 68,* 44–55.

Author Index

Subject Index